Hegel's Theory of Madness

SUNY Series in Hegelian Studies
William Desmond, Editor

HEGEL'S
THEORY OF
M A D N E S S

Daniel Berthold-Bond

STATE UNIVERSITY OF NEW YORK PRESS

Published by
State University of New York Press, Albany

For information, address State University of New York Press,
State University Plaza, Albany, N.Y., 12246

Production by Diane Ganeles
Marketing by Bernadette LaManna

Library of Congress Cataloging-in-Publication Data

Berthold-Bond, Daniel, 1953–
    Hegel's theory of madness / Daniel Berthold-Bond.
        p.   cm. — (SUNY series in Hegelian studies)
    Includes bibliographical references and index.
    ISBN 0-7914-2505-3 (alk. paper). — ISBN 0-7914-2506-1 (pbk. :
alk. paper)
    1. Hegel, Georg Whilhelm Friedrich, 1770–1831—Views on mental
illness.   2. Psychiatry—Philosophy.   3. Mental illness.   I. Title.
II. Series
RC437.5.B47   1995
616.89′001—dc20   94-32809
                                                     CIP

10 9 8 7 6 5 4 3 2 1

For Lily

"I just can't give my mind up" about you,
to adapt one of your own phrases!

Verrücktheit ist einer in der
Entwicklung der Seele notwendig
hervortretenden Form oder Stufe.

Insanity is a necessarily occurring
form or stage in the development of
the soul.

(Hegel, *Encyclopedia of the
Philosophical Sciences*)

Contents

Acknowledgments

This book was inspired by a casual conversation many years ago with a remarkable man at Yale University, John Smith, with whom I studied Hegel. After a class in which we covered Hegel's "Anthropology" lectures from the *Encyclopædia,* he mentioned that he wished someone would devote some time one day to the discussion of madness which was placed so improbably in the midst of these lectures. After nearly ten years of gestation, I have turned John's casual remark into an invitation, and now have the chance to thank him once again for all he has meant to me. Thanks also go to my father, Fred Berthold, for remaining after all this time my most gracious reader. My students at Bard College also deserve my gratitude for perpetually forcing me to rethink assumptions, for their illuminating confusions no less than for their insightful readings, and for their independence of mind. Finally, heartfelt thanks to my wife Annie and my daughter Lily for being just exactly who they are.

Various parts of this book previously appeared in other forms: parts of chapter 3 as "The Decentering of Reason: Hegel's Theory of Madness" in *International Studies in Philosophy* 25 (1993); parts of chapter 4 as "The Two Faces of Desire: Evolution and Nostalgia in Hegel's Phenomenology of Desire" in *Clio* 19 (1990); parts of chapter 5 as "Hegel, Nietzsche and Freud on Madness and the Unconscious" in *The Journal of Speculative Philosophy* 5 (1991); parts of chapter 6 as "Intentionality and Madness in Hegel's Psychology of Action" in *International Philosophical Quarterly* 32 (1992); and parts of chapter 7 in "Hegel on Madness and Tragedy," *History of Philosophy Quarterly* 11 (1994).

Abbreviations

All references to Hegel's works will be cited in the text using the following abbreviations. For details, see the Bibliography.

A   *Hegel's Aesthetics: Lectures on Fine Art,* 2 vols.

F&K   *Faith and Knowledge*

JR   *Jenaer Realphilosophie (1805–1806)*

HP   *Lectures on the History of Philosophy,* 3 vols.

HW   *Hegel's Werke,* 18 vols., ed. P. Marheineke, et al., Duncker und Humblot Verlag

L   *The Science of Logic*

LR   *Lectures on the Philosophy of Religion* (the lectures of 1827)

NL   *Essay on Natural Law*

PCR   *The Positivity of the Christian Religion,* in Knox and Kroner, *Hegel's Early Theological Writings*

PH   *Philosophy of History,* 3 vols.

PM*   *Philosophy of Mind,* vol. 3 of the *Encyclopædia of the Philosophical Sciences*

PN*   *Philosophy of Nature,* vol. 2 of the *Encyclopædia*

PR/1817–19   *Philosophie des Rechts: Die Mitschriften Wannen-*
               mann (Heidelberg 1817–1818) und Homeyer (Berlin
               1818–1819)

PR/1819–20   *Philosophie des Rechts: Die Vorlesung von 1819–20*

PR*   *Philosophy of Right*

PS   *Phenomenology of Spirit*

RH   *Reason in History,* the Introduction to the *Lectures*
               on the Philosophy of History

SC   "The Spirit of Christianity and its Fate," in Knox
               and Kroner, *Early Theological Writings*

SL*   *Logic* ("shorter" *Logic*), vol. 1 of the *Encyclopædia*

VR   *Vorlesungen über Rechtsphilosophie,* 6 vols.

W   *Werke,* 20 vols., ed. Eva Moldenhauer and Karl
               Markus Michel, Suhrkamp Verlag

---

* References to these works are to sections ('§'), not pages. I have
indicated where citations from these works are from Hegel's "remarks" on the text (*Anmerkungen,* designated 'A'), or from passages added to the texts by various editors from student notes and
lecture manuscripts (*Zusätze,* designated 'Z'). See the following
'Note on the *Zusätze*' for comments on their status.

Note on the *Zusätze*
to Hegel's Lectures

Since I will be relying on several of the *Zusätze,* or additions, to lectures Hegel delivered at Heidelberg and Berlin—particularly the lectures on "Anthropology" he gave in conjunction with his courses on the *Enzyklopädie der philosophischen Wissenschaften im Grundrisse*—a word about the status of the *Zusätze* is in order. These passages were added to the *Enzyklopädie* and the *Grundlinien der Philosophie des Rechts* after Hegel's death by a variety of editors: in the case of the *Enzyklopädie,* Leopold von Henning (the *Logik*), Hegel's teaching assistant at Berlin who later lectured at the University on Goethe's theory of color; the scholar Ludwig Boumann (the *Philosophie des Geistes*); and the philosopher Karl Ludwig Michelet (the *Naturphilosophie*); and for the *Philosophie des Rechts,* Eduard Gans, the legal philosopher, first secretary general of the Hegelian Society for Scientific Criticism, and later one of Karl Marx's teachers at Berlin. The editors relied on Hegel's lecture manuscripts and the detailed notes they and other students (Major Karl von Griesheim, Heinrich Hotho, H. von Kehler, F. W. A. Mullach, Carl Gustav Homeyer, David Strauss, and others) had taken on the lectures. Hegel's posthumously published lectures on religion, art, the philosophy of history, and the history of philosophy were similarly compiled from Hegel's lecture manuscripts and auditors' transcripts and notebooks (*Nachschriften*), published first in an edition of Hegel's complete works by an Association of Friends of the Deceased (*Freunde des Verewigten*) (*Werke,* 18 vols., ed. P. Marheineke, J. Schulze, E. Gans, L. von Henning, H. Hotho, K. Michelet, F. Förster, Berlin: Duncker und Humblot, 1832–45).

There has been considerable debate about the value of these additions. Nicolin and Pöggeler, who omit the *Zusätze* from their edition of the *Enzyklopädie* (Hamburg: Felix Meiner, 1959), are particularly troubled by the way the Friends of the departed Hegel often conflated material from lectures given over a long period of time (from 1816 to 1830), thus failing to respect the development of Hegel's thought (see their *Einleitung,* xlv–vi). Johannes Hoffmeister offers similar criticisms of Eduard Gans for his method of selection of the *Zusätze* for the *Philosophie des Rechts* (Hoffmeister ed., Hamburg: Meiner Verlag, 1955, *Einleitung,* xiiff), and Bernhard Lakebrink, in his later edition of the *Philosophie des Rechts* (Stuttgart: Philipp Reclam, 1970), regards the *Zusätze* to be much inferior, both "linguistically and intellectually," to Hegel's original text (*Einleitung,* 4).

But the view that the *Zusätze* are invaluable and largely trustworthy reflections of Hegel's lectures is held by many others. Theodore Geraets, W. A. Suchting, and H. S. Harris, translators of Hegel's *Encyclopaedia Logic* (Cambridge: Hackett, 1991), conclude that "there is no serious doubt that [in the *Zusätze*] we have a generally reliable record of what Hegel said" (viii). J. N. Findlay believes that "without such material as is provided by the editorial *Zusätze,* [the *Encyclopædia*] would be largely uninterpretable, a monumental inscription in Linear B" (Foreword to Hegel's *Philosophy of Nature,* Oxford: Clarendon, 1970, vii). See also Findlay's Forewords to the "shorter" (*Encyclopædia*) *Logic* (Oxford: Clarendon, 1975) and *Philosophy of Mind* (Oxford: Clarendon, 1971), and M. J. Petry's Introduction to *Hegel's Philosophy of Subjective Spirit,* 3 vols. (Dordrecht, Holland: D. Reidel, 1979, 1: cx–cxv).

Without a reliance on the *Zusätze* to Hegel's "Anthropology" lectures, especially the long addition to § 408 of the *Enzyklopädie* (30 pages in Boumann's original edition, HW 7: part 2, 198–228), where the most extensive comments on mental derangement occur, a book on Hegel's theory of madness would be diminished greatly. Since Boumann's main sources for these *Zusätze*—the lecture manuscripts of Hegel and the transcripts of Hotho, Kehler, Griesheim, and Boumann himself—correspond with each other quite significantly in their basic presentation of ideas, there is sufficient reason to be confident in their authority and value. (See Heinrich Hotho, *Philosophie des Geistes, nach dem Vortrage des herrn Professor Hegel, im Sommer 1822,* and Karl von Griesheim, *Philosophie des Geistes, vorgelesen von Professor Hegel, Sommer 1825,* Staatsbibliothek Preussischer Kulturbesitz, Handschriftenabteilung, Archivstrasse 12–14, 1 Berlin 33; and H. von Kehler, *Philosophie des Geistes nach Hegel, Sommer 1825,* Universitätsbibliothek, Goethealle 6, 69 Jena.) For detailed comments on specific passages from the "Anthropology" *Zusätze* and their method of composition, see M. J. Petry's extensive Notes to *Hegel's Philosophy of Subjective Spirit* 2: 431–634.

CHAPTER ONE

Introduction

Canst thou not minister to a mind
    diseased;
Pluck from the misery a rooted
    sorrow;
Raze out the written troubles of the
    brain;
And, with some sweet oblivious
    antidote
Cleanse the stuffed bosom of that
    perilous stuff
Which weighs upon the heart?

          (Shakespeare, *Macbeth*)

During the period from 1816 to 1830, first at Heidelberg and later at Berlin, Hegel lectured regularly on the topic of madness or mental derangement (*Verrücktheit*). Unfortunately, the only remarks he published on this theme were contained in a mere two-page section of the highly condensed version of his lectures, the *Encyclopædia of the Philosophical Sciences* (published first in 1817, with subsequent editions in 1827 and 1830). This no doubt explains why virtually no notice was taken of Hegel's theory of madness by his contemporaries. One author, a physician writing of Hegel's general philosophy of medicine, lamented in 1829 that:

> the system of Hegel, recently epoch-making in . . . North German scientific culture, and already applied in many ways to theology, jurisprudence, history in general, as well as to the history of philosophy especially and to aesthetics, has not been considered or noted by . . . physicians.[1]

In 1845, fourteen years after Hegel's death from cholera, one of Hegel's students, Ludwig Boumann,[2] published some thirty pages of *Zusätze*, or 'additions' to the *Encyclopædia* discussion of madness (HW 7: 198–228), based on Hegel's lecture manuscripts and the detailed notes Boumann and other students had taken on the lectures.[3] The expanded discussion presents not only Hegel's general theory of madness, but also a classificatory system, remarks on causation and therapy, numerous summaries of case histories, and comments on current debates and controversies within psychiatric medicine.

Even still, Hegel's ideas attracted almost no attention. Indeed, as Dietrich von Engelhardt notes, "in the comprehensive works on the history and systematics of the concept of illness, Hegel has not been included."[4] Similarly, Hegel remains conspicuously absent from the host of recently published works on the history of insanity beginning with those of Michel Foucault in the 1960s, including works which especially emphasize the importance of the period of the early nineteenth century.[5] And even within Hegel scholarship itself, very little notice has been given to Hegel's theory of madness.[6]

It may be that even the enlarged discussion of madness afforded by Boumann's additions has appeared too slim to merit much attention. Or perhaps the fact that Hegel situates his discussion within the "Anthropology" section of his *Encyclopædia* has led to its marginalization, given that anthropology for Hegel deals merely with the 'soul,' which has not yet developed into the truly 'spiritual' consciousness which preoccupies him in the main body of his philosophical project. Thus W. T. Stace can write that Hegel's remarks on insanity "appear to be parenthetical, and to have no connection with the course of the dialectic."[7] The fact that Hegel himself refers to madness in any explicit way only tangentially and in passing in his other writings would certainly appear to add weight to the attitude of neglect. But whatever the reasons for the inattention Hegel's theory of madness has suffered, a closer look is in order.

The *Encyclopædia* passages are in fact so suggestive that there are good reasons for according to insanity a much more important role within the larger scheme of Hegel's philosophy than the space he allots to it might suggest.[8] Most importantly, we may note Hegel's claim that "insanity [is] an essential . . . [and] necessarily occurring form or stage . . . in the development of the soul" (PM § 408 Z). His point, of course, is not that we are all inevitably destined to derangement, but rather that madness represents a

constantly threatening and yet seductive possibility prepared for
by our encounter with the fundamentally alienating character of
life. Further, like Freud some eighty years later, Hegel saw madness as a reversion to and recovery of psychic origins: in madness,
the mind "sinks back" into the earliest phases of the development
of the soul, the domain of the unconscious play of instincts, or what
he calls "the life of feeling" (*Gefühlsleben*) (PM §§ 403–408). As
such, the study of madness promises a privileged point of access to
what we might call a primordial ontology, or an ontology of origins.
Moreover, since Hegel believes that the "feeling soul" (*die fühlende
Seele*) is never somehow overcome in the normal course of ego-development, but is retained and integrated within the rational self,
this primordial ontology may also serve to illuminate the anatomy
of the 'normal' (or as Hegel says, the 'developed' or 'rational') mind
in new ways.

This last point is particularly important. One of the most fascinating aspects of Hegel's theory of madness is that insanity and
rationality are not in fact conceived of as opposites, but in important respects as kindred phenomena, sharing many of the same
underlying structures, each illuminating their 'other' in significant
ways. The healthy mind is still grappling with the same sorts of
contradictions and feelings of alienation, the same "infinite pain"
(PM § 382), which characterizes insanity. The fact that madness is
the mirror of the developed consciousness—inverted and distorted
in many respects, to be sure, incorporating the structures of rationality within a different construction of the relation between the
self and its world—explains why Hegel views the surpassing of disease by health as always one which preserves within itself the possibility of a regression: "insanity is not a . . . *loss* of reason," he
says, "but only derangement, only a contradiction in a still subsisting reason," so that madness has "the healthy . . . consciousness
for its presupposition" (PM §§ 408 & Z).

Hegel believes that there are certain essential tensions—"contradictions" and "oppositions" as he calls them—inherent in madness which are "still preserved" and mirrored in the rational mind
(PM § 408 Z): for example, the tensions between the unconscious
and the conscious, between nature and spirit, and between the
inner world of instinct and the outer world of 'otherness' which
stands opposed to our desire. These oppositions are ineluctable features of all mind, and since they appear much more vividly in madness, a study of madness affords us with a particularly illuminating perspective from which to view the 'normal.' Darrel

Christensen goes so far as to say that "the phenomenology of the diseased mind is the same as the phenomenology of the normal mind," and that "the formal characteristics of mental diseases are the same as the formal characteristics of normal thought" except for the presence of "an archaic content" in madness.[9] Whether the phenomenological structures of mental health and illness are in fact essentially identical for Hegel will have to be explored in detail, but at the very least it is clear that they are intimately related. Just as Freud was later to take it as a first principle of his psychoanalytic theory that "in order to arrive at what is normal and apparently so simple, we shall have to study the pathological with its distortions and exaggerations,"[10] a close reading of Hegel's analysis of the diseased mind promises a fascinating entry to his phenomenology of rational consciousness.

With this suggestion in mind, it would be a mistake to see mastery and slavery, stoicism, skepticism, despair (the "unhappy consciousness"), the law of the heart, absolute freedom and terror, the beautiful soul—and many of the other forms of consciousness which together make up the gallery of the shapes of spirit in Hegel's *Phenomenology*—as ways of being which have no point of contact with his discussion of madness. It is true that he sees mental disease as a particular shape of mind which occurs at a level of life which is "immersed in nature" and hence is not fully spiritual, and which is surpassed by truly rational consciousness. This may be why there are so few references to insanity outside of Hegel's anthropology; the phenomenology of the developed consciousness will require a different vocabulary to describe its inner conflicts than the language appropriate to insanity, as the spheres of spirit and nature enclose importantly different forms of experience and theaters of action. But again, madness has the healthy consciousness as its 'presupposition,' and in rationality we can hear the echo of the language of madness, the vestige of our archaic past which we all retain within us, which allows us to uncover striking points of contact between madness and these other shapes of experience. Indeed, we will see that many of the portraits Hegel draws of particularly alienated forms of consciousness, where the inner turmoil of the rational mind forces consciousness to become radically decentered and dislocated, are so close to the portrait he gives of madness that the line of demarcation separating them becomes all but erased.

The relationship of mirroring between madness and the 'normal' mind allows for new perspectives not only on different phenomenological shapes of consciousness, but on many other themes which are central to Hegel's larger philosophical project, ranging from the most central assumptions of his metaphysics to his philosophy of language, his aesthetics, his conception of the nature of history and time, his theories of labor, desire and human intentionality, and his reflections on poverty and social marginalization. The purpose of this book will be to explore these connections between Hegel's theory of insanity and other basic themes of his philosophy by situating his analysis of madness within several contexts: within the "Anthropology" discussion of the 'feeling soul,' where Hegel works out a sophisticated ontology of mental derangement; within the history of medical psychology during the great reform period of the turn of the eighteenth century when Hegel was writing; within a comparison to Hegel's phenomenology of the developed consciousness, where so many of the same mental and experiential structures as are found in madness reoccur; and within the broadest scope of Hegel's metaphysics, epistemology, aesthetics, and political philosophy, in order to exploit the promise of his theory of madness to reveal new perspectives on themes which are most central to his philosophic vision.

Chapter 2 will locate Hegel's theory of madness within the history of early nineteenth century philosophical and medical conceptions of insanity. This was a time of enormous upheaval in the social and medical perceptions of madness, and in the practices of classification, diagnosis, and treatment. We will look at some of the most important controversies of the period, most notably those between empirical and Romantic medicine and between 'somatic' and 'psychic' theories of mental illness, and show how Hegel's own 'speculative' theory of madness sought to fashion what he called a "middle path" between these contesting factions. We will introduce the primary elements of Hegel's ontology of madness as they emerge in his "Anthropology" discussion of 'the feeling soul,' and conclude with a look at his position on the early nineteenth century fascination of psychology with animal magnetism, or Mesmerism.

In chapter 3, the provisional sketch of Hegel's theory offered in the previous chapter will be fleshed out by examining in more detail such key ideas as regression, separation from reality, dream-consciousness, and the place of the unconscious in the economy of the instincts. These ideas will then be applied to an explicit comparison of the phenomenological structures of madness with those of the developed consciousness, centering on Hegel's account of stoicism, skepticism, and despair. Along the way, we will discuss the relationship between Hegel's purely formal ontology of madness and his personal acquaintance with insanity through the illnesses of his sister Christiane and his close friend, the poet Friedrich Hölderlin. Finally, it will be argued that Hegel's conception of madness sheds new light on his commitment to an 'idealist' philosophy, since in important ways madness is diagnosed as a sort of failed idealism which by contrast helps to deepen our understanding of the values of Hegel's own philosophic system.

Chapter 4 will concentrate on Hegel's theory of desire, most particularly on that aspect of desire which is nostalgic and regressive, tempting consciousness to abandon its immersion in the everyday world and to "sink back," as Hegel puts it, to the archaic past of the soul. It is this nostalgic face of desire which plays for Hegel the same role as the concepts of regression and the death instinct would later for Freud, and we will explore this comparison in some detail. The chapter will close by examining Hegel's interpretation of the biblical story of the Fall, showing how his allegorical reading relies strongly on a conception of nostalgic desire which is central to his anatomy of the etiology of or 'fall' into madness.

Chapter 5 will expand on the theme of the unconscious in Hegel's account of madness, placing Hegel in dialogue with the later theories of Nietzsche and Freud, and focusing on such issues as the line of distinction between health and illness, the analogy of madness to dreaming, the nature of sublimation and repression, and the concept of insanity as a double personality. Chapter 6 will turn outwards, in a sense, moving away from the psychic unconscious to a consideration of Hegel's theory of conscious intentionality. The argument of the chapter, however, will be that even in the most intentional action, Hegel detects the crucial presence of what is unintended or hidden from conscious sight, so that at least in some sense the role of the unconscious remains important even in the course of our entirely 'normal' day-to-day experience. This theme will be investigated through an interpretation of several of the most important features of Hegel's theory of intentionality: his conception of the circular nature of action, his critique of anti-consequentialist ethical theories, his portrait of alienation, and his theory of language. The purpose of the chapter will be to draw some conclusions about just how much madness and the rational mind share with respect to the vicissitudes of the unconscious.

Our discussion will then turn, in chapter 7, to an examination of the connections between madness and tragedy. While these are not connections Hegel tends to draw himself, it will be argued that his theory of tragedy reveals a form of action that in important respects exists very much on the borderline between health and illness. By existing in the between-space of sanity and madness, tragic action serves to highlight the overlapping structures of mental derangement and the developed, rational consciousness in a particularly forceful way. We will compare madness and tragedy as forms of acute alienation in response to the experience of what Hegel terms "the broken world," and as sharing an ontology of inward 'doubleness' or self-division which in turn entails a radical reorganization of the relation to the outer world. In addition, by looking at Hegel's readings of various Sophoclean tragedies, we will examine the close association between madness and tragic action in their struggles with guilt and evil, in their reliance upon the unconscious, and in their similar dislocations from historical time.

Finally, in chapter 8 we will consider the implications of an important, and in many ways puzzling, absence in Hegel's theory of madness: an account of the social, political, and historical contexts in which insanity becomes defined and managed. We will examine the ways in which Hegel's uncharacteristic silence on historical and cultural themes opens his discussion of madness to the critiques of two of the most important twentieth century writers on the history of psychiatry and the concept of mental illness: Michel Foucault and Thomas Szasz, who argue in different ways that madness is not in fact a medical phenomenon at all, but a phenomenon of social engineering, moral re-education, and the politically instigated labeling and 'correction' of behaviors viewed as threatening to the dominant order of society. We will look carefully at Hegel's reliance on the therapeutic theory and practice made famous by the French physician Philippe Pinel, who instituted what he called a 'moral therapy' in his directorship of the asylum of Bicêtre in Paris in the years following the French Revolution, and seek to resolve the extent to which Hegel's own understanding of moral therapy leaves him vulnerable to the sorts of attacks 'social labeling' theorists like Foucault and Szasz level against Pinel.

It will be argued that Hegel's ontology of madness would be importantly strengthened if it could be made compatible with a labeling perspective, so that insanity would be analyzed from a double point of view, as an actual medical phenomenon requiring an ontological description, but also as a phenomenon in part subject to cultural construction, requiring a description of the historically changing social and political contexts in which madness becomes redefined. And it will be suggested that in fact there is a way of reconstructing Hegel's theory of madness so that such a reconciliation is possible, if we apply the analysis he develops in his political philosophy of poverty and destitution to his ontology of insanity. While this reconstruction would leave writers like Foucault and Szasz unsatisfied, given their uncompromising reduction of madness to a purely socially constituted phenomenon, it would not only preserve the subtlety and force of Hegel's ontology of madness, but would make it more in tune with such basic commitments of his larger philosophy as his theory of recognition—that self-identity is shaped in significant ways by how and what I am recognized as being—and his emphasis on historical and social reality as the context in which phenomenological structures of consciousness are made determinate and concrete.

The last thirty years have seen a steadily growing fascination with the study of madness and the institution of psychiatry on the part of sociologists, historians, legal scholars, philosophers, feminist theorists, and writers situating themselves in the terrain of post-modernism. Much of the interest has been spurred by a series of heretical anti-psychiatric writings which appeared in the 1960s—Foucault's *Madness and Civilization* and *The Birth of the Clinic,* Szasz's *The Myth of Mental Illness, Psychiatric Justice,* and *Law, Liberty, and Psychiatry,* R. D. Laing's *The Divided Self* and *The Politics of Experience,* David Cooper's *Dialectics of Liberation* and *Psychiatry and Anti-Psychiatry,* and Thomas Scheff's *Being Mentally Ill*—as well as by studies of psychiatric institutions such as Erving Goffman's *Asylums* and David Rothman's *Discovery of the Asylum.* There is now a huge literature on madness, perhaps particularly within the field of the sociology of medicine, but also including contributions by Marxists, Freudians and post-Freudian psychoanalytic theorists, civil libertarians, and philosophers from within both the analytic and continental traditions. In delving into Hegel's much-neglected theory of madness, we will gain not only some new perspectives on his own larger philosophy, but also prepare the way for a dialogue with this widespread contemporary interest in the theme of insanity and its social, medical, and philosophical history.

CHAPTER TWO

Hagel's Place in Early Nineteenth Century Views of Madness

A physician boasted to Nicocles that his art was of great authority. "It is so, indeed," said Nicocles, "that can with impunity kill so many people."

(Montaigne, *Essays*, 1580)

In the present enlightened age, it is to be hoped that something more effectual may be done towards the improvement of the healing art, than to indulge with the splenetic Montaigne, in contemptuous and ridiculous sarcasms upon the vanity of its pretensions.

(Philippe Pinel, *A Treatise on Insanity*, 1801)

The purpose of this chapter is mainly historical in emphasis. Our discussion will introduce some of the basic features of Hegel's account of *Verrücktheit*, but the theoretical and philosophical underpinnings of these ideas will be presented in a preliminary way, simply in order to provide the context for our historical discussion, and will be fleshed out in detail only in later chapters. In the present chapter, we will see that Hegel's theory of madness holds an interesting and noteworthy place in the history of early nineteenth century philosophical and medical literature on insanity, due to its careful positioning in the middle ground between competing schools of thought.[1] This period was marked by often strident controversy between empirical and Romantic medicine, between 'somatic' and 'psychic' theories of mental illness, and between physical and psychological methods of therapy.

Hegel carried on an extensive correspondence with many of the actors on every side of these debates, and was thoroughly acquainted with the relevant literature. One writer asserts that

"Hegel possessed all the medical knowledge available in his time, and in that he exceeded many of his contemporaries, physicians and [philosophical] writers [alike]."[24] In a fashion so typical of his philosophic temperament, Hegel rejected each of these camps as 'one-sided,' and sought to develop a position which might reconcile the oppositions in a higher dialectical synthesis.

We will begin by sketching out the lines of division between the various competing schools of the time, and Hegel's attempt to mediate between them. We will then situate his discussion of madness within the context of his "Anthropology," and look at his position on the early nineteenth-century fascination of psychology with animal magnetism and Mesmerism, since this serves as an important point of access to his idea of 'diseases of the soul.' Throughout, the attempt will be to place Hegel's discussion within the historical setting of late eighteenth- and early nineteenth-century psychiatry and philosophy of medicine, and to emphasize the historically unusual character of his attempt to mediate between opposing and even hostile schools of thought.

Hegel's Middle Path

The Turning Point

Historians of madness all point to the late eighteenth century as a crucial turning-point in the social and medical perception of insanity. Indeed, many argue that it is really only during this period that madness comes to be regarded as a medical phenomenon at all. During the preceding century, dating from the 1656 founding of the Hôpital Général in Paris, the insane were locked away, along with criminals and the indigent, in places of confinement which were established under the police power of the state with a judicial rather than a medical function.[3] The Royal Edict of 1656 assured that the directors of these establishments would have at their disposal "stakes, irons, prisons, and dungeons in the said Hôpital Général . . . so much as they deem necessary."[4]

By the 1780s, a growing number of reports detailing the horrors of these 'hospitals' were published in France, England, and Germany. We may cite brief statements from three of the most important reformers of the turn of the eighteenth century to get a sense of the climate of moral offense. Philippe Pinel, known as the 'liberator of the insane' for his development of a 'moral treatment' and his removing the chains from the inmates during his tenure as chief physician first at the Hôpital Général of Bicêtre and later at La Salpêtrière from 1793 until his death in 1826, writes in his *Medical and Philosophic Treatise on Mental Alienation (Traité médico-philosophique de l'aliénation mentale,* 1801) of the state of the Hôpital Général prior to his directorship:

> The managers of the . . . public asylums for maniacs . . . , who are frequently men of little knowledge and less humanity, have been permitted to exercise towards their innocent prisoners a most arbitrary system of cruelty and violence.[5]

Johann Christian Reil, considered the founder of German psychiatry and responsible for the first reforms of the German asylums for the insane, remarks in his *Rhapsodies on the Application of Psychical Therapy to Insanity (Rhapsodien über die Anwendung der psychischen Kurmethode auf Geisteszerrüttungen,* 1803):

> We lock up these unfortunate creatures like criminals in mad-boxes . . . or in the damp cellars of jails . . . and let them, chained in irons, rot in their own filth. . . . The guards are usually unfeeling, cruel men . . . who in their control over madmen have seldom stepped outside the circle drawn by their whip.[6]

And Jean-Etienne-Dominique Esquirol, a student of Pinel's, a physician at La Salpêtrière beginning in 1810, and the person most responsible for the 1838 legal reforms on insanity in France, described his impressions of asylums he had visited in thirteen cities:

> These unfortunates are . . . worse off than beasts. . . . I saw them in narrow, stinking holes without air or light, chained in caves in which one would hesitate to lock up those wild beasts that a profligate administration maintains at great expense in [the zoos of] the capitals.[7]

One last eyewitness account is worth quoting, describing the treatment of a patient under the care of the famous British clergyman and physician Francis Willis (1718–1807) at his privately owned madhouse on the outskirts of London:

> The unhappy patient . . . was no longer treated as a human being. His body was immediately encased in a machine which left no liberty of motion. He was sometimes chained to a stake. He was frequently beaten and starved, and at best he was kept in subjection by menacing and violent language.[8]

When we reflect that the eyewitness was the Countess of Harcourt and the patient no less than King George III, it becomes all the more sobering to imagine the 'treatment' of the general population of the madhouses, which consisted mainly of the poor, the indigent, and the socially disenfranchised.

Beginning in the 1790s, first in France and later in England and Germany, a new sensibility emerged which was characterized by the transformed image of the insane as suffering from *medical illness,* which would require the transfiguration of the prisons that housed them into *medical* asylums and retreats. On March 27, 1790, the Revolutionary Constituent Assembly in Paris announced a law which mandated that:

> Persons detained because of a state of insanity . . . will be examined by doctors who . . . will enquire into the true situation of those sick so that, in accordance with the decision taken about their condition, they are either freed or cared for in hospitals that will be designated for this purpose.[9]

The asylum was henceforth to constitute "a truly medical environment."[10] As Foucault notes, with the insane now placed under the supervision of physicians and the environment of internment now mediated by medical categories, "mental *disease,* with the meanings we now give it, is made possible" for the first time.[11]

Contesting Factions

While there is a real question about just how much the actual condition of the insane changed with the new reforms, there can be no doubt that on the level of theoretical discourse, madness had undergone a fundamental alteration. And with the medicalization of the discourse about madness, there emerged an increasingly polarized debate between contesting factions about how to conceive the nature of mental disease. By the time of Hegel's lectures on madness (1816–30), the lines of dispute had been firmly drawn between 'somaticists' who regarded insanity as a disease of the body and 'psychists' who viewed it as a disease of the soul, as well as between practitioners of empirical medicine who insisted on a purely clinical procedure of description, diagnosis, and treatment, and adherents of Romantic medicine who argued that madness (and indeed all illness) could only be fully understood within a metaphysical system. A closer look at the lines of contention will help us to judge more clearly the direction Hegel takes in his own account of madness.

The first point to be made is that the two distinctions, between somatic and psychic medicine, and between empirical and Romantic medicine, do not exactly overlap. In fact, many Romantics sided more with a somatic approach to disease: Johann Christian Reil's *Rhapsodies,* for example, which became a classic of Romantic medicine, for all its poetic, literary, and speculative style, was straightforwardly materialistic and somatically based. Further, the psychists often presented their views in the language of empiricism: Karl Ideler's *Foundations of Psychiatry (Grundriss der Seelenheilkunde),* one of the most important texts produced by the psychic school, adopts the procedure of strict "empirical psychology."[12] Thus Hegel's critique of contemporary psychiatry will be complex, directed against all of the various combinations of somatic-empirical, somatic-Romantic, psychic-empirical, and psychic-Romantic theories.

ROMANTIC AND EMPIRICAL MEDICINE. Romantic medicine, to begin here, was greatly influenced by the Scottish physician John Brown (1735–1788), whose 1780 *Elementa medicinæ* postulated that Life is nothing but essential, innate "vital energy" or "excitability," and that disease is either a sthenic (excessive) or asthenic (diminished) redistribution of the normal intensity of the healthy organism.[13] Brown was important for such Romantic physicians as Adalbert Marcus, Andreas Röschlaub, Karl Neumann, Karl von Eschenmayer, Johann Christian Heinroth, Karl Windischmann, Lorenz Oken, Alexander Haindorf, Johann Reil, and many others,[14] as well as for the poet Novalis and the philosopher Schelling (Hegel's classmate at Tübingen, his associate at Jena, and his close friend until their break around 1807). Schelling's own metaphysical conception of nature was a further major influence.[15] Schelling's brother Karl was himself a practicing Romantic (or 'philosophical') physician who published two articles on the cosmological significance of animal magnetism,[16] and who treated Hegel's sister Christiane for 'hysteria' over a period of ten years (1822–32) after she had spent a year in the Zwiefalten asylum, using herbs and the "gentle" principles of Pinelian therapy.[17]

The Romantic physicians based their theories on broad metaphysical, cosmological, theological, and even aesthetic speculations. Frequent preoccupations were the historicality of illness (what Heinroth called an "evolutionary history of mental disorders,"[18] whereby a proper taxonomy, or 'nosology' of diseases was to be determined by tracing out the sequence of their emergence in history);[19] the religious significance of illness (hence the 'theological psychiatry' of Heinroth, Karl Windischmann, Franz von Baader, Ludwig Friedländer, and Johann Nepomuk Ringseis);[20] the tendency to idealize illness as providing poetic, mystical insight into higher truths; and the related view of illness as a return to an original and privileged state of nature from which we have been alienated by a repressive and essentially diseased civilization. The return, to be sure, is mediated by pathology, but the physician is guided by what Reil calls in his *Rhapsodien* the attempt to "recreate" the madman "in terms of natural history."[21]

All this met with unmitigated disdain from the proponents of empirical medicine. Christoph Hufeland spoke in 1800 of the "fruitless speculation" of the Romantics. A. F. Hecker warned in 1805 of the "slippery ice, . . . the thorns, cliffs and rushing forest streams of the most recent philosophies," whose "mania for systems" must be countered by a purely descriptive, clinically-oriented empirical medicine. In 1816, a pseudonymously published "Complaint" by one 'Candidus' referred to the "fantasies and errors of young and old which [the Romantic, speculative] philosophy of nature ha[s] caused in Germany." And in 1823, the anatomist Phillip Karl Hartmann denounced the "subjugat[ion] of medicine" by the fantastical systems of the Romantic physicians and philosophers.[22]

Empirical medicine in the late eighteenth and early nineteenth centuries traced its lineage back a century to the work of such writers as the English physician Thomas Sydenham, who in the 1680s adopted the procedure of classifying diseases like plants, in terms of their purely external features, "with the same care which we see exhibited by botanists in their phytologies," since we can never delve more deeply than to "the superficies of bodies, not [to] the minute processes in nature's 'abyss of cause.' " Just as Hufeland and the other empirical psychologists of the nineteenth century would 200 years later, Sydenham spoke of the dangers of "curious and irrelevant speculations" into the *meanings* of disease.[23] Sydenham's more famous friend and fellow member of the Royal Society, John Locke, echoed this warning in his unfinished work on *De arte medica,* where he spoke against those whose researches into medicine were overly "curious in imagining the secret workmanship of nature and [who], . . . putting all these fancies together, fashion themselves systems and hypotheses" which have "diverted their enquiries from the knowledge of things."[24]

All through the eighteenth century, similar arguments were made, and by Hegel's time were commonplace. The clinical study of symptoms, the growing interest in post-mortem examinations of the mentally ill, and the exclusive reliance on physical methods of therapy (both drugs such as arsenic, belladonna, camphor, and opium, and physical procedures such as blood-letting, purging, castration, and the use of electricity), were basic commitments of nineteenth century empirical medicine, attested to in such works as John Haslam's *Observations on Insanity* (1805), Andrew Marshal's *The Morbid Anatomy of the Brain* (1815), and P. J. Schneider's *Pharmacology* (*Entwurf zu einer Heilmittellehre gegen psychischen Krankheiten,* 1824).[25]

THE SOMATIC AND PSYCHIC SCHOOLS. Turning now to the distinction between the 'somatic' and 'psychic' schools of psychiatric medicine, we may say in general that the somatists argued against the adoption of any psychology that was thought to be independent of principles of physiology (although these principles could be derived either empirically or metaphysically), while the psychists insisted precisely on an independent psychology. Thus the somatist Franz Joseph Gall's monumental six volume work, *On the Functions of the Brain* (*Sur les fonctions du cerveau et sur celles de chacune de ses parties,* 1809), sought to explain the various forms of insanity according to principles of cerebro-anatomy, and specifically according to the assumptions of 'cranioscopy' or phrenology (where the contours of the skull betoken the 'contours,' so to speak, of the soul or spirit).[26] Gall's lectures at Vienna were finally condemned in 1802 by the Austrian government for their reputedly anti-religious implications, but his work remained influential.

François Broussais, an important figure in the development of the French somatic school (Castel calls him the "prophet of 'physiology' "[27]) argued in 1828, as Klaus Doerner summarizes, that "concepts like ego, consciousness, rationality, and mental disease had to be deontologized, since they were actions of the nervous and constantly changing brain matter."[28] The French physician and anatomist Antoine Laurent Jessé Bayle, using findings from post-mortem studies of the insane, concluded in 1822 that the mental symptoms of madness were caused by pathological inflammation of the brain membrane.[29] And in 1830, just a year before Hegel's death, Maximilian Jacobi's book, *Observations on Pathology* (*Beobachtungen über die Pathologie und Therapie der mit Irresein verbundenen Krankheiten*) appeared, giving perhaps the clearest statement of the somatic position that all mental disorder is merely the symptomatic expression of an underlying physical-neurological disorder. Jacobi was the director of an asylum in Siegburg, and the somatic school counted among its members many other asylum directors.[30]

On the other hand, psychists like Karl Ideler (1795–1860), chief physician in the department of mental diseases at Charité Hospital in Berlin and director of its psychiatric clinic, argued that any purely materialistic medicine would necessarily fail to offer a convincing explanation of the vicissitudes of madness; that conscious life cannot be reduced to bodily processes, but rather the "psyche is autonomous"; that mental illness is a purely psychological phenomenon, a disease of the soul, dependent upon passions and drives which are "essential drives of the mind" prior to any physiological determinations.[31] Earlier, Johann Heinroth (1773–1843) developed a 'theological psychiatry' which portrayed madness as moral and religious transgression, so that "all evil, including the disturbances of psychic life, [are attributable] to sin."[32] Heinroth's psychology therefore strenuously resisted reducing such "disturbances" to neurological-anatomical factors: "*das Körperliche Leiden dabei ist nicht mehr als ein zufälliges und sekundäres zu betrachten*" (physical affliction is nothing more than a contingent and secondary consideration).[33] Earlier still, Johann Langermann, a disciple of Kant and Fichte and an important figure in the movement for asylum reform in Bayreuth, published a work on melancholy (1797) in which he took all materialistic, somatic medicine to task (including animal magnetism and homeopathy), and insisted that mental disease is a disorder of the spirit.[34] And in 1789, Andrew Harper concluded, in his *Observations on Insanity,* that "actual insanity . . . seldom arises from any other source than a defection in the mind alone."[35]

To underscore the complicated relationships between the empirical, Romantic, somatic, and psychic factions, we may note that (1) while certainly many of the somatists were aligned with the empiricists (for example, Hufeland, Hecker, Hartmann, and Bayle), (2) so were some of the psychists (Ideler stands out here); and (3) while many Romantics were psychists (for example, Heinroth, Windischmann, and Ringseis), there were actually probably more Romantic (or 'philosophical') somatists: Reil and Brown we have mentioned, but also Gall, as we can see in the title of his *Philosophical and Medical Investigations on Nature and Art (Philosophisch-medicinische Untersuchungen über Natur und Kunst)*, Broussais, whose *Irritation and Madness (De l'irritation et de la folie,* 1828) picks up John Brown's Romantic-somatic category of 'excitability' or 'irritability,' and the physician Alexander Haindorf, whose *Attempt at a Pathology and Therapy of the Spiritual and Mental Disorders (Versuch einer Pathologie und*

Therapie der Geistes- und Gemütskrankheiten, 1811) presented detailed empirical accounts of the nervous system wed to an elaborate Romantic paradigm.

HEGEL'S SPECULATIVE PHILOSOPHY OF MEDICINE. We are now in a position to see where Hegel fits into this complicated picture. Towards the beginning of the Introduction to his *Philosophy of Mind* (the third volume of his *Encyclopædia,* in which the discussion of madness appears), Hegel describes the traditional opposition in psychology between Pneumatology, or Rational Psychology, and Empirical Psychology. Rational psychology is "an abstract and generalizing metaphysic," concerned only with "the supposedly unmanifested essence . . . of mind," adopting a purely *a priori* treatment of psychology; while empirical psychology "deals with the 'concrete' mind," or "the contingent particularity of mind," rejecting "any attempt at a 'speculative' treatment." Between the two, "in the middle," as he says, stands Hegel's own approach to psychology, which he calls the "genuinely speculative" method (PM § 378 & Z).[36]

Hegel's middle way may be seen with respect to both the empirical/Romantic and the somatic/psychic dualisms we have been looking at. His polemics against Romanticism are well known,[37] but it may be helpful to relate his critique directly to Romantic medicine. Hegel in fact echoes the language of the empirical physician A. F. Hecker's 1805 description of the "slippery ice, . . . the thorns, cliffs and rushing forest streams" of Romantic medicine, in writing (just a year later) of the Romantics' "wild forest stream that threatens to sow confusion in reason and science."[38] In his *Philosophy of Nature* (volume two of the *Encyclopædia*), he remarks that the Romantics Oken, Troxler, and Schelling have "lapsed completely into an empty formalism" (PN § 359 Z), and refers to John Brown's Romantic theory of 'excitability':

> Of all the concoctions . . . in the sciences, none is more unphilosophical than the introduction of such formal and material relationships as the theory of stimulation. . . . The result of this is to reduce all distinctions within the organism to the formalis[tic principles] of . . . increase or decrease, of intensification or attenuation. . . . A theory of medicine built on these arid determinations . . . [results in a] crude and thoroughly unphilosophical procedure. (PN § 359)

The "empty formalism" of Romantic medicine is its construction of *a priori* metaphysical systems which are then simply imposed on the diagnostic and classificatory tasks of medicine.[39] In a passage from his 'shorter' *Logic* (the first volume of the *Encyclopædia*), Hegel refers to the Romantics as presenting *a priori* principles which become "self-complacent, . . . so much at home [in the element of thought] that [this thinking] feels an innate indifference to descend to particulars, . . . [and] never gets further than the universality of Ideas. . . . [Such systems are] justly open to the charge of formalism." Hegel concludes this passage by insisting that "Philosophy, then, owes its development to the empirical sciences" (SL § 12).

For all those, beginning with Marx and continuing through twentieth century analytic critics, who believe that this "self-complacency" of *a priori* principles describes precisely Hegel's own 'speculative' philosophy, a passage from Hegel's *Lectures on the Philosophy of History* leaves us in no doubt as to his view of this procedure. Hegel is speaking here of the speculative approach to history, and he brings up just the criticism Marx and Engels were to make famous against him, namely that speculative philosophy appears to "dwell in the region of self-produced ideas, without reference to actuality. . . . [According to this characterization], speculation might be expected to . . . force [the concrete historical data] into conformity with a tyrannous idea, and to construe it, as the phrase is, *a priori*" (RH 8). But, Hegel says, any close reader of his own philosophy of history will see that this is a completely mistaken idea of the methodology of speculative science, and that its starting-point is precisely the empirical record. He makes this point again in his *Philosophy of Nature,* in speaking of the speculative approach to the physical world (which includes the human body and its illnesses):

> Not only must philosophy be in agreement with our empirical knowledge of Nature, but the *origin* and *formation* of the Philosophy of Nature presupposes and is conditioned by [the] empirical. (PN § 246)

There are many similar passages extolling the importance of the empirical and warning against the lures of Romantic abstraction and formalism throughout Hegel's works. But we must note that in most of these passages, Hegel goes on to warn against the dangers of the opposite extreme as well, when empiricism arrogates to itself the whole of science. Thus in his 'shorter' *Logic,* he writes that "The principle of Experience carries with it the unspeakably important condition that . . . we must be in contact, . . . [or] in touch with . . . facts," but remarks that these empirical facts remain mere brute data, without interconnection or explanatory value, until they are "taken up" by "speculative thinking" (SL §§ 7, 9). A few pages later Hegel returns to this idea: "Philosophy is the child of experience, and owes its rise to *a posteriori* fact. . . . But there is also an *a priori* aspect of thought," in which the merely "immediate" character of the concrete is raised to the element of "universality" (SL § 12). Hegel distinguishes between the starting-point, or "origin" of a science, which must rest firmly upon the empirical, and the science itself, which must rest upon speculative "notions" (*Begriffe*) (see PN § 246)—that is, upon philosophic insight.

The 'notion' of illness, for example, will not be a simple listing of external features of disease, a clinical portrait of symptoms, a sort of 'botany' of illness à la Sydenham, but will require a conceptual, theoretical, *philosophical* discernment of the underlying, inner meanings of disease. Freud, almost one hundred years later, spoke in a similar way of the "attitude [of] contemporary psychiatry" towards the neuroses: "Psychiatry gives names to the different obsessions but says nothing further about them," refusing to delve into "the sense of symptoms."[40] For Freud no less than for Hegel, a full account of mental illness will require an *ontology* of the psyche which rests upon 'notional thinking,' however differently the theoretical constructs in which Freudian and Hegelian notions such as repression, substitute-formation, projection, regression, and the unconscious may be situated.

It is just this notional thinking which is absent in the idea of empirical medicine, so that we can observe only "the superfices of bodies" (Sydenham), and must exclude any attempt to gather the meanings of symptoms. Or as the phrenologist Gall put it: "I leave unsought the nature of the soul as of the body. . . . I confine myself to phenomena."[41] In a letter to his friend Windischmann, the Romantic physician, Hegel writes that empirical medicine is "forced to talk of people's suffering in such an external fashion" that it can "no longer find any point of attachment" to "what is inner and operating from within outward."[42] It is this 'inner' world of illness that requires philosophical, speculative insight.

We get a good sense of Hegel's commitment to an ontology, or what might be called a *logic of the interior* of illness in his method of classification of the forms of madness. Petry points out that Hegel was writing during a time of "terminological chaos" in the classification of mental illness. "The truth of the matter was that the medical knowledge of the day, unlike the botanical and zoological knowledge, was incapable of providing a satisfactory empirical foundation for the sort of elaborate classificatory systems being formulated."[43] Hegel's own classificatory scheme was relatively austere, most importantly because it did not set out to detail all of the endless varieties of clinical symptoms, but was based on a logic, or ontology, of the essential character of madness. Hegel writes:

> The various forms of insanity . . . are usually classified not so much according to an *inner* characteristic as according to the *manifestations* of this illness; but this is inadequate for the philosophical treatment of the subject. We must recognize that even insanity is a state which is differentiated within itself [i.e., in its essence] in a necessary and therefore rational manner. (PM § 408 Z)

Thus while Hegel sees "the particular content" of madness to be "something infinitely manifold and therefore contingent"—the proper subject of study for clinical, empirical research—the key to a philosophically adequate classification of insanity is to provide an account of the logical possibilities of expression within the essence of madness itself. The essence of madness is the "state in which the mind is shut up within itself, has sunk into itself, whose peculiarity . . . consists in its being no longer in immediate contact with actuality but in having positively separated itself from it" (PM § 408 Z). The three main forms of insanity that Hegel discusses (see Figure 1 below)—*der Blödsinn* (idiocy), *die Narrheit* (madness proper), and *die Tollheit* or *der Wahnsinn* (mania or frenzy)—are the three logical expressions of this state of withdrawal and separation. In 'idiocy'—analogous to modern diagnostic classifications of organic brain syndromes and mental retardation—which Hegel sees as mainly incurable, there is a more or less complete separation from reality and depletion of the capacities of rationality and volition. In madness proper—most analogous perhaps to the modern category of the obsessional neuroses—the mind becomes "imprisoned" in a particular fixed idea to which it "accords an objective significance." In mania or frenzy—which would include the current classifications of manic-depressive or bipolar disorders, dementia, paranoia, and schizophrenia—consciousness becomes explicitly aware of the "contradiction" between its withdrawal into the life of the feeling soul and the vestige of its own "objective consciousness," so that there is a "despairing effort to overcome the discord . . . and to restore its . . . self-identity" (PM § 408 Z).

Hegel's Typology	Pinel's Typology
Die Verrücktheit	*Aliénation mentale*

I. Der Blödsinn (idiocy)	I. La mélancolie (melancholia)
a. (Idiocy proper)	II. Manie sans délire (mania without
i. Natürlichen Blödsinn (natural	delirium)
idiocy: cretinism)	III. Manie avec délire (mania with
ii. (Exogenous or acquired idiocy)	delirium: manic frenzy, the
b. Die Zerstreutheit (the distracted mind)	'normal' form of madness)
c. Die Faselei (the rambling mind)	IV. La démence (dementia)
II. Die eigentlich Narrheit (madness or folly	V. L'Idiotism (idiocy)
proper)	a. (Innate, or natural idiocy:
a. Der Lebensüberdruß (world-weariness)	cretinism)
b. Die Melancholie (melancholia)	b. (Acquired idiocy)
III. Die Tollheit oder der Wahnsinn (mania	
or frenzy)	

Figure 1: Comparison of Hegel's and Pinel's Typologies of Madness

Hegel's classification system was partly influenced by Pinel's. He identified basically the same forms of madness, although (1) he did not see melancholy as a distinct illness, but as a species of *Narrheit* (madness or "folly" proper); (2) he saw Pinel's "dementia" as a particular form of "idiocy" (*die Faselei,* or "the rambling mind"); (3) he disagreed that manic frenzy (Pinel's *manie avec délire,* Hegel's *Tollheit* or *Wahnsinn*) was the 'normal' form, emphasizing *Narrheit* instead; and (4) while Pinel's classification begins with those forms of madness in which bodily processes are least implicated (melancholy and "mania without delirium"), moving to those where organic factors are most present (dementia and "idiocy"), Hegel's scheme works in just the opposite direction. Most importantly, Pinel does not see his classificatory system as based on any philosophical theory whatsoever, but as the result of clinical observation pure and simple. He is impatient with "the arbitrary distributions of nosologists" which are "far from being the result of accurate observation and experience," and resolves:

> to adopt that method of investigation which has invariably succeeded in all the departments of natural history, viz. to notice successively every fact, without any other object than that of collecting materials for future use. . . . With this in view, I first of all

[look to] . . . the symptoms of my patients.[44]

Hegel's classification of madness, on the other hand, is straightforwardly philosophical, in the sense that it develops an ontology of
what madness *means* as the framework in which the "infinitely
manifold" data of psychiatric symptoms may be explained.[45]

Hegel's commitment to the need for philosophical insight into
mental illness does not lead him quite so far as his predecessor
Kant, who felt that we should not refer the insane "to the medical
faculty, but must refer him to the philosophical faculty," since
"physicians and physiologists are generally still not advanced
enough to see deeply into the mechanism inside a human being."[46]
In 1904, the clinical physician Adolf Meyer scorned Kant's appropriation of the "diseases of the mind" for the philosopher, and included Hegel in his dismissal of all "philosophical medicine":

> An essentially speculative philosophy of a Hegel had to show the
> futility of a method which did not shape thought according to ac-
> tual experience, but, on the contrary, created a set of methods of
> thought which it forced on the facts, without any consideration for
> the pluralism or multiplicity of experience.[47]

Hegel, however, himself warns that philosophy can never 'deduce'
all the multiplicity of diseases, their etiologies and courses, or their
clinical symptoms. We have already noted Hegel's serious reservations about the Romantic 'philosophical' medicine, and his commitment to the important role of empirical-clinical research. Still,
philosophical insight is necessary, since clinical method can only
provide the starting point for understanding illness, and its observations stand in need of the theoretical framework which only a
genuinely speculative philosophy of the psyche can supply.

Thus Hegel consistently places himself in the between-space
of empirical and Romantic conceptions. As Von Engelhardt says,
"Hegel takes issue . . . with both the empirical and the romantic
views toward research into nature and medicine," and argues for
the "need for some combination of empirical work and speculation."[48] We see this middle perspective in Hegel's ambivalence towards the Romantic physician John Brown, whom on the one hand
we have already seen Hegel to criticize for his overly abstract and
formalistic theory, but whom on the other hand Hegel praises for
"direct[ing] attention beyond what was merely particular and specific both in diseases and remedies, to the *universal* in them as the
essential element" (PN § 373). True, Brown's insight is not tied sufficiently to the concrete, but it does at least emphasize the limita-

tions of the strictly empirical approach. For Hegel, both are necessary: "In the progress of philosophical knowledge, we must not only
give an account of the object *as determined by its Notion*"—the
speculative contribution—"but we must also name the *empirical*
appearance corresponding to it, and we must show that the appearance does, in fact, correspond to its Notion"—the clinical contribution (PN § 246A).

In an article comparing Brown's and Hegel's theories of medicine, Thomas Bole makes a helpful distinction between two forms
of speculative theory: *metaphysical* speculation, which characterizes Brown's system, and *logical* speculation, which Bole sees as
the defining characteristic of Hegel's position. What distinguishes
any speculative theory, whether metaphysical or logical, from empirical theories is that speculative theories are in principle not fal-
sifiable by particular facts. But while Brown adopts *a priori* principles from which he claims to be able to deduce the empirical
phenomena of disease, Hegel

> was concerned not with dictating *a priori* laws governing empir-
> ical data, but with sketching the logical geography explored by
> medicine. As an hypothesis not about empirical data, but about
> empirical hypotheses, [Hegel's speculative theory] was 'meta-em-
> pirical,' but not metaphysical.[49]

The problem with Brown's theory was that, while it promised
a complete deduction of the empirical data, it was actually remark-
ably unable to account for many of the empirical facts of disease, so
that Brown was constantly forced into arguing that we should disregard particular phenomena as insignificant.[50] Hegel, on the other
hand, never saw it as the business of speculation to deduce the empirical facts of disease, but, taking the facts as given, to develop a
series of hypotheses about the nature of health and illness which
could explain their significance. Hegel's speculative system of medicine is 'logical,' rather than metaphysical, then, in the sense that
it suggests a conceptual scheme in which empirical hypotheses and
data have meaning, and not in making empirical claims itself.

As for Hegel's middle path between the somatic and psychic
schools, throughout his discussion of madness he insists that "insanity must be grasped essentially as an illness *at once mental and
physical*" (PM § 408 Z), and that "mental illness is not merely to be
compared with physical illness, but is more or less bound up with
it" (PM § 406 Z). Any purely psychological account of madness will

contradict the basic principle of Hegel's ontology, that Nature, or the physical, is the "presupposition" of Mind, or the spiritual (PN Intro). Hegel is ultimately not a mind/body dualist at all, since for him the body is an essential aspect of the soul: the mind and body are a "community," not to be conceived as "antithetical" or "independent" of each other (PM § 389).[51] Thus in his *Philosophy of Right,* in the midst of his account of freedom and slavery, he insists that to attack or enslave another's body is directly to violate their soul:

> While I am alive, my soul . . . and my body are not separated; my body is the embodiment of my freedom. . . . It is therefore only abstract sophistical reasoning which can so distinguish body and soul as to hold that the 'thing-in-itself,' the soul, is not touched or attacked if the body is maltreated and the existent embodiment of personality is subjected to the power of another (PR § 48).

Given Hegel's account of the intimate community of mind and body, the somatic aspect of insanity clearly must be accounted for. On the other hand, nothing is more ludicrous to Hegel than strict materialism (see, e.g., SL § 38 Z), and any reduction of madness to exclusively material factors will fail to see that all mental illness is a struggle between physical and spiritual dimensions of the soul. Thus psychiatry must find a middle path: just as mind is the "unity of thought and being" (PM § 389 Z), of the mental and the physical, we stand in need of a mediating psychology which will account for the complex interplay between mental and physical aspects of madness.

This middle path can be seen clearly in Hegel's remarks on therapeutics. "The curative method," Hegel says:

> is partly physical and partly psychological. In some cases the former alone is sufficient; but in most cases it is necessary to supplement this by psychological treatment which, in its turn, can sometimes effect a cure by itself. There is no known remedy universally applicable for the physical side of treatment.

Thus while physical treatments should be explored, the current state of empirical medicine is much too uncertain to rely on exclusively. Finally, "the most effective treatment is always psychological." Specifically, Hegel strongly endorses Pinel's so-called 'moral treatment' of the insane, which begins from the premise that "the insane are still moral beings" who can be reasoned with.

The temptation to rely exclusively on physiological methods of therapy tends to deny the psychological component of mental illness, to overlook the moral nature of the insane, and to justify all the horrors of Bedlam (PM § 408 Z).

While Pinel's influence on Hegel was largely confined to the topic of therapeutics, it is worth noting that Pinel himself occupied an essentially middle position between the somatic and psychic schools. Unlike Hegel, Pinel did not work out much of a theoretical justification for this middle path. Indeed he was greatly skeptical of the "metaphysical discussions and ideological ramblings" into which he saw theoretical psychiatry falling,[52] and prided himself on a purely descriptive, empirical psychology. But the basis for Hegel's mediating psychology was already implicit in Pinel. On the one hand, Pinel was convinced that physical processes were implicated in madness:

> In order that intelligence should be intact, and should exercise its full power, . . . it is necessary that the organs from which [the faculties and sentiments of the soul] are derived should be sound; but when these are altered, perturbations in the faculties and sentiments immediately set in.[53]

On the other hand, Pinel was wary of relying too heavily on physical therapies such as drugs and bloodletting, and argued that precisely the success of 'moral' or purely psychological treatments strongly suggested physical causes were not the most important. "The successful application of moral regimen exclusively gives great weight to the supposition that in a majority of instances, there is no organic lesion of the brain nor of the cranium."[54]

Thus it may well be that Hegel found support for his own middle path in Pinel. It remained for Hegel to provide the philosophical framework in which this mediating psychology could take on an explanatory value.

Hegel's Anthropology of Madness:
The Reversion of the Mind to Nature

Regression, Displacement, Dream

Hegel's discussion of madness occurs within the "Anthropology" chapter of his *Philosophy of Mind (Philosophie des Geistes)*. The subject of the "Anthropology" is the "soul," which Hegel describes as "natural mind," or "mind which is still in the grip of Nature" (PM § 387 Z).[55] What this means is that at the level of the soul, the I or self has not yet developed into full conscious awareness of itself and its surrounding world. Indeed, much like Freud's anatomy of "primary narcissism," the soul for Hegel does not distinguish between inner and outer at all: the soul is a "differenceless unity," prior to any opposition between interior and external realities (PM § 398 Z). The soul is the pre-conscious state of the mind, the "form of the dull stirring, the inarticulate breathing of the spirit through its unconscious and unintelligent individuality" (*in seiner bewußt- und verstandlosen Individualität*) (PM § 400).

Hegel's theory of madness thus locates mental illness within the soul, and relies heavily on a psychology of the unconscious. Anticipating Freud, Hegel sees madness as a regressive turn backwards into archaic states of the mind, a "reversion" or "sinking back" of the developed, rational consciousness into the more primitive world of instincts and drives, or what Hegel calls "the life of feeling" (*Gefühlsleben*). In insanity, the "reversion to mere nature" displaces the normal principles of rational consciousness—what Freud calls "the laws of the ego" and the "reality principle"—and liberates the feelings, passions, and instincts of the soul: "the earthly elements are set free" and the "natural self . . . gains mastery over the objective, rational . . . consciousness" (PM § 408 & Z).

The most general characteristic of madness is this motion of withdrawal into the soul, or the unconscious life of feeling, and the corresponding displacement of the usual relationship with reality. The "sinking of the soul into its inwardness . . . cut[s] off [consciousness] from its connection with the outside world," so that the soul "contemplates its individual world not *outside,* but *within* itself" (PM § 406 Z). Or as Freud says, "material reality" is replaced by "psychical reality."[56] In this state of "commun[ing] merely with its interior states," Hegel continues, "the opposition between itself"—the soul—"and that which is for it"—the world, or reality—"remains shut up within it" (PM § 402 Z). Reality thus becomes a projected image of the "earthly elements" or passions and drives of the soul, "a shadow cast by the mind's own light—a show or illusion which the mind imposes as a barrier" (PM § 386) between itself and the external world from which it has withdrawn in an attempt to escape some experience of pain and alienation.

Freud's definition of neurosis closely echoes Hegel's view. He speaks of "the low valuation of reality, the neglect of the distinction between [reality] and phantasy," and the "path of regression" taken by the libido which has been "repulsed by reality" and must seek satisfaction through a "withdrawal from the ego and its laws."[57] Indeed, it is striking to see how close Hegel's picture of madness comes to the account Freud would begin developing of regression, the displacement of the reality principle, projection, and the unconscious some eighty years later. Further, Hegel already drew attention to the importance of the phenomenon of fixation, which Freud was to make a central concept in his anatomy of the neuroses. Just as for Freud a particular neurosis is to be explained by a fixation of the libido upon a specific unconscious wish or repressed archaic memory, Hegel speaks of the variety of shapes that madness takes as manifestations of the soul's becoming "engrossed with a single phase of feeling," or "imprisoned" in and "dominated by" a "fixed element" or "fixed idea" of the unconscious (PM § 408 & Z).[58]

Perhaps most striking of all is the fact that Hegel anticipates Freud in emphasizing the fundamental role of dreams in his development of a psychology of madness. It is well known that Freud attributed his greatest insights into mental illness to his discovery of a dream-theory. For Hegel, too, the nature of dreams holds an eminent place in the explanation of insanity. Within Hegel's metaphysics, nature is defined metaphorically as the state of spirit sleeping (PR § 258 Z). That is, the full development of spirit into its conscious life is not yet present in nature, which in its shape as the human soul is the unconscious. The soul, then, "is only the *sleep* of mind" (PM § 389). When consciousness sleeps, it "returns back" from its engagement in the external world to the domain of the soul, of unconscious drives and feelings which are expressed in dreams (PM § 398). As Freud says, when I dream, "I want to know nothing of the external world."[59] Dreaming abandons all the objective connections and causal associations between perceptions which are present in waking life, and adopts a system of symbolic "picture-thinking" (*Vorstellungsdenken*) which "wrests things completely out of their concrete context" so that "everything drifts apart, criss-crosses in the wildest disorder," and "objects lose all necessary, objective, rational connection and are associated only in an entirely superficial, contingent and subjective manner" (PM § 398 Z).

Like Freud, Hegel sees the "return" to dream-life as a necessary and rejuvenating feature of normal existence. But in madness, when consciousness reverts back to the state of the soul and becomes "engrossed" or "imprisoned" in this state, the mind is trapped in the dream state. Madness is a "*dreaming while awake*"

(PM § 408 Z), and "between [health] and insanity the difference is like that between waking and dreaming: only that in insanity the dream falls within the waking limits" (PM § 408).

Hegel and the Romantics

While Hegel's philosophy of madness is remarkable for its prefiguring of key elements of Freudian psychoanalytic theory, it is also very much in dialogue with his contemporaries. For example, the depiction of madness as a sort of 'dreaming while awake' incorporates a very common image of eighteenth and early nineteenth century psychic and Romantic theories of mental illness. Michel Foucault calls attention to the intimate connection between dreams and madness beginning in the eighteenth century. Madness is "the night of the mind" in which the self is "confiscated" by the dream-image, "imprison[ed] . . . in the circle of an erroneous consciousness."[60] The early eighteenth century Scottish physician and poet Archibald Pitcairne says that "Delirium is the dream of waking persons."[61] Even Kant uses this image; in his 1764 essay on the *Illnesses of the Brain* (*Versuch über die Krankheiten des Kopfes*) he writes that "*Der Verrückte ist also ein Träumer im Wachen.*"[62] And at the same time that Hegel was lecturing on madness, the Romantic theological psychiatrist Dietrich Kieser wrote of madness as belonging to "the nocturnal aspect" and the "sleeping" of the soul.[63]

Hegel, it is true, developed a much more elaborate theory of the nature and function of dreams than his predecessors, and situated it within a quite detailed psychology or 'anthropology' of the soul rather than relying on largely metaphorical and poetic descriptions. But the basic equation of madness with dreaming was clearly indebted to an already established tradition.

Further, Hegel's general account of madness as a process of reversion or sinking back into nature recalls the Romantic portrayal of the insane as having returned to an original state of nature. There are, however, some important differences to be noted. First, unlike the Romantics, Hegel did not idealize nature as a more 'innocent' and 'uncorrupted' state from which we have been dispossessed through the Fall into an alienating civilization. Hegel concedes that the history of culture is a path of struggle and a scene of pain and unhappiness, and that madness can be caused by "the violent upheaval and putting out of joint of the general state of the world." He cites as an example the period of the French Revolution, where "the almost complete collapse of civil society caused many people to become insane" (PM § 408 Z). But in general, the causes of insanity, where an individual withdraws back into nature and becomes imprisoned in the dream-life of the soul, must be traced to idiosyncrasies of individual psychology and not to larger cultural states of affairs.

Hegel sees the Romantics as overvaluing nature at the expense of culture. Nature, for Hegel, is the incomplete, the as-yet-undeveloped, the mere potentiality of spirit—spirit asleep and inarticulate, awaiting education into the language of rationality and culture that is its destiny and truth. Thus he denies that madness is a state in which the mind is open to higher truths and poetic insights. Madness is in fact a desperate "struggle for liberation" (PM § 402 Z) from nature, from the "dark, infernal powers" of the unconscious (PM § 408 Z) which assume mastery over the mind and prevent a genuine integration of the life of feeling and instinct with rationality and social consciousness.

Finally, Hegel entirely rejects the Romantic penchant for historicizing mental illness,[64] so that each particular form of madness is postulated as having arisen during a specific historical period. Not only does Hegel see this tendency as a perfect example of Romantic abstraction and formalism gone wild, but his whole theory of the nature of the soul is in principle opposed to it. The soul, for Hegel, is essentially pre-historical, in the same sense that the libido is pre-historical for Freud. Just as Freud sees mental illness as taking us back to the archaic past, to the play of instincts and drives which is prior to all human socialization, Hegel sees the "life of feeling" which is peculiar to the soul as the "innermost, unconscious instinct" of nature, which is prior to all history (RH 30). For genuine history to arise, we must move from the purely instinctive, pre-rational standpoint of the soul to the standpoint of culture, from nature to spirit, from dream to reason. Nature, to which we return in madness, is the "still unconscious dullness" of spirit, which has no historical content but is only the "pre-history" of culture (RH 71–75). Thus to center one's explanatory account of madness around a theory of the historical emergence of forms of insanity is to fundamentally misconstrue the nature of mental illness. The Romantic historicizing of madness obscures the origins of insanity in the 'dark, infernal' regions of the soul which are shut off from the very possibility of genuinely historical expression.

Hegel, the Somatic / Psychic Controversy, and Animal Magnetism

Hegel's theory of madness was also in close dialogue with those involved in the somatic/psychic controversy of the early nineteenth century. We have already noted Hegel's belief that "insanity must be grasped essentially as an illness *at once mental and physical.*" But further, his account of madness is directly modeled on his exposition of bodily disease (PN §§ 371–74). In purely physical illnesses, the bodily organism is overpowered by inorganic nature. "It finds itself in a state of *disease* when one of its systems or organs, stimulated into conflict with the inorganic power, establishes itself in isolation and persists in its particular activity against the activity of the whole, the fluidity [*Flüßigkeit*] and all-pervading process of which is thus obstructed" (PN § 371). For example, the blood may become "inflamed, and then it is active on its own account," independent of the healthy functioning of the total organism, or the stomach may become "overloaded" so that "the digestive apparatus functions as an isolated, independent activity, mak[ing] itself the center" of the organism, and "is no longer a moment of the whole but dominates it" (PN § 371 Z).

So too in the 'diseases of the soul,' the proper 'fluidity' of the mind is disrupted through the reversion to the life of feeling, which isolates one aspect of the soul over against the integrated unity of the mind. When the self becomes "engrossed with a single phase of feeling, it fails to assign that phase its proper place" within the harmony of the mind, and "finds itself in contradiction between the totality systematized in its [healthy] consciousness and the single phase or fixed idea which is not reduced to its proper place" (PM § 408). For example, in melancholy, a form of *Narrheit* or "madness proper," the individual is "imprison[ed] in the fixed idea of the loathsomeness of life," and "constantly broods over its unhappy idea" to the exclusion of all else, becoming "unable to rise to spontaneous thought and action" (PM § 408 Z).

This modeling of mental illness on the pattern of physical illness was typical of the somatic school. Further, Hegel's description of madness as a reversion to nature directly implicates what he calls the "element of corporeality" in the life of the soul (PM § 408). In keeping with this, he insisted that further research into the connection between madness and "a morbid condition of the nervous system" (PM § 408) should be encouraged, and in his *Philosophy of Nature* he gives a quite lengthy account of the current state of knowledge of anatomical neurology (PN § 354).

On the other hand, Hegel was opposed to any attempt simply to reduce madness to neurological or somatic considerations. For again, body and mind are not to be conceived as opposites in the life of the soul, but are in some sense 'intertwined.' "Insanity is therefore a *psychical* disease," Hegel says, by which he means "a disease of body and mind alike: the commencement may appear to start from the one more than the other, and so also may the cure" (PM § 408). We can only fully understand madness when we adopt an integrative approach, a 'middle' path between the exclusively somatic and the exclusively psychical positions, and account for the way in which insanity represents both a crisis of the spirit and a 'fixation' of unconscious, essentially physical determinations of drives and instincts.

Hegel's middle position in the debate between the somatists and psychists may be highlighted by looking at his stance on animal magnetism, or Mesmerism, which stood at the center of the controversy between the two schools. Franz Anton Mesmer (1734–1815) came to fame in 1774 in Vienna with the use of a magnet to cure a girl suffering from hysteria, and his method soon became the topic of heated debate. In 1777, he was forced to leave Vienna for Paris due to suspicions of fraud. In 1784, a Royal Commission headed by Benjamin Franklin, and including the scientists Bailly and Lavoisier and the physician Guillotin, was established in France to investigate Mesmerism. The report debunked animal magnetism as a sham, *"un système absolument dénué de preuves."*[65] Later, an 1812 commission of the Prussian government, led by the empirical physician Christian Hufeland, published a positive report, and in 1831, the year of Hegel's death, the French Royal Academy of Sciences stated that "far from setting limits to this part of physiological science, we hope that a new field has been opened up to it."[66] Enthusiastic supporters of Mesmer included Lafayette and George Washington.[67] As for the medical community, it was about equally divided between those who saw magnetism as a hoax—what Doerner calls "that spectacular and scandalous epitome of office-hour psychiatry"[68]—and those who regarded it as a miraculous advancement of psychiatric medicine.

Hegel, at any rate, was convinced. "In modern times, men of unimpeachable integrity have performed so many cures by magnetic treatment that anyone forming an unbiased judgment can no longer doubt the curative power of animal magnetism" (PM § 406 Z). He carried on a considerable correspondence with practitioners and theoreticians of Mesmerism, including his former Dutch student Peter van Ghert, the Romantic theologian and philosopher Karl Windischmann, and both the Romantic idealist philosopher Friedrich Schelling and his brother Karl, the Romantic physician who was to treat Hegel's sister for hysteria. Friedrich, who also piqued Hegel's interest in water divining,[69] in fact nearly lost his teaching position at Jena after misdiagnosing the daughter of Caroline von Schlegel as suffering from a nervous disorder, for which he recommended magnetic therapy, when in fact she had a simple, but nearly fatal, case of dysentery.[70]

The question for Hegel was not whether animal magnetism worked—on this point he was entirely satisfied—but how. Contemporary explanations were split between somatic and psychical accounts. Somatists, whether empirical physicians like Hufeland or Romantic physicians like Karl von Eschenmayer (a follower of Schelling's and chair of the department of philosophy at Tübingen), described animal magnetism as operating on a purely bodily level; psychists like van Ghert, Windischmann, Gotthilf von Schubert, Joseph Ennemoser, and Ferdinand Rungee claimed that magnetism was a straightforwardly spiritualistic phenomenon.

Both alternatives left Hegel unconvinced. The best explanations were no explanations at all: the Frenchman Armand Puységur, the marquis de Chastenet, who implausibly combined the careers of artillery officer and Romantic-psychist author—and who performed many magnetic cures himself—exclaimed in 1807: "*Je n'ai pas aujourd'hui plus de moyens de rendre raison des phénomènes du magnétisme animal;* il existe, parce il existe[!]" (At the moment I can only explain animal magnetism in this way: *it exists because it exists*).[71] Hegel believed that animal magnetism was bound to remain a mystery for both strict materialism and strict spiritualism. In a letter to van Ghert, he says that while Mesmerism must be seen as being effective at a physical level, it is "not open to ordinary physiological interpretations."[72]

This again seems to prefigure Freud, who felt that unconscious drives implied somatic factors but could not be fully explained by them. While Freud totally rejected Mesmer's theory of magnetism—"[Mesmer's] theory has become so alien to our contemporary mode of scientific thought that it may be considered as eliminated"[73]—he studied with the great neurologist and hypnotist Jean Charcot in Paris, and struggled during the 1880s and 90s to reconcile Charcot's somatic theory of hypnotism with a psychological (or "suggestion") theory,[74] which might finally "strip the manifestations of hypnotism of their strangeness."[75] While neither Hegel nor Freud could endorse a purely neurological account, Hegel was convinced that entirely spiritualistic theories, for their part, reduced animal magnetism to "magic." Indeed magnetism abandons "practical common sense" to utter "confusion," and appears as an "incredible miracle." Finally, what is needed is a fundamentally new orientation: Mesmerism "necessitates the advance from ordinary psychology to the comprehension afforded by speculative philosophy for which alone animal magnetism is not an incomprehensible miracle" (PM § 379 Z).

What the speculative philosophy of medicine provides is a way to account for seemingly bizarre capacities of the magnetized subject which so contradict the operations of the 'normal' mind and "the ordinary course of nature"—the evident "liberation" of the mind from "the bondage" to "spatial and temporal relations," as for example the ability to perceive tastes and smells which are present in the magnetizer with whom she stands *en rapport,* or to perceive sights without the eyes or light (PM §§ 379, 406 & Z). They key is found in the fact that the magnetic state is, strictly speaking, a state of disease:

> the magnetic state is an *illness*; for in general the essence of disease must be held to consist in the isolation of a particular system of the organism from the general physiological life, and in virtue of this *alienation* of the particular system from the general life, the [organism] exhibits its . . . impotence and dependence on an *alien* power. (PM § 406 Z)

As in all illness, animal magnetism effects the isolation of one aspect of the organism from the whole; here, the subject returns to and becomes engrossed in the life of the feeling soul which we have seen to be precisely the course followed in the onset of madness. And just as in all mental disease, in animal magnetism the liberation of the unconscious dimension of the psyche effects a displacement of the usual causal and associative connections of the rational mind; the life of feeling is "without any distinctions between subjective and objective, between intelligent personality and objective world, and without . . . any definite points of attachment" to the "ordinary course of nature" (PM § 406). Finally, as in madness proper, the magnetic state is a reversion to the domain of sleep and dream; the magnetized subject is the "somnambulist," "plunged . . . into the state where he is wrapped up in his undifferentiated natural life, i.e., into sleep" (PM § 406 Z).

With the reversion to the unconscious life of feeling, where none of the ordinary laws of waking consciousness and perception obtain, the bizarre, topsyturvy world of dream-life provides its own "laws," just as in certain forms of madness the mind is subject to "a perfect type of chaos" where the conditions of external reality are

"unconsciously turn[ed] topsyturvy" (PM § 408 Z). The mind is liberated from the usual parameters of causal connection and spatio-
temporal ordering, since the dream-life of the feeling soul respects
none of these categories in any ordinary way. Hence the seemingly
bizarre phenomena of the somnambulist state (however mysterious
the actual physiological mechanisms which make these phenomena
possible may remain to the current state of anatomical science).[76]

There remains one crucial point to be gleaned from the explanation of the magnetic state as a form of disease, which has to do
with the relationship between the magnetizer and the magnetized
subject. I am not thinking here of the therapeutic relation between
the two, although Hegel makes some interesting remarks on this
as well (PM § 406 Z; PN § 373 Z). Rather, the point I have in mind
returns us to Hegel's notion that magnetism is a form of "alienation" of the magnetized subject, whereby the subject "exhibits its
. . . impotence and dependence on an *alien* power." This alien
power is of course the magnetizer, with whom the subject is able to
enter into "rapport" through the hypnotically induced sleep state
(PM § 406). Thus there is effectively a "duplication of the personality" of the subject (PM § 406 Z), whereby the subject is alienated
from her own waking personality and comes under the power of
the personality of the magnetizer.

What is so interesting about this is that Hegel's general account of madness also relies upon the idea that the insane take on
a sort of 'double personality.' By sinking back to the unconscious
life of the soul, the insane individual "is driven out of its [rational]
mind, [and] is shifted out from the center of its actual world." And
yet there is nearly always (except in the severest cases of brain lesions) the retention of a vestige of that rational consciousness.
"Since [the insane self] still retains a consciousness of [its lost]
world, it has two centers, one in the remainder of its rational consciousness and the other in its deranged idea." Thus "the insane
subject is in communion with himself in the negative of himself,"
and is a "subject disrupted into *two different personalities*" (PM §
408 Z). The implications of this idea of the double personality of the
insane for Hegel's adoption of the Pinelian therapeutics of moral
treatment are clear. "It is the merit of Pinel . . . to have grasped
this residue of rationality in lunatics and maniacs as the foundation of treatment," so that a dialogue between the rational "center"
of the personality and the therapist works towards a "drawing outwards" of the self from the center of its "diseased subjectivity" back
"towards the real world" (PM § 408 Z).

Madness is thus a sort of tortured dialogue between the dream-life of the unconscious and the echo of the rational self. In animal magnetism (and in successful psychiatric therapies), this conflictual dialogue becomes a harmonious rapport between two actually distinct selves. In both states the self becomes subject to an 'alien power,' only in madness this power is the rational self's own unconscious 'other,' the feeling-life of the soul from which spirit once emerged in the course of its development and to which it now returns in a desperate withdrawal from its everyday world.

In the debate between the somatic and psychical interpretations of animal magnetism, then, Hegel's speculative philosophy seeks to find a middle course between overly spiritualistic accounts which finally reduce the phenomenon to magic by overlooking the underlying physical dynamics of the unconscious, and overly materialistic accounts which fail to do justice to such psychological dynamics as the 'reversion' or 'sinking inward' of consciousness, the nature of dream imagery, and the psychical bond of rapport (the doubling of the personality) between the magnetizer and the somnambulist. This is entirely in keeping with Hegel's larger endeavor to mediate the conflicts amongst Romantics, empiricists, psychists, and somatists in the field of psychiatry. His development of a speculative philosophy of medicine allowed him simultaneously to call into question the one-sidedness of the 'ordinary psychologies' of the day while also acknowledging the importance of many of their findings and hypotheses. He was able to give due credit to the need for empirical research while offering an ontology or speculative logic of madness which provided an explanatory framework for comprehending the empirical data. And his insistence that insanity was a disease "at once mental and physical" made it possible to encourage the work of the anatomical neurologists without prejudice to a deeper exploration of the psychological dynamics of madness.

CHAPTER THREE

Madness as the Decentering of Reason

I have been confirmed in my idea that the study of madness—alienation in the deepest sense of the term—was at the center of an anthropology, of a study of man. The asylum is the refuge for those who can no longer be made to live in our interhuman environment. Thus it is a way of understanding this environment indirectly, as well as the problems it constantly poses for normal men.

(Jean Hyppolite, *Figures de la pensée philosophique*)

Psycho-analysis has demonstrated that there is no fundamental difference, but only one of degree, between the mental life of normal people, of neurotics and of psychotics. A normal person has to pass through the same repressions and has to struggle with the same substitutive structures; the only difference is that he deals with these events with less trouble and better success.

(Sigmund Freud, *On Psycho-analysis*)

One of the features of Hegel's conception of madness which sets it apart from other theories of the turn of the eighteenth century is his phenomenological approach.[1] While his middle path between opposing paradigms seeks to acknowledge important insights of both empirical and philosophical psychologies, his own speculative philosophy of medicine does not simply integrate both sides of this opposition, but goes beyond them. It is largely Hegel's grounding of his philosophy of madness in what he views as a fundamentally new method of analysis, that of phenomenology, which accounts for this.

In an advertisement placed by the publishers of the *Phenomenology of Spirit* in a Jena cultural journal (*Intelligenzblatt der*

Jenaischen Allgemeinen Litteraturzeitung) of October 28, 1807, Hegel offers his own account of phenomenology as a "replace[ment] [of] psychological explanations as well as the more abstract discussions of the foundation of knowledge."[2] Traditional methods of psychology and epistemology are seen by Hegel as overly formalistic, tending to abstract features of the mind away from the concrete experience of consciousness in its encounters with the world. The task of phenomenology, the advertisement continues, is to describe "the wealth of appearances [*Reichtum der Erscheinungen*] in which spirit presents itself, . . . brought into a scientific order."[3] Phenomenology is thus an (ontological, speculative) logic of the appearance of shapes and structures of consciousness in its varied experience of the world.[4]

Key to Hegel's phenomenology is his attempt to demonstrate that these shapes and structures are not unchanging, static categories or faculties of the mind, but that they evolve through experience from more primitive, incomplete forms into successively more developed and complete forms according to certain dialectical patterns. As Hegel puts it in the advertisement for the *Phenomenology*, his new science will exhibit the manner in which the shapes of consciousness continually "dissolve and pass over into higher ones which constitute their next truth."[5] This 'dissolving' (*sich auflösen*) and 'passing over' (*übergehen*), however, is a process which always retains its past history; the initial shapes are not simply replaced by new ones, but are *aufgehoben*, integrated and preserved within the more complete configurations of consciousness into which they evolve.

These commitments of Hegel's phenomenology help explain the intimate interplay between the concepts of health and illness, of 'normalcy' and its derangement, in his philosophy of madness. Most importantly, they explain his claim that madness has "the healthy . . . consciousness for its *presupposition*" (PM § 408 Z). The healthy consciousness—"the self-possessed and healthy subject" (*das gesund und besonnen Subjekt*) or "the fully furnished [*gebildete*] self of intelligent [*verständigen*] consciousness" (PM § 408)—is the shape of consciousness which has evolved out of the original form of all human existence as the 'feeling soul' (immersed in nature, instinct, and the unconscious), and madness is a movement backwards to origins, a return out of developed consciousness back to the life of feeling. As such, madness cannot be explained from within itself, according to a phenomenology unique to itself; our explanations must always have reference to the phenomenology of the healthy mind. In short, the different forms of madness are each modifications of certain fundamental structures of the developed, 'normal' mind.

The present chapter will explore this interconnection between the phenomenologies of madness and the healthy mind in two ways. First, after expanding on several of the basic themes of Hegel's theory of *Verrücktheit* which were introduced in a provisional way in chapter 2, we will explicitly compare the phenomenological structures of madness with those of the developed consciousness. The comparison will center on Hegel's account of desire as the fundamental underlying nature of consciousness, and on three of the most paradigmatic shapes of the developed consciousness: stoicism, skepticism, and despair (the unhappy consciousness). The purpose of this comparison will be to show how there are substantial and revealing parallels between the structures of the mad and healthy selves, and yet that Hegel finally situates the two within importantly different phenomenological spaces. The discussion of phenomenological structures of madness will also give us occasion to compare this highly formal philosophic endeavor with Hegel's personal encounter with the insanity of his sister Christiane and his close friend Friedrich Hölderlin, and to raise the question of how fully Hegel's public, philosophic discourse on madness squares with his private experience of the suffering of the insane.

The second main concern of the chapter will be to suggest that the close relationship between Hegel's accounts of madness and rationality enables a new point of access to his idealism. It will be argued that the closeness of these states extends to their sharing, in certain ways, the basic world-view of idealism, the view that reality is in important respects constituted by the mind. By seeing how Hegel's theory of madness may be read as the diagnosis of a fantastic and ultimately failed form of idealism, we will be able to place the commitments and values of his own idealism in sharper focus.

The Anatomy of Madness

Hegel's classification of the forms of madness rejects the common method of centering on symptoms, and looks instead at what he calls the "inner characteristics" of madness (PM § 408 Z). That is, Hegel offers an ontology of insanity, which focuses on the way disease is a modification of constitutive structures of the mind rather than concentrating on the museum of external signs. Each of the three major forms of *Verrücktheit—Blödsinn* (idiocy, imbecility), *Narrheit* ("madness proper"), and *Tollheit* or *Wahnsinn* (mania, frenzy)—are particular variations of his general ontology of madness as a 'sinking inward' of the mind into itself and a corresponding break with the normal relations to reality. To cite again Hegel's basic definition of madness, it is "a state in which the mind is shut up within itself, has sunk into itself, whose peculiarity . . . consists in its being no longer in immediate contact with actuality but in having positively separated itself from it" (PM § 408 Z). In chapter 2 we looked briefly at how Hegel distinguishes these three forms.[6] The present discussion will seek to flesh out the two most general features of the ontology of madness: withdrawal and separation from reality. We will see later that these are features which also play a significant role in Hegel's ontology of the 'normal' mind.

Withdrawal, Separation, and Decentering

Let us begin by looking more closely at the nature of withdrawal in madness, the 'sinking inward' of the mind into itself. We have seen that Hegel's phenomenology of the developed, rational mind seeks to show how this consciousness preserves within itself its origins in nature, the life of feeling, so that it is a unity of reason and nature, mind and body, thought and feeling, consciousness and the unconscious. Madness is a disruption of this unity, where archaic feeling states become autonomous, or "are set free in [a] reversion to mere nature," and the mind becomes "engrossed" or "fixed" within its original shape, the feeling soul (PM § 408). Fundamental to this reversion and fixation is that "the soul . . . contemplates its individual world not *outside*, but *within* itself" (PM § 406 Z). There is a rupture of the relation to the external world, where the mind "communes merely with its *interior* states" (PM § 402 Z), and has thus become delivered over to a "psychical self-imprisonment" (PM § 408 Z). The movement of withdrawal is a response to the experience of pain and alienation in the self's encounter with its world, just as we will see that the fundamental response of all desiring consciousness to the failure of finding unity with its world is to retreat inward.

Trapped within itself, cut off from objective reality, which is seen only as the theater of its own pain, and from which the self seeks solace from in the womblike seclusion of its interiority, insanity substitutes for the connection with reality its own subjective, projected reality, a "shadow cast by the mind's own light" (PM § 385 Z). Thus in the mad self's "negation of the real" (PM § 403), reality is not *nothing*, a sheer absence, but redefined, reconstructed and projected by fantasy. Reality as 'other,' as external and threatening, is negated, but replaced by the dream of the mind in an effort to overcome that otherness. Just as Freud speaks of "two realities" in his *Interpretation of Dreams*, "psychical reality" and "material reality,"[7] the reality of dreams and the unconscious on the one hand and the reality of rationality and the external world on the other, madness for Hegel is the displacing of the objective reality of the external world with the subjective reality of the inner world.

It is this action of displacement of the external which accounts for the presence of *two centers* of reality in insanity, which we have already noted to be a crucial characteristic of Hegel's ontology of madness. The first center is the displaced, forgotten—or rather, only dimly recalled, as in a dream—center of objective externality, while the second is the constructed, projected center of subjective interiority. The mad self is "imprisoned in a particular, merely subjective idea, . . . driven out of its [rational] mind, [and is thus] shifted out from the center of its actual world and . . . has two centers" (PM § 408 Z), the displaced, de-centered, lost, but still recollected trace of its rationality, and the new center of its deranged consciousness. We have also noted that this doubling of reality corresponds to a doubling of the personality of the insane subject. Caught between the recollection of the objective world and the now dominant world of its subjective construction, the absence of a unified world is mirrored in the absence of *self*-unification, and the individual experiences herself as "a subject disrupted into two different personalities" (PM § 408 Z).

We will see shortly that this notion of doubleness—indeed of a *double* doubleness, where the divided world is complimented by a divided self—not only plays an essential role in Hegel's anatomy of madness, but is equally fundamental to his phenomenology of the rational spirit. The experience of doubleness, and the essentially ambiguous (*zweideutig*) character of both consciousness and reality, is a constantly recurring theme in Hegel's dialectic. Hence this will be one important place to examine significant similarities between the formal structures of madness and those of the rational consciousness. This shared ground, however, while extensive, is not complete; madness and rationality are not so distant from each other as to be opposites, but neither do they collapse into each other. The key difference is that madness occurs in the domain of the 'feeling soul' (*die fühlende Seele*), which is spirit in *nature*, a domain existing ontologically prior to, or better, 'underneath,' the developed, rational shape of consciousness. Insanity is a return of the developed mind back to nature and the life of feeling (*Gefühlsleben*), which underlies rationality but has been covered over and transfigured, or *aufgehoben*, by it.

In this turn backwards of madness, the self in a sense internalizes the master/slave dialectic of struggle for domination, where the 'other' it seeks to overcome is precisely its own rational nature, which in the course of things had gradually gained preeminence over the original state of the infant as 'nature' (the life of feeling or instinct). Madness is precipitated when the self comes to feel betrayed by its rational nature, by its failure to find a way to rationally reconcile itself with the world. And the self which seeks liberation into mastery is precisely the more primitive, archaic 'feeling soul' or 'natural self' which previously had been submerged. In madness, "the natural self . . . gains mastery over the objective, rational, concrete consciousness," and the "earthly elements" of the soul (*das Irdische*) "are set free" (PM § 408 and Z). The life of feeling, passion, the instincts—the underworld or underground, as it were, of the psyche, intimately connected with the body, the human shape of nature—asserts its claims to the soul over the claims of rationality, and assumes the position of power.

Madness, however, is subject to a similar ironic twist, or reversal, as occurs in the master/slave dialectic, where the master, in achieving victory over the other, the slave, in fact enslaves himself. The mad self, in overcoming the otherness of the rational world, is delivered over to a "psychical self-imprisonment" within the "abyss" of its feeling soul (PM § 408 Z). And just as the master, revealed in her victory as a slave, must struggle to liberate herself, madness assumes the form of a "struggle for liberation" from its bondage to the life of feeling and instinct.

Feeling and Language

We will say more about Hegel's association of feeling with nature in chapter 7, where the importance of nature in madness will be examined through a comparison with his account of nature on the tragic stage. For now we may note that the identification of feeling with nature serves to situate feeling within the element of the 'immediate' which has not yet developed into its full spiritual form. Rationality is intrinsically mediational for Hegel; it is concerned with dialectical engagement with the other, and implies community, relationship, and dialogue. Immediacy, on the other hand, entails isolation, seclusion, privacy, the self withdrawn into the narcissistic cocoon of 'I am I.' Hegel writes in his *Phenomenology* that "the situation in which consciousness knows itself to be at home is . . . one marked by the absence of spirit" (PS 15). In this sense, we might say that the reversion of the mind back into the life of feeling represents an immediate sense of 'at-homeness' which is prior to the development into fully spiritual consciousness.

Feeling is a sort of private language for Hegel,[8] and hence is linguistically as well as ontologically prior to our species-being. This explains why Hegel does so much to distance himself from the Romantic infatuation with feeling (*"Gefühl ist alles,"* as Goethe liked to say), as for example in the Preface to the *Phenomenology* where he writes that the person who "makes his appeal to feeling, . . . is finished and done with anyone who does not agree"; they have "nothing [at all] to say to anyone who does not find and feel the same in himself" (PS 43). Only where there is something to say can nature be transformed into spirit and feeling into reason. Only in the publicity of language, in which the particular, isolated 'I' vanishes' and becomes for-others in a common world, can spirit find its true element.

This withdrawal of madness into a private language of feeling creates the major impediment to the therapeutic relation. Jean Hyppolite refers to the extreme point of madness as the point at which the self "does not wish to speak anymore," where the self "withdraws [in]to itself and rejects all communication," and sees this as the fulfillment of "the death instinct."[9] We will see in the next chapter that for Hegel, too, the death instinct is very much present in the dynamics of madness. We have already hinted, at the close of chapter 2, at what nevertheless makes the therapeutic relation possible for Hegel—or, put otherwise, how Hegel can see madness as a struggle for liberation notwithstanding its imprisonment in a sphere which rejects (or rather, privatizes) language— namely, the fact that in all madness there remains a vestige of rationality, a 'second center' of the personality which the therapist can speak to and seek to draw out into dialogue. We will return to this basic assumption of Hegel's therapeutics in our final chapter.

Nature, Dream, and the Unconscious

The privacy of the language of feeling involves a replacement of the rational scheme of causal connections between the mind and the world with a logic of its own, a logic of feeling, which is "self-supporting and independent of" the rational threads connecting the self to the external world (PM § 406). What occurs here is much like what Freud sees as happening in dreams, where there is a withdrawal from the logic of connections pertaining in the external world, and the development of a new language with its own unconscious mechanisms. And indeed we have seen that Hegel uses the image of the dream, with the associated nocturnal imagery of darkness and sleep, to describe the life of feeling.

Nature itself is referred to as "mind asleep" (PR § 258 Z), and for the feeling soul "the world outside it and its relationship to that world is under a veil, and the soul is thus sunk in sleep" (PM § 406). Now while Hegel anticipates Freud's view that sleep is a necessary "rehabilitation" from the turmoil of life,[10] madness is a desperate attempt to heal the wounds of alienation by a permanent withdrawal into the world of sleep: madness is a *dreaming while awake* (PM § 408 Z). This image is very common in the psychological literature of the eighteenth and early nineteenth centuries,[11] along with the general association of madness with "the nocturnal aspect" of the soul, and the idea of cure as an "awakening."[12] Madness is thus a sort of darkening of the world—a "veiling" of the world of daylight (PM § 406)—where the more primitive 'earthly elements' of the soul which hold dominion over the world of sleep are emancipated, and where the language of conscious rationality is replaced by the language of dream life.

The analogy of madness to dreaming and the inscribing of madness within the world of the night points to the crucial role of the unconscious in Hegel's anatomy of insanity, just as Freud sees the dream as the key to the discovery of the vicissitudes of the unconscious. As Darrel Christensen says, "[Hegel], like Freud, holds that dreams and symptoms are to be understood in their own language as exhibiting contents of the mind below the level of conscious awareness."[13] We will explore the theme of the unconscious fully in chapter 5, but may point out here that the feeling soul is described by Hegel as "the stage of [mind's] darkness" precisely because the "light" of consciousness is not yet explicit (PM § 404). Thus Hyppolite is right to see Hegel's account of the "natural" self as entailing as "one of its fundamental traits," a "radical unconsciousness": the self "sees only through a veil, in a state of non-seeing."[14] *Gefühlsleben,* mind sunk into the darkness of sleep, is the unconscious power of instinct.

We can see this association of nature with the unconscious clearly, for example, in Hegel's discussion of what he calls "the living work of art" (*das lebendige Kunstwerk*) in his *Phenomenology,* where he offers his interpretation of the Bacchic and Eleusinian cults of the Greeks. These festivals celebrate the sense of unity with nature, "the untamed revelry of nature," in the pre-linguistic symbolism of the body (dance, frenzy), where "the self . . . is beside itself . . . in corporeal beauty." This ecstatic movement, where the mind is outside itself in its immersion in nature, is seen as the "satisfied night" of the unconscious: the "sun" of consciousness is a perpetual " 'setting' or going-down" into the "nether darkness" and "night of concealment" of the unconscious (PS 436–39). The living work of art is superseded by the "spiritual work of art" (*das geistige Kunstwerk*), in which language replaces the symbolism of nature and the body, poetry replaces Bacchic enthusiasm, consciousness replaces the unconscious. Similarly, Hegel's famous analysis of Sophocles' *Antigone,* a topic we will explore at length in chapter 7, reveals an association of the life of feeling (chauvinistically inscribed as the feminine) with darkness, the nether world, and the unconscious (PS 267ff).

Madness and the Developed Consciousness

As we turn now to draw out some of the connections between Hegel's account of madness and his phenomenology of the developed consciousness, it is important to stress that at the heart of Hegel's philosophy is his theory of the dialectical character of reality, which characterizes all human life as a process of evolution through strife. The being of consciousness is never a state of repose, but involves the perpetual dissolution (*Auflösung*) and dismemberment (*Zerrissenheit*) of its self-identity, since consciousness is animated by an internal drive to reach out beyond—and hence to uproot—its present reality toward a fuller self-determination. Hence "the life of spirit is not the life that shrinks from . . . the tremendous power of the negative . . . and keeps itself untouched by devastation [*Verwüstung*], but rather the life that endures it and maintains itself in it" (PS 19 / W 3: 36). This means that human consciousness is continually subject to the experience of "infinite pain" (PM § 382), and the reversion of spirit into madness is only one of a number of strategies consciousness may take in its struggle with this pain.

Desire

To get a clearer sense of why Hegel describes spirit as continually abandoned to the encounter with pain and alienation, and how this abandonment reveals a largely shared ontology of the mad and rational selves, we need to say a word about his phenomenology of desire. A much fuller account of desire will occupy us in the next chapter, where an argument linking the nostalgic dimension of desire with madness will be developed, but for now we may content ourselves with a few general remarks. Desire, for Hegel, is ontologically constitutive of human consciousness: "Self consciousness *is* desire" (PS 109). Now desire is essentially a desire for unity, both the unity of the self with the world it inhabits (the desire to overcome the sense of disparity between what the world is and what we wish it to be), and the unity of the self with itself (the desire to overcome the sense of disparity between what we are and what we wish to be).

Crucial to Hegel's anatomy of desire is his argument that consciousness cannot achieve this unity on its own; the narcissistic standpoint of 'I am I' is empty, without content (except as fantasy), and hence is intrinsically unstable, forcing consciousness out of itself to acknowledge an other. Even God, in Hegel's view, requires an other, which is the secret meaning of his creation of the world, as a mirror in which he may find himself doubled (see e.g. HP 1: 75). So too the profound need which motivates the creation of art is the drive that human beings have for a "duplication" of the self, the impulse of "bringing what is in [us] into sight" so that we may recognize the self in what we produce (A 1: 32). Hence just as we have seen there to be an intrinsic doubleness characteristic of madness, in its two centers of reality and its doubling of the personality, some sort of doubleness is present in all consciousness as a consequence of its desiring nature. Further, as with madness, this is a double doubleness, not simply an experience of the double center of reality—the experience of the disparity between the inner and the outer worlds—but a reduplication of the self as well.

But in duplicating the self, in finding the self outside itself in its other, consciousness is confronted with alienation: it is opposed to itself, experiences disunity, and is henceforth driven by the effort to consume or assimilate its other so as to recover its lost unity. Desire is thus a vicious cycle of yearning, a movement outwards, a cathexis (binding) of an other so as to satisfy its need for content, and yet, in the confrontation with alienation, an anxious attempt to retreat to itself so as to protect itself from the pain of self-opposition.

Despair

While we see this double movement of externalization and retreat in all the shapes of consciousness, it is the *Gestalt* of despair which epitomizes it most perfectly, and which serves as the clearest point of comparison with madness. Hegel's commitment to an account of human existence as subject to 'infinite pain' is what motivates him to see the state of despair, or the 'unhappy consciousness,' as the central shape of consciousness in its quest for unity,[15] and we might say that madness is the most extreme gesture open to consciousness when it is unable to resolve its despair.

The unhappy consciousness is the pain of the self that fails to reach unity with itself, the "grief and longing" (PS 456f) of the self which yearns for unity but experiences only inner division and estrangement. "The unhappy consciousness," Hegel writes, "is the tragic fate of the . . . self that aims to be absolute" (PS 455)—the age-old longing of human beings to become God, to become complete and whole, to overcome our sense of alienation from our world, the anxiety of yearning for unity but constantly being forced to acknowledge the pain of failing to reach it.

Two formal structures of despair call for special attention. First, despair is the experience of *internal* division: it recognizes the other—which is essentially outer reality as a whole—as its own essence, as what is fundamental to its own existence, but experiences this other as constantly escaping it, just as Sartre says that our existence constantly escapes coinciding with our essence.[16] As much as we may seek to define ourselves as an abiding essence, we are "condemned to be free," as Sartre puts it,[17] condemned, that is, to perpetual self-becoming, which is implied by our finite and temporal nature—we are always radically incomplete unto ourselves. Thus the unhappy consciousness, like the mad self, is a *double personality*, a "duplication of self-consciousness within itself," which, however, is experienced only as "self-contradiction" (PS 126). It has two centers of itself within itself, which never overlap: the self experienced as finite, mutable, and subject to the whims of contingency, and an opposing self it also identifies with, at least by way of desire, the self as whole, immutable, and self-identical. As Jean

Hyppolite puts it, "every self-consciousness is double for itself: it is God and man," or master and slave, "at the heart of a single consciousness."[18]

Second, the response to this painful experience of inner division is the act of *projection*, the projection outward onto a 'beyond' (as God, or essence) of its desire for self-identity and completeness. Hence Alexandre Kojève writes that the despairing consciousness "imagines an 'other world' which is 'beyond' the natural world of the senses; . . . in *this* world everything is slavery, [for] . . . freedom is real [only] in the beyond."[19] Consciousness is never what it is; as pure subjectivity it is pure negativity, becoming, transformation, self-transcendence; and in despair, which is precisely the acute recognition of this absence of unity, it projects its own image of itself as immutable, whole, and free outward onto an ideal reality. The unhappy consciousness is thus the agonizing desire of spirit struggling to fulfill this ideal of self-identity and unity but always finding it to be elusive.

It is hard not to be struck by how closely these formal structures of despair are paralleled in the formal structures of insanity. Indeed, Hegel uses virtually identical language in his description of the deepest form of madness (*Tollheit, Wahnsinn*) to that of his discussion of the unhappy consciousness. The mad self "is aware of the disruption of his consciousness into two mutually contradictory modes," and "obtains the unhappy feeling of his self-contradiction; . . . here we see the soul in the more or less despairing effort to overcome [its] discord . . . and to restore its . . . self-identity" (PM § 408 Z). The mad self has separated itself from actuality, from the world, just as despair is animated by the painful recognition of its division from reality or essence. Stanley Rosen's description of despair as a "radical homelessness" where consciousness "lacks an 'objective correlative' " and "can only dream and suffer"[20] is equally as telling a description of madness, which has forsaken its objective home and withdrawn into the dreamlife of the interior.[21] Finally, along with the unhappy sense of inward division and homelessness, the key gesture of madness in response to its sense of pain is *projective wish-fulfillment*: the insane self projects its inward dreams of unity onto the world and treats them as real, just as in despair the desire for self-wholeness is projected onto a 'beyond.'

Are We All Mad?

This parallelism of madness and despair gives cause for reflection. Given that despair is posited by Hegel as the central form of consciousness; and given that the structures of despair and madness dovetail so closely; then, much as Freud is forced to admit that "a healthy person, too, is virtually a neurotic"[22]—or, more strongly, "you may quite well say that we are *all* ill"[23]—should we not also see Hegel's philosophy as entailing that we are all mad? This is in fact the conclusion that Jean Hyppolite draws in a typically provocative article on "Hegel's Phenomenology and Psychoanalysis." He analyzes the essential doubleness of consciousness that we have seen to be entailed by the ontology of desire as itself the heart of madness: "The essence of man is to be mad [for Hegel], that is, to be himself in the other, to be himself by this very otherness." And Hyppolite further sees the act of projection which is intrinsic to despair, the "casting out" of the self of its "feeling of deep upheaval," as "man's inherent madness."[24]

I wish to disagree with Hyppolite here, and argue that there is an important difference between despair and madness, but not without first strengthening his case. Hyppolite does not look at the *Encyclopædia* discussion of madness, but draws his conclusions from his reading of the *Phenomenology*. And it is true that Hegel employs the language of *Verrücktheit* at important junctures of that text. For example, "skepticism" is described at one point as an "unconscious, thoughtless rambling" (*bewußtlose Faselei*) (PS 125 / W 3: 162), and *Faselei* is a subcategory of *Blödsinn*, one of the three main categories in Hegel's typology of insanity; the "law of the heart" is delivered over to "frenzy" *(Wahnsinn,* a major category of insanity), and is characterized as "derangement" *(die Verrücktheit des Bewußtseins)* (PS 225 / W 3: 280); the attitude of "virtue" is an internal contradiction which culminates in madness (*Verrücktheit*) (PS 229 / W 3: 285); the standpoint of "absolute freedom and terror," with its "fury of destruction" (PS 359), is explicitly diagnosed in the *Encyclopædia* as a form of *Wahnsinn* (PM § 408 Z); and the "beautiful soul" is a "lost soul" consumed by a yearning for unity which it cannot attain, becoming "disordered to the point of madness" (*zur Verrücktheit zerrüttet und zerfließt in sehnsüchtiger Schwindsucht*) (PS 407 / W 3: 491). Further, Hegel occasionally seems to directly support Hyppolite's discovery of madness in the very ontology of desire, as for example in a passage from the *History of Philosophy* where he speaks of how the essential human yearning for unity leads to "extravagant" efforts which "constantly pass into madness (*Verrücktheit)"* (HP 3: 510 / W 20: 418).

Nevertheless, Hegel is explicit in the *Encyclopædia* that not every relationship to the self as other is an indication of madness: "We must distinguish this negative of the soul characteristic of insanity from [an] other kind of negative; . . . we need not therefore be mad" simply because of this negative self-relation or double personality (PM § 408 Z). What distinguishes madness from despair is that madness occurs when the mind has been forced back into 'the feeling soul,' the domain of nature and the unconscious, whereas the consuming grief of despair occurs at the level of "the intellectual and rational consciousness" (PM § 408 Z). Thus while for Hegel despair is an absolutely necessary shape of consciousness, not only formally (as a logically necessary stage of his phenomenology) but actually, for all consciousness, madness is only formally necessary (a logically necessary potentiality of spirit), but not a state which we all will fall into:

> This interpretation of insanity as a necessarily occurring form or stage in the development of the soul is naturally not to be understood as if we were asserting that *every* mind . . . must go through this stage. . . . Such an assertion would be as absurd as to assume that because . . . crime is considered as a necessary manifestation of the human will, therefore to commit crime is an inevitable necessity for *every* individual. Crime and insanity are extremes which the human mind *in general* has to overcome in the course of its development, but which do not appear as extremes in every individual (PM § 408 Z).

Despair is a necessary experience of consciousness because of the ontology of desire: "Reason *must* withdraw from the happy state" of perceived unity with its world (PS 214), since every achievement of self-identity is constantly unsettled by the necessity of the independence of the other as the condition for recognizing the self. Madness, on the other hand, is an extreme consequence of this experience of alienation, when the mind becomes 'extravagant' in its desperate attempt to flee the pain of existence, and where rational connection with the world has become not simply precarious but radically obscured.

The references to insanity in the *Phenomenology* punctuate points at which the rational consciousness has been driven beyond itself, or better, *back* from itself, in a regressive escape to a fundamentally different way of being, the way of nature and feeling and the unconscious. Madness in this way holds a fascinatingly complex position in Hegel's philosophy: it both shares the formal structures of normal, rational consciousness (yearning, self-division, withdrawal, projection) and yet occupies a categorically different space, the space of feeling rather than reason, of nature rather than spirit. Further, insanity is not an actually necessary destiny for all consciousness, unlike despair, and yet it is constantly prepared for by despair, which in its grief solicits consciousness to 'sink back' to an inwardness which is more primitive than reason.

Madness in Relation to Stoicism, Skepticism, and the Unhappy Consciousness

We are now in a better position to draw some conclusions about the relation between madness and developed consciousness. Madness is a reversion to nature, much as Freud sees neurosis as a regression to and fixation on an archaic unconscious content (a 'reversion' to and 'imprisonment' in a 'feeling state' for Hegel), which involves a dislocation from the language of reason, and hence a breakdown of the connections between the inner world of consciousness and the objective outer world. This description allows us to see some important differences between madness and the developed consciousness, differences which occur *within* the structures of withdrawal, the resulting double centering of reality, and the movement of projection that pertain to them both. A brief return to Hegel's account of despair, along with a look at the two shapes of consciousness which precede it in the *Phenomenology*—stoicism and skepticism—will help to illuminate these differences.

Stoicism, skepticism, and the unhappy consciousness are the first three configurations of selfhood Hegel discusses which involve the relation of a single consciousness, or state of mind, to an alien and threatening environment, and as such stand as analogues to the situation of madness. Their presence at the beginning of Hegel's anatomy of self-consciousness also reveals their privileged status as paradigms for subsequent forms of experience; they are repeatedly recovered, recapitulated, and elaborated upon in the course of the mind's exploration of possible ways to define itself and its relation to the world. The master/slave dialectic which precedes them (and in this sense underlies them) also reveals interesting parallels with insanity. We have already alluded to some of these earlier in this chapter, but will defer further examination of this comparison until later, since the analogy to madness is complicated by the presence in the master/slave relationship of two selves.[25] This duality is itself suggestive, as we have noted, given Hegel's emphasis on the 'double personality' of the insane, but for now a more straightforward comparison with paradigmatic shapes of the single consciousness will best serve our purposes.

In general, this triad of shapes of consciousness—stoicism, skepticism, and despair—unlike madness, is animated by an intense concern for the relation with externality. Even in the movement of withdrawal, stoicism, skepticism, and the unhappy consciousness are ultimately seeking union with the other, and all are mediated by language, by reason, rather than feeling.

Stoicism, like madness, represents the movement of withdrawal from the experience of the dismembered world, the world which holds for it only pain. As Hyppolite puts it, the stoic "leaves existence on one side and poses itself on the other,"[26] just as we have seen the mad self to situate itself on the 'other side' of reality. There is in fact a studied attitude of indifference to the external world in stoicism, what Joseph Flay calls a "contempt for the vagaries of life" and a "refusal to deal with the contingencies and realities of life," so that "access to reality is effectively denied."[27] It is a yearning for unity, and for freedom, but a yearning which despairs of having its freedom acknowledged in the social and political world, a world in which it feels forsaken, lost, not-at-home. The external world is negated, and the stoic seeks to achieve a wholly inward peace, turning to the freedom of its own thought. "In thought," the stoic believes, "I am not in an *other* but remain simply and solely in communion with myself" (PS 120). All this sounds much like what occurs in madness, particularly if we see this radical interiorization of stoicism as a sort of dreaming, as for example Stanley Rosen does,[28] and yet there are two crucial differences.

First, if the stoic dreams, she does so in a different language than that of madness: the stoic seeks her freedom in thought rather than feeling—in the universal language of *Begriffe* (e.g., the concepts of virtue, of wisdom, of truth) rather than the utterly private and prelinguistic cathexes of feeling-states. As such, she remains within the general life of reason, even though this is reason without the power to actualize itself through externalization. Second, Hegel views stoicism as an inherently unstable state of mind; it is profoundly incomplete and hollow, unable to gain what it desires, its sense of unity and freedom, since it is incapable of generating any content for its thought apart from the outer world which it has negated. The stoic consciousness is thus fundamentally impotent, while the mad self has a relative potency and stability. For Hegel, thought requires otherness, since it is intrinsically universal, a being-with-others, and becomes empty when removed into the narcissistic interiority of 'I am I.' Feeling, however, is intrinsically private, and is relatively removed from the need for the mediation of universal, socially determined connections in order to have a content—it is, as we have seen, "self-supporting and independent of" the external world. Thus the mad self is able to create a world out of the projection of its feelings. It *has* a world, a content—not an objective, rational world to be sure, but nevertheless a world, a world as rich as the world of dreams.[29]

Similarly, skepticism, which is the attempt to annihilate polemically the otherness of the world, of everything which appears to stand over against consciousness as independent of it, succumbs to paralysis precisely because it is so closely bound to otherness—it is constantly concerned with what it is not in order to destroy it, but can produce no positive content itself. In reducing everything outside itself to nothing, it has reduced itself to nothing as well. Skepticism thus "culminates in solipsism," as Kojève points out,[30] much as madness is a fundamentally self-enclosed state, and yet the skeptic's solipsism is ironically—or even comically[31]—obsessed with otherness, with what lies outside it, precisely since it seeks to gain its self-identity and freedom through the persistent destruction of the abiding character of the world. Unlike skepticism, madness is neither as obsessed with externality nor as simply destructive in its negation of reality, since it is also constructive: it is not tied to the domain of reason which requires the other to acknowledge the self, but finds its home in the unconscious life of feeling, which has at its disposal the archaic, preconceptual content of nature, instinct, and feeling, which it uses to construct an alternative reality to the one which it withdraws from.[32]

Finally, if we look at the double center of reality and the resulting gesture of projection characteristic of the unhappy consciousness, there are again important differences from what occurs within the formally similar structures of madness. The two centers of despair are those of existence and essence, finitude and the infinite, the sense of the self as doomed to perpetual becoming and the ideal of the self as achieving the peace of being. In despair, we project the ideal of the self onto a "beyond," the image of God or essence or reality unencumbered by becoming and mortality. But, in the first place, this is not the projection of a fantasy—Hegel would disagree strenuously with the great atheist thinkers like Feuerbach, Marx, Nietzsche, Freud and Sartre who followed him—but of a dimension of the self which we truly are, although we feel painfully divided from it. Of course, even our fantasies may indicate essential aspects of the human spirit, but in the same way that dreams (for Hegel) illustrate the pre-conscious domain of the feeling soul rather than intrinsically rational and thus fully spiritual potentialities. Madness, again, is a "necessary and essential" shape of spirit, but as indicating the shape of the soul prior to its evolution into rationality.

Second, the guiding drive of despair is precisely a struggle for liberation from our enclosure within individual subjectivity, so as to achieve unity with what we experience as other, while in madness, the self seeks to entirely negate the other. As Rosen points out, while despair begins "with a loss of the world as stable dwelling, it is marked by a struggle to reappropriate the world."[33] It is precisely this reappropriation which madness refuses, seeking rather a substitute world of fantasy. The final point to note is that despair reaches its height in an attempt to destroy the body, the "enemy of desire" we find lurking within ourselves as mere nature, and which we experience as the source of our finitude (see PS 135–36). In madness, on the contrary, we affirm our being as *homo natura,* so that the body becomes the center of our search for unity and freedom, through the projective wish-fulfillment of feeling.

It is true that the shapes of developed consciousness struggling with the pain of existence can pass over into madness. The essential 'negativity' to which the self is destined in its striving for unity prepares the possibility for the path of despair to turn towards the path of insanity, where the self has become radically disoriented and dislocated from its world. But we should see that this change of paths involves an alteration of the phenomenology of consciousness as well: the formal structures of withdrawal, the doubling of reality, and projection remain similar, and yet they circumscribe opposed spheres of life, the life of reason and the life of feeling.

The Intimacy of Madness: Christiane, Hölderlin, and the Limits of an Ontology of Madness

Be a philosopher; but, amidst all your philosophy, be still a man.

(David Hume, *An Enquiry Concerning Human Understanding*)

Before turning to the final section of this chapter, where we will investigate the ways in which Hegel's discussion of madness allows new insight into his idealist philosophy, the time has come to pause and consider a fundamental question about Hegel's anatomy of madness. The question to be posed takes its inspiration from Søren Kierkegaard, Hegel's master tormentor, his Aristophanes, his Inquisitor extraordinarius, against whom the great legion of Hegel's other tormentors (from Feuerbach and Marx through Karl Popper and Hans Reichenbach and all the myriad of twentieth-century analytic philosophers) must be measured. The consummate artistry of Kierkegaard's irony was never more inventive than in its application to the proposition that the Hegelian 'System' systematically overlooks and represses the concrete existential reality of the individual, by privileging a "logic of the concept," so that all that really matters is the dialectical play of conceptual categories. But such a play of concepts, after all, takes place "only on paper," utterly "indifferent to existence," and gains its logical force precisely due to the fantasy of being blissfully unencumbered by any concern for the actual lives of human beings.[34] Adapting this view to the matter at hand, we may ask whether Hegel's ontology of madness, for all the impressive show of such conceptual categories as regression, doubling, and projection, and for all the intricate dialectical interplay of the principles of a 'speculative' theory of illness, does not cover over and leave silent what might be called the existential intimacy of madness, the horror and tragedy of the concretely lived experience of the insane.

We will return to this question more fully later, both in chapter 7 when we explore the intertwining of madness with tragedy, and in chapter 8 when we consider the claims of people like Michel Foucault who speak of the ways in which the medicalization of madness "merciless[ly]" silences the voices of the insane through "an act of sovereign reason."[35] But already we have gathered a good enough picture of some of the most basic structural elements of Hegel's account of insanity to consider this question in at least a provisional way.

A very important recent book on Hegel by William Desmond, *Beyond Hegel and Dialectic,* provides us with an excellent point of access to the question we are posing. Himself partly inspired by Kierkegaard, Desmond argues that Hegel's dialectic tends to reduce thinking to self-thinking, that dialectical mediation is always finally the mediation of the self with itself, and thus that 'otherness' is never fully recognized in a fundamental sense, but always sublated and brought back into the self-unified concept of philosophic thought. Desmond notes Aristotle's intuition that "the least number, strictly speaking, is two,"[36] and asks rhetorically whether

"Hegel [can] really count to two, or count to a real two? . . . Hegel does not finally count beyond one at all."[37] And this 'one,' of course, is nothing but the all-encompassing unity of reason and the logical concept. What then happens to the purported 'other' of rationality? What are we to make of madness?

In thinking through Desmond's argument, my purpose is not to challenge his overall critique of Hegelian dialectic, but to take seriously its implications for Hegel's theory of madness. I should say, however, that while I feel Desmond's interpretation of Hegel is extremely provocative and well worth pursuing, I finally side with commentators such as Robert Williams who argue that "Hegel does not collapse the other into the same, [or] mediation into self-mediation." I agree with Williams that for Hegel, "the other cannot be brought into immediate or full presence except by reducing the other to self-sameness," and that Hegel is very concerned to show how "the attempt to do so is inherently one-sided and leads to coercion, the life and death struggle, murder, or enslavement."[38] Williams is right to insist that Hegel anticipates the Heideggerian ideal of a *Gelassenheit* or "releasement" of the other: "Genuine reciprocal recognition requires [in Hegel's view] a renunciation of seizing-upon the other . . . and reducing him [or her] to my own possibilities. . . . The other is not eliminated, but rather released and allowed to be (*entlassen*)."[39]

There *is* respect for genuine otherness in Hegel, and his notion of recognition of the other is not simply a surreptitious attempt to cancel the independence of the other and sublate it into self-unity. The unity Hegel looks for is always a 'unity of difference' or a 'difference within unity' which resists all efforts to enclose otherness within the narcissistic greed of the 'I am I.' Desmond's argument, however, is both subtle and far-reaching, and my present comments seek no more than to mark out the differences of where we stand, and are hardly meant to imply that we may so easily dispose of his critique.

The question Desmond's analysis leaves for Hegel's theory of madness is whether Hegel is really able to account for the existentially concrete 'otherness' of insanity. When Desmond considers the role of otherness and doubleness in the unhappy consciousness, he finds that Hegel is not ultimately interested in despair's yearning sense of a 'beyond' with which it cannot coincide; this 'beyond' is no real double or other to consciousness, but only a "mirror" of its own nature which it must seek to recover so as to unify itself internally.[40] Any persistent sense of the 'beyond' as an otherness which radically transcends consciousness itself "will be marked down [by Hegel] as a dialectical failure."[41] Only when the despairing consciousness is comprehended as an effort to restore the unity of reason with itself can it be understood fully.

Applying this analysis to madness, one might say that Hegel's talk of the 'double center' of insanity is deceptive, since there is no *real* doubleness, no real opposition between reason and any radical otherness of reason which could be understood apart from its constant reference to the 'center' of reason which always remains within it. Madness is a regression back from reason into a state of being—that of the feeling soul—which itself is the 'presupposition' and origin from which rational consciousness emerges, and the entire struggle of madness is a struggle towards restoration of the unity of reason with itself. To follow this line of argument further, there is no authentic counting to two in Hegel's theory of madness, no genuine emergence of the existential horror of insanity, but only the facade of a 'doubleness' and 'otherness' which is dialectically destined to be overcome by what we have already noted to be Hegel's conceptualization of madness as "not a . . . *loss* of reason, . . . but only derangement, only a contradiction in a still subsisting reason" (PM § 408).

While Desmond is most interested in uncovering how the Hegelian dialectic ultimately is unable to account for the existential 'otherness' of *evil*—an argument we will return to in chapter 7—in one place he indirectly applies his analysis to the issue of madness. In speaking of the failure of Hegelian dialectic to truly incorporate the horror and "idiocy" of evil ("in the Greek sense of *idios,* its otherness to the public universal")[42]—since evil is radically "other to logos, other to [dialectical] structure"[43]—he remarks that *outside of his philosophy,* Hegel certainly did have a sense of this radical otherness. To catch sight of Hegel's own sense of the 'idiocy' of otherness—the irreducible intimacy of the grief and sense of being crushed by evil—we need only look at his correspondence. In his letters, "there we meet the private Hegel," immersed in "the intimacy of the existential. . . . In his letters there is no dialectical consolation when dealing with the death of children,"[44] for example, and moreover, no sign of confidence in the logic of the concept when it comes to his feelings about the madness of his sister Christiane. "Hegel was deeply moved, indeed I suspect was at a loss for what to think regarding his own sister's breakdown. . . . We do not find any facile reasonableness. We find hints of a noble pessimism before some of life's inevitabilities." Most telling, perhaps,

Desmond wonders about the complete *silence* on Hegel's part regarding the madness of his friend, the great poet Hölderlin:

> Was the more intimate Hegel here at a loss too, before the existential breakdown of a beloved [friend], a breakdown that was not merely dialectical? Was the howl of the disordered mind, and especially the madness of an intimate, a friend, something he could not accommodate in his logic?[45]

The question of whether and to what extent Hegel is only able to account for madness within an ontology so indebted to a logic of rationality that he must effectively silence the voices of the insane and ignore the existential reality of madness will be addressed more fully in our concluding chapter. It should be pointed out here, however, that the central conviction of Hegel's ontology of madness, that the insane are still rational beings, was partly intended to resist precisely the recurring *dehumanization* of the mad by earlier views which conceived of madness in terms of demonology or bestiality. Thus only by refusing to make the insane into the *complete* 'other' of rationality can we prevent their complete descent into silence. Whether Hegel ironically achieves an alternative version of silencing the insane by going too far in the opposite direction, by refusing to allow insanity a space of its own outside the limits of accepted rational categories—so that, as Foucault puts it, "the language of psychiatry, which is a monologue of reason *about* madness, has been established only on the basis of such a silence"[46]—needs careful thinking through. We will not finally come to terms with this question until later, but we can make a beginning here by picking up on Desmond's reference to Hegel's feelings for Christiane and his silence about Hölderlin, and the implication that there is a revealing and troubling split between his onto-logical account of madness and his private, existential response to it.

Hegel's sister Christiane (1773–1832) was afflicted with periods of mental illness throughout the last twenty years or so of her life, and finally committed suicide. She was diagnosed with 'hysteria' (*Hysterie*), which Hegel speaks of in an 1820 letter to his cousin, the Reverend Göriz, as a form of "derangement" (*Verrücktheit*) marked by a "physical condition . . . which effects a release of the inner passions"[47]—note here Hegel's typical reference to the presence of both physical and affective states—and which he seems to associate with 'mania' or *die Tollheit*.[48] During the early stages of Christiane's illness, Hegel invited her to "move

in with us permanently," to "regard my home . . . as a haven open
to you, . . . to offer you peace and contentment."[49] Later, after a particularly severe recurrence, Hegel proposed a Pinelian course of
"loving care combined with medical treatment," then in 1821
arranged for Christiane's commitment to the asylum in Zweifalten,
and a year later, on her release, for her treatment by his former
friend Friedrich Schelling's brother Karl. A year after Hegel's own
death in 1831, Christiane, moved by her grief at her brother's
passing and her continuing inner torments, took her life.[50]

Desmond is absolutely correct to suspect that Hegel was "at a
loss for what to think" about his sister Christiane's mental breakdown. In the same letter to Göriz in which Hegel writes of his
hopes for a Pinelian therapy, he explicitly says that "I do not know
what I am to say" of his sister's "unfortunate condition." "This
news [of her most recent breakdown] has moved me deeply. Of all
the things that can affect a human being, this is the hardest to
take." There is no question at all that Hegel does not remain the
philosophic dialectician in his personal relations with Christiane
and in the intimacy of his confronting her pain. The question becomes why then he does not allow this intimacy to enter his philosophy, why we are given only logic, ontology, and dialectic, and not
the *experience* of suffering that he clearly knew in his own life.

In the first place, it is important to note just how often Hegel
does refer to the existential anguish of such states of being as madness and despair in his philosophy; no one could read Hegel's texts
and miss the repeated language of "pain," "suffering," "sorrow" and
"anguish." But doesn't this language get swept up into logical-di-
alectical categories? Doesn't the "slaughterbench of human history," the "pathway of despair," and the "infinite pain" of existence
become conceptualized as so many expressions of the "logic of negativity" which moves the dialectic along its merry way? Doesn't the
very possibility of Hegel—or any of the rest of us—being "deeply
moved" get forgotten? Doesn't the possibility of "not knowing what
I am to say" become moot? That is, doesn't Hegel *always* have
something to say in his philosophy, isn't he never at a loss to provide the appropriate logical category by which we may comprehend
the 'negativity' of life?

Hegel, I propose, would have been astonished by such questions. It is as if he were to have forgotten Hume's warning not to
forget, in the midst of our philosophic enterprises, that we are still
human. This is just what Kierkegaard and his pseudonyms sometimes accuse Hegel of forgetting: according to Johannes Climacus,

the 'author' of the *Concluding Unscientific Postscript,* whose very title challenges the (purported!) Hegelian scientization of existence, Hegel does "his utmost to forget that he is an existing individual, by which he becomes a comic figure, since existence has the remarkable trait of compelling an existing individual to exist whether he wills it or not."[51] Desmond, for his part, knows full well that Hegel never forgot his humanity; it is there to be seen in all its pathos in Hegel's letters. But Desmond does seem to be accusing Hegel *the philosopher* for leaving no room for genuine pathos *in* his philosophy.

To this accusation, Hegel would, I am sure, plead 'guilty,' but would hardly see it as something to 'accuse' philosophic discourse with. The absolutely personal and inherently intimate encounter with life's sorrows can never in principle be 'logicized' or philosophically comprehended, any more, for example, than a speculative medicine could ever hope to deduce the empirical symptoms of disease. Philosophies which seek to comprehend or deduce the purely personal are precisely those which lead to the most dangerous sort of reductionism. At those moments when we "have nothing to say," because we can only feel and suffer, were we to speak nevertheless, were we to translate the intimacy of the experience of grief into philosophic discourse, we would transgress against a domain of experience which demands of us that we refuse to speak philosophically.

This hardly implies, however, that a philosopher should not speak at all about pain and suffering. He or she must only be careful not to confuse the domain of philosophic discourse with the actual experience of anguish, to pretend as if the ontological inquiry were fully capturing the intimacy of suffering. Hegel is no more guilty of such confusion than is Kierkegaard, or his pseudonym Anti-Climacus, in writing *The Sickness Unto Death* (edited, we must note, by "S. Kierkegaard"). *The Sickness Unto Death* presents us with at least as many ontological and dialectical principles, categories, and schematisms of despair as does Hegel's account of the unhappy consciousness and madness. The purpose of such accounts—and it is perfectly clear from Anti-Climacus' whole procedure that he shares this purpose—is to present the formal, structural features of an ontology which can offer explanatory value for the human tendency toward certain states. This is a philosophic enterprise, and a useful one, for just because no philosophic enterprise can ever prepare us for the actual experience of despair or madness, nothing short of such an enterprise could ever explain and give meaning to what it is in the nature of human Being that makes it susceptible to these experiences.

Just as Desmond is right to interpret Hegel's "loss for what to think" about his sister Christiane as the admission of a purely personal dimension of the confrontation with suffering, I believe he is on the right track to interpret Hegel's silence about Hölderlin as a sign of his acknowledgment that "he could not accommodate" the intimacy of his pain over his friend's madness "in his logic." But again, this does not imply a weakness of his logic, as though an ideal logic would be one which included this intimacy: this is precisely the pretension which a logic must steadfastly refuse.

Hölderlin (1770–1843) became a close friend of Hegel's (and Schelling's) at Tübingen where they were students at the University from 1788-1793.[52] In 1796, Hölderlin helped land Hegel a job as a tutor in Frankfurt, where Hölderlin himself had just become a tutor to the children of the banker Jacob Gontard (whose wife Susette became Hölderlin's "Diotima," initiating him into the mysteries of love[53]). As early as 1801, Hölderlin had a presentiment of his impending madness, and in 1802, the year Susette Gontard died, Hölderlin suffered his first severe breakdown. His illness progressed over the next few years (just the period during which he wrote his most sublime poetry) until he was institutionalized in the psychiatric ward of the Autenreithsche Klinik at Tübingen in 1806, and a year later in the now famous *Turm* or tower in the home of the carpenter Ernst Zimmer, where he lived out the remaining thirty-six years of his life.[54] Hölderlin's illness was diagnosed as severe 'frenzy' (*Wahnsinn*), just that form of madness which Hegel takes to be most philosophically significant in his *Encyclopædia,* and which corresponds with the modern classification of schizophrenia. Indeed, beginning with Wilhelm Lange's 1909 *Pathographie* of Hölderlin, nearly all such studies specify his illness as catatonic schizophrenia.[55]

Hegel apparently never visited his friend after Hölderlin's final breakdown, nor are there any direct references to him in any of Hegel's works; even in his letters Hegel only refers to his friend's "sad condition" twice (once in 1803 to Schelling, and once in 1807 to Hölderlin's most loyal friend, Isaak von Sinclair), and then only in passing.[56] Thus Hegel seems to have been quite unlike the faithful friend of Hölderlin's *Empedokles,* Pausanias, who says to Empedokles:

Daring to tread the sanctum of the abyss
Where, patient, Earth conceals her heart from day
And the dark Mother will confide to you
Her sufferings, her griefs, O son of Night,
Of Aether, even then I'd follow you down.[57]

Hegel does not follow Hölderlin down to the Autenreithsche Klinik or the *Turm*, does not share the sufferings and griefs of his friend, the son of Night who has tread the sanctum of the abyss, does not write to him, does not visit him, barely mentions him. But if Desmond is right, this is no symptom of a cold indifference, but precisely a sign of being overwhelmed, of being too deeply moved to speak. Appearances notwithstanding, it might be that "Hegel never ceased to love Hölderlin," as Christoph Jamme says[58]—and more, that his silence was an indication of his love. Alan Olson, in his splendid book on *Hegel and the Spirit,* greatly expands this argument in a chapter on "Madness" where he seeks to show that the whole *Encyclopædia* discussion of insanity was in part an indirect, "sublated" response to Hölderlin's illness.

Olson argues that "Hegel was so deeply disturbed by his friend's rapid emotional and mental deterioration that he repressed all [direct] reference," but that nevertheless "indirect allusion" is made to Hölderlin "in [Hegel's] extensive, albeit somewhat odd, philosophical treatment of madness in the *Enzyklopädie*"[59]— that in fact, the whole *Encyclopædia* discussion is an *encyklos* or "circl[ing] round" the fate of Hölderlin and "an attempt to come to terms somehow" with Hölderlin's madness.[60] On the empirical level, Olson provides such intriguing evidence as the perfect resemblance between Hegel's otherwise peculiar remark that "big muscular men with black hair" appear to be most susceptible to the madness of frenzy (*Wahnsinn*) (see PM § 408 Z) and the description of Hölderlin in his 1802 passport: he is "a large, muscular man of six feet" and a "fair-skinned, brown-eyed brunette."[61] More generally, Olson points out how the general task of the *Encyclopædia* discussion to explain the regressive turn back from sanity into insanity "clearly calls to mind the condition of Hölderlin."[62] Further, and most provocatively, he suggests that Hegel's larger philosophic project was conceived as an attempt to move in an opposite direction of "transcendence" from that of his Romantic poet friend Hölderlin, the "beautiful soul" (*die schöne Seele* which so preoccupies Hegel in his *Phenomenology*) whose sublime consciousness "withers and dies the moment the world intrudes on its being." As such, Hölderlin "remained Hegel's *daimon,* his existential Other, and this concerned, even frightened, Hegel deeply throughout his life."[63]

Whether or not it was what Olson calls "Hegel's persistent fear of Madness"[64] which kept him from being Hölderlin's Pausanias, Olson's reading gives great weight to the idea that Hegel's silence over his friend was a silence born—as with his sister Christiane—of "not know[ing] what [he is] to say." What Hegel *does* say of madness in the philosophic discourse of the *Encyclopædia* is not an attempt to accommodate his inarticulate pain into the consoling logic of a speculative ontology of madness— nor should it be—but an attempt to explain the ontological condition of human Being which makes the existential pain of madness possible. If, as Olson suggests, there is some sense in which this amounts to a 'sublation' of Hegel's relation to Hölderlin, I would only say that it is not an attempt to sublate or deflect the pain of the encounter itself. Here, on the level of the experience of pain, Hegel's silence is more eloquent than his philosophy, and must necessarily be so, for on this level the philosopher must be careful to have nothing to say. This is absolutely not to minimize the value of a philosophical ontology of madness, but rather to hear the wisdom of Kant's dictum that once the important work of science is accomplished, we must be able to "deny knowledge in order to make room for . . ." —well, Kant says "faith,"[65] but for our purposes, we may say "the idiotic," or "existential intimacy," or perhaps simply "silence."

Earlier in this chapter we spoke of madness as a sort of private language, and said that in Hegel's view, "only where there is something to say can nature be transformed into spirit and feeling into reason." On one level, the philosophical 'silence' of Hegel's private confrontation with the intimacy of grief—his "not know[ing] what [he is] to say" about his sister Christiane, for example—is reminiscent of the 'private language' of madness, in that both dwell with feelings and are responses to a break-down of the ability to rationally comprehend the intimacy of suffering. But on another level, we must be careful not to confuse Hegel's *philosophical* silence with the inability to have anything to say at all. Hegel does speak, after all, to his sister, and to such people as his friend Heinrich Beer, whose child's death leads Hegel to write a letter expressing his "incalculable pain" at "the crushing blow of misfortune" and offering to "hold your hand in the depth of a pain borne of friendship."[66] The holding of Beer's hand expresses a pre-linguistic gesture of concern (and a rather touching one for such a staid Prussian gentleman), but the writing of the letter shows that Hegel felt there was still something possible, and very important, to convey in language, in the very midst of a letter which had the great wisdom to remain *philosophically* silent.

Madness and Hegel's Idealism

More than shedding new light on different shapes of consciousness which make up the phenomenological gallery of spirit, Hegel's discussion of madness allows us a new way of approaching some of the most basic metaphysical assumptions of his 'absolute idealist' philosophy. Just as Hegel's idealism postulates that the world is in an important sense a projection of mind, so too a fundamental characteristic of madness is the gesture of projecting a reality. In fact we might speak of *two* idealisms present in Hegel's writing, the true idealism he associates with his philosophic system and the fantastic idealism of madness. Thus in understanding Hegel's diagnosis of the failure inherent in the false idealism of insanity, we may gain a deeper interpretation of the notoriously complex vicissitudes and contours of his own idealism.

The Quest for Unity in the Midst of Discord[67]

The aim of Hegel's absolute idealist system is to show that all dualistic philosophy is ultimately false—that the purportedly common-sense hypothesis of an external world which is entirely 'other' from the mind is an illusion. Thus in the closing lines of the Introduction to his *Phenomenology,* Hegel anticipates that "consciousness will arrive at a point at which it gets rid of its semblance of being burdened with something alien" (PS 56). And in his *Encyclopædia* logic, he writes that "the aim of knowledge is to divest the objective [external] world that stands opposed to us of its strangeness, and, as the phrase is, to find ourselves at home in it: which means no more than to trace the objective world back to . . . our innermost self" (SL § 194 Z).

It is important to interject here a warning against reading Hegel's idealist vocabulary as an attempt to seduce us into the airy reaches of a reality wholly created by the mind, disencumbered by the inconvenience of an actually existing external world. Hegel's critique of dualism, his talk of the world as a projection of mind, and his imperative to trace the world back to consciousness does not imply—as one common reading of his idealism would have it, most recently reasserted in Robert Pippin's *Hegel's Idealism,* which has justifiably provoked much debate[68]—that he means to reject the standpoint of realism. Hegel never denies that there is an external material world, nor that there are fundamental ways in which this world is independent of our cognitive and linguistic activities. Nor does he ever deny that our knowledge must begin with our experience of that world. On the contrary, "cognition . . . demand[s] the surrender to the life of the object" (PS 32). While this object ultimately must be conceptualized, and in this sense be 'constituted' by consciousness, in order for it to have significance, it is not created *ex nihilo* by the mind. Thus Hegel is untiring in his argument against all philosophical positions which assert that "the thing in itself is nothing, but has meaning only in relation to the 'I'" (PS 481), and against what he (perhaps incorrectly) takes to be the Kantian position of "holding that both the form and the matter of knowledge are supplied by the Ego" (SL §42 Z), a position which ignores the "'given' in sensation" by "reducing objectivity directly to . . . an ideal factor" (F&K 154).

Kenneth Westphal has gone a long way in his book on *Hegel's Epistemological Realism* to show that Hegelian idealism is not a sort of grudging accommodation of realism, but entirely entails it.[69] I agree with Westphal, and have argued elsewhere[70] that we must take Hegel's claim seriously that his philosophy is an attempt to make "the two methods of realism and idealism overlap one another" (HP 3: 164). From this perspective, while the aim of knowledge is to "behold the self in the object" (PS 417), this first of all absolutely requires an external world and an independent object to which we must "surrender" ourselves.[71] This should come as no surprise to us after our discussion in the last chapter of Hegel's critique of John Brown's abstraction away from the concrete empirical data of illness and his attempt to reach a middle path of reconciliation between empirical and Romantic medicine.

For the purposes of our present discussion, the important point is to see that Hegel's rejection of dualism is not a denial of the existence of an independent external world, nor a reduction of the world to an idea. It is a rejection of the view that the mental and the physical, the inner and the outer, the self and its world, are ultimately alien to each other, two fundamentally different substances or essences or realities. His argument is that the world becomes fully real or actual (*Wirklich*) only to the extent that it is conceptualized by (and in this sense traced back to) the mind. The difference between the idealisms of madness and rationality will largely be determined by contrasting means of conceptualization.

It is clear that Hegel's view of the human project of reconciling thought with reality would not be seen as a *task* if there were an immediately given harmony of the inner and outer worlds. Hegel's philosophy thus describes the quest of consciousness to overcome the experience of dualism, to find itself at home, united and in harmony with its world, a quest which is motivated precisely by the recurring experience of *dis*-unity. The path of consciousness is a path of constant loss and despair, where every achievement of happiness, the perception of unity, is undermined by the "slaughterbench" of happiness (RH 27) which is the inflexible law of human history.

Hegel's idealism thus presents us with the dilemma of insisting, on the one hand, on the ultimate unity of human consciousness with its world, but on the other hand, on the perpetual ephemerality of attempts at reconciliation. One is reminded of Albert Camus' definition of the absurd, which he sees as the central existential fact of the human condition: the absurd, he says, is the expression of a "divorce between man and his life, the actor and his setting." It is the experience of a fundamental dichotomy:

> Man stands face to face with the irrational; he feels within him his longing for happiness and for reason. The absurd is born of this confrontation between the human need [for reason and meaning] and the unreasonable silence of the world.[72]

This seems very much of a spirit with Hegel's own words in his *History of Philosophy* when he speaks of the essential "negativity" of human subjectivity, which "signifies the lack of a firm and steady basis, but likewise the desire for such," so that "it evermore remains a yearning" (HP 3: 510).

It is just this conflict between the yearning for unity and the experience of discord which leads Hegel to describe mind as "infinite pain." Further, this recurring pain inherent in the human situation is why he views the state of despair as the central shape of consciousness in its quest for unity, and why he sees the possibility of madness, where the mind can no longer cope with the encounter with despair, as a constantly present possibility of human experience.

Idealism, Madness, and History

Central to Hegel's description of madness as an imprisonment in the night of the mind is that insanity entails the erosion of the edifice of idealism, the relation of the self to its world—or rather, the substitution of a false, dream-constructed idealism on the toppled remains of true idealism. The world of night is an obscuring of the distinction between self and world, where the "soul is immersed in its [own] differenceless unity" (PM § 398 Z). All interest in the external world has been negated, and the mad self, like the dreaming self, becomes a world unto itself: there is an *immediate* identity of self and 'world,' where the world is simply the interior mirror of the self's fantasy and desire. This is mad idealism, the achievement of the identity of self and other through the negation of the external other and the construction of a purely internal mirror.

This is why Hegel says of the proposition, "What I think is true"—which when understood correctly expresses the goal of idealism, the "perfect unity of thought and being"—that it "receives in the mentally deranged a wrong, an irrational meaning" (PM § 408 Z). Truth and reality are reduced to the merely subjective fantasies projected by our feeling soul. This is also why Hegel makes the striking claim that in madness "there is something akin to philosophy," which is however only the "pathological" mirror of true idealism (PM § 379 Z). All mind is a craving for unity, for an identity of thought and being, of inner and outer, but it is only through the long struggle of rational consciousness with its sense of separation from its world that this unity may be achieved. The unity of madness forsakes this struggle, turning away from the pain it entails, and retreats to the world of dreams in which it constructs an all-too-immediate harmony, for the mad self "communes merely with its *interior* states: the opposition between itself and that which is *for* it [the world], remains still shut up within it" (PM § 402 Z).

We get a good sense of Hegel's view of the sort of relationship between thought and being which pertains to true idealism from a passage in his *Phenomenology* where he compares the internal and external worlds to:

a double gallery of pictures, [each] of which [is] the reflection of the other: the one, the gallery of external circumstances which . . . circumscribe the individual, the other, the same gallery translated into the form in which those circumstances are present in the conscious individual . . . [who] *transforms* [the world]. . . . Individuality is itself the cycle of its action in which it has exhibited itself as an actual world, and as simply and solely the unity of the world as *given* and the world it has *made*.

For the rational mind, this is "a unity whose sides do not fall apart . . . into a world that *in itself* is already given, and an individuality existing *on its own account*" (PS 185). Such a view would be that of strict dualism, where there is no possibility of a 'translation' or 'transformation' of the external by the internal. In madness, however, the two sides do fall apart, so that they have no connection. Madness is "without any definite points of attachment" between subject and object (PM 406); "in this diseased frame of mind the [individual] will not give up his subjectivity, [and] is unable to overcome his repugnance to the actual world" (PM § 396 Z). The world is experienced as the sheer necessity of fate, an inhospitable world of suffering which the self has no power to transform, and the mad self retreats into a way of being which exists "on its own account." Madness thus initially accepts the standpoint of strict dualism, experiences the incommensurability of the inner and outer, and resolves the impasse by a psychological negation of the external and a corresponding withdrawal into itself. The double gallery has been reduced to a single gallery, the gallery of the night of the mind which only dreams its emancipation from suffering.

Madness is a profound disillusionment with the self's ability to transform the world, an inability to see the world not merely as 'given' but also as made. This points to the importance which Hegel attaches to labor for the cure of madness, a topic which will occupy us in greater length in chapter 8. "By working, [madmen] are forced out of their diseased subjectivity and impelled towards the real world" (PM § 408 Z). As Georg Lukács says, "The growth of self-consciousness is bound up with work."[7] Labor is capable of overcoming and transforming the alien character of the world, shaping it into a reflection of our rational, inter-subjective consciousness.

Hegel's theory of labor implies a very important difference between madness and the developed consciousness. Only through labor is history possible, since labor is what transforms the existing world as 'given.' Kojève makes this connection between labor and history a cornerstone of his famous reading of Hegel's *Phenomenology*: "Where there is work, there is necessarily change, progress, historical evolution," Kojève writes. Even more strongly, "[the] creative education of man by work creates history—i.e., human time."[74] Thus, for Hegel, only under the perspective of true idealism is history conceivable: the world is "actually *projected out of myself*"(PM § 402 Z), not as a creation *ex nihilo*, and not as the fantasy of our mere wishes or feelings, but as the struggle to transform the given historical environment in which we are grounded, and hence by taking that environment as the objective ground of our struggle. The withdrawal of madness into the darkness of nature allows only an internal 'history,' a dream-history, precisely because it retreats from the ground of the given. In severing its connections with the external, the mad self cuts itself off from the conditions for history and is abandoned to the caprice, accident, and fantasy which characterize the life of feeling.

This dislocation of history is seen in the disruption of temporality that Hegel identifies as a common feature of madness. Madness, he believes, is often brought about through the experience of the "upheaval and putting out of joint of the general state of the world," where "the individual lives with his feelings exclusively in the *past* and is thus unable to find himself in the *present*" (PM § 408 Z). Thus just as Freud sees neurosis as a return to infancy, in which the body, instinct, the archaic content of primitive nature and impulse become the center of the neurotic's life, so too Hegel sees an imprisonment in the past, and hence an abrogation of history, as typical of the ontology of insanity.

We will see in the next chapter that madness is in important respects a nostalgic return to the myth of Eden, the primitive unity of the garden of 'nature' prior to the world of spirit which appears only with the Fall into labor and history. Hegel speaks of the legend of a "primary, paradisical state of man" at one with nature, as the purportedly pre-historical phase of human life (RH 71–75). But the destiny of mind is to become historical, to leave the garden of instinct, the unconscious life of feeling, and to search for a "second harmony"—a true idealism, or unity of mind and world, which forsakes the immediate harmony of nature by transforming the world through labor (SL § 24 Z).

It is important to note, however, that Hegel sees times of happiness as being just as unhistorical as the temporality of madness. "History is not the soil of happiness; the periods of happiness are blank pages in it" (RH 33). Happiness is only possible when desire has been fulfilled, when satisfaction is reached. History, on the other hand, requires the sense of opposition and disruption, the experience of dichotomy between the inner and outer worlds, which is the condition for the impulse to transformation. We must never forget that Hegel's vision of the ultimate unity of thought and being is described as a *task*, a task which must be perpetually renewed, just as desire perpetually renews itself in every experience of satisfaction. For "all existing reality [is] unstable and disunited"

(RH 38), entailing that consciousness constantly be uprooted from its periodic achievement of harmony and stability. Thus despair is a natural consequence of human history, and is continually regenerated. And with despair, we must recognize that madness, despair's secret sharer, its darker mirror, is also a constantly regenerated possibility.

CHAPTER FOUR

Madness and the Second Face of Desire

We may assume that as soon as a given state of things is upset there arises an instinct to recreate it.

(Sigmund Freud, *New Introductory Lectures on Psychoanalysis*)

In chapter 3, we saw how Hegel's anatomy of desire as a primary structure of human consciousness helped explain the self's recurring encounter with despair and the resulting temptation towards a regression into madness as a strategy for coping. As desire, consciousness is delivered over to a state of perpetual unrest, constantly yearning for self-unification and reconciliation with its world, yet abandoned to the disruption of every temporary achievement of satisfaction. In the present chapter, we will explore in more detail the dynamics by which this disquieting sense of homelessness into which we are thrown by desire may lead to a search for the archaic home of all consciousness in the pre-rational life of the soul, the primitive 'life of feeling' which is the territory of madness. This will entail an examination of the regressive, nostalgic aspect of desire, which in Hegel's phenomenology competes with a progressive, evolutionary impulse, much as in Freudian theory the death instinct is in contest with the instinct of life. This darker side of desire performs the work of decentering by which consciousness becomes dislocated from the rational threads of connection to the outer world; it exploits our yearning for wholeness and redemption from the experience of alienation by luring us onto the path of regression where consciousness re-enters the world of the unconscious from which it had previously emerged in the course of its development.

We will first trace out the internally double nature of desire—

as progressive and regressive, evolutionary and nostalgic—through a variety of important passages in Hegel's texts, showing how the darker, regressive impulse is always already present as a potentiality within its evolutionary opposite. Then in section 2 we will look at the crucial passage from the *Phenomenology* where Hegel defines self-consciousness as desire, and draw out some of the consequences of his discussion through a comparison with Freud's theories of narcissism and the death instinct. In the final section we will turn to Hegel's fascinating treatment of the biblical story of the Fall in his *Encyclopædia*, showing how he uses the Genesis narrative as an allegory for his concepts of evolution and nostalgia. Each of these themes—narcissism, the death instinct, and the Fall—will deepen our understanding of how madness emerges at the perimeter of the entirely normal psychology of desiring consciousness.

As we begin to explore the key theme of 'two faces' of desire in Hegel's phenomenology, an important caveat needs to be made. The very language of 'two faces' will be misleading if we forget that for all of Hegel's fascination with dualisms and dichotomies, he was finally a philosopher of mediation. Mind and body, freedom and necessity, thought and being, self and other—Hegel ultimately transfigures each of these dualities into a unity, and this is also true of the two dimensions of desire. Thus nostalgic desire becomes sublimated and transformed into the crucially *recollective* nature of philosophic wisdom, which is united with the dialectically progressive character of spirit in Hegel's famous description of "Absolute Knowledge" (PS 479–93).[1] This does not mean, however, that Hegel ever diminishes the value of examining terms in their opposition: quite the contrary, it is only through such an examination that the essential 'negativity' of life can be exposed. With regard to desire, which is such a key element of Hegel's phenomenology, it is imperative to trace out the internally ambiguous and conflictual character of desire as both progressive and nostalgic, since this ambiguity has far-reaching implications for his anatomy of madness. The present chapter will be involved mainly in this task of examining the oppositional, even dualistic logic of desire. Hence the need for the warning: if we forget Hegel's final commitment to unification and mediation, we not only misread the structure of his dialectic, but close off the possibility of a coherent notion of therapeutics in which the 'two faces' of desire may become reconciled.

The Two Faces of Desire

On the most general level, we can see the importance of the concept of desire for Hegel in his appropriation of Aristotle's analysis of being as a desiring of form by matter, where this desire is the life-force of all being towards becoming and development. For our purposes, however, it is not so much Hegel's metaphysics of desire—desire as the 'impulse' or 'force' or 'power' which vitalizes all substance—which is of interest, as it is the role of desire in his phenomenology of human consciousness. Here, Hegel takes as his starting point the principle that "self-consciousness is desire" (PS 105, 109). Desire is the power or force which drives the self beyond itself, beyond every particular state of satisfaction and security and certainty, revealing satisfaction to be a self-consuming and ephemeral experience which is undermined by the perpetual regeneration of desire. Desire discloses the gap between the actuality and potentiality of the self and is what determines the self as a constant process of metamorphosis and transcendence, as it recurringly seeks to close this gap.

This element of desire as transcendence is what helps account for the evolutionary character of Hegel's dialectic, the fact that the inevitable dissatisfaction with present actuality will force spirit to develop and progress through the exploration of more complete and fulfilling possibilities of its being. But there is another dimension of desire as well, one that is often overlooked or forgotten due to Hegel's emphasis on evolution. This second face of desire is present throughout the breathtaking vicissitudes of Hegel's dialectic, and has the exactly opposite character to the nature of desire as transcendence: it is retrogressive and nostalgic, calling spirit away from the strife of evolution back to a past which it yearns for as a scene of peace and repose. It is precisely the victory of this second face of desire over the impulse toward evolution which provokes the turn backwards into the primordial life of feeling in madness.

As we will see, Hegel regards the fundamental object of all desire to be *unity*, the overcoming of disparity between actuality and possibility, is and ought, reality and ideality. And yet unity is a perpetually vanishing achievement; the character of spirit as transcendence means that every position of security and certainty it attains on its path of becoming will be lost. The dialectical nature of reality condemns the self to a state of restlessness (PS 6, 12), and, at its extreme, to despair (PS 49) and even madness. Out of this scene of disquiet and loss, there is generated an inevitable desire

for peace, a nostalgic desire for a return to the initial state of security which preceded the despairing cycle of becoming.

Thus, like the Freudian death instinct, which competes with
the instinct of life and growth and calls the self to a path of regression to a state of rest, this second, nostalgic face of desire is an
ever-present counterpoint to the impulse to development and evolution. It is ultimately an expression of what the great majority of
philosophers throughout the ages have called the universal desire
of human beings for happiness. For Hegel, however, happiness is
"the mere abstract and merely imagined universality of things desired, a universality which only ought to be" (PM § 480)—a
yearning for a fictive state of ultimate satisfaction, the fantasy of a
return to Eden, or to use Freud's vocabulary, the wish for a return
to the womb. As Stanley Rosen puts it, the historical search of
human beings for happiness confronts us with "the tragic record of
. . . efforts to overcome alienation by a return to paradise."[2]
Madness is a significant entry in that tragic record, being one of
the most drastic engagements of the death instinct, one of the most
desperate of all Eden-quests.

A famous passage from the *Lectures on the Philosophy of
History* leaves us in no doubt as to Hegel's feelings about the
prospects for achieving lasting happiness: "History," Hegel writes,
is "the slaughter-bench at which the happiness of peoples . . . has
been victimized" (PH 21). Hegel thus foreshadows Kierkegaard's
conviction, given voice by his pseudonym Anti-Climacus in *The
Sickness Unto Death,* that:

> happiness is not a characteristic of spirit, and in the remote
> depths, in the most inward parts, in the hidden recesses of happi-
> ness, there dwells also the anxious dread which is despair.[3]

But the mere fact that what this second face of desire seeks is
incapable of satisfaction in no way diminishes its force and reality.
Thus Hegel's frequent talk of the *necessity* of the development and
evolution of spirit (e.g., PS 50, 51; SL § 25) must be understood in
terms of an ideal necessity, which is not a necessity for any particular individual or society. This is very clear from Hegel's discussion of madness, which is precisely a reversion or sinking-back of
consciousness into a prior phase of being which gave a sense of security. And Hegel insists that madness is a completely natural, indeed even a necessarily occurring possibility of consciousness as a
response to the alienation and despair caused by the demands of

self-development (PM § 408 Z). Nostalgia, whether qualified as madness or not, is always on the borderline of disease for Hegel. It is not simply a transient turn of mind which distracts us in moments of melancholy, but a way of thinking and feeling which perpetually threatens our whole state of being with the desire for retreat and regression to a simpler, happier world, and a corresponding rejection of the world we happen to live in. Madness is only the most intense and desperate state in which this nostalgic way of being is attested to.

'I am I,' Narcissism, and the Death Instinct

Consciousness and Self-Consciousness

Hegel first defines the self as desire in the section of his *Phenomenology* where he describes the transition from the standpoint of *consciousness* to that of *self-*consciousness.[4] Put briefly, consciousness for Hegel is the relation of the human subject to an object which is experienced as external to it, while self-consciousness is the relation of the subject to her*self* through her relation to the object. "The existence of the world becomes for self-consciousness [his or her] own truth and presence; [self-consciousness] is certain of experiencing only itself therein" (PS 140). Consciousness thus entails the sense of division or disunity between self and world, while self-consciousness is in principle the standpoint of reunification.

The regressive movement of madness, for its part, will *not* involve a move backwards from the standpoint of self-consciousness to that of consciousness, since it is precisely the experience of standing opposed to an external world (which is the experience of consciousness) that is evaded in madness. No, madness will share with the perspective of *self-*consciousness the effort to divest the external world of its strangeness, but with this crucial difference: the mad self does not seek to find itself at home in that world, to reconcile itself with externality, but rather to break with that world, to efface it, and to substitute for the external a wholly inner construction of reality. Madness is thus not a regression to the oppositional stance of consciousness, but a reversion to the feeling soul, which radically reconfigures the unificational quest of self-consciousness, displacing the search for unity with the external other onto a search for unity within its own instincts and their projected fantasy life.

As we turn to see how Hegel elucidates this regressive path of madness in terms of a nostalgic desire for a primordial unity, it is interesting to have in mind Jacques Lacan's critique of Hegel's anatomy of desire. Lacan reevaluates Hegel's ontology of desire from within (his own idiosyncratic appropriation of) the perspective of psychoanalysis, and criticizes Hegel for ignoring the essentially unconscious origin of desire. Hegel's great "error in the *Phenomenology of Mind* [*Spirit*]," Lacan says, is "the promotion of consciousness as being essential to the subject in the historical after-effects of the Cartesian *cogito*," which amounts to a "deceptive accentuation of the transparency of the I in action at the expense of the opacity of the signifier [namely, the unconscious] that determines the I."[5] Desire, Lacan argues, must be seen as fundamentally prior to the rational, self-conscious subject, and as expressing a longing for the recovery of the unconscious origin of life. Hegel's analysis of desire, for Lacan, remains trapped within an entirely logocentric, egocentric definition, effecting a "logicizing reduction" which cuts us off from inquiry into the unconscious.[6]

In the next chapter, we will see that there is indeed a sense in which Hegel privileges consciousness over the unconscious, and to this extent we should certainly grant Lacan his point. On the other hand, it is difficult to see this as a symptom of Hegel's debt to the Cartesian tradition of exalting the transparency of the ego, for two reasons. First, Hegel's phenomenology operates according to the technique of disrupting the subjective feeling of certainty (*Gewißheit*)—our "clear and distinct ideas," to use Descartes' phrase—in each successive shape of consciousness. It is precisely the feeling of the mind's transparency to itself which this technique discloses as deceptive. Thus the path of consciousness is one of constant loss of security and of continual frustration of the project of mastering its own contents. More important for our present purposes, however, is a second reason for reservation about Lacan's critique: notwithstanding the relative importance Hegel grants to consciousness over the unconscious in his phenomenology of the rational, or 'developed' mind, it is by no means the case that he essentially ignores the unconscious dimension of desire. We could make no sense of Hegel's account of madness if Lacan were right. In fact, we will see that Hegel significantly anticipates Lacan's own description of desire as the nostalgic yearning to recover unconscious origins. Further, this yearning is not only present in madness for Hegel, so it is not the case that we could grudgingly grant Hegel some passing interest in the unconscious, but

only at the margins of mental life. Madness is only the extreme expression of a universal human desire for recovery of a primitive unity of the instincts rooted in our very nature, the unconscious domain of the soul which Hegel insists is the original presupposition of all conscious life.[7]

The Lure of a Primordial Unity

The 'ideal of self-consciousness, the perfect unity of self and world where nothing stands opposed to the self, is described by Hegel as "the motionless tautology of 'I am I'" (PS 105). It is important to note that this is only the initial, undeveloped, naive expression of self-consciousness. Self-consciousness proper will emerge out of the self-destruction of the 'I am I' as it is undermined by desire, which forces the self outward. But the 'I am I,' the certainty of self which recognizes no challenge to its autonomy, never relinquishes its allure: it is the scene of embryonic security and primordial peace which will serve as the object of all nostalgic desire. As such, within the very ideal of self-consciousness there rests the impetus towards regression, which, when it comes to dominate the quest for unity, assumes the form of a temptation into madness.

Hegel's description of the 'I am I,' and his subsequent analysis of the inherent instability of this standpoint due to the nature of self-consciousness as desire, bears striking resemblance to the account of narcissism offered by Freud more than a century later. In his 1914 paper "On Narcissism," Freud expresses his view that "The development of the ego consists in a departure from a *primary narcissism* and gives rise to a vigorous attempt to recover that state."[8] This 'primary narcissism' is described as a "primordial unity" of libido, a complete interpenetration of ego- and object-instincts, where no distinction is made between inner and outer reality: there is no Other but only Self. The parallel with Hegel's account of the 'I am I' seems obvious, and the similarities continue in Freud's theory of the inevitable departure of the ego from its primal scene of unity and satisfaction. The ego cannot in fact gratify itself; it needs the other and must "yield up," as Freud puts it, some of its inwardly absorbed, ego-bound libido onto the other.[9] In "thrusting forth [its libido] upon the external world," the distinction between ego and other, or self and world, first arises, and with it the long course of ego-development is initiated.[10] In Hegelian terms, this is the movement of the externalization of desire, which underlies the *Bildung* or education or acculturation into rationality, submerging

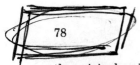

the original unity of the feeling soul beneath the gradually ac-
quired structures of reason.

For Hegel just as much as Freud, the self-satisfaction of the 'I
am I' is a vanishing moment, an intrinsically transient and self-
consuming state. It is illuminating to compare this vanishing of
the 'I am I' with what occurs in the first category of Hegel's logic,
Being (*Sein*), which like the 'I am I' is a completely empty self-identity. As Parmenides says in his poem, *The Way of Truth:*

> Being has no coming-into-being and no destruction, for it is whole
> . . . , without motion, and without end. . . . Nor is Being divisible,
> since it is all alike . . . And remaining the same in the same place,
> it rests by itself and thus remains there fixed.[11]

According to Hegel, however, such a definition of being is exactly the same as the definition of *nothing*— "it is a blank . . .
featurelessness," an "empty word," an "inchoate thought" (SL §§
85, 86; L 78). The truth of being is in fact *becoming*, the reaching
out beyond its abstract unity to self-determination, and in an analogous way the truth of the 'I am I' is desire: "self-consciousness is
desire" (PS 109). What the self desires, its complete unity with itself, it cannot achieve, for it is without content—it is empty, featureless, inchoate—and needs the other to recognize and affirm it:
"Self-consciousness exists in and for itself when, and by the fact
that, it so exists for another; that is, it exists only in being acknowledged" (PS 111). In this sense, the goal of psychiatric therapy
will be to reestablish the condition of trust by which the mad self
may once again seek acknowledgment by an other.

Self-unity is always the primary object of desire,[12] but due to
the hollowness of the narcissistic ego, desire also requires otherness. As Judith Butler puts it, while desire is always "reflexive," a
"pursuit of itself," it is also "intentional," always a "desire *of* or *for*
an other."[13] In the very act by which self-consciousness seeks to destroy the independence of the other so as to confirm its own autonomy, it unwittingly acknowledges the importance of the other
for its own satisfaction: "Desire and the self-certainty obtained in
its gratification are conditioned by the object, for self-certainty
comes [only] from superseding [seeking to destroy] this other" (PS
109). In positing the necessary other of itself, self-consciousness experiences disunity, and is henceforth driven by the effort to consume or assimilate its other so as to recover its lost unity.[14]

Already in the infant's scream, which Hegel alludes to in his

Philosophy of Mind just a few sections before his discussion of madness begins, we see the demand for satisfaction which is at once essentially narcissistic—"the independence of the outer world is non-existent" for the child, and serves only to satisfy his or her desires (PM § 396 Z)—and yet, inevitably, at the same time this very demand reveals the essential dependence of the child on the other. Desire is first of all the desire for unity, for independence from all otherness, and yet in spite of itself it is driven beyond its limits, compelled to reach out beyond the emptiness of its inner world to the outer world which alone can provide it a content and meaning. Desire is in this way a "greedy emptiness," to borrow a particularly apt phrase from Alexandre Kojève, an "emptiness greedy for content."[15]

In this double action of the self by which it posits the other so as to satisfy its need for content and yet seeks to consume the other so as to recover its self-identity, we see the two faces of desire, the one reaching towards the world in which it must act out its destiny, and the other seeking to retreat to the security of a primitive unity. This doubleness of desire accounts for the double center of reality and the double personality of the mad self, which we have explored earlier. The nostalgic face of desire is the dominant force of madness, which centers reality within the archaic feeling soul, while the evolutionary face of desire is the still present, although now decentered and submerged, trace of rationality.

The Death Instinct and the Work of Destruction

For both Hegel and Freud, there is an intimate connection between these two forms of desire. As we have seen, Freud sees the origin of ego-development in the first 'yielding up' or externalization of libido onto an other. But while this is a necessary action, it is also profoundly disquieting, since it demands that the ego limit itself according to the requirements of the reality principle. Hence the ego is subject to a recurring re-engagement of its desire to recover the state of primary narcissism. Freud goes so far as to say that the whole course of ego-development is in fact an attempt, perpetually frustrated and yet constantly re-engaged, to return to this unity.[16] The nostalgic face of desire thus accompanies and seeks to gain dominance over the developmental face of desire, a circumstance which eventually led Freud to postulate the existence of a death instinct operating in contest with the instinct of life.

In the 1920s, Freud came to revise his earlier theory of the ego

and sexual instincts and the primacy of the pleasure principle, due
to his discovery of the frequency of what he termed the "compulsion to repeat" in both neurotic[17] and non-neurotic[18] behavior. The
compulsion to repeat is the characteristic of all the instincts to
recreate and restore an earlier state of things so as to master and
remove a traumatic experience. The death instinct, or "instinct of
destruction," is described as "the most universal endeavor of all
living substance . . . to return to the quiescence of the inorganic
world," the yearning to "reach [the] ancient goal . . . [of the] initial
state from which the living entity has . . . departed and to which it
is striving to return by the circuitous paths along which its development leads."[19] Thus all development is only a circuitous course of
regression, an attempt to return to and recover the origin, the state
of peace prior to the inevitable pain of disunion which characterizes our life as human beings. From the moment that the infant enters the world "so unwillingly,"[20] the life instinct (Eros, the instinct
towards growth) is threatened by an opposing nostalgic instinct
which seeks to destroy the other which confronts it so as to return
to the primitive unity of primary narcissism, and ultimately, to the
state before life itself, to nothingness.

The Hegelian counterpart to Freud's death instinct can be
seen in the element of desire which seeks the destruction of the
other. The impulse to destruction is indeed inherent in the very nature of desire, which is forced to acknowledge an other to itself
against its own narcissistic wishes, since the other is necessary for
content and recognition and yet at the same time disrupts the self's
sense of unity by standing against it. Desire thus becomes an
"agency of destruction," as Butler puts it,[21] an attempt to transform the other by negating or annihilating its independence.

While Hegel's most famous example of this destructive character of desire is surely his anatomy of the master/slave dialectic—
a life and death struggle where the master eventually dominates
the other by reducing him or her to the status of a mere 'thing'—we
can see the impulse to destruction all through the multiplicity of
'shapes' or *Gestalten* which populate Hegel's *Phenomenology*. We
can see it, for example, in the stoic's attempt to recover the standpoint of 'I am I' through a withdrawal and retreat from the world
which she treats as though it were nothing, in the skeptic's attempt to "annihilate the being of the world" (PS 123), in the "law of
the heart's" effort to make the cruel and heartless reality of the
world submit to her own inner conscience, in the conflict between
the "human and divine laws," which "attain their true end only in

so far as both sides suffer the same destruction" (PS 285), and in the rage and "fury of destruction" (PS 359) enacted by the reign of terror during the French Revolution. In all of these cases, the work of destruction is brought to bear on the world, the other of consciousness, for the express purpose of recovering the lost sense of unity for which the human spirit yearns.

In madness, too, there is an intrinsically destructive impulse involved in the severing (*Trennung*) or breaking (*Zerbrechung*) of connections with objective reality. In chapter 3, we described the regressive turn of madness as an internalization of the master/slave dialectic where the feeling soul comes to dominate and subjugate the rational self, so that "the natural self gains the mastery over the objective, rational, concrete consciousness" (PM § 408 Z). And Hegel directly uses the language of destruction in his account of mania (*Tollheit*): this is the self who "has a vivid feeling of the contradiction between his merely subjective idea"—his fantasy-projection of reality—"and the objective world, and yet cannot rid himself of this idea but is fully intent on making it an actuality"— on *living* his fantasy—and "on *destroying* what is actual" (*das Wirkliche vernichten*) (PM § 408 Z).

The Role of Destruction in Despair and Madness

A particularly forceful example of this impulse towards destruction can be seen in Hegel's analysis of despair, or the unhappy consciousness, which we have seen to be so close to madness in important respects. We may recall that Hegel interprets despair as "the tragic fate of the certainty of self that aims to be absolute" (PS 455), essentially, the yearning to become God and thereby to become whole, and to overcome our sense of vulnerability and impotence at the hands of fate. The desire to become God might be described as the deepest expression of our nostalgic desire for unity, and the despairing consciousness is precisely the experience of the impossibility of satisfying this desire: it is "the knowledge of *total* loss . . . the loss of [its] certainty of itself . . . the grief which expresses itself in the hard saying that 'God is dead'" (PS 455).

The response of the unhappy consciousness to this experience of loss is especially interesting. At its height, despair turns to asceticism, which is an attempt to destroy desire itself.[22] Desire, as we have seen, inevitably disrupts the security and peace of self-consciousness and throws it into a struggle with otherness. Every satisfaction is self-consuming and begets a new desire, and with it, a regeneration of alienation. The despairing soul thus comes to see its desire as the enemy lurking within it, the source of its wretchedness, which it seeks to destroy through rituals of mortification and sacrifice (PS 135–36). The constant disappointment of the nostalgic desire for deliverance from the restlessness and inner division of spirit, and for a restitution of its lost sense of security and peace, thus leads in despair to an enactment of the Freudian death instinct as self-consciousness seeks to destroy the very source of its life.

It was argued in chapter 3 that despair holds a particularly important place in our consideration of Hegel's account of madness, since it shows in a striking way how some of the central phenomenological structures of madness are already present within the structures of rational consciousness. It was also argued, however, that there are crucial differences within this shared ground, and we are now in a position to see these differences from a new light. Like despair, madness might be characterized as a desire to become God, understood as the nostalgic yearning for complete unity and peace. But the despairing consciousness experiences the impossibility of this ambition, and turns against its own desire as its strategy for overcoming the grief which follows from this experience of impossibility and loss. This is certainly an engagement of the death instinct, and yet a quite different engagement than we see in madness. For the mad self does not seek to destroy its own desire, but to emancipate its desire from any pretense of finding unity with what lies outside it.

Madness is the liberation of desire as pure nostalgia, unencumbered by the unhappy consciousness' absorption in the constantly ephemeral effort to reconcile itself with otherness, with reality, with God understood as the abiding essence of the external world. The death instinct of madness is thus more extreme than that of despair: by radically severing itself from the relation to otherness—objectivity, externality, reality—it seeks a return to just what despair turns against as the enemy within, the 'earthly elements' of the soul, the archaic womb of nature, the life of the body, instinct, passion, and feeling.

Of course, we have also seen that Hegel undermines the attempt of madness to achieve a state of pure nostalgic recovery of the primitive, in insisting on the 'double center of reality' present in all madness: try though it may to perfect the work of the death instinct, the mad self cannot completely destroy the trace of its own rationality. Thus just as despair must fail to destroy its own desire, madness must fail to annihilate its own rationality, so that both despair and madness are states which in principle contain the seeds of their own self-overcoming and point beyond themselves towards the possibility of recovery. Just how Hegel conceives of the mechanisms of recovery will be a major focus of our final chapter.

The Other Face of Desire: the Power of Evolution

In coming to see the essentially destructive character of nostalgic desire, which so clearly anticipates Freud's postulation of a primitive death instinct, we must not lose sight of the fact that Hegel himself almost always emphasizes the positive, evolutionary character of desire in his philosophy. We have already noted that for Hegel spirit does not "shrink" from devastation, but "endures it and maintains itself in it." Indeed it is precisely in the "labor of negativity," the inevitable dismemberment of every state of repose and satisfaction, that spirit has life: spirit is "pure, simple negativity, and is for this very reason the bifurcation of the simple," a "self-othering" (*Sichanderswerdens*) (PS 10 / W 3: 23) which negates all unity and destroys every effort of the 'I am I' to assert its claims. This is why, short of suicide, both the self-destructive effort of the unhappy consciousness and the other-destructive effort of madness are bound to fail. In despair, the enemy, desire, "renews himself in his defeat" (PS 136), since the peace of narcissistic unity which despair seeks is internally unstable and destined to point beyond itself. And in madness, the enemy, rationality itself, remains present in spite of its subjugation, and haunts the project of a return to pure interiority, insinuating itself as a second center of reality in the very midst of the self's attempt to forget it.

While the restless, self-alienating character of spirit reveals "all existing reality [to be] unstable and disunited" (RH 38), Hegel sees this process as the necessary condition for evolution. The disquiet and discord of spirit is not a symptom of disease but of an "impulse of *perfectibility*" (PH 54). Disease, on the contrary, is present in satisfaction and repose: periods of satisfaction are signs of spirit in the throes of decline and self-destruction, when it has "used up and exhausted itself" (RH 38). It is a central principle of Hegel's philosophy that every satisfaction brings on death (PH 74), which is why "periods of happiness are blank pages in [history], periods of harmony, when antithesis is in abeyance" (PH 26f). The nostalgic desire for harmony is an acting out of the death instinct, and yet like the Phoenix which is "continuously preparing its own

pyre and consuming itself," this act of destruction and death is always a prelude to the reincarnation of life: "from its ashes the new,
rejuvenated, fresh life continually arises" (RH 89).

Thus "life proceeds from death," Hegel writes (PH 77); spirit's
cyclical recovery of satisfaction and harmony is itself cyclically
transcended by the desire of perfectibility which presses spirit on
to fuller explorations of its possibilities. Here Hegel departs from
Freud's frankly bleak and pessimistic reading of the death instinct,
which, by the time of his *Civilization and its Discontents* (1930), on
the eve of the ascendence of Hitler, is envisioned as a sheer act of
destruction threatening culture with disintegration. Hegel, writing
one hundred years earlier, saw his own age as the "birth-time" of a
"new world" out of the destructive cauldron of the French
Revolution (PS 6f), and emphasized the power of the life instinct to
emerge from death.[23] Hegel says this notwithstanding the fact
that, as we saw in chapter 2, he regarded the period of the French
Revolution as one of an "almost complete collapse of civil society
[which] caused many people to become insane" (PM §408 Z). Hegel
was like Luther, who spoke of learning "to hear in God's mighty No
his mighty Yes," and who adopted as one of his favorite scriptures
the lines from Samuel, "the Lord kills and He gives life" (1 Samuel
2: 6).[24] Hegel's metaphor of the Phoenix-like nature of spirit echoes
Samuel, and his commitment to hearing always the Yes in the
midst of the No, affirmation and rebirth at the heart of negation
and death, reflects his conviction that the evolutionary impulse of
desire can, and generally does, master its nostalgic, destructive
counterpart.

Thus attempts like those of Gilles Deleuze to characterize
Hegelian desire as entirely negativistic—something which is always reactive, ultimately a form of *ressentiment* which reduces to a
Nietzschean 'slave' mentality, and incapable of a truly life-affirming impulse which is crucial for human emancipation—does
not do justice to the progressive, liberatory power of desire that
Hegel insists on.[25] It is true that this evolutionary face of desire is
always in dialectical tension with the nostalgic face, and always ac-
companied by a 'labor of negativity,' but it is only because there is
an impulse to perfectibility, a genuinely life-affirming direction-
ality to desire, that we can explain the repeated rising of the
Phoenix in human history.

Still, it is to be hoped that we have already gained some sense
of the power of nostalgia in Hegel's phenomenology of desire, and
while Hegel's whole philosophy is committed to an emphasis on

evolution and progress, it would be a mistake to minimize the threat of the regressive, destructive face of desire, or the careful attention Hegel gave to it. Thus readings of Hegel which lead in just the opposite direction from Deleuze's are equally misleading. So, for example, Wilfried Ver Eecke, inspired by Lacan, contrasts Hegel and Freud on the grounds that while "Freud was preoccupied with persons whose way of life did not satisfy desire,"

> Hegel immediately drops a figure whose failure he unveiled and begins the analysis of another figure who has integrated a new element in order to see if this new figure can [be more successful at] satisfy[ing] human desire. Freud stays with his neurotic, who is lost in his own rituals or symptoms and searches with him in a long therapy for a way to restructure his life.[26]

While it is true that Hegel's phenomenological method constantly pushes forward, the implication that he becomes impatient with "failures" (to use Ver Eecke's term), discarding all regressive and maladaptive figures of consciousness in a restless search for ever healthier, more successful ones, cannot be accepted. That Hegel, unlike Freud, had no psycho-therapeutic practice in which he would "stay" with individual patients for the long haul towards cure, is not the issue. Hegel is as preoccupied with the darker side of human desire as is Freud, and he is tireless in showing how shapes of consciousness which have been revealed as unstable and self-destructive nevertheless are recurring patterns of life. The attitudes of mastery and slavery, of stoicism and skepticism, of despair or the unhappy consciousness, are not dropped by the wayside of Hegel's philosophy, but constantly reappear and re-echo throughout his dialectic. Hegel's whole *Phenomenology* is itself a long therapy of spirit, a concernful dwelling with human consciousness along its path of sorrow and labor of self-transfiguration.

Just as Freud sees Eros as being in constant struggle with Death, Hegel insists that "spirit is at war with itself" (PH 55). Just as the master/slave dialectic is never completely left behind but re-emerges in new shapes and disguises, spirit is embroiled in a constant life and death struggle between the two faces of of desire. It is this inescapable condition of struggle which leads Hegel to describe madness as a 'necessarily occurring' possibility of consciousness, even in the midst of his emphasis on the essentially progressive, evolutionary impulse of spirit. We may now turn, in the final section of the chapter, to explore further the terms of this struggle by looking at Hegel's reading of the biblical story of the Fall.

The Fall

There is a long history of debate among commentators on Hegel as to how to understand his frequent use of Christian imagery. Some read this imagery as a purely mythological, symbolic, figurative covering over what they consider to be his basically secular and even atheistic philosophy.[27] Others are astonished by such a suggestion and believe, as William Werkmeister says, that "Hegel's basic orientation, his whole mode of thinking, is essentially religious."[28] I do not propose to enter into this intriguing debate here, but will only point out that in the context of our imminent discussion of the biblical story of the Fall of Man, Hegel invariably refers to the Genesis account as an "allegory" or "legend" or even a "myth" or "mythology" (e.g., SL § 24 Z; PM § 405 Z; PH 57f). He warns us that we must not allow ourselves to become overly enthralled by the letter of the Word but must philosophically interpret its spirit. In the long passage from the 'shorter' *Logic* where we encounter Hegel's most focused discussion of the Fall, we are told at several crucial junctures of the biblical account that the literal reading of the story can only mislead us. Nevertheless, we "cannot afford to neglect these popular conceptions" and myths of religion:

> The tales and allegories of religion, which have enjoyed for thousands of years the veneration of nations, are not to be set aside as antiquated even now. (SL § 24 Z)[29]

Eden: Nature, Innocence, and Evil

We can see by even a cursory glance how well the story of the Fall serves as an allegory for Hegel's phenomenology of desire. Eden is the innocence of a "natural harmony" which is "disrupted" by the temptation of desire, where human beings fall into "disunion" and subsequently seek, through fulfilling the mandate of the Curse—to labor, to "work in the sweat of [their] brow"—to reach a "second harmony." Freud's account of the displacement of the ego from its primary narcissism and its "vigorous attempt to recover it," and Hegel's analogous account of the downfall of the 'I am I' through the constant regeneration of desire and the nostalgic yearning to reclaim its lost innocence, both can be seen as transcriptions of this ancient biblical story.

Eden represents for Hegel the standpoint of immediate knowledge, a non-reflective and complacent sense of orientation in the world where there is no trace of disunity between consciousness and object, self and other, mind and reality. Everything is familiar and in its place, nothing is alien or threatening. But for Hegel, mere familiarity is the very poorest form of understanding:

> The commonest way in which we deceive either ourselves or others about understanding is by assuming something as familiar. . . . Such knowing never gets anywhere, and it knows not why. (PS 18)

The state of 'natural harmony' is thus destined to collapse, for it is really only deception and ignorance, and more, *evil*. This is the first of several twists or reversals Hegel introduces into the Eden story: innocence is so far from blessedness that it is more appropriately seen as evil. We will see in chapter 7 that this account of evil will have important implications for Hegel's conception of madness, which in one place he describes as the state in which "the evil genius of man gains the upper hand" (PM § 408). For now, I wish only to caution that Hegel's occasional association of madness with evil cannot be understood in a common, moralistic sense, but will depend on a rather idiosyncratic interpretation of evil.

We already begin to get a hint of this idiosyncrasy in some of the harshest words of the *Phenomenology,* where Hegel tells us that "innocence is merely non-action, like the mere being of a stone, not even that of a child" (PS 282). And here in his 'shorter' *Logic,* he writes that:

> the very notion of spirit is enough to show that man is evil by nature, and it is an error to imagine that he could ever be otherwise. To such an extent as man is and acts like a creature of nature, his whole behavior is what it ought not to be. For the spirit it is a duty to be free, and to realize itself by its own act. Nature is for man only the starting-point which he has to transform.

'Evil,' then, is really something like *incompleteness* for Hegel, or that which stands at the beginning, awaiting development. Nature is 'evil' in the sense that it is only the potentiality of spirit, and innocence itself is really 'evil' in the same way; it is uneducated, naive, unencumbered by the labor of its own transformation. The human spirit cannot be content with its natural condition of innocence (ignorance), but is internally stirred towards knowledge. Hence the words of Genesis, that God has forbidden Adam and Eve the fruit of the tree of knowledge, "evidently assume that man [and woman are] not intended to seek knowledge, and ought to remain in the state of innocence"—*but these words cannot be right*. "It is a mistake to regard the natural and immediate harmony as the right state," or to see "the only way of being . . . restored to peace" as a "surrender [of] all claims to think or know"; for the dignity and destiny of human beings lies in the search for knowledge. A literal reading of Genesis would, from a Hegelian perspective, force us to see God's intention for His creation as an imprisonment in ignorance—really, in evil—and perhaps even in madness, insofar as Eden is precisely the image which lures the nostalgic desire of madness back to its immersion in nature.

Thus as a corollary to Hegel's first reversal of Genesis, his principle that innocence is evil, we see his second reversal: the Fall is not so much the birth of original sin—indeed Hegel explicitly associates original sin with the natural, immediate state of innocence and harmony which precedes the Fall—as it is the path to the liberation from evil, the path of redemption, the "principle of restoration." The loss of innocence begets disunion—an "inward breach" and "schism," where our original harmony is "sundered," revealing a "severed life"—and yet this "step into opposition" is the "awakening of consciousness," the first step towards the "education and culture" (*Bildung*) of human consciousness. The desire for knowledge, the impulse to perfectibility, dislocates the desire for unity and security, awakening us from the dream-life of satisfaction into the strife of evolution. This impulse is precisely what the therapist will seek to revitalize in her discourse with the insane, thereby awakening the mad self from its dream state.

The Serpent and the Curse

The significance of this reading of the Fall of Man within Hegel's larger philosophic project can be seen very clearly already in the *Phenomenology,* written some ten years before the first edition of the *Encyclopædia* appeared in print. In his Introduction to the *Phenomenology,* Hegel presents his task as tracing out "the path of the natural consciousness which presses forward to true knowledge" (PS 49), and this "natural consciousness" is precisely the "immediate knowledge" Hegel refers to in his *Encyclopædia* to describe our original innocence. But this initial, naive, non-reflective consciousness is destined to lose its innocence: "Natural consciousness will show itself . . . not to be real knowledge," it will be "driven beyond it[self] . . . and this uprooting entails its death" (PS 49, 51). As we have seen, all satisfaction entails death, and yet this destruction itself engenders evolution: "Thus consciousness suffers this violence at its own hands: it spoils its own limited satisfaction" (PS 51) so that spirit may "liberate itself from this [mere] semblance" of knowledge (PS 48) and initiate the "labor of its own transformation" (PS 6).

In the Genesis story, the source of the disruption of Adam's and Eve's natural unity is the external agency of the serpent. Hegel cannot allow this, however, but introduces his third reversal of the biblical legend by insisting that: "The truth is that the step into opposition, the awakening of consciousness, follows from the very nature of man; and the same history repeats itself in every son [and daughter] of Adam [and Eve]." The security of our ignorance is internally uprooted by desire, the inner tempter. Our desire for growth, for knowledge, destroys the contentment and consolation of our natural consciousness, "so that it may purify itself for the life of the spirit" through the path of its self-education (PS 49f). As Hegel says in his *Philosophy of Mind,* human beings are capable of "acquir[ing] knowledge of the Truth only when that original paradisiacal unity of man with Nature ha[s] been *disrupted*" (PM § 405 Z).

But while the destructive, violent disruption of our original harmony is the necessary condition for evolution, it is clear that this is no easy path. The Curse demands that human beings "bring forth in sorrow," and, to cite Hegel's famous words from the Introduction to the *Phenomenology,* this makes the path of evolution a "pathway of doubt, or more precisely . . . the way of despair" (PS 49). As such, the very moment that the "desire of perfectibility" destroys the natural harmony of our immediate state of innocence, it brings to life the nostalgic desire to recover it, the second face of desire which henceforth will engage in an unceasing struggle with the impulse to evolution. Doubt, despair, and madness—the triple companions on the path of education—each become allies of nostalgia: doubt, when it is incorporated into the skeptic's nihilistic effort to destroy all otherness; despair, when it turns into the grief of the unhappy consciousness, with its desperate attempt to recover wholeness through the destruction of its life-force; and madness, when the self seeks to heal the pain of existence by radically reorienting itself, severing its connections from the reality of the external world and retreating inward into a reality of dreams and shadows. The biblical Curse upon human beings, the payment for their desire for evolution, is that they must bring forth in sorrow, so that every progress towards enlightenment and liberation from ignorance will be attended by a further loss of security and the generation of new discords. The nostalgic desire for a regression to innocence and peace is thus the unintended twin to the desire for evolution which issues from the birthpangs of sorrow of the Fall.

Forgetfulness

Hegel himself notes that the violence which "consciousness suffers at its own hands" as a consequence of the uprooting of its natural harmony by the desire for perfectibility creates anxiety, which "may well make [consciousness] retreat . . . and strive to hold on to what it is in danger of losing [viz., its natural unity]." But, he continues:

> it can find no peace. If it wishes to remain in a state of unthinking inertia, then thought troubles its thoughtlessness, and its own unrest disturbs its inertia. (PS 51)

Yet while consciousness can find no peace, since its desire disrupts the inertia of every satisfaction, the anxiety which attends this disruption insures that it will seek all the more persistently for a recovery of its inertia. This is no doubt why it is such an important principle of Hegel's phenomenology that consciousness "is always reaching this result, learning from experience what is true in it, but equally . . . always forgetting it and starting the movement all over again" (PS 64). Forgetfulness is the act of nostalgia seeking to heal the wounds suffered by spirit on its path of evolution by recovering its lost innocence. It is significant that Hegel sees madness itself as a supreme act of forgetting: the mad self is "obsessed with [its] subjectivity, and in the process *forgetting* the objective world." This forgetfulness manifests itself in the falling apart of the ordinary causal and temporal connections of rational thought, connections which can no longer be "held together," but which become lost in "the abyss of indeterminateness" (PM § 408 Z). Lost in a profound forgetfulness, fallen back into the darkness and dream life of the sleeping soul, the nostalgic desire for the narcoleptic peace of Eden has enraptured the mad self to the point where it must, as it were, start the movement of life all over again, begin again, as the infant began, the path of awakening into rationality and spirit.

We might picture one traditional reading of the biblical promise of salvation as a rebirth into innocence through a sort of baptism of forgetfulness. If salvation "redeems and dismantles, as it were, the hopeless history of the world," as Karl Löwith puts it,[30] so that history becomes a mere "interim" which human beings will be saved from, as Reinhold Niebuhr says,[31] then the "new world" prophesied in the Book of Revelation might be seen as a return to Eden, and the world of human history banished to forgetfulness in an act of apocalyptic purification. "For the first heaven and the first earth," the heaven and earth of human history, "were passed away," John writes of his Revelation:

> And God shall wipe away all tears from their eyes; and there shall be no more death, neither sorrow, nor crying, neither shall there be any more pain: for the former things are passed away. (Revelation 21: 1, 4)

It is not hard to see in the words of Revelation the answer to the grief and longing of the unhappy consciousness which yearns for unity, the achievement of the nostalgic yearning for deliverance from the pain of history—the slaughterbench of happiness—and the restoration of the innocence of Eden.[32] But Hegel cannot accept this reading, for again, "innocence is like the mere being of a stone, not even that of a child." Spirit has life only by maintaining itself in "the tremendous power of the negative," and any return to the satisfaction of Eden, so far from issuing in new life, would insure the final victory of the death instinct and a capitulation to madness.

This is why Hegel insists in his discussion of the Fall that the "second harmony" which spirit works towards after the loss of its "natural harmony" is not a mere return to innocence but the achievement of a fundamentally transformed spirit, spirit which has become educated, spirit in possession of philosophic wisdom (SL § 24 Z). Hegel was an unmerciful critic of the Romantic seduction of a 'return to nature' and the idealization of the 'noble savage.'[33] Spirit has as its vocation the ceaseless labor of self-transcendence and evolution, and any effort to restore our 'natural consciousness' is a symptom of the death instinct, and ultimately, a symptom of madness, which sinks back to a prior state of being in an attempt to ward off the pain of disunity. Indeed the goal of madness is precisely the goal of all nostalgic desire, to recreate a condition of unity. Madness recreates in fantasy the world as a projection of its inner desires: "The madman considers his subjective world as fully real and actual" (PM § 408 Z), thus removing the source of alienation and discord he experienced in the otherness of the external world, the world of sorrow and pain.

Labor

In closing our discussion of the Fall, it must be stressed that when Hegel speaks of the 'second harmony' or 'restoration' of unity which is the goal of the evolutionary strife of spirit, he adamantly denies that this achievement of unity between consciousness and its world could ever occur through a sinking back to the inertia of innocence. Rather, this unity requires labor (*Arbeit*). Human beings must work in the sweat of their brow and hence transform their ignorance into knowledge, and remake the narcissistic unity of their self-absorption into the spiritual unity of the human community. Labor is what liberates the slave (in principle) from her bonds by shaping and transforming the natural world through her own activity. Similarly, we will see in chapter 8 that Hegel sees labor as one of the most effective cures of madness, since "by working, [the insane] are forced out of their diseased subjectivity and impelled towards the real world" (PM § 408 Z). Labor is what is capable of overcoming and transforming the alien character of the world, shaping it into an image of our desire for progress. Thus while labor is the Curse placed upon Adam and Eve, and "is the result of the disunion," the Fall from the natural harmony of Eden, "it is also the victory over it; . . . [human beings] can only satisfy [their] wants by [themselves] producing and transforming the necessary means" (SL § 24 Z).

Hegel's inspirational teaching of the liberating power of labor, which promises us the satisfaction of our desire for unity by calling us to a transformation of the self through education and a shaping of the world into a rational society, is the natural outcome of his faith in evolution. And yet we must not forget the power of nostalgia. Labor, as Marx insisted, may well be liberating in principle, but it is very often alienating in practice. This is clearly the situation of the slave in the *Phenomenology*, who removes her chains in theory but retains them in reality, since the product of her labor is owned and enjoyed by the master. This is just what leads the slave to stoicism, the retreat from the cruel and heartless condition of reality into the self-absorbed and impotent realm of freedom *in thought alone* (PS 120–22).

So too, the unhappy consciousness discovers in its labor only its own nothingness, since it cannot empower itself to remake the alien world (PS 132–34). And when we turn to our discussion of Hegel's theory of the cure of madness, we will have to ask serious questions about the efficacy of labor for 'forcing' the insane out of their diseased state and 'impelling' them towards a reintegration with rationality. For example, many of the questions Michel Foucault raises about Pinel's 'moral treatment' through labor, which Foucault sees as a form par excellence of alienated labor, a "coercive education" into social norms and a "therapeutics into repression,"[34] will have to be considered with respect to Hegel, who, as we have already noted, was greatly influenced by Pinel. Alienated labor is the experience of division between self and world where the desire for unity is perpetually frustrated. Here labor does not confirm our freedom, but rather only reconfirms our estrangement from a world which is experienced as "the irrational void of necessity" (PS 443), where the individual "sees itself destroyed by the negative essence [the alienating power of the external world] confronting it" (PS 219).

The strife and discord which is intrinsic to the evolution of spirit thus ensures the recurring experience of alienation, and with it, the seductive lure of nostalgia, the attempted retreat backwards to our lost innocence through the work of destruction. The evolutionary face of desire leads to the uprooting of every achievement of satisfaction and happiness, and thus at the heart of progress there "dwells also the anxious dread which is despair" (to recall Kierkegaard's words), or the grief and longing of the unhappy consciousness which yearns to be absolute but experiences only loss and division, and which is on the border of madness. As such, no account of the evolution of spirit can avoid coming to grips with the second face of desire, the face of nostalgia, the face of the death instinct. However optimistic and inspiring Hegel's phenomenology of human history, his reader is constrained to recall the power of this dimension of desire, and the powerful pull of despair and madness which accompany our struggle with the 'infinite pain' of spirit's struggle for growth and evolution.

CHAPTER FIVE

Madness and the Unconscious

With few exceptions, philosophers have taken up one or other of the two following positions [on the unconscious]. Either their unconscious has been something mystical, something intangible and undemonstrable, . . . or they have [simply] identified the mental with the conscious and have proceeded to infer from this that what is unconscious cannot be mental or a subject for psychology. These opinions must be put down to the fact that philosophers have formed their judgment on the unconscious without being acquainted with the phenomena of unconscious mental activity, and therefore without any suspicion of how far unconscious phenomena resemble conscious ones or of the respects in which they differ from them.

(Freud, *The Claims of Psycho-analysis*
to Scientific Interest)

Consciousness is the mere surface of our mind, of which, as of the earth, we do not know the inside but only the crust.

(Arthur Schopenhauer, *The World as*
Will and Representation)

Hegel's analysis of madness as a regression to the sphere of the feeling soul, where dreams, fantasy-projection, and the play of instincts predominate, clearly situates the psychic space of *Verrücktheit* within the unconscious. Thus Hegel's philosophy of madness of necessity will be a depth psychology, an exploration of the dynamics of psychic life beneath the surface of consciousness. In the present chapter we will flesh out the role of the unconscious in Hegel's theory of madness against the backdrop of general features of two subsequent and much more widely known depth psychologies: those of Nietzsche and Freud. By allowing Hegel to enter into dialogue with the more fully developed theories of Nietzsche and Freud, we may gain a clearer sense of his own contributions.

Placing Hegel in Dialogue with Nietzsche and Freud

Hegel does not often directly refer to the unconscious in his writings, and does not explicitly develop this concept as a central principle of his phenomenology. We might therefore think that Hegel is simply one more of "the philosophers" so frequently criticized by Nietzsche and Freud, who, as Freud says, "protest that they could not conceive of such a monstrosity as the unconscious," and are thus doomed to a fundamental misunderstanding of human experience.[1] Nietzsche writes in a similar vein:

> The unconscious disguise of physiological needs under the [philosopher's] cloaks of the objective, ideal, [and] purely spiritual goes to frightening lengths—and often I have asked myself whether . . . [the whole of] philosophy has not been . *a misunderstanding of the body.*[2]

And yet it is simply not true that Hegel "totally lacked the Freudian idea of . . . the unconscious," as one commentator suggests,[3] at least if "the Freudian idea of the unconscious" is taken in a general sense. I am persuaded, on the contrary, of the validity of Errol Harris's judgment that "some may dispute the interpretation which attributes to Hegel a theory of the unconscious, but there are passages which can hardly be otherwise understood."[4] Willem DeVries reaches a similar conclusion when he asserts that "Hegel's concept of feeling is one of the earliest modern attempts we can find to work out a theory of our preconscious mental activity," a theory which "infer[s] the existence and nature of unconscious psychological activities from the data of pathology."[5]

Certainly Hegel's notion of the 'feeling soul' as the *'bewußtlosen Individualität'* of spirit is in accord with the very general description Freud gives of the unconscious in his 1933 *New Introductory Lectures on Psychoanalysis*: "The oldest and best meaning of the word 'unconscious' is the descriptive one; we call a psychical process unconscious whose existence we are obliged to assume—for some such reason as that we infer it from its effects—but of which we are not directly aware."[6] Of course, this definition is so broad that it is hardly enough in itself to allow us to draw any substantial comparisons. Freud himself goes on to say that this description alone would not give "the right to introduce the concept of an unconscious into psychology," and that much greater specificity is needed.[7] One of the main tasks of the present chapter will be to show that Hegel's notion of a regression or 'sinking back' of the mind to an archaic feeling-state in fact shares a great deal of the specific features of Freud's theory.

Naturally, there may be disputes about how well Hegel's theory corresponds with many of the technical features of Freud's account—which, it should be said, changed over time—for example, the relation of the unconscious to a 'preconscious' system, the specific dynamics of repression and censorship,[8] and the mechanisms of symbolic expression, not to speak of Freud's emphasis on the libidinal or sexual character of the unconscious.[9] And of course Freud systematized his theory of the unconscious at enormously greater length than did Hegel. But something very much the same as the Freudian concept of the unconscious does emerge, albeit infrequently, within Hegel's phenomenology of the developed consciousness, for example, in his doctrine of the 'cunning of reason' (*List der Vernunft*),[10] and in his theory of guilt and intentionality.[11] More importantly, however, we have already seen that the unconscious plays a central role in his portrait of insanity, and it is here that a comparison of Hegel with Freud—and with Nietzsche as well, who also makes the emphasis on unconscious processes central to his "new psychology"—becomes particularly interesting.

We will see that while in important respects these three writers offer competing psychologies, there are substantial parallels as well. For example, all three propose an understanding of illness as essential for an appreciation of health. Further, all regard the unconscious as crucial to the development of a decisively new orientation for psychology. Finally, all link this new psychological orientation to the need for a physiology: the unconscious points towards the domain of the body, nature, instinct. As Nietzsche says, the new psychology will be a "*physio*-psychology, . . . daring to descend to the depths," and will "translate man back into nature," into the "eternal basic text of *homo natura*," recovering the biological roots of human experience from their exile by the puritanical and spiritualistic tradition of philosophy.[12]

Thus just as Freud adopts as the motto for his *Interpretation of Dreams* Virgil's dictum that "if I cannot bend the higher powers, I will move the infernal regions"—the higher powers being the sphere of consciousness and rationality, whose structures cannot be fully understood without tracing them back to the "infernal regions" of the unconscious—we have seen that Hegel speaks of madness as a reversion to the unconscious where "the earthly elements" of the body have their home, and "the dark, infernal powers of the heart are set free" (PM § 408 & Z). Only a phenomenology of these infernal regions will allow for a full explanation of mental life.

There are, of course, important and far-reaching differences between the theories of Hegel, Nietzsche, and Freud on illness and the unconscious, and we will especially stress three such oppositions in this chapter. First, Nietzsche and Freud both effect a reversal of the values Hegel assigns to consciousness and the unconsciousness, or rationality and instinct. Consciousness is a mere surface, a disguise, parable, and façade covering over the true depth of the psyche, the unconscious. Thus Freud:

> Consciousness is the *surface* of the mental apparatus.[13]

> It is essential to abandon the overvaluation of the property of being conscious. . . . The unconscious is the true psychical reality.[14]

And Nietzsche:

> The world of which we can become conscious is only a surface-and sign-world.[15]
>
> All our so-called consciousness is a more or less fantastic commentary on an unknown, perhaps unknowable, but felt text.[16]

For Hegel, on the other hand, the unconscious is the merely immediate stage of spirit, spirit asleep, the inarticulate voice of nature awaiting education into the language of rationality which is its destiny and truth. In this sense it is the *unconscious* that is a mere disguise, and consciousness or rationality that is the genuine text of the psyche. Thus Hegel would tend to reverse Nietzsche's view (shared by Freud) that "thoughts are the shadows of our feelings."[17] In his 'shorter' *Logic,* for instance, Hegel says that feelings assume their "proper light" (emerging, to reverse Nietzsche's metaphor, from their shadow-state), only when they are "translated into the form of thought: . . . to think things over [Nachdenken] is . . . to transform feelings . . . into thoughts" (SL § 5). So while Nietzsche calls for a translation of the language of conscious thought back into the text of nature, Hegel engages in the much more traditional philosophic enterprise of translating nature into the text of thought.

In this sense we must grant Jacques Lacan's claim, mentioned in chapter 4, that Hegel "promote[s] consciousness as being essential to the subject." What cannot be granted are Lacan's stronger claims, that this amounts to a Cartesian-like faith in the transparency of consciousness, and that Hegel is engaged in a "logicizing reduction" of the mind which precludes inquiry into the unconscious. Despite Hegel's more traditional standpoint in relation to Nietzsche and Freud, he would agree on the intimate connection between thought and feeling, consciousness and the unconscious. Nature, the domain of spirit sleeping and hence unconscious to itself, is a "riddle," Hegel says, since while it *appears* alien to spirit, it is spirit's *presupposition* (PN Intro). Given this relationship of presupposition, we must avoid the all-too-common strategy of disassociating the two spheres of being, constructing a pure philosophy of the rational mind which avoids inquiry into the riddle of nature, the shadow world which in fact is the place of spirit's origins.

A second difference is that the line of demarcation between madness and health is more clearly drawn by Hegel than it is by either Nietzsche or Freud, for whom this line is at best tenuous. This will lead us to question whether Hegel has not inscribed the boundaries of rationality and its derangement too quickly and too distinctly—whether his own phenomenology does not suggest a less definite line of separation between the two.

Third, Nietzsche must be distinguished from Hegel and Freud in terms of his evaluation of illness. Specifically, illness is not necessarily pathological for Nietzsche. In speaking of his own illness, he writes that "even in times of grave illness I did not become pathological."[18] Indeed, we will see that Nietzsche views a certain form of illness as essential to health. Further, Nietzsche tends to locate the source of disease not in the unconscious, as Hegel and Freud do, but in consciousness. Consciousness itself is often described as a disease and a pathological state.[19] As such, Nietzsche will often stand as counterpoint rather than companion to Hegel and Freud in their thoughts on illness.

The Definition of Madness:
Regression, Separation, Nostalgia

Hegel and Freud

There is no evidence that Freud, who was known for his deep suspicion of all 'speculative' metaphysical systems,[20] was influenced by Hegel, or even that he knew very much about him. Freud refers to Hegel only once in his writings, and then indirectly: in his *Interpretation of Dreams,* in the midst of a cataloguing of the "unusual unanimity" of the "authorities" in their "very low opinion of mental activity in dreams," he mentions that "Spitta [1882] quotes Hegel as saying that dreams are devoid of all objective and reasonable coherence."[21] The absence of influence notwithstanding, we have already suggested that Hegel's remarks on dreams often are very close in spirit to Freudian insights, and more strongly, that Freud's definition of neurosis is a very close echo of Hegel's view of madness. Just as Hegel emphasizes a regressive withdrawal or 'sinking back' of the developed mind into a more primitive sphere of mental life, Freud speaks of the "path of regression" taken by the libido which has been "repulsed by reality" and must seek satisfaction through a "withdrawal from the ego and its laws."[22] And just as Hegel stresses the separation of the mind from 'contact with actuality,' Freud repeatedly refers to "the low valuation of reality, the neglect of the distinction between [reality] and fantasy."[23]

FEATURES OF THE UNCONSCIOUS. The place to which the mind retreats in madness is also the same in Hegel's and Freud's theories, what Hegel calls the 'life of feeling' (*Gefühlsleben*), the domain of the unconscious, the body, nature, and instinct, a domain in which a fundamentally new form of discourse obtains, displacing the language of the the 'waking' mind by a more archaic language characteristic of dreams and fantasy. To get a sense of just how close Hegel's account of the unconscious domain of the feeling soul is to Freud's own conception, we may turn to Freud's important 1915 "metapsychological" paper on "The Unconscious" (*Das Unbewußte*),[24] where he details the essential features of the unconscious "mental system."

The two most central characteristics of the unconscious, Freud says, are wishes grounded in instinctual impulses, and the absence of relation to outer reality, which is replaced by the internal, psychical reality of wishes and instincts.[25] Hegel does not often directly speak of wishes, but we have seen he does emphasize the fixation on 'subjective ideas' which are rooted in archaic feelings or impulses. And we have noted several times that he exactly anticipates Freud's notion of a break from external reality, the severing of connections with the outer world. Indeed, as Willem DeVries points out, in Hegel's idea of the feeling soul there is simply no concept of an external world, nor in fact any concept of the self or the non-self[26]—concepts which are also absent in Freud's notion of the unconscious.

Freud states further that in the unconscious there is no sense of contradiction: "Instinctual impulses are co-ordinate with one another, exist side by side without being influenced by one another, and are exempt from mutual contradiction."[27] This is true for Hegel as well. As we have seen, Hegel views the life of feeling as "in a remarkable degree self-supporting and independent" of the "causally connected scheme of things" which is so basic to the life of conscious rationality. There is no "compliance with the laws and relations of the intellect," no grounding in "the ordinary course of nature" (PM §406). In the absence of all such rational interconnections of experience, the feeling soul is characterized by a radical "immediacy" (PM §§ 405, 406). This immediacy leads Hegel to say that the typical "contradiction" between different aspects of experience which are a feature of the mediational, developed consciousness, "does not concern what we call the feeling soul" (PM § 402 Z).

The remaining two features of the unconscious Freud mentions in his 1915 essay are "timelessness"—"the processes of the [unconscious] system are not ordered temporally, are not altered by the passage of time; they have no reference to time at all"—and the "mobility" of instinctual cathexes, namely the remarkable condensation of ideas and displacement of affect from one idea to another.[28] We noted in passing in our discussion of animal magnetism in chapter 2 that the magnetic state involves the "liberation" of the mind from "the bondage" to "spatial and temporal relations," but we will defer fuller discussion of the role of time in Hegel's account of madness until chapter 7, where we will see several similarities to Freud's notion of the 'timelessness' of the unconscious mental processes.[29] As for the presence of condensation and displacement—Freud's "primary processes" as opposed to the mediational, causally ordered "secondary processes" of the ego[30]—Hegel's identification of the natural soul with the state of dreaming, where fundamentally different laws of association of ideas obtain, is consistent with Freud's account, although Hegel does not work out the dynamics of these associative processes in nearly the same detail.

HEALTH AND ILLNESS. Hegel's and Freud's characterizations of mental illness in terms of regression shows that they both see madness as presupposing a healthy consciousness. "Insanity must be discussed before the healthy . . . consciousness," Hegel says in his *Philosophy of Mind*, since the 'natural self' or 'feeling soul' to which insanity returns is developmentally prior to the rational consciousness. But insanity "has [the healthy] consciousness for its *presupposition*," precisely because madness only can be understood as a return, a reversion back to a prior state (PM § 408 Z). Insanity is a response to the healthy mind's encounter with an experience of pain with which it cannot cope. In this sense, madness is ironically a *therapeutic* attempt, an effort to heal what Hegel calls the "wounds of spirit" through a self-protective gesture of retreat. Freud elaborates this therapeutic motivation of illness in his notion of "the need for illness" and "secondary gain,"[31] and it is a basic assumption underlying Hegel's view of madness as a strategy of defense against intense suffering and alienation.

But there is an even stronger relation between the mad and healthy selves than the fact that madness presupposes health: insanity and rationality share some of the same basic underlying structures. As we saw in chapter 4, both Hegel and Freud regard the basic desire of all mind to be the striving for a reconciliation and unity between the inner and outer worlds, subject and object, self and other, and yet they both feel that all mind is perpetually confronted with the experience of disunity and contradiction. And both posit a basic duality of instinct (Freud's Eros and Death) and desire (Hegel's evolutionary and nostalgic impulses) which operate in a conflictually interactive way to respond to this confrontation with disunity.[32] In all consciousness, whether healthy or ill, there is a fundamental impulse towards withdrawal and regression competing with an impulse toward development and growth.

Again, both Hegel and Freud see the regressive feature of instinct or desire to be entirely normal, a response to what Hegel calls the essential human "craving . . . for unity" (PM § 379). Similarly, Freud explains the "oceanic feeling" of "being one with the external world as a whole" as a nostalgic vestige of the first period of infancy, where the ego does not yet distinguish anything outside itself, a sort of perfect image of the 'I am I.'[33] The death instinct is a constantly seductive Siren's song, echoing the universal human desire to restore this state of primary narcissism, the original scene of unity. In madness, the power of the death instinct, or Hegel's second face of desire, becomes dominant, leading the rational consciousness back to the archaic world of the unconscious. As for the life instinct, in madness it is displaced from its search for unity in the external world and now assumes the function of projecting its desires in fantasy.

Both Hegel and Freud view consciousness as being delivered over to a fundamental experience of anxiety in its inevitable encounter with discord and estrangement.[34] The stark words of Freud's *Civilization and its Discontents*, that "all the regulations of the universe run counter to . . . the intention that man should be 'happy,' "[35] recall the Hegelian characterization of history as "the slaughterbench at which the happiness of peoples . . . [is] victimized" (PH 21). Anxiety explains the presence within consciousness of the nostalgic yearning for an idealized past, the sense of the ego being haunted by the (at least unconscious) recollection of its primary narcissism. Consciousness can never entirely exorcise its desire for a recovery of its lost primordial unity.

This is the paradox at the heart of Hegelian desire and Freudian instinct, that while we can never achieve a permanent state of happiness, yet, as Freud insists, "we must not, cannot, give up our efforts" to achieve it.[36] What results is a continually renewed temptation to withdrawal, the gesture of retreat away from the disheartening world of external reality into the internal world of the mind. We see this in Hegel's account of stoicism—which serves as the paradigm for all of the successive movements of withdrawal in further shapes of consciousness—where the stoic seeks to recover the standpoint of the 'I am I' through a retreat from the world that causes it so much pain. And we see it in Freud's hypothesis of a "compulsion to repeat," which animates the instincts with a retrogressive urge to recover the "ancient goal" of quiescence.[37] This basic structural dynamic of the mind, the desire for unity which leads to the movement of withdrawal, is, again, the fundamental structure of madness.

A question which both Hegel and Freud must face, given their view of the overlapping of the formal structures of instinct and desire in mental disease and health, is just how distinct these two states are. In his *Encyclopædia* discussion of madness, Hegel gives the appearance of not really taking this question seriously. Madness occurs when the rational mind has reverted to the life of feeling, and where the connections to reality have been severed, while the healthy mind retains these rational threads of association to reality. What could be clearer? But Hegel should have considered this question more carefully,[38] since his phenomenology of the developed, rational consciousness is so strongly committed to showing how the connections between self and world are never stable. The goal of the unity of consciousness and reality is constantly undermined, beset again and again by the essential 'negativity' of life which entails an 'infinite pain.' The path of consciousness seeking its reconciliation with reality is a road of loss, a "pathway of despair," to repeat Hegel's well known image. We need not go as far as Jean Hyppolite, who, as we have noted, sees this essential negativity of life as itself entailing that "the essence of man is to be mad [for Hegel]." It does seem plausible, however, to assume that the struggle of the rational mind with its experience of despair will constantly threaten consciousness with the possibility of becoming radically dislocated from its world, and beckon the mind to sink back into madness.

Freud takes the question of the distinction between health and disease more seriously than Hegel, and tends to see the substantial mirroring of the formal structures of these states as blurring the line of demarcation. The difference between madness and health is essentially a practical rather than a theoretical one, having to do simply with a matter of degree: "If you take up a theoretical point of view and disregard this matter of quantity [degree], you may quite well say that we are *all* ill—that is, neurotic."[39]

Enter Nietzsche

ILLNESS AND "THE GREAT HEALTH". It is at this juncture, where the line separating illness from health has become obscure, that we must turn to Nietzsche. If anything, Nietzsche's position is even stronger than Freud's:

> Health as such does not exist. It is your goal that determines what health ought to mean even for your body. . . . The concept of normal health . . . must be given up.[40]

> By now we have learned better than to speak of healthy and sick as of an antithesis.[41]

> Health and sickness are not essentially different.[42]

We have delayed Nietzsche's entry into the dialogue with Hegel and Freud until this point because, typically, he is much more elusive in his definitions of health and illness.[43] One might try to discover similarities with Hegel's and Freud's characterizations of mental disease in terms of the double movement of withdrawal and separation from reality. For example, Nietzsche is grateful to his own experience with illness for its reinforcement of his tendency towards isolation and solitude—his 'pathos of distance' from others, his dislocation from the human-all-too-human world of conventional values. His illness allows for a new form of experience; he lives in a different world, "an as yet undiscovered country whose boundaries nobody has surveyed yet, ... [so] strange, questionable, terrible . . . that [his] craving to possess it has got beside itself."[44]

What complicates the comparison with Hegel and Freud is that Nietzsche also calls this "illness" his "great health" (*die grosse Gesundheit*).[45] The great health is "a new health,"[46] quite different from the common concept of health which essentially sanctifies the status quo and regards as sick "any inconvenient disturber of the peace."[47] The great health is one "that one does not merely have but also acquires continually, and must acquire because one gives it up again and again, and must give it up."[48] By this valuation, genuine health *incorporates disease* as its closest companion, its necessary other.

> Finally, the great question [is] . . . whether we can really dispense with illness . . . and whether our thirst for knowledge and self-knowledge in particular does not require the sick soul as much as the healthy, and whether, in brief, the will to health alone is not a prejudice, cowardice, and perhaps a bit of very subtle barbarism and backwardness.[49]

The great health sees disease as necessary for self-transcendence, as an education into new ways to see and create. It is a "health which cannot do without even illness itself, as an instrument and fishhook of knowledge, . . . which permits paths to many opposing ways of thought."[50] Disease is the descent or going-under (*Untergang*) which is necessary for health: only "from such abysses, from such severe sickness," is one able to "return newborn, having shed one's skin."[51]

Nietzsche thus revalues the opposition between health and disease, reconstructing the pedestrian definition of health as herd morality and disease as any way of thinking which puts the common value of 'rationality' into question. Nietzsche's revalued disease, the disease which is essential to the great health, is that which allows a closer contact with the depths, an *Untergang* (going under) into the domain of nature, where we may shed the skin of conventional mores and tap the source of a more elemental creativity. What is truly sick is that which seeks to repress nature, the body, the un-conscious world of instinct, of which our rational, logical schemes are merely epiphenomenal sign-languages. The common ideal of health, which for Nietzsche is pathology, is a sort of 'vampirism' which sucks the lifeblood of the body—the will, instinct, passion, feeling—and leaves only the corpse of 'pure spirit,' a sheer surface without depth, a hollow husk of consciousness which has utterly repressed its darker but more vital unconscious origin.

THE CRITIQUE OF METAPHYSICAL CONSTRUCTIONS OF REALITY. Nietzsche in fact replaces the age-old motivating drive of philos-ophy, the will-to-truth, with the *will to health,*[2] and calls for a "philosophical *physician*" to replace the metaphysician and logi-cian.[53] Freud is like Nietzsche here, in that they both see the tradi-tional philosophic will-to-truth as a fantastic falsification of the es-sential subjectivity of reality. Metaphysical *Weltanschauungen,* the constructs of the will-to-truth, are no more than projected wish-ful-fillments of the philosophers' yearning for ultimate answers in a world which remains mockingly silent.[54] We must, as Freud says, "transform metaphysics into metapsychology,"[55] translating the mythologies of philosophic *Weltanschauungen* into the 'true psy-chical reality' of the inner world of unconscious instinct. Hence the priority of the physician over the philosopher, and the deposing of the pursuit of Truth with the agenda of diagnosing the causes of cultural pathology, the sources of decadence, weariness, nihilism, *ressentiment,* and guilt.

Hegel, of course, has gone down in the annals of the history of philosophy as the consummate *Weltanschauung*-builder, the pur-suer of Absolute Truth in the grand style. And as such he is seen as the archetypal opponent of the Nietzschean and Freudian critiques of philosophy. Yet we must be cautious, for Hegel also effects a revaluation of truth.[56] Truth no longer resides in the serene immo-bility of Platonic forms, nor in the cosmic eternity of the rational-ists' eye of God, nor in the brute givenness of the empiricists' Nature. Truth is a becoming, with an intrinsic historicity. And it is just this dynamic, Bacchanalian character of truth which results in the essential negativity of human history, the perpetual loss and death of our successive constructions of reality. Human existence is a pathway of doubt and despair, a theater of suffering, a slaughter-bench of happiness, a constant reopening of the 'wounds of spirit.' We would surely need to look much more closely at Hegel's phe-nomenological method to determine to what extent it could be seen as the work of a 'philosophical physician.' But however we finally decide this question, Hegel's interest in the darker side of the human spirit—spirit in its negativity, dismemberment, and infinite pain—positions him more closely with Nietzsche's and Freud's concerns than might be supposed by a too hasty caricature.

Madness, Dreams, and Sublimation.

We have already sufficiently detailed the parallels between Hegel and Freud on the most general features of madness: the reversion to nature, the break from the usual connections with reality, the fixation on "feeling states" or instinctual cathexes, the important role of the body—the fact that mental illness is " bound up" with the body, as Hegel say, or as Freud says, that mental illness has an "organic foundation"[57]—as well as the identification of the 'unconscious mental system' or the '*bewußtlosen Individualität*' as the psychical center of madness, and the crucial role of dreams, the projected images of 'the night of the mind,' as central symbols of the unconscious. We have seen how with the movement of withdrawal and rupture from reality, Hegel and Freud argue that the language of rationality is replaced by a more primitive, archaic discourse of unconscious wishes, fantasies, and drives, which in madness as in dreams are projected onto reality as substitutes. We have also briefly indicated how Nietzsche's view of illness effects an important reversal of some of these basic commitments of Hegel and Freud. The scope of this reversal may be explored more fully by looking at Nietzsche's view of dreams, and the important relation between dreaming, sublimation, and art.

Dreams and Art

In at least one place Nietzsche links "the fantasizing of dreams and insanity" together,[58] which might suggest a closeness to Hegel and Freud. But more usually, he effects a reversal, so typical of his thinking, whereby the reality projected by dreams in no way stands in a less privileged position than the reality of waking life. Thus in his *Daybreak*—the very work in which the above passage occurs— he writes that "there is no *essential* difference between waking and dreaming . . . [since even] our moral judgments and evaluations are only images and fantasies based on a physiological process unknown to us."[59] Once the myth of a Reality in itself has been put into question—or actually "abolished," as Nietzsche proposes in *The*

Twilight of the Idols[60]—there remains only dream, reality as projected by the mind.

Nietzsche's claim that there is no clear distinction between dreaming and waking directly mirrors his view that "health and sickness are not essentially different." Unlike Hegel and Freud, then, dreams will not hold any straightforward explanatory value for illness. We need a more subtle typology of dreams, just as we must distinguish between the illness which accompanies the great health and the neurotic illness of, for example, religion. In an analogous way, we may make value judgments between different types of dreams—not, to be sure, by appealing to the standard of Reality, but on an essentially *aesthetic* basis. "It is only as an aesthetic phenomenon that existence and the world may be eternally justified," Nietzsche proclaims in a much-quoted passage from the *Birth of Tragedy*.[61] As creative projections of values, all dreams are aesthetic phenomena, and the question then becomes whether our dreams are a form of self-affirmation or self-denial, and whether they appropriate and express the "eternal basic text of *homo natura*" or seek an escape from it. This is reflected in Nietzsche's contrast between truly healthy artists and the "artists of decadence" in his *Will to Power*. The artists of decadence "fundamentally have a *nihilistic* attitude toward life" as opposed to "those imposing artists . . . who bestow upon things their own power and self-redemption," who "express their innermost experience in the symbolism of every work of art they produce," and whose creativity is a form of affirmation and "gratitude for their existence."[62]

In *The Birth of Tragedy*, Nietzsche argues that art holds the power to heal and redeem us from the "horror and absurdity of existence,"[63] but only if dream is united with nature, Apollo with Dionysus, the "beautiful illusion of the inner [dream] world of fantasy"[64] with the primal unconscious force of nature which is the heart of all great art. When dream is detached from nature, as Nietzsche argues occurred in Greek tragedy with Euripides, who purportedly substituted an "aesthetic Socratism" for Dionysian nature, a glorification of rationality, logic, and the "cool clarity of *consciousness*"[65] for the Bacchanalian forces of the unconscious, art becomes sick.[66]

Art, Sublimation, and Repression

Nietzsche's distance from Hegel and Freud on the nature of illness comes into further focus when we look at the way that 'nature,' 'feeling,' and 'instinct' are described. All three associate the domain of the unconscious and instinct with the *particularity* of human life as opposed to our social being. It is true that both Freud and Nietzsche recognize a collective character of our unconscious—both, for example, speak of our dreams as expressing the phylogenetic prehistory of human instincts.[67] And for Hegel too there are certainly universal features of feeling. The point is that these features express our private interests, the laws of the individual heart: feeling is the terrain of seclusion, subjectivity, isolation. As such, feeling precludes community and communication; it speaks a private, pre-rational language. The life of feeling is in this way a sort of pre-historical way of being, as the "innermost, unconscious instinct" of nature, which is prior to all socialization (RH 30). For fully historical existence to be possible, we must move from the standpoint of 'I' to that of 'We,' which requires, Hegel insists, that the purely private, isolating language of feeling submit itself to *sacrifice, renunciation,* and *surrender (Aufopferung, Verzicht, Aufgabe)* (see PS 136–39, 212f / W 3: 175–78, 265). Similarly, to regress back from reason to feeling, from history to fantasy, is the emergence of disease.[68]

At least at first glance, it would seem that Freud and Nietzsche depart from Hegel on this point, and would view his call for the sacrifice of the particularity of feeling as simply a call for repression, and hence as an invitation to disease itself. For Nietzsche, the "slanderers of nature"[69] who sacrifice the body and fight against instinct as a sickness, are the heralds of decadence, weariness, *ressentiment,* and neurosis. Their "priestly medicine" is a disguised "lust for nothingness" that is itself the greatest illness of all.[70] If "nothing else [is] 'given' as real except our world of desires and passions,"[71] then to renounce this reality is to repress life itself and become sick. And Freud sees the essential neurosis of civilization as resulting from the "psychologically unrealistic" demands of the social repression of our instincts.[72]

There is a real difference between Hegel, Nietzsche and Freud here, but it is not as simple as it might seem. For Hegel's recurring claim that a sacrifice and renunciation of particularity and 'the heart' is necessary in order for universality and reason to emerge is not in fact a call for the annihilation of nature, but for its *Aufhebung* or sublimation.[73] Again, nature is the 'presupposition' of spirit, and as such must be preserved, or incorporated, or 'taken up' *(auf-gehoben)* in the transition from feeling to reason. "Everything spiritual, every content of consciousness, anything that is product and subject of thought . . . must also, and originally does, exist in the mode of feeling" (RH 17). The 'sacrifice' of feeling is thus in fact its sublimation. Feeling is dethroned but not destroyed, nor can it ever be destroyed except in the illusions of ascetic self-mortification, which is just as ill for Hegel as it is for Nietzsche and Freud. Thus in his analysis of the unhappy consciousness, Hegel describes ascetic mortification as a will to nothingness, "a personality brooding over itself, as wretched as it is impoverished" (PS 135f). And in his early work on *The Positivity of the Christian Religion,* he is even more assertive: asceticism, he says, is a "self-deception" which pursues a "false tranquility," but "sinks into helplessness, anxiety, and self-distrust, a psychical state which often develops into madness" (PCR § 29).

The fact is that all three writers insist on the need for a sublimation of feeling. For Hegel, this is perhaps seen most clearly in his aesthetics. Art is the expression of the human impulse to produce itself, to rediscover or "recognize again [its] own self," to find itself "duplicated" or mirrored in the external world (A 1: 31). This expression is the representation of human feelings and passions, but not through any direct discharge—not through what John Dewey calls "an instantaneous emission," a mere "inner seething" and inchoate "babbling."[74] Rather, art is the objectification and reconstruction of passion, which allows for its *Aufhebung* or sublimation (A 1: 48 / W 13: 73). What was previously shut up in the privacy and subjectivity of the unconscious becomes an "address" or "call" or "question" (*Frage, Anrede, Ruf*) posed to the conscious mind (A 1: 71/ W 13: 102), "call[ing] forth" from the "depths" of the soul "a sound and an echo in the spirit" (A 1: 39). Passion which is unsublimated "engrosses the *whole man,* so that he loses the power to tear himself free, . . . [and] he has no longer any will beyond this single passion" (A 1: 48), just as in madness we are 'imprisoned' in the life of feeling. By sublimating passion, art frees us from the enslavement to the body—again, not by eliminating the body but by transfiguring it. To quote Dewey again, aesthetic "expression is the clarification of turbid emotion; our appetites know themselves when they are reflected in the mirror of art, and as they know themselves they are transfigured."[75]

Freud also sees art as the sublimation of instinct: "Artistic talent and capacity are intimately connected with sublimation."[76] As Paul Ricoeur points out, "The work of art enter[s] the field of psychoanalysis as the analogue of dreams and the neuroses."[77] All three involve a liberation from the tension of unfulfilled wishes and instincts through substitute formation. But while dreams and the neuroses function by way of regression, art frees the mind from the inhibition and repression of the dream work and neurotic symptomatology by the creative 'deflection' or 'transformation' of instinct. Thus in his *Leonardo* study, Freud says that in art, the "libido evades the fate of repression"—and hence illness—"by being sublimated from the very beginning into curiosity and by becoming attached to the powerful instinct" for creativity. "The quality of neurosis is absent, . . . and the instinct can operate freely."[78] Products of art, unlike those of dreams, are not illusions for Freud: both involve a transposing of unconscious conflicts and desires onto fantasies, but, as Ricoeur says, the artist "finds a way back to reality from this world of fantasy: he creates a new reality, the work of art."[79] Art is in fact an important feature of Freud's notion of "the education to reality" in that it contributes to the very production of reality. Its 'fantasies' are not nostalgic but progressive: in the work of art, a reality is created in which the past is overcome, just as Leonardo's renderings of the Mona Lisa's smile suggest to Freud that the artist has "denied the unhappiness of his erotic life and has triumphed over it in his art."[80]

Finally, Nietzsche regards the sublimation of passion and instinct as crucial to health as well.[81] And as for Hegel and Freud, he looks to art as a paradigm of sublimation. "Every artist knows how far from any feeling of letting himself go his 'most natural' state is"—the goal is not a *"laisser aller"* but rather an "education" and "discipline" of the passions; not a crude revelling in nature but self-conquest, self-elevation, self-transcendence.[82] "In man *creature* and *creator* are united: in man there is material, fragment, excess, clay, . . . chaos; but in man there is also creator, form-giver," the artistic force by which the chaos of nature is "formed, broken, forged, torn, burnt, made incandescent, and purified."[83] Sublimation is the refinement, cultivation, assimilation, channeling, integration, and "spiritualization" (*Vergeistigung*) of nature. It is contrasted to repression in that sublimation is a form of "employing" and "economizing" "those impetuous torrents of the soul that are so often dangerous and overwhelming," rather than "enfeebling" them and "wanting to make them dry up."[84]

The Status of Privacy and Community

Thus Hegel is really much closer to Nietzsche and Freud with regard to his interpretation of the feeling soul than appears at first glance. For all three, sublimation is a middle path between the *laisser aller* of nature and its repression, and to leave this path in either direction is to risk illness. The real differences lie elsewhere. First, while Hegel sees the sublimation of feeling as entailing a movement away from the particularity and privacy of the heart, Nietzsche's psychology of sublimation is committed to preserving and nourishing this privacy. Nietzsche idealizes the hermit, who lives in "the desolate regions," who needs his masks and conceal-ments, his "citadel of secrecy," who prizes interiority over commu-nity and silence over language.[85] "All community makes men—somehow, somewhere, sometime 'common,' " "unclean," unhealthy.[86] Nietzsche's great "nausea" is in fact his "nausea over man," which can be cured only by solitude, a "return to myself."[87]

Second, while Freud does not share Nietzsche's idealization of the private individual, he is often equally skeptical of the possi-bility of a genuinely healthy construction of our social being. For Freud, "every individual is virtually an enemy of culture,"[88] and every social sublimation of instinct is inherently unstable, pre-cisely because it demands so much by way of sacrifice.[89] Hegel is more optimistic here, seeing the human struggle for community and social synthesis as a genuinely achievable goal, and indeed as a goal which has been achieved in every great epoch of world his-tory. But even here we must be careful not to reduce Hegel to the sort of cartoon image which compares his optimism to "Voltaire's Doctor Pangloss [who] sees only the harmony of all things."[90] Hegel is not ignorant of the force of the death instinct, the destructive power which lies so closely at the heart of desire. He insists on the contrary that history is the slaughterbench of happiness, that spirit exists only in "the power of the negative" whereby it must confront itself again and again "in utter dismemberment" (PS 19). Our social being is not easily won, and Hegel knows full well the possibility of pathology arising in civilization, as for example in his interpretation of the French revolution, where the desire to con-struct a genuinely universal will of the people resulted in the law of the guillotine and reign of terror that he explicitly diagnoses as madness (PS 355–363; PM § 408 Z).

The Double Center of Madness

We have seen that Hegel's and Freud's basic characterization of mental illness as a withdrawal or retreat into the life of feeling and the unconscious, and a resulting severing of the connections to reality, leads to a view of madness as entailing what Hegel calls a 'double center' of reality and a 'double personality.' To cite again the key passage:

> [The mad self] is driven out of its [rational] mind, shifted out from the center of its actual world and, since it also still retains a consciousness of this world, has two centers, one in the remainder of its *rational* consciousness and the other in its *deranged* idea.
>
> . . . The insane subject is therefore in communion with himself in the negative of himself. . . . Consequently, though the insane person is *in himself* or *implicitly* one and the same subject, yet he does not know himself objectively as a self-accordant . . . subject, but as a subject disrupted into two different personalities (PM § 408 Z).

Freud also sees mental illness as situated within a doubled center of reality, the world from which the ego has withdrawn but still retains a tenuous relation to, and the substitution formations enacted by the projections of unconscious wishes. Similarly, Freud compares the neurotic to the dreamer, both of whom are like "two separate people," the one representing the wishes of the unconscious and the other the wishes of the censoring agency of consciousness and the reality principle.[91]

Nietzsche, as we should expect, holds a more ambiguous position. On the one hand, since he effects an erasure of the distinction between waking and dreaming, and between reality and appearance, the idea of a double center of reality becomes questionable. The objective, external reality of which Hegel and Freud speak so confidently, which is displaced by the fantastic realities of madness, is 'abolished' by Nietzsche and can no longer serve as a standard by which to measure its 'other,' the reality projected by the mind. On the other hand, Nietzsche does partly recover the distinction between two centers of reality in his diagnosis of neurotic illness. For example, he anticipates the major features of Freud's analysis of religion as a neurosis, which seeks to replace the reality of the earth with the myth of heaven, the reality of the body with the illusion of the eternal soul, and the reality of this world with the superstition of another world. Thus there *are* certain givens of reality for Nietzsche, against which a certain kind of mental projection may be described in the language of myth, illusion, and superstition.

But there is an even deeper sense in which Nietzsche may be seen to share the Hegelian and Freudian notion of a double center of reality as a model for understanding illness. When he turns to a description of the dialectical relation between his own health and illness, Nietzsche directly appropriates the language of a "dual series of experiences" and a corresponding double personality:

> For a [truly] healthy person, . . . being sick can even become an energetic *stimulus* for life, for living *more*. . . . A long, all too long, series of years signifies recovery for me; unfortunately it also signifies relapse, decay, the periodicity of a kind of decadence. . . . Looking from the perspective of the sick toward *healthier* concepts and values and, conversely, looking again from the fullness and self-assurance of a *rich* life down into the secret work of the instinct of decadence—in this I have had the longest training. . . . Now I know how . . to *reverse perspectives*. . . . I have a subtler sense of smell for the signs of ascent and decline . . . I know both, I am both. . . . This *dual* series of experiences, this access to apparently separate worlds, is repeated in my nature in every respect: I am a *Doppelgänger*, I have a 'second' face in addition to the first.[92]

This intimate interweaving of health and illness, this double strand of personality, these two faces and double perspectives and two separate worlds of the *Doppelgänger*, reveals both Nietzsche's closeness to and his departure from Hegel and Freud. Like them, Nietzsche sees a double center of reality as entailed by the descent into illness. But while Hegel and Freud diagnose this as pathology, Nietzsche sees it as the potentiality for a great health. Illness which is not simply a neurotic denial of instinct, but which brings us closer to the world of the body and nature, also brings us closer to the source of all human creativity. This is why it is "impossible to be an artist and not to be sick."[93] This idea is explored in a provocative passage in the *Twilight of the Idols* titled "Toward a Psychology of the Artist" where Nietzsche says that art requires frenzy:

> If there is to be art, if there is to be any aesthetic doing and seeing, one physiological condition is indispensable: frenzy. Frenzy must first have enhanced the excitability of the whole machine; else there is no art. . . . What is essential in such frenzy is the feeling of increased strength and fullness. . . . In this state one enriches everything out of one's own fullness: whatever one sees, whatever one wills, is seen swelled, taut, strong, overloaded with

strength. A man in this state transforms things until they mirror his power—until they are reflections of his perfection.[94]

Hegel, we may recall, categorizes frenzy as the deepest form of madness, precisely where the double center of reality is most extreme: "The maniac himself has a vivid feeling of the contradiction between his merely subjective idea and the objective world," between his absorption in the "dark, infernal powers of the heart" and the structures of reason. But the condition for sublimation of these powers of the heart is greatly attenuated in madness, precisely because the mind becomes fixated on unconscious impulses and does not want to let go, does not want to emerge outwards from its imprisonment. For Nietzsche, on the other hand, the artist is precisely the person who can—indeed who must—risk the descent into the conflictual doubleness of frenzy, and who has the power to liberate the creative forces of unconscious drives from any imprisonment or paralyzing fixation. If Hegel sees labor as the key to a transformation of the diseased subjectivity of the soul back into actuality, Nietzsche, we might say, sees illness itself as the condition for the transformative labor of art.

It is hardly the case that either Hegel or Freud denies an essential ontological duality of consciousness, or sees health as an overcoming of this duality. Freud's whole psychoanalytic theory insists on a basic doubleness of the life of the mind, a dynamic interplay between conscious and unconscious structures, and defines neurosis as the repression of instinct. As for Hegel, his phenomenology is committed to what Friedrich Grimmlinger calls a "*notwendige Zweideutigkeit*" and "*Doppeltheit*" which is internal to all mind.[95] The self discovers itself only in its relation to itself *as other*; it is in the gesture of self-externalization, *sich Entäußerung,* becoming-other, and the subsequent doubling of the center of our experience, that the self exists. Further, the unconscious is one of the central elements of the self's duality for Hegel, just as it is for Nietzsche and Freud. Unconscious intentions, the motivating forces of our desires, passions, and instincts, are interwoven with conscious intentions in every human action, as the warp and woof of our history (RH 26–31). There is always a "latent, unconscious" feature of action (RH 35) which accounts for the "double meaning" of the deed and the fact that the self "become[s] a riddle to itself" (PS 220). The unconscious, nature, is our internal riddle, and Hegel no more sees the solution to this riddle to be the denial of the unconscious than does Nietzsche or Freud.[96] We cannot remove the warp of history from its woof: feeling must be integrated into rationality, nature must be sublimated into the life of spirit.

What Hegel and Freud both deny is that the reversion or *Untergang* into nature is the key to genuine health. Nietzsche sees this going-under as the necessary propaedeutic to a casting-off of the constricting shackles of socially constructed norms and a revaluation of decadent values. Hegel and Freud, on the other hand, see our social being as our truly human essence, so that a reversion to the domain of instinct will be an imprisonment in a pre-rational, pre-social, and hence essentially pre-human level of life. This is why we have seen Hegel to insist that the person who "makes his appeal to feeling is finished and done with anyone who does not agree; he only has to explain that he has nothing more to say to anyone who does not find and feel the same in himself" (PS 43).

In comparing Hegel's theory of madness and the unconscious to those of Nietzsche and Freud, certainly we must not minimize the differences—for example, Nietzsche's and Freud's reversal of the values of consciousness and the unconscious, Nietzsche's revaluation of the relation between illness and health and his idealization of seclusion, and Hegel's relative optimism about our social being. Still, such a comparison shows that Hegel anticipates many of the same themes which were to occupy Nietzsche and Freud in their new psychologies of the depths: the view of madness as a response to the essential negativity of life, the characteristics of withdrawal and the decentering of reality, the conflictual duality of instinct or desire, the structures of nostalgia, narcissism and the death instinct, the importance of dreams as a model for understanding the unconscious and illness, and the crucial role of sublimation.

We need not follow Nathan Fialko's sweeping claim that "the system of Hegel contains, in fact, all the ideas that modern psychiatry has evolved"[97] in order to trace out noteworthy lines of connection. It would be a great mistake, in fact, to assent to such a picture. In the first place, even in 1930 when Fialko made this claim, there was of course no singular modern 'psychiatry' but a proliferation of competing systems. While we have seen that Hegel's theory is remarkable for its mediating position between widely different nineteenth-century medical models, it would be misleading to think that he would view his position as 'containing' the basic commitments of behaviorism, for example, or even of much of Freudian psychoanalytic theory. The Hegelian anatomy of madness is no more a complete anticipation of modern psychiatries than are post-

Platonic philosophies merely a series of footnotes to Plato. Nevertheless, Hegel's theory clearly involves significant foreshadowings of concepts and methods of explanation which later became integral to certain modern psychiatric models, and this relationship of foreshadowing invites us to resituate the Hegelian anthropology of the soul within a tradition from which it has previously been largely excluded.

CHAPTER SIX

Madness, Action, and Intentionality

Th' entente is al.

(Chaucer, *Troilus and Criseyde*)

The intention as the whole origin and pre-history of an action—almost to the present day this prejudice dominated moral praise, blame, judgment, and philosophy on earth.

(Nietzsche, *Beyond Good and Evil*)

[The intellect] does not penetrate into the secret workshop of the will's decisions. . . . In fact, the intellect remains so much excluded from the real resolutions and secret decisions of its own will that sometimes it can only get to know them, like those of a stranger, by spying out and taking unawares; and it must surprise the will in the act of expressing itself, in order merely to discover its real intentions.

(Arthur Schopenhauer, *The World as Will and Representation*)

The present chapter will further extend our examination of Hegel's psychology of the unconscious by delving into a number of basic features of his philosophy of action and intentionality. We will see that for Hegel, all human action inherently involves a crucial element of *un*-intentional meanings, whether on the side of motives or consequences. Madness is only the extremest expression of unintentionality, where the basic meanings of action originate from the unconscious life of feeling or instinct. And while not every human act involves unintended meanings in this radical sense of being rooted in the depths of unconscious wishes and instincts—it is hardly necessary to suppose, for example, that in writing *The*

Satanic Verses, Salman Rushdie unconsciously harbored a wish for the Ayatollah Khomeini to place a bounty on his life or for Saudi Arabia to declare a *jihad* against literary modernism—still, the fact that for Hegel every action must be understood to include a fundamentally unintentional content helps to illuminate a certain continuity between madness and 'normalcy,' and the value of a depth psychology even for the 'normal' mind. This is just as it should be for a philosopher who understands the insane mind to "presuppose" a healthy consciousness and to be "only a contradiction in a still subsisting reason" (PM § 408).

The role of the unintentional within the entirely 'normal' orbit of human experience is highlighted in a number of important themes in Hegel's philosophy: in his hypothesis of a circular structure of action, in his critique of purely intentional ethical positions, in his ontology of alienation, and in his philosophy of language. Accordingly, we will first look at these four themes, seeking to understand the place of unintentionality in Hegel's philosophy of the 'normal,' before turning to look at the dynamics of the unintentional within the sphere of madness, and seeking to draw some conclusions about the continuities and discontinuities between the role of the unconscious in health and illness.

The Idea of Un-Intentionality

In one of the more arresting passages of his *Beyond Good and Evil,* Nietzsche presents us with a breathtaking three-stage history of morality: in the "pre-moral" phase, the value of an action is determined entirely by its *consequences*; in the moral period per se, what counts is the *intention* behind the act; and finally, in the "extra-moral" stage which Nietzsche is advocating, "the decisive value of an action lies precisely in what is *unintentional* in it. . . ."[1] While such heresy is to be expected from Nietzsche, that "immoralist with a good conscience," the purpose of this chapter will be to show that there is an important sense in which Hegel, the great eulogizer of the majesty of Reason, largely anticipated this heresy.

Nietzsche's point in declaring the decisive role of the unintentional is to stress the basic commitment of his new depth psychology, that consciousness is only a surface, covering over the much more basic unconscious origin of all thought and action. The above passage continues:

everything about [action] that is intentional, everything about it that can be seen, known, 'conscious,' still belongs to its surface and skin—which, like every skin, betrays something but *conceals* even more. In short, we believe that the intention is merely a sign and symptom that still requires interpretation. . . .

Insofar as Hegel sketches out a psychology of the feeling soul that foreshadows the Nietzschean and Freudian calls for a depth psychology,[2] an investigation of the pre-rational realm of unconscious motivations and drives, he too is interested in the unintentional character of action. Moreover, it is not simply in the domain of madness, where the self imprisons itself in the life of feeling, that the unintentional is an important feature of action for Hegel; we will see that he claims *all* action has a crucially unintentional aspect. Now, since the unintentional is bound up with the unconscious (although not always in the same ways, as we will see), and since all action involves an unintentional dimension, this entails, as Darrel Christensen points out, that Hegel would entirely agree with Freud's (and Nietzsche's) view of the unconscious having "a continuing function in even the normal and mature consciousness."[3] It is not only abnormal psychology, but all psychology, which must recover the domain of the unconscious, and with it the unintentional, if we are to fully understand human action and values. Thus any philosophy of mind or any ethics which mainly emphasizes conscious intentions will inevitably fail to provide an adequate psychology.[4]

Two quick qualifications are needed before we go on. First, it would be wrong to imply that Hegel exactly shares the Nietzschean and Freudian view that, as Freud puts it, "the unconscious is the *true* psychical reality."[5] We noted in the previous chapter that both Nietzsche and Freud tend to see consciousness as a mere 'surface,' a sort of disguise and facade covering over what alone is fully real, the unconscious. For Hegel, the most fully real dimension of the mind is consciousness, or rationality. And yet we have a completely misleading picture of Hegelian psychology if we do not see that there is a sense in which he also identifies consciousness as a surface (albeit not a *mere* surface), the sense in which consciousness is developmentally subsequent to the domain of nature, instinct, feeling, and the unconscious. In his "Anthropology" discussion of the 'soul' and the 'life of feeling' where the unconscious dominates, he explicitly states that "everything that [later] emerges in conscious intelligence and in reason has its source and origin" in "the heart, in . . . feeling" (PM § 400). Thus while Hegel must remain one of those whom Nietzsche and Freud criticize for overvaluing consciousness, he certainly does not devalue the unconscious. In no sense may he be counted among those philosophers we have seen Freud to scorn who "protest that they could not conceive of such a monstrosity as the unconscious." Hegel not only conceives of the unconscious, but makes it an integral feature of his phenomenology of action.

This first qualification leads to the second: just as Hegel acknowledges the fundamental role of the unconscious without, however, deeming it the ultimate psychical reality, so too he is serious in his anticipation of Nietzsche's admonition to account for the unintentional value of an action without, however, going so far as to call this the 'decisive' value of action. Most importantly, Hegel would be very critical of Nietzsche's downplaying of consequentialism, the so-called 'pre-historical' phase of morality. As skeptical as Hegel is of any account of action that overlooks the unconscious, we will see that he is equally dubious of all moral theories that minimize consequences. Such theories displace the value of the external world, evading the crucial role of 'otherness' for constituting the self, and imply an ethics of sheer interiority which results in an ultimately destructive narcissism that borders on madness.

As we turn now to explore Hegel's theory of the unintentional, it should be warned that exactly what relationship(s) the unintentional has with the unconscious will be left open until late in our discussion. The unintentional will always *at least* be 'unconscious' in the minimal sense of being something unsuspected, something which we are unaware of, or have not foreseen. But whether there is a deeper sense in which the unintentional is rooted in an actual unconscious motivation will not be assumed, nor even addressed, until after we have sketched out the basic role of unintentionality in Hegel's theory of action, his critique of anti-consequentialism, his account of alienation, and his thoughts on the nature of language.

The Anatomy of Un-Intentionality

The Circle of Action

In the introduction to his lectures on the *Philosophy of History,* in the midst of a discussion of the historical significance of individual action, Hegel writes that "in [every] simple act, something further may be implicated than lies in the intention and consciousness of the agent." This is because "the deed immediately establishes a train of circumstances not directly connected with it, . . . [not, that is, contained] in the design of the [person] who committed it." Hence "the substance of the act [its consequences] recoils upon the perpetrator, reacts upon him and destroys him" (RH 35–36). This passage articulates Hegel's basic theory of the structure of action as involving a 'recoil' (*Rückschlag*) of consequences back upon the intentions of the actor. All action is a *circle* (see, e.g., PS 240),[6] wherein our conscious purposes are projected outwards, in a deed whose consequences inevitably express something beyond what was intended; the deed therefore recoils back upon the purpose, throwing it into question, exposing the disparity between its intended meaning and its actual outcome, 'destroying' the actor by revealing the unavoidable guilt[7] entailed by action, the inevitable distortion of what is willed through its very externalization and expression.

This is certainly complicated, and we might well count ourselves fortunate that Hegel gives a concrete example—a rare enough occurrence for him—to explicate his meaning. It turns out, however, that his choice of examples is somewhat unfortunate, inviting misleading conclusions. In the same passage from the *Philosophy of History,* he speaks of a man who sets fire to the house of a person who has wronged him. The man's intention is simple revenge, but other houses catch fire too, and the property and lives of innocent people are destroyed (RH 35–36). Here we certainly have a clear example of an action recoiling back upon the intention and exposing guilt, and yet we might be led to think that Hegel's idea of the circle of action only applied to the deeds of arsonists and other criminals (it is only simple justice that *their* deeds recoil and reveal guilt). Additionally, we might suppose that the disparity between conscious intention (here, revenge) and consequences (harming innocent people) simply results from a culpable lack of forethought (the man should have realized the danger). But this is not so. *All* intentionality is incomplete, unable to anticipate and encompass the full train of consequences, unable through any sheer exertion of will to force the world to become a simple mirror of our purposes. Hence all intentionality is subject to the 'recoil' of action, and to guilt. As we have seen, Hegel believes that "innocence is merely non-action, like the mere being of a stone, not even that of a child" (PS 282).

An important principle of Hegel's view of the circle of action is that all action involves a "double meaning" (*Doppelsinn, Zweideutigkeit*). Already in the master/slave dialectic that inaugurates the discussion of human action in the *Phenomenology*, Hegel presents us with a whole series of ambiguities or double meanings entailed by the attempt to gain recognition—an attempt which Hegel sees as the essential desire and intention of all self-consciousness. The most fundamental of these double meanings is that in order for the self to gain recognition (the intention), it must first of all "come out of itself" (*außer sich gekommen*) to enter into relation with an other (it must act), and yet in this very process of externalization (*Entäußerung*) "it has lost itself" (PS 111 / W 3: 146). The consequence of acknowledging an other for the purpose of affirming one's own autonomy is that our autonomy is put into question, threatened, destroyed: we now exist for-another and not simply for-ourself. The consequences have recoiled back on the intention; action is an externalization (*Entäußerung*) which is always an alienation (*Entfremdung*).

In his discussion of "The Actualization of Rational Self-Consciousness through Its Own Activity" in the *Phenomenology*, action is again described as having a "double meaning" (*Doppelsinn*). The original intention becomes subject to an "inversion" (*Verkehrung*)—this is the 'recoil' of action—through being put into effect: "the consequences of its deeds are for [consciousness] not the deeds themselves." That is, we desperately want to count our intention *as itself* being the deed, since we fail to recognize what we *meant* to bring about in what *is* brought about. The world appears as "absolutely *alien* to [the actor]," an "empty and alien necessity." We experience estrangement, division, self-doubt, and "consciousness, therefore, . . . has really become a riddle to itself" (PS 220–221 / W 3: 274).

There are several aspects of this basic sketch of the circle of action which call for special attention: the implications for Hegel's view of anti-consequentialist moral positions; the importance of the 'recoil' or 'inversion' of action for Hegel's portrait of human alienation; the clues offered for Hegel's theory of the unconscious by the fact that the actor becomes a 'riddle' to herself; and the way Hegel's theory of intentionality is closely linked with his philosophy of language.

Hegel's Critique of Anti-Consequentialism

We have seen that all action involves the implication of consequences, and hence of meanings, beyond what "lies in the intention and consciousness of the agent." Action necessarily entails what is *un*-intended. As Hegel says in the *Phenomenology,* consciousness "goes beyond itself in [its] work" (PS 243); work, or action, is the transcendence of intentionality. Moreover, we cannot subtract this transcendence from the meaning of an act—so as to hold on to our intention as the sole bearer of significance—without falling into solipsism and self-deception. Consciousness cannot know itself until it acts: "An individual cannot know what he really is until he has made himself a reality through action" (PS 240); "The self knows itself as actual only as a *transcended* self" (PS 299).

This explains Hegel's thoroughgoing criticism of all anti-consequentialist moral positions, of all ethics of interiority. Beginning with his account of stoicism, the essentially nostalgic attempt to recover the narcissistic unity of the self with itself, the "motionless tautological" stance of 'I am I,' through a constant withdrawal and retreat from the world which the stoic treats as though it were nothing (PS 119–122); and continuing through such shapes of consciousness as the "law of the heart," which is reduced to a "rage and frenzy of self-conceit" when its actions inevitably contradict (recoil against, or as Hegel says in this section, reverse and invert [*umkehren, verkehren*]) the intentions of its private con-science (PS 221–28 / W 3: 275–83); and the "honest consciousness" which consoles itself for all the failures of its action with the purity of its own "good intentions" (PS 247ff); and the "beautiful soul" which "makes duty a mere matter of words," since it "*does not act*" but only intends (PS 403)—through all these configurations of moral consciousness we have hypocrisy, "the hypocrisy which wants its judging [intending] to be taken for an actual deed" (PS 403). Or as Nietzsche says, such a person "believes sincerely that willing *suffices* for action."[8] Hegel's harsh remarks about the 'beautiful soul' express very clearly the crux of his critique of all consciousness which defines itself solely by the integrity of its intentions:

> [Such a consciousness] lacks the power to externalize itself. . . . It lives in dread of besmirching the splendour of its inner being by action . . .; and, in order to preserve the purity of its heart, it flees from contact with the actual world, and persists in its self-willed impotence. . . . Its activity is a yearning which merely loses itself as consciousness becomes an object devoid of substance . . . and finds itself only as a lost soul: . . . its light dies away within it, and it vanishes like a shapeless vapour that dissolves into thin air. (PS 399f)

It is important to mention that Hegel's position is by no means one which completely discounts the role of intentionality. Thus, for example, while Hegel is very critical of Kant's anti-consequentialism, seeing it as an "empty formalism" which condemns us to a "never-ending ought-to-be" ungrounded in concrete reality (see PR §§ 135ff; PS 236, 252ff, 364ff; PM §§ 507ff), still, he entirely agrees with Kant that the utilitarian abandonment of concern with intentionality amounts to a dehumanization of the moral project (see PS 353ff).[9] The point of Hegel's critique of purely intentional moral theories is that they are incomplete and hence disingenuous. In failing to account for the whole structure of action,[10] we are not only given a deceptive picture of action, but a picture which lures us away from engagement in the external world, which entices us into the attitude of withdrawal into ourselves, and which tends to create a fatalistic attitude by portraying the world as an alien, indifferent sphere of cold necessity.

It is just this attitude which becomes intensified in madness, according to Hegel, given the extreme movement of regression by which the mind becomes "shut up within itself." We may say, then, that any ethics of interiority is on the borderline of madness for Hegel. In this regard, it is telling that Hegel sees three of the main guises of the moral consciousness—the 'law of the heart,' 'virtue,' and the 'beautiful soul'—to be closely associated with madness: as we noted in chapter 3, the law of the heart descends into "frenzy" and "derangement"; virtue is a self-divided consciousness whose extreme expression is madness (*Verrücktheit*); and the beautiful soul's flight from the external world and impotent search for self-unification entails a "disorder[ing] to the point of madness."

The Recoil of Action and Alienation

The recoil of consequences back on intentions engenders, as we have seen, a double meaning of action, one meaning which corresponds to the inner world of intentions, and another, contradictory meaning which conforms to the external world of effects. More generally, this doubleness characteristic of action is a basic feature of Hegel's ontology of human existence, which is first of all an ontology of alienation. For Hegel, spirit is "pure, simple negativity, and is for this very reason the bifurcation of the simple," a "self-othering" (*Sichanderswerdens*) (PS 10 / W 3: 23) which negates all unity and destroys every effort of the 'I am I' to assert its claims. Our very being is an unrest, a disquiet, a constant reaching out beyond itself, a transcendence of all stability, a decentering of all unity. In this way, the double meaning intrinsic to action reveals a deeper double meaning, or double center, of experience—the decentering of alienation, the division of the self from itself, the ephemerality of any experience of self-coinciding or satisfaction. All satisfaction brings on death; we live only insofar as desire is regenerated, and thus insofar as otherness and disunity are perpetually recreated.[11]

The inevitable failure of intentionality to control the course of events, which reflects the larger fact of alienation, is epitomized in the experience of despair, the 'grief and longing' of the unhappy consciousness. One of the recurring features of the unhappy consciousness is in fact the experience of a recoil of our action back upon our intentions. For example, what we intend when we combat our finitude—the 'enemy' of instinctual drives and desires within us—is to experience ourselves as more sublime, as beings who transcend our nature as incarnated subjects, and to coincide with our image of the self as an immortal spirit. But what we actually accomplish in the act of self-mortification is only the heightened sense of our own embodiment: "This enemy renews himself in his defeat, and consciousness, in fixing its attention on him [with such serious concern], far from freeing itself from him, really remains for ever in contact with him, and for ever sees itself as defiled" (PS 136).

Or when despair becomes a sort of "musical thinking" (*musikalisches Denken*), displacing all cognitive, conceptual engagement with our sense of division, and giving the self over to the attempt to simply *feel* a unity with the world—the intention is again foiled by the fact that all we can feel is our own "agonizingly self-divided" consciousness, the "infinite yearning" for an "unattainable beyond" (PS 131). Every effort to reconcile the sense of division between our existence and our essence, finitude and the infinite, self and world, ends in bewilderment (*Verwirrung*) and inversion (*Verkehrung*) (W 3: 163).

It is precisely this despairing recognition of our fundamental self-estrangement, reflected in the guilt-laden disparity between inner intentions and external events, which is the ontological and psychological ground in which the possibility of madness is rooted. Madness is the most radical form of alienation, the extreme experience of decentered, self-divided existence. The intentionality of madness is displaced onto the purely 'subjective ideas' of fantasies, where we attempt to leave behind the original 'center' of existence, the external world, keeping it completely on the outside of our experience, precisely so as to evade the recoil back upon our intentions, or fantasies, of any objective consequences.

Intentionality and Language

> As long as we have to use language in one way or another, we cannot help feeling a certain split taking place within ourselves, which is contradiction.
>
> (Daisetz Suzuki, *Zen and Japanese Culture*)[12]

A further theme that helps illuminate Hegel's idea of the circle of action is the connection between his theory of intentionality and his philosophy of language. If we look at the language employed by the moral consciousness which emphasizes intentionality over consequences, we see that "moral consciousness . . . is still *dumb*, shut up with itself within its inner life" (PS 396). Pure intentionality is ultimately silent, precisely because "language is self-consciousness existing *for others*, . . . [where] the self separates itself from itself" by expressing itself (PS 395). It is just this existence-for-others which mere intentionality seeks to avoid, since it wants to guard itself against the recoil of consequences it does not desire. Language is "at once the externalization and the vanishing of this particular 'I.' . . . The 'I' that utters itself is *heard*, . . . [and this] means that its *real existence* [as a private, particular 'I'] *dies away*," becoming other to itself, immersed in a communal space, a being-among-others (PS 308f). Language for Hegel is the very existence or "being-there" of spirit (*das Dasein des Geistes*) (W 3: 478): "We see language as the existence of spirit. Language is self-consciousness existing for others, . . . the self that separates itself from itself, which as pure 'I' = 'I' becomes objective to itself" (PS 395).[13]

The 'vanishing' of mere particularity through language is the vanishing of the pretense of intentionality to be complete unto itself. "Language," Hegel says, "is more truthful" than mere intentionality: "in [language], we ourselves directly refute what we *mean* to say" (PS 60). As Heidegger says in his discussion of Hegel's theory of language, "Language repudiates our intention."[14] The first example Hegel gives of this in the *Phenomenology* is in his analysis of the standpoint of "sense-certainty" (*sinnliche Gewißheit*), which is basically the position of common sense realism, that there is an immediate correspondence of a given, brute datum, a 'this-here-now,' with our sensible perception of it. Hegel seeks to reveal the intention behind the language of sense-certainty, the language of 'this-here-now,' as being refuted in the very moment it is put into words.

Anticipating Moritz Schlick's acknowledgement that the "immediate sensation" which is to be the foundation of knowledge "cannot be written down, for as soon as I inscribe the demonstratives 'here,' 'now,' they lose their meaning,"[15] Hegel asks just what the 'this-here-now' *is*. "In order to test the truth of this sense-certainty," namely that *this* thing or event, *here*, is *now*, "a simple experiment will suffice. We write down this truth," or "we utter" it; "a truth cannot lose anything by being written down" or spoken. But when we "look again at the written [or spoken] truth we shall have to say that it has become stale," that, in fact, "it proves itself to be something that is *not*" (PS 60). In the very act of being put into language, the 'this-here-now' is no more, it is always already past, or "vanished," to use Hegel's word. As Charles Taylor puts it, "I cannot know even what I mean if all I can say is 'this' or 'here.' . . . For it to mean something for me, and not just be an empty word, there must be something else I could say to give a shape, a scope, to this 'now.' "[16] What is said is 'more truthful' than what we mean to say: our language exhibits the unintelligibility of just what we intended to have stand as the most essential character of perceptual experience, the brute sense datum.[17]

This is the first of a long series of examples in the *Phenomenology* of the recoil of language back upon intentions. Throughout the many shapes of consciousness Hegel explores in this text, what is meant is disclosed as at best an incomplete rendition of what is actually sayable, and what is sayable is shown to reveal a much fuller 'truthfulness' about experience. What is merely "meant *cannot be reached* by language" (PS 66). This is at least partly because what we mean or intend is private, determined by our subjective desires and purposes which are meant to be protected from the distortion which inevitably results from externalization. Language, however, is externalization, expression, being-for-others, and hence has a universal signification which contradicts any purely private intention.

In an important section of the *Encyclopædia* on the relation between memory and words, Hegel remarks on Mesmer's experiment in attempting "to think without words." Such a procedure is "manifestly irrational," Hegel asserts, "a procedure which, as Mesmer himself admitted, almost drove him insane." Hegel goes on to speak more generally about the power of the word, saying that it is:

ridiculous to regard as a defect of thought and a misfortune, the fact that it is tied to a word; for although the common opinion is that it is just the *ineffable* that is the most excellent, yet this opinion, cherished by conceit, is unfounded, since what is ineffable is, in truth, only something obscure, fermenting, something which gains clarity only when it is able to put itself into words. Accordingly, the word gives to thoughts their highest and truest existence. (PM § 462 Z)

One might say that just as Mesmer was "almost driven insane" by his effort to think without words, madness itself is from Hegel's perspective an attempt to achieve the ineffable, to think without language, or rather an attempt to speak a purely private language. Jacques Lacan's critique of Hegel's reputedly logocentric characterization of desire, and his alternative configuration of desire as an essentially nostalgic longing for recovery of an original scene of unity (see chapter 4), ironically leads him to a view of language which precisely corresponds to Hegel's estimation of the predicament of Mesmer and the insane. For Lacan, as Judith Butler puts it, "linguistic signification is a series of substitutions" for pre-linguistic, unconscious intentions, "that can never reclaim an original meaning. In effect, to be in language means to be infinitely displaced from original meaning."[18] It is just this melancholic, even tragic perspective on language which motivates the yearning for retrieval of a pre-linguistic origin—a yearning which Lacan himself acknowledges is impossible of fulfillment.

In important respects, Hegel's theory of language is echoed in the phenomenology of Jean-Paul Sartre, in the section of *Being and Nothingness* on "Concrete Relations with Others." It is worthwhile to pause briefly to sketch out this comparison, given that Sartre finally draws quite different conclusions than Hegel does from an essentially shared starting point. Like Hegel, Sartre stresses the ephemerality of intended meaning (*le sens*), and the priority of expression:

> By the sole fact that whatever I may do, my acts freely conceived and executed, my projects launched toward my possibilities have outside of them a meaning which escapes me and which I [nevertheless] experience.

> Thus the 'meaning' of my expressions always escapes me. I never know exactly if I signify what I wish to signify. . . .

> As soon as I express myself, I can only guess at the meaning of what I express—i.e., the meaning of what I am—since in this perspective to express and to be are one.[19]

We see from this last passage that just as Hegel draws an ontological consequence from his reflections on language—"we see language as the existence of spirit"—Sartre regards language as ontologically constitutive. Insofar as human consciousness is a being-for-others, and "language is not a phenomenon added on to being-for-others . . . [but rather] *is* originally being-for-others," it follows that "I *am* language" (*je* suis *langage*).[20]

The crucial difference between Hegel and Sartre emerges in their contrasting evaluations of the basic externalizing and therefore alienating character of language, the fact that language, as Sartre puts it, is a "flight outside myself" (*fuite hors de moi*),[21] calling the self's private meanings into question and disclosing the self as unavoidably subject to a public space of signification. For Sartre, language ultimately reveals the limitations of my freedom, my being as transcendence, by confirming my entrapment within the category of being-for-others. All language is a "stealing of thought" (*un vol de pensée*)[22] by an other who constitutes its meaning, and to that extent constitutes me as well. In speaking, I become subject to the other's gaze, which is an insurmountable obstacle to my free being-for-self, forcing me to confront my ineluctable 'facticity,' my thing-ness, my being as object for an other. Even the language of love, which is *meant* to express the ideal of the reciprocal recognition of each other's freedom, becomes embroiled in this conflict, and ultimately becomes simply the language of seduction and beguilement, a version of the Hegelian master/slave dialectic of struggle for capture and possession of the other.[23]

For Hegel, on the other hand, the alienating character of language is finally emancipatory. Hegel would certainly agree with Sartre that in being thrown outside the self through expression, freedom is called into question, but he would characterize this as merely the freedom of the 'I am I,' of pure being-for-self, of sheer particularity, which for Hegel is not finally our truest being nor consequently our truest freedom. As we saw in the last chapter, Hegel's phenomenology is fundamentally opposed to the Nietzschean privileging of privacy and self-enclosure and committed to a definition of human being as the striving for community: "Human nature only really exists in an achieved community of minds" (PS 43). Pure being-for-self has nothing to say to others, but language is 'more honest' than our essentially nostalgic, regressive desire for complete interiority and self-sufficiency. Language is an emancipation from the inarticulate particularity of the 'I,' an entering into community which is the space in which genuine freedom and self-identity must be sought and struggled for.

Hegel's theory of language is also well worth comparing to Wittgenstein's, most specifically to Wittgenstein's stance against the possibility of a private language. Hegel and Wittgenstein present largely analogous arguments against the positivist-empiricist description of the relationship between language and reality; they each insist that the meanings of words are not determined by the things they refer to but by linguistic practices or rules of usage; and both conclude, to use Wittgenstein's formulation, that "It is only in a language that I can mean something" in a coherent way.[24]

Charles Taylor was the first of several commentators to note the similarity between Hegel's and Wittgenstein's thinking on language when he spoke in his 1972 essay on "The Opening Arguments of the *Phenomenology*" of "a degree of affinity" between Hegel's analysis of sense-certainty in the *Phenomenology* and Wittgenstein's arguments in the *Philosophical Investigations*. Taylor shows convincingly that both Hegel's and Wittgenstein's analyses "turn on the basic starting point that to know is to be able to say."[25] We may add that just as Hegel refers to the purely private and merely intended as an "inchoate word" and a "blank space," Wittgenstein says that a word which was "intelligible to me alone" could be expressed only as "an inarticulate sound." Even here, though, "such a sound is an expression [*Ausdruck*] only as it occurs in a particular language-game," that is, in a common language. Apart from such expression, the word would have no "justification."[26]

In the context of his exposure of the disparity between meaning and language in sense-certainty, Hegel refers to "the divine nature" of language, that it "directly revers[es] the meaning of what is said, . . . making it into something else, and thus not letting what is meant get into words at all" (PS 66).[27] Thus just as the consequences of every action 'recoil' against intentions, so too language 'reverses' meaning, exposing the inherent incompleteness and impotence of what is merely intended.[28]

This divine recoil of language is exemplified in Hegel's advocacy of a fundamentally new approach to grammar, one which casts suspicion on the subject-predicate propositional form and proposes the use of the "speculative" or "philosophical proposition" (PS 36–40).[29] The subject-predicate model of language is misleading for Hegel because it seduces us into thinking of language as the direct, immediate expression of meaning, of subjects which either 'contain' their predicates, or at least are fully captured and mirrored by their predicates. But again, language always points beyond the apparently transparent and stable character of meaning or intention, which entails that predicates recoil back against the subject, casting it into question: the subject "suffers, as we might put it, a counterthrust [*Gegenstoß*]" (PS 37 / W 3: 58). Hegel gives the example of the proposition "God is being":

> The predicate is 'being'; it has the significance of something substantial in which the subject is dissolved. 'Being' is here meant to be not a predicate, but rather the essence; it seems, consequently, that God ceases to be what he is from his position in the proposition, viz. a fixed subject. Here thinking, instead of making progress in the transition from subject to predicate, in reality feels itself checked [*gehemmt*] by the loss of the subject, and, missing it, is thrown back [*zurückgeworfen*] on to the thought of the subject [seeking a new way of understanding it]. (PS 38 / W 3: 59)

It is precisely the 'inhibition' (*Hemmung*) of thought effected by the ambiguity and instability of the speculative proposition that Hegel sees as responsible for the sense of obscurity and disorientation people find in reading (speculative) philosophy:

> [This] inhibition of thought is in large measure the source of the complaints regarding the unintelligibility of philosophical writings from individuals who otherwise possess the educational requirements for understanding them. Here we see the reason behind one particular complaint so often made against them: that so much has to be read over and over before it can be understood—a complaint whose burden is presumed to be quite outrageous, and, if justified, to admit of no defence. (PS 39)

The source of this complaint is our common-sense assumption that meaning is directly expressible in language, our belief that the proposition is a "firm objective basis" (*festen gegenständlichen Boden*) upon which intention is transparently displayed, and hence our deep consternation when we learn that philosophically understood, the proposition entails an inevitable recoil of language back upon intentionality:

> [W]hat this [complaint] amounts to [is that] the philosophical proposition, since it *is* a proposition, leads one to believe that the usual subject-predicate relation obtains. . . . But the philosophical content destroys (*zerstört*) this attitude and this opinion (*Meinung*). We learn by experience that we meant something other than we meant to mean (*die Meinung erfährt, daß es anders*

gemeint ist, als sie meinte), and this correction of our meaning compels our knowing to go back (*zurückzukommen*) to the proposition and understand it in some other way. (PS 39 / W 3: 60)

When Hegel wrote in the draft of an 1805 letter to Heinrich Voss, a translator of Homer, that he "wish[ed] to try to teach philosophy to speak German,"[30] he was expressing what he was to call two years later, in the Preface to the *Phenomenology,* his desire to utilize the "plastic" nature of the German language to "destroy" the apparently transparent character of the propositional form (PS 38, 39), just as we have seen him say that in all action, consequences recoil back on intentions and "destroy" the actor.[31]

The Unintentional and the Unconscious

In all of the various aspects of Hegel's theory of the circle of action we have discussed, the 'unintentional' has been described simply as the undesired, unforeseen consequences of an intentional act. Thus we do not yet have anything approaching what Nietzsche meant when he wrote that "the decisive value of an action lies precisely in what is *unintentional* in it"; Nietzsche is referring to unconscious motives, motives which lie in the depths of our primordial, pre-linguistic, pre-rational passions and drives. Obviously, simply to be unaware that 'x' will occur as the result of an intention being put into effect is not to say that 'x' was unconsciously intended. Put in another way, when Hegel says that "In [every] simple act, something further may be implicated than lies in the intention and consciousness of the agent," this does not necessarily imply that the "something further"—the actual consequence—was contained as a motive in the unconscious.

It seems implausible, for example, to assume that the arsonist Hegel refers to in his *Philosophy of History* necessarily unconsciously intended to have his fire spread beyond the home of the person who wronged him. Perhaps he did: this isn't impossible to imagine, but it does strain credulity to suppose that he necessarily did. Or is Hegel suggesting something like the inordinately severe doctrine Jean Paul Sartre later developed, which proposes that human beings are responsible for whatever happens to them—even the "coefficient of adversity," the most contingent effects of happenstance—since, deny it or not, we have chosen whatever befalls us: "there are no *accidents* in a life," Sartre writes, and hence "no excuses." Thus, for example, "in war there are no innocent victims" and in a deep sense "I choose" even my "being born."[32] True, unlike Hegel, Sartre rejects the notion of a psychical unconscious, so that for him in some sense we consciously intend or choose whatever occurs in our lives. Does Hegel, for his part, share the Sartrean view of radical responsibility for all the consequences of our actions while differing only in ascribing intentionality to the unconscious?

Not at all. Much of Hegel's theory of action can be read as adopting a view of the unintentional as simply being that which is undesired and unforeseen, without any reference to a psychical unconscious (that is, to a Nietzschean or Freudian notion of the unconscious). Certainly, his basic critique of non-consequentialist ethics does not require a depth psychology, and it is entirely possible to read his theory of alienation without allusion to the unconscious. On the other hand, it is clear from Hegel's theory of madness that Hegel does have a theory of the unconscious, and that at least in madness, the 'unintentional' has a Nietzschean/Freudian character. At least in madness, there are motives we do not consciously intend which are nevertheless present in the unconscious, and which are necessary for a full explanation of our actions.

By way of experiment, then, it might be interesting to see whether Hegel's larger theory of action is amenable to depth psychology, with its emphasis on the role of unconscious motives— without, again, implying that the unintentional dimension Hegel ascribes to all action will always require the presence of unconscious motives. If so, then this might allow Hegel to avoid the charge of oversimplification that Nietzsche complains of when he says that "All psychology so far has got stuck in moral prejudices and fears; it has not dared to descend into the depths,"[33] and that Freud complains of when he speaks of the ignorance of "philosophers, for whom 'conscious' and 'mental' [are simply] identical."[34] This would also make it possible for Hegel to escape the awkward situation of requiring two quite different psychologies of action, one for madness—where the unconscious is a central principle of explanation—and another for 'normal' or 'rational' action, where a logic of purely conscious intentions would be sufficient. Such a double psychology would be disconcerting given that Hegel often insists on the parallelism of mental structures between madness and the developed consciousness.

A good place to begin, in order to test our hypothesis, is to return to the discussion in the *Philosophy of History* where Hegel is concerned with the 'recoil' of action on intentions. Shortly before this passage, he writes that "world history does not begin with any conscious aim; . . . [its aim is at first present] only in an implicit form, namely as Nature—as an innermost, unconscious instinct. And the whole business of history . . . is to bring [this unconscious instinct] into consciousness" (RH 30). He goes on to speak of the "unconscious impulse" of the "natural will," that is, of "instinct [and] passion," which serves as the means by which the hidden purposes of the *Weltgeist* are brought into consciousness and realized (RH 31ff).

This is one of many places where Hegel seems to be personifying *Weltgeschichte* and the *Weltgeist,* and this no doubt raises difficulties for any attempt to draw inferences about a psychology of the unconscious which could apply to individual human beings. But first, note that the unconscious which Hegel ascribes to the *Weltgeist* is precisely the "natural will"—the instincts and passions—of concrete human individuals. *Human* 'nature' is the unconscious face of world history. The human motives and intentions which are the means to actualizing history are originally unconscious, not merely in the sense of our being unaware of their full consequences, but in the much deeper sense of originating in the body, which for Hegel is the domain of 'nature.' Here we can see Hegel anticipating Nietzsche's call for a *"physio-psychology"* which "translate[s] man back into nature." In this sense, when Hegel says that consciousness "has really become a riddle to itself" insofar as its intentions are always subject to a recoil of consequences, it is tempting to see the source of this riddle (or at least a frequently contributing factor) to be 'nature,' the domain of spirit's unconscious life—all the more so since Hegel actually refers to nature as a "riddle" (e.g. PN Intro).[35]

The implication of this interpretation is not that every human act must be understood in terms of unconscious motives. All action, for Hegel, involves the contribution of unintended consequences, but there is no reason to suppose that Hegel sees these as always foreshadowed in the unconscious. Rather, the point is that since we are all creatures of nature as well as rational beings, we are all subject to the vicissitudes of unconscious drives of which we are unaware, and which in certain sorts of situations play a significant role. To cite two examples which will occupy us in greater detail in the next chapter, it may be that Hegel's analysis of Oedipus as caught in "an antithesis of the conscious and the unconscious" (PS 280) implies the presence of actual unconscious motives operating in contradiction to his conscious intentions. Antigone, on the other hand, is seen as fully conscious of the crime entailed by the burial of her brother: there is no unconscious motive here, even though Hegel believes her act still creates unintended consequences, not the breaking of Creon's edict, which she does knowingly, but the exposure of her own sense of law, "divine law," as incomplete and one-sided (PS 284). Thus while the unintentional is a constant presence in action, it is not always present in the form of unconscious motives.

There are further grounds for drawing conclusions about individual psychology from Hegel's statements about the 'unconscious impulses' of the *Weltgeist*. While Hegel is speaking of *Weltgeschichte* in the cited passage, similar remarks are repeated elsewhere with respect to individual history. Thus, for example, we have seen that in his discussion of the biblical story of the Fall, Hegel describes the "natural unity" of the Garden, where Adam and Eve are "creatures of nature," as an entirely pre-reflective absorption in the life of the instincts. Here there is not yet any history, since there is no genuine labor: labor is the curse upon human beings which arises with our surrender to desire. Only then do we have the "awakening of consciousness," and the condition for historical action. Thus just as *Weltgeschichte* begins in the form of "Nature as . . . unconscious instinct, and the whole business of history . . . is to bring [this unconscious instinct] into consciousness" (RH 30), so too, each and every human individual must repeat the history of Adam's and Eve's transformation of unconscious nature through labor.

This "awakening of consciousness" begets disunion—an "inward breach" and "schism," where we "step into opposition" with the original harmony of our unconscious life, and henceforth live a "severed life" (SL § 24 Z). This language of opposition and schism recalls Hegel's description of the 'double meaning' of action, the double center of alienated experience which occurs as the result of the disparity between external events and internal motives. In the discussion of the Fall, the fall into labor, or action, initiates the awakening of consciousness and effects the doubling and dividing of the self between its historical being and its unconscious nature. Insofar as Hegel sees the story of the Fall as an allegory for the continuous need to 'transform nature' through labor in order to perpetually create history, it does not seem so outlandish to suppose that 'nature,' the unconscious impulses of the human psyche, must play a significant role in the circle of action, by which historical transformation is brought about.

Madness and Unintentionality

Hegel's analysis of madness emphasizes the same basic gesture of withdrawal into interiority that is also a recurring movement of all consciousness in response to the experience of alienation. Stoicism, the unhappy consciousness, the law of the heart, and the beautiful soul are each typical expressions of a nostalgic desire to recover the ephemeral state of self-unity, to overcome the sense of estrangement and disruption which emerge through action. For this very reason, these shapes of consciousness are on the borderline of madness for Hegel.

While we have argued that it may be possible to see much of conscious intentionality as involving a contribution from the unconscious, the intentionality of madness, according to Hegel, is entirely displaced onto the unconscious life of feeling and instinct. Intentions are dream-like, in the same sense that Freud sees mental illness as sharing with dreams the characteristic of a "withdrawal from the ego and its laws," and the development of a fundamentally different language, with its own unconscious mechanisms. Thus madness represents the most radical instance of the 'unintentional.'

The connection between the unintentionality of madness and the nature of language is an important one. Even someone like Michel Foucault, who argues that theories of insanity have tended to see "language [as] the first and last structure of madness, its constituent form," stresses that these theories envision the particular nature of the language of madness to be fundamentally different: "Such discourse is both the silent language by which the mind speaks to itself in the truth proper to it, and the visible articulation in the movements of the body," a form of "immediate communication," a discourse of delirium.[36] The language of madness is thus marked by privacy, immediacy, and soliloquy—what appears on the outside as either silence or delirium—and by the centrality of the body, or the pre-conscious (and thus *consciously* unintentional) domain of instinct which is its proper truth.

Freud discusses the idea of a different language of the unconscious as early as his *Interpretation of Dreams,* and in his 1913 paper on *The Claims of Psycho-analysis to Scientific Interest* he includes a section on "The Philological Interest of Psycho-analysis" where he describes the interpretive work of psychoanalysis as being "first and foremost translations from an alien method of ex-

pression into one which is familiar to us," or a translation of the
" 'language of dreams' into our waking speech." He argues that the
language of the unconscious "forms part of a highly archaic system
of expression" marked by symbolism, the uniting of contrary meanings, and a general sense of elliptical expression and omission of
connecting links.[37] Hegel's notion of the archaic dream state of
madness and the displacement of rational threads of association
between ideas anticipates Freud here. In the context of Hegel's
theory of language, we might say that by replacing the usual features of language, madness seeks to avoid the recoil of language
back upon intentions, just as more generally its withdrawal into
the interior life of the feeling soul is an effort to escape the alienating confrontation with externality.

But of course *all* language is expression, and thus subject to
the disparity between intentionality and what is expressed. As
Freud points out, for example, the 'manifest' dream, the actually
expressed images of the dream, by no means directly expresses the
'latent' dream-thought, the original wishes or drives which become
expressed in the manifest dream.[38] Thus there will always be a recoil of language back upon intentions, even in dreams and madness. The point is that in madness, language is interiorized; it is
really a soliloquy of the mind, a sort of private language, so that
the 'recoil' or 'counterthrust' of what is expressed back upon what
is intended remains enclosed within the fantasy life of the self. The
goal of therapy will then be to externalize, or to 'translate,' the interior language of madness into the publicity of common language,
or into 'waking speech' as Freud says.

As we should expect, in madness there is a radicalization of
the solipsism and deception Hegel associates with all purely interior experience. In madness, "the mind is . . . nestled in its interior
life" to such an extent that it "is at home only in its subjective
ideas." Without interest in external reality, the insane are "led to
create some content or other from [their] own resources and to regard this purely subjective content as objective" (PM § 408 Z)—a
situation which parallels the "hypocrisy" Hegel saw in every moral
position "which wants its judging [intending] to be taken for an actual deed."

But in madness, the withdrawal into self-imprisonment is so
extreme that the very possibility of a recoil of consequences back
on motives is thrown into question, at least, as we have just remarked with respect to the privitization of language in madness, in

any common way. The circle of action is wholly inward, since, as we have seen, the mad self "communes merely with its *interior* states" (PM § 402 Z). Here there is no acknowledgement of the legitimate presence of an external world into which intentions are projected through actions. Rather, the dreams of the unconscious are projected into an internal fantasy world—a "shadow cast by the mind's own light"—which remains under the subject's control. This account is very close to Freud's notion of fantasy-projection, a process of replacing the threatening reality of the external world with a 'reality' constructed out of the wishes and superstitions of the unconscious.[39] In such a thoroughly internalized construction of reality, there can be no experience of recoil as it is present in the rational consciousness, and strictly speaking, no possibility of the experience of guilt, since as far as consciousness is concerned, there is no disparity between an inner and an outer world: there *is no outer world.*[40]

Similarly, the 'double meanings' and 'double center' of experience which we have seen to be so important in Hegel's theory of the circle of action, must be fundamentally displaced in madness. Given the negation of external reality, the only remaining ground for doubleness is within the space of consciousness' own self-imprisonment. Actually, if the "negation of the real" (PM § 403) in madness were to be perfectly complete, there could be no real duality even within consciousness, since the value of fantasy projection is precisely its ability to effect a coinciding of intention and reality. This is why it is so crucial to Hegel's account of madness that external reality does retain a certain sort of presence in madness, in the shape of a more or less dimly recollected trace, like a shadow or echo of its former reality.

It is the presence, albeit the dim and repressed presence, of a recollected image of reality which holds the hope for a cure of madness, according to Hegel. While the subject of Hegel's therapeutics must await a fuller discussion in chapter 8, we may note here how closely his theory of the cure of madness fits in with his phenomenology of action and his critique of non-consequentialist moralities. We have already indicated, in chapter 2, how impressed Hegel was with the so-called 'moral treatment' advocated by Philippe Pinel, which spurned the common therapies of purging, whirling chairs, narcotic drugs, and punitive incarceration, and emphasized rather the importance of labor. And in chapter 4 we noted how Hegel views labor as equally capable of liberating the slave and the insane, just as it liberates or 'awakens' Adam and Eve from their immersion in nature, through its power of creatively transforming the alienating character of the external world.

Hegel is entirely sensitive to the motives which lead human beings to withdraw into themselves—it is Hegel, after all, who describes the path of consciousness towards self-development as a path of doubt and loss and despair, and who speaks of history as the 'slaughterbench' of human happiness. Yet his philosophy is finally one which calls us to externalization, to expression, to labor, the very actions which confront us with the conditions of alienation, of the recoil of consequences back on intentions, of ambiguity, double meaning, self-division, and guilt. Hegel is not being perverse here; his invitation to alienation is not made out of a fondness for torment. Rather, he is concerned with what he sees as the essentially pathological character of radical withdrawal, wherein we persist in a state of "self-willed impotence," of sheer yearning, of profound hollowness, and of abnegation of our implicit destiny as human beings to create, to become, to transform ourselves and our world. The withdrawn soul is a "lost soul," and a wasted soul; "its light dies away within it" (PS 400). To act is to become thrown into alienation, to be sure: "Action is itself nothing else but negativity" (PS 238), the disruption and loss of what is merely meant or intended or desired. But to act is also the necessary condition for creation. When "spirit becomes an 'other' to itself" through action, "and enter[s] into [concrete] existence, it *creates* a world" (PS 467).

But Hegel is not a naive optimist any more than he is a lover of torment for its own sake. He is fully aware of the powerfully nostalgic dimension of human desire, that side of desire which longs for peace and security, which yearns for redemption from the suffering and alienation inherent in action, and which lures us back into withdrawal, to isolation, to self-imprisonment, and, at its most desperate extreme, to madness. Thus while the *Phenomenology* tells the story of the evolution of consciousness through progressively richer shapes of being, it is punctuated by recurring gestures of withdrawal, and Hegel never claims there is any psychological necessity that consciousness must emerge out of such states. There is only a 'logical' necessity for consciousness to progress, a necessity 'on paper' we might say, in the sense that Hegel believes there are inherent contradictions involved in every configuration of withdrawal from the world, contradictions which logically only can be resolved through action, expression, externalization. But this logical necessity is by no means a psychological necessity, which accounts for the fact that in the midst of an essentially evolutionary philosophy of action, Hegel is very much concerned to provide an anatomy of shapes of consciousness which break under the pressure of the wheel of action, and lure us into dream and darkness, where the light dies away within us, and we fall back onto the hypocrisy (and at times, even the madness) of a merely intended life.

CHAPTER SEVEN

Madness and Tragedy

[N]ow the awful dirge begins,
the fiend, the fury,
singing, wailing in me now,
shrieking madness!

(Euripides, *Hecuba* ll. 683–86)[1]

Ajax, ill to cure,
Sits by, and holy madness is his consort. . . .
Better if he
Were hidden in Hades, now his mind is gone . . . .

(Sophocles, *Ajax* ll. 610, 635)

[W]hat madness came upon you!

(Sophocles, *Oedipus the King* l. 1300)

That way madness lies.

(Shakespeare, *King Lear*)

It is a basic argument of this book that madness and the 'normal' mind are not sheer opposites for Hegel. Not only does Hegel refer to madness as a 'necessary' and 'essential' stage in the phenomenology of human consciousness, but there are certain basic structures of madness which are equally structures of the developed, rational mind. In the present chapter, we will explore this shared ground further by looking at a variety of intersections between Hegel's account of madness and his theory of tragedy. Like despair, which exists on the borderline between madness and rationality, tragic action, while not pathological in principle, shares many of the same mental structures and strategies as madness. It is striking, indeed, to see how frequently the language of madness is evoked on the tragic stage. As Bennett Simon remarks of the ancient Greek stage, not only is "madness in metaphorical terms . . . extremely common in the plays of the three great tragedians, . . . but frank clinical madness, complete with hallucinations and delusions, . . . is also rather common."[2]

Paul Ricoeur says something very important when he comments, "No other philosophy has ever equalled [Hegel's] endeavor to integrate tragedy to logic."[3] While Ricoeur is using 'tragedy' in a metaphorical sense, the point of the forthcoming argument will be that even in the narrower, literal sense, Hegel's interpretation of tragic drama—especially when understood in conjunction with his theory of madness—may be shown to cast new light on some of the central commitments of his larger (phenomeno-) logical vision.

We will see that both madness and tragic action involve ontologies of disunion—both are inwardly divided, doubled forms of consciousness—and as such highlight Hegel's elaboration of an ontology of alienation at the center of his phenomenology. Further, within this divided state, both exhibit Hegel's idea of a double center of reality, the reality of the inner world and that of the outer world, in particularly poignant ways: outer reality is experienced as the dreadful world of an alien fate, and in their confrontations with fate, both the mad and tragic selves recenter their desires and designs around an inner reality which is essentially dislocated from the outer world. This recentering in turn uncovers a world of constant inversion, reversal, and peripety, a world and a way of acting which is perpetually inscribed within double meanings and ambiguous implications. Additionally, it is just this inwardly divided and inverted world which enables the phenomena of madness and tragic action to reveal the human struggle with guilt and the nature of evil in especially dramatic ways. And finally, madness and tragedy each involve an intimate relation to 'nature,' to the domain of feeling, passion, and unconscious drives, and allow us to see how Hegel develops a depth psychology to explore the dynamics of unconscious mental life.

On the Borderline:
The Between-Space of Madness and 'Normalcy'

It is not only a study of madness which allows us to look at what Freud calls the "distortions and exaggerations" of psychic life in order to gain insight into the 'normal.' Hegel's philosophy is one which emphasizes the inherently alienating character of life. The path of development of consciousness is one of loss, doubt, and despair, and the life of spirit is continually confronted by "the tremendous power of the negative," or more starkly put, by "devastation" (*Verwüstung*) (PS 19 / W 3: 36). As such, consciousness is delivered over to a state of yearning for wholeness, for peace, for redemption from discord, without ever being able to achieve it in any lasting way. This leads to the construction of strategies for realizing harmony which often become desperate.

This is in fact the origin of many forms of madness, according to Hegel, when consciousness sinks back into disease in response to the devastation of its desires. But there are what we might call 'transitional' or 'borderline' strategies as well, desperate to be sure, yet still located by Hegel within the terrain of the 'normal' or rational consciousness. These are extreme forms of alienated existence which cling to rationality but must struggle with the alluring promise of release that madness offers. Hence Hegel's belief that "the extravagances of subjectivity constantly pass into madness" (PH 3: 510).

The forms of consciousness which occupy positions on the borderline between the 'normal' and the 'deranged' offer sufficient "distortions and exaggerations" in their own right to provide, along with madness, the desired goal of a point of access to the 'normal' through the distortion of the normal. But more, their peculiar positioning within the between-space of the rational and mad souls promises a unique vantage point from which to examine the intersection of rationality and madness, a psychical interstice in which we are forced to question what really separates the two.

We have already discussed a number of examples of such transitional or borderline states; we have noted that Hegel uses the language of *Verrücktheit* in his analyses of stoicism, skepticism, despair, the law of the heart, virtue, absolute freedom and terror, and the beautiful soul. In the present chapter, we will explore a comparison of madness with tragic action, which also exists on the border of madness, and which not only plays a key role in Hegel's phenomenological project, but also has a larger metaphysical and aesthetic significance.

While the immediate goal of the chapter will be to investigate a number of the most striking connections between madness and tragedy, with a view to further deepening our understanding of Hegel's theory of mental derangement, we will also be reinforcing the secondary task of this book, which is to lay the foundation for a fresh look at Hegel's anatomy of the 'normal' mind. For again, neither madness nor tragedy are so much opposite ways of being to that of the fully rational consciousness, as they are distorted images of it. This is what allows Sophocles' Odysseus, for example, to look upon Ajax's madness and see there his own "dim shape" and "shadow" (*Ajax* l. 126). As such, madness and tragedy highlight in a graphic way basic features of the everyday world of 'normal' experience: we are all inwardly divided and doubled selves; we all exist within a double center of reality and must struggle with the sense of an alien fate; we all act within a world of double meanings, of ambiguity, inversion and reversal; we are all subjects of guilt in our very being; and we are all creatures of nature as well as spirit, of unconscious motives and drives as well as conscious intentions.

The Ontology of Disunion

The Broken World

Both tragedy and madness are responses to what Hegel calls in his *Aesthetics* the "oppositions of this chaotic universe," oppositions which ensure that spirit cannot "escape the misfortune [*Unglück*] and calamity"—or perhaps, the ill health (Hegel's word is *Unheil*)—"of the finite realm" (A 1: 178 / W 13: 234). Of course, to experience the world as a divided and broken place is not itself peculiar to madness or tragedy. Human consciousness is a yearning for unity, a profound desire to become "conscious of itself as its own world, and of the world as itself" (PS 263)—a sort of nostalgic craving for that 'oceanic feeling' of oneness which Freud interprets as our most primordial wish. Yet this yearning is perpetually frustrated by the encounter with discord, opposition, and estrangement. The world is never a simple mirror of our inner desires, but throws them into question, setting them in opposition to the desires and values of others, and revealing the disparity between the merely personal and the social character of being, between our interior lives and our confrontation with otherness.

Further, the broken and divided character of the world effects a similar inner division of consciousness. The "gulf" between "inward strivings and external reality" (HP 1: 52) means that satisfaction can only be achieved momentarily, that fulfillment is ephemeral, that desire is constantly rekindled, and that consciousness experiences itself as inwardly torn between its desire for wholeness and its feeling of being dispossessed. The whole course of Hegel's *Phenomenology* may be read as an account of different therapeutic efforts on the part of consciousness to heal the wounds of the spirit, to struggle for a sense of reconciliation of its inner division.

But while madness and tragedy fall within the universal experience of a broken world, and share with all forms of consciousness the struggle to heal their inner disunity, they are extreme cases, and thus greatly magnify the contours of Hegel's phenomenological landscape of alienation. A brief recollection of some of the key ideas in Hegel's definition of madness, and an exploration of parallel features in his definition of tragedy, will allow us to compare the place of the ontology of disunion in these two dramatic forms of alienation.

Madness and The Tragic Collision of Opposites

We have seen that while Hegel is concerned to show throughout his discussion of *Verrücktheit* that madness incorporates many of the same psychological mechanisms as the fully rational consciousness, he describes insanity as a final capitulation in the face of the alienating character of existence, where the mind 'reverts back' to and becomes 'engrossed' in a more primitive way of being, the 'life of feeling,' radically separating itself from external reality, which is experienced as a theater of infinite pain.

At first glance, it might seem as though madness successfully solves the problem of alienation, since in displacing its connections with the external world, it achieves the desired state of self-reunification through a projective dream life which directly expresses its desires. But although we have noted that Hegel foreshadows Freud in seeing madness as a therapeutic attempt, he also anticipates Freud's view that the attempt is doomed to fail. This is no more a moral judgment on Hegel's part than it is on Freud's: neither takes the position that just because madness is pathological, it must be condemned as a failure on ethical grounds.[4] Rather, Hegel argues that the effort of madness utterly to remove external reality, completely to obliterate the laws of the ego and the reality principle, and fully to replace the discourse of rationality with a competing, pre-rational discourse of fantasy, cannot be achieved. Madness can go a long way in this project, but reality and rationality can at most be radically dislocated and displaced, never fully effaced; the "rational nature" of the insane cannot be "entirely destroyed" (PM § 408 Z). But since rationality remains, albeit in a weakened and vulnerable form, and with it an at least tenuous connection with reality, the condition of alienation remains as well; madness remains inwardly divided, a double personality with a double center of reality.

A similar intensification of the ontology of disunion, with the resulting doubling of the center of reality, is present in Hegel's account of tragic action. Unlike the relatively self-contained nature of Hegel's discussion of madness, his treatment of tragedy is much more wide-ranging, from the systematic analysis of Greek and modern tragic literature in his *Lectures on Aesthetics*, to the account of the tragic character of certain forms of ethical action and religious experience in his *Phenomenology*, with briefer comments in his early essay on *Natural Law*, in his *Philosophy of Right*, and in his Berlin lecture cycles on the *Philosophy of History*, the *Philosophy of Religion*, and the *History of Philosophy*.[5]

Throughout his various discussions of tragic action, the theme of ontological disunion is paramount. Tragedy is a form of 'collision' of opposites, a scene of conflict and contradiction between equally justified principles. In ancient Greek tragedy, these principles are "substantive and independently justified [ethical] powers"—for example, those of private conscience and social custom, the religious and the secular, family and the state, love and duty, nature and culture—which are embodied in individual actors whose characters directly express these larger, cosmic forces (A 2: 1194 ff). In modern (or Romantic) tragedy, where emphasis is placed much more strongly on the "subjective inner life of the character" (A 2: 1223), the conflict "lies essentially in the character to which the individuals adhere in their passion" (A 2: 1226).[6] But in all cases, the tragic stage is a theater of the doubling of reality through the collision of unreconciled oppositions; the world is "rent asunder" in tragic action (PS 265).

We see this double center of reality in both of the basic forms of ancient tragic collision Hegel identifies, represented by Sophocles' *Antigone* and *Oedipus the King*, respectively. In *Antigone* the opposition is between the demands of social-political life and those of the family; between the divinities of light and darkness, the "daylight" gods of the state and the "nether" gods of instinct, feeling, and blood ties; and between what Hegel configures as the masculine and the feminine powers of life (A 1: 221, 464; A 2: 1213; PS 267ff, 284). In *Oedipus the King* the collision is between the principles of consciousness and the unconscious, be-

tween what is open and what is hidden, between volitional and unintentional acts (A 1: 207; A 2: 1214; PS 283f, 446–48; LR 354n).

We will return to say more about these two plays later, but we
can already see some similarities between the ontology of disunion
in tragic action and in madness. Just as madness presents a world
which is doubled between the desires of internal reality and the re-
lentlessly alienating force of external reality, tragic action is situated in a world which is divided against itself, between the tragic
actor's "pathos"[7]—that is, the "power[s] of the heart," or the "essential needs [Bedürfniße] of the human heart" (A 1: 232, 220 / W 13:
286)—and the opposing authority of external reality which is experienced as "the eternal necessity of a dreadful fate" (PS 279). Just
as madness "clings to itself and has its objectivity within itself," recentering reality within the "fixed idea" of its own interior life (PM
§ 408 Z), the tragic actor is centered in "the firmness of *one* 'pathos'
which remains true to itself" (A 1: 240)—Antigone, for example, in
the 'pathos' of family, of instinct, of the gods of the underworld, and
Oedipus in the 'pathos' of the dominion of consciousness, the sover-
eignty of what is open to sight. And just as madness cannot escape
alienation, but is haunted by the trace of reality and rationality it
seeks so desperately to efface, the tragic actor is undone by the
center of existence which opposes it—Antigone by light, Oedipus
by darkness, Antigone by the power of the political state, Oedipus
by the power of the unconscious.

Similarly, just as the doubling of the center of reality in madness effects a corresponding splitting of consciousness into a double
personality, the collisional nature of reality in tragedy also reveals
an inward duality of character. Given Hegel's claim that modern, or
Romantic, tragedy locates the conflict of powers within the character itself, while in ancient tragedy, the tragic character is "one in
himself," unified by a single 'pathos' (A 1: 240; and see A 2: 1206,
1225–6), this double personality of the tragic actor is in principle
more clearly present in modern tragedy—for example, in Hamlet's
spirit of revenge and his debilitating inertia; in Macbeth's commitment to evil and his simultaneous revulsion by it, in his inclination
to brutality and his desire to resist it; in Othello's powerful faith
and the doubt which unhinges it, in his great love and the corrosive
jealousy which destroys it; in Caesar's wisdom and self-deception,
in his courage and superstition; in Cleopatra's paradoxical nature
as both harlot and goddess, simultaneously corrupt and holy; and in
Iago's lament that "I am not what I am" (*Othello* I, i).

And yet it is possible to see this doubleness in all tragic figures—

certainly in Oedipus, who is torn between what he knows and what he is, who is the subject of a "double striking curse," with "darkness on his eyes, that now have such straight vision," who knows not "where he lives, nor whom he lives with" (*Oedipus the King* ll. 414–19), whose mother/wife Jocasta invokes the gods to "keep you from the knowledge of who you are" (*Oedipus the King* l. 1068).[8] And Antigone too is a double self, a self divided between her past history and the self so transformed by the crisis of her brother's unburied corpse, the self who was betrothed to Haemon and the self who goes to the "marriage chamber" of her tomb (*Antigone* l. 891).

Indeed, while Hegel says that ancient tragic characters "firmly identify themselves with the one ethical 'pathos' which alone corresponds to their own already established nature" (A 2: 1226), these characters are tragic precisely because they are engaged in intimate struggle with their opposite. Oedipus adheres tenaciously to the rights of consciousness, but his very actions solicit the opposite power, that of the unconscious, which finally destroys him. Antigone unbudgingly clings to the 'pathos' of blood ties, but her character is equally defined by her 'other,' by her confrontation with the laws of social and political reality which circumscribe her destiny. Again, this is analogous to the situation in madness, where the insane, despite their imprisonment within a fixed idea, are nevertheless double personalities precisely because of the continued relation to otherness, to what surrounds, as a sort of constantly encroaching negative space, the fixity of their internal dream lives.

Madness, Tragedy, and Despair

The kinship of madness and tragedy through their related ontologies of disunion can also be seen in their shared affinity with the state of despair. In our previous discussions of the unhappy consciousness we saw how Hegel conceives of despair as a continually present possibility, indeed as the "center" and "birthpang" of all the shapes of spirit (PS 456f), expressing the fundamental fact of consciousness' inner division (*Entzweiung*). This self is torn between the sense of its own finitude, of being caught up in the consuming fire of change—"bound upon a wheel of fire," as Lear says (IV, vi)—in a world of accident and caprice, and its desire for self-identity, for immutability, for completeness—the desire, ultimately, for the divine, for what Hegel calls the "tragic" desire "to be absolute" (PS 455). It is in this sense that Hegel sees Goethe's *Faust* as an "absolutely philosophical tragedy," showing "the tragic quest for harmony between the Absolute . . . and the individual's knowledge and will" (A 2: 1224). Despair reflects the sense of loss of the divine, the forfeiture of a world redeemed from alienation and protected from the irrational force of contingency. It is the "grief which expresses itself in the cruel words that 'God is Dead' " (PS 455).

We encounter the 'cruel words' of despair many times in the language of tragedy.[9] Euripides, like his contemporaries Thucydides and Plato, was deeply suspicious of the nostalgic invocation of a pantheon of gods whose irrationality and arbitrariness had become embodied in the destructive madness of the Peloponnesian Wars. Of the three great ancient Greek tragedians, Euripides was perhaps the most stark in his expression of this language of despair. His Hecuba perfectly represents Euripides' sense of the tragic absence of the divine:

> O Zeus, what can I say?
> That you look on man
> and care?
>   Or do we, holding that the gods exist,
> deceive ourselves with unsubstantial dreams
> and lies, while random careless chance and change
> alone control the world? (*Hecuba* ll. 488–92)

> O gods! Do I call upon those gods for help?
> I cried to them before now, and they would not hear.
> Come then, hurl ourselves into the pyre. Best now
> to die in the flaming ruins of our father's house! (*Trojan Women* ll. 1280–83)

Hecuba looks at a world divested of divine compassion, seeing only a "ruined land, ashes and smoke, wasted, wilderness of war," and hearing only the "ringing echo of terror" which haunts the godless world (*Hecuba* ll. 480, 1110). In such a world, the overlapping of tragedy and madness becomes complete: "our fortune's course / of action is the reeling way a madman takes" (*Trojan Women* ll. 1204–5). Madness is a central theme of Euripides' *Heracles, Orestes,* and the *Bacchae* as well.

But we need not rely exclusively on Euripides—Hegel's least favorite Greek tragedian, incidentally[10]—to see how central the theme of a disparity between the human and divine was to the Greek tragic stage. It is Sophocles' *Antigone* which Hegel takes as the prototype for the collision between 'human law' and 'divine law' that he sees as the fundamental opposition of Greek tragedy. We may also think of Sophocles' Oedipus, who had always accounted himself blessed by the gods, but is revealed as "the most accursed, whom God too hates / above all men on earth" (*Oedipus the King* l. 1345); and Ajax, who is made insane by Athena, and hears the fiendish "sweet laughter" of the gods reverberating over the blood-drenched stage of human action (*Ajax* l. 79); and Heracles, who encounters the divine in terms of torture and madness: "Torture, torture is all [Zeus] gives me! . . . / this inexorable flowering of madness," without prospect of any healer, any "craftsman surgeon" (*Women of Trachis* ll. 995–1001). Similarly, Aeschylus presents the theme of dislocation from the divine, resulting in illness: a "sickness that fights all remedy" (*Libation Bearers* l. 470), where, as Cassandra says, all is "useless; there is no god of healing in this story" (*Agamemnon* l. 1248). Like madness, the tragic experience of a world divested of any rational order begets a struggle with illness and a forlorn yearning for healing.

As for madness, we have seen how Hegel's description directly appropriates the language he uses to define the unhappy consciousness: his portrayal of despair as "the duplication of self-consciousness within itself," which is experienced only as "self-contradiction," is mirrored virtually exactly in his description of madness as a "disruption of consciousness into two mutually contradictory modes." We might see madness, like tragedy, as an intensification of the despairing response to a god-forsaken world. Indeed, Hegel sees religious disillusionment as a powerful cause of madness, when "the individual is plunged into absolute uncertainty whether God's grace has been granted to him," effecting a "derangement of [the] person's individual world" (PM § 408 Z). Madness is an attempt at self-empowerment where the power of the divine is experienced as either absent or irrational, an attempt to *become* God in a fantastic effort to fill the void expressed by the cruel words of despair, that "God is dead." This attempt at empowerment and self-deification is seen in the mad self's negation of the external world, the scene of god-forsaken fate, and in the internalization and reconstruction of reality through dreams, by which madness seeks to create and rule a world of its own.

This dream-project of madness goes beyond what we find in tragedy, insofar as the forces represented by the tragic protagonist's 'pathos' are universal ethical principles and not fantasies. Still, we can see how tragedy lies on the border of madness when we note how the tragic protagonist, like the mad self, tends to negate the reality of the world which confronts him or her: the

tragic character has "drowned in [a] Stygian water . . . all independence of the objective, actual world" (PS 281), so that the reality he
or she is in collision with "vanishes" into "oblivion" (PS 448). To
cite but two examples: Clytaemestra, standing over the bloody
corpses of Agamemnon and Cassandra, seeks to obliterate the guilt
of her act when she says to the chorus:

> You can praise or blame me as you wish;
> it is all one to me. That man is Agamemnon,
> my husband; he is dead; the work of this right hand
> that struck in strength of righteousness. And that
>   is that. (*Agamemnon* ll. 1403–1406)

Similarly, Antigone says impatiently to Creon:

> Why are you waiting [to pronounce my doom]?
> Nothing that you say fits with my thought. I pray it
> never will.
> Nor will you ever like to hear my words. (*Antigone* ll. 499–501)

By erasing all justification of the opposing center of reality,
tragedy effects a decentering of reality which is analogous to that
of madness, resulting in a similar attempt to remake the world, to
project the tragic actor's own vision of reality onto existence. And
just as with madness, the decentering project of tragic action is
never conclusive, never complete, never capable of perfectly eliminating the force of reality which stands against it. It is destined to
remain in collision with its antithesis, ordained to a double center
of existence and an ontology of disunion.

Submersion, Darkness, and the
Infernal Powers of Nature

The action of decentering reality in response to the alienating
character of the world leads to a further point of comparison between madness and tragedy: the way in which this decentering enterprise involves a motion of withdrawal and submersion of consciousness into itself. Both madness and tragic action share with
despair the "*pain* of the spirit that wrestle[s], but without success,
to reach out into objectivity" (PS 410)—both yearn for but fail to
achieve a coinciding of their inner desires with the course of the
world. As a result, both initiate a movement of internalization of

reality. Madness, we know, is directly described by Hegel as a "sinking of the soul into its inwardness," where consciousness "contemplates its individual world not *outside,* but *within* itself." As for tragic action, this involves an analogous "withdrawal from [the] truth . . . [of] the real world," a "mourn[ing] over the loss of its world" which leads to the creation of a reality "which is raised above the real world" (PS 425f).[11]

The movement of withdrawal can take many forms, both in tragedy and in madness. For example, the typology of madness Hegel presents in his "Anthropology" categorizes insanity very largely according to specific shapes of withdrawal: the mind may withdraw into a relatively indeterminate, "vacuous" state (as in cretinism, or "natural idiocy" [*der Blödsinn*]); or into "distractedness" (*die Zerstreutheit*), where it becomes so absorbed by a certain feeling or idea that it is unaware of the course of events outside it; or into "rambling" (*die Faselei*), where it cannot concentrate its attention on anything, but sinks into a "perfect type of chaos"; or into a particular period of the past; or into an obsession with a specific delusion (that one is God, or a king, or a grain of barley, or is made of glass); and so on (PM § 408 Z).

In tragedy, one of Hegel's central examples of withdrawal is Hamlet, who exemplifies the intensified version of a common state of being, that of "the beautiful soul" (*die schöne Seele*). The beautiful soul lives in dread of acting: "it flees from contact with the actual world," and becomes absorbed in a state of "self-willed impotence" (PS 400 / W 3: 484). Hamlet, the tragic representative of the beautiful soul, has, like the mad self, sunken into himself (*in sich versunken*) (W 14: 208), and "persists in the inactivity of a beautiful inner [*innerlichen*] soul which cannot make itself actual or engage in the relationships of his present world" (A 1: 584; and see A 2: 1225–6).

The particular shape of withdrawal which holds the most interest for a comparison of madness with tragedy is the sinking inward and submersion of consciousness into 'nature,' the basically pre-rational level of mental life, the life of feeling which Hegel associates with darkness and dream: the domain of the unconscious, of instinct, of the body. The withdrawals of the mad and tragic selves into nature are both voyages into those "infernal regions" of the unconscious Freud refers to in his *Interpretation of Dreams.* Thus, just as in insanity the "earthly elements" of nature are liberated—"the dark, infernal powers of the heart are set free" (PM § 408 Z)—so too in tragedy, Hegel believes we are continually confronted by a collision of the laws of the 'upper,' 'daylight' world of consciousness with the laws of the 'lower,' 'nether' world of instinct and passion. Antigone, to cite Hegel's favorite example of this, reveres "the underworld gods of Hades, the inner gods of feeling, love, and kinship [des Bluts], not the daylight gods of free self-conscious national and political life" (A 1: 464 / W 14: 60).[12]

The Return to Origins, a Place Prior to Time

In a sense, madness is a return to origins, to that "eternal basic text of homo natura" Nietzsche speaks of as lying beneath all the masks and cloaks and surfaces of consciousness. We noted in chapter 5 that along with such features as the disconnection from external reality, the primacy of instinctual impulses, the absence of any sense of contradiction, and the striking "mobility" of instinctual attachments, Freud sees "timelessness" as one of the defining characteristics of the unconscious: unconscious processes "have no reference to time at all." We may now see how Hegel's own interpretation of madness as a return to origins emphasizes timelessness as well. The infernal regions of nature are inherently prior to time, to genuinely human time, or history. This explains Hegel's disenchantment with the Romantic physician's penchant for historicizing illness, as we saw in chapter 2. To seek to locate the different forms of madness within specific historical periods is to adopt temporal categories for explaining a phenomenon which is essentially opposed to temporality. Hegel's well-known claim that spirit "traverses" a temporal sequence, that its "motion" is a movement "in time, and the 'shapes' . . . of spirit display themselves in a temporal succession" (PS 413) is true for the shapes of spirit, or rational self-consciousness, and cannot be transposed onto the sphere of Gefühlsleben where the forms of madness find expression, without historicizing what is a fundamentally ahistorical way of being. As Marcuse puts it, for Hegel "only spirit can be 'in time' and 'appear' in time."[13] What precedes spirit, and what reverts back from spirit to an origin prior to spirit, can only be misunderstood by comparison with historical and temporal ways of being.

For Hegel, time is the expression of "pure freedom in face of an 'other' " (PS 413), an undoubtedly difficult concept which, however, at least entails the notion of consciousness (which alone can be free, for Hegel) determining itself—or, to use Marcuse's phrase, "bringing itself forth"[14]—in relation to what is external to it. Self-constitution within a being-towards-the-world, which for Hegel is ultimately labor, is the condition for temporality. A stone, as

Marcuse points out, lacks the "form" of temporality precisely because a stone "cannot shape and express itself in time,"[15] cannot bring itself forth into the world, cannot constitute itself through labor, but is eternally constituted by laws which are external to it. It is, of course, *subject* to time, but it is not a temporal being in the sense Hegel reserves for the term. As for madness, while it is surely not comparable to the being of the stone, neither will Hegel allow us to see it as "pure freedom in face of an 'other'," or as the labor of self-constitution in relation to the external. The gesture of radical dislocation from the external which defines the regressive motion of madness precludes any such conception.

Finally, we may see Hegel's anticipation of Freud's insistence on the 'timelessness' of unconscious mental processes in his conception of historical existence as beginning in the form of "nature, as an innermost, unconscious instinct" and progressing through a process of "bringing [this unconscious instinct] into consciousness" by the transformative character of labor. Such a conception directly prepares the way for an explanation of madness—the reversion of mind into nature, the return to the darkness of our origins—as effecting an abandonment of history, a paralysis of our ability to transform nature through labor. History, temporality, and labor may be spoken of with respect to madness only metaphorically, in the sense that we might describe madness as achieving the construction of a 'history' of the soul's interior and a labor of fantasy as a substitute for the social character of history and labor which characterizes the enterprise of rationality.

Physis and Nomos

Hegel's theory of tragedy also emphasizes the role of a reversion to nature, with the associated nocturnal imagery of darkness. To this end, he exploits the tragic theatre's preoccupation with a dissonance between *physis* (nature) and *nomos* (custom, culture, convention, law), and the recurring theme of the tragic actor's alienation from the outer world of custom and corresponding identification with the internal world of nature. We may note that this theme is often directly linked in tragedy with the anatomy of madness, as in Lear, and, on the Greek stage, in Medea and Ajax and in the frequent dramatizations of possession, either by Dionysian frenzy (for example, Pentheus) or by the infecting power of the Erinys (for example, Eteocles, Clytaemestra and Orestes). The infliction of madness is indeed one of the specialties of the furies, the archetypal creatures of nature:

Over the beast doomed to the fire
this is the chant, scatter of wits,
frenzy and fear, hurting the heart,
song of the Furies
binding brain and blighting blood
in its stringless melody. (*Eumenides* ll. 328–33 and 341–46 [re-
peated])

While Hegel is most interested in the tragic dissonance between culture and nature as it occurs in Greek drama, it is also
clearly present in modern tragedy. Macbeth, for example, though
he may "look like the innocent flower," preserving the mask of civilization, is really "the serpent under't" (I, v), and Lady Macbeth's
famous "damned spot" of blood may serve as an emblem of her reversion to nature. Similarly, Hamlet is drawn to "some vicious
mole of nature" within his soul (I, iv), and Lear's exile from his
Kingdom into the "all-shaking thunder" of nature (III, ii)—an exile
which coincides with his madness—also discloses the process of
dislocation of *nomos* by *physis*.

On the ancient Greek stage, the tension between culture and
nature provides the dialectical backdrop for nearly all the sur-
viving tragedies. For example, the thematic framework of
Aeschylus' *Oresteia* is the conflict between a yearning for some rational order of custom and the persistent undermining of this desire by the descent into the blood-rites of nature. And Euripides'
character of Medea embodies, as William Arrowsmith puts it, "the
blinding force of life itself, stripped of any mediating morality or
humanizing screen; naked, unimpeded, elemental *eros*; intense,
chaotic, and cruel; the primitive, pre-moral, pre-cultural condition
of man and the world."[16]

AJAX AND ANTIGONE. It is really the tragedies of Sophocles,
however, which most draw Hegel's attention to this theme. We will
speak of *Oedipus the King* in next section, and concentrate here on
the *Ajax* and the *Antigone*. The *Ajax* is interesting because of the
direct association between the movement of withdrawal into nature and the theme of madness. As Michael Davis points out in his
essay on "Politics and Madness," there is an important relationship
in the *Ajax* between the language of 'inside' and 'outside' and the
categories of sanity and madness.[17] On the surface, it is when
someone is 'outside' himself that he is mad, out of his mind. And
yet with Ajax there is a certain reversal of the usual relation between inner and outer. The sane Ajax appears to entirely lack an
inside: he is all outer, everything must be directly visible to be real

to him, and no distinction is acknowledged between the way things appear on the outside and the way things are. It is thus paradoxically the sane Ajax who is 'out of his mind.' Athena's act of revenge on Ajax is precisely to bestow upon him an interior, and hence to force him *into himself.* Ajax's acquisition of an interior throws him back into the previously denied world of nature, a world, like that of madness, of darkness: Ajax's vision is "darkened," he exists now under the "terrible yoke of blindness," and he is forced to speak of the "darkness that is my light" (*Ajax* ll. 85, 123, 394). He becomes a "dim shape" and "weightless shadow" (*Ajax* ll. 121–26), like the ethereal figures of dream images.

Indeed the nature to which Ajax reverts is not simply *like* the world of madness; for him, the two coincide. For Ajax there is no possibility of integration of inner and outer, nature and culture, body and spirit. The reversal and inversion of his self is so abrupt, so unprepared for, and exposes a region of being which had been so thoroughly repressed, that his delivery over to *physis* is immediately a deliverance to madness. Ajax was so much a stranger to himself, so convinced that his own nature could only coincide with his (equally blunt) conception of custom and law, that the move inward to a previously opaque, more elemental region of nature, left him without defense—he who in the outer world was the most brilliant of defensive warriors.

This language of darkness associated with the tragic figure's reversion to nature is worked out most fully by Hegel in his discussion of the *Antigone,* where the central tragic collision is between the forces of human and divine law. Recall that Hegel defines 'human law' as the law of the state, which he associates with daylight, openness to view, and the upper world of culture. 'Divine law' is the law of individual conscience, tied in Antigone to family relations, and associated with darkness, hiddenness, and the underworld of nature. Hegel's descriptions of Antigone's tragic position as representative of divine law recapitulate almost exactly the language he uses to describe the sinking of the self into madness: Antigone's 'pathos,' her defining character, is her identification with *Gefühlsleben,* the life of feeling, the heart, intuition, instinct, and dream, with the associated primal images of earth, blood, the underworld, and night-time.

It is true that Creon, who remains in the daylight world, is also a tragic figure for Hegel. Hence submersion into nature is by no means a necessary feature of tragic action, and in this respect tragedy differs from madness, where such a submersion is essential. Rather, Creon is destroyed precisely because of his unwilling-ness to acknowledge the justice of the netherworld, his opposite. But while Hegel insists, against readings which see Creon as simply a tyrant who acts unjustly,[18] that Creon too is a genuinely tragic figure, he focuses his attention much more fully on the psy-chology of Antigone. Creon is in some respects more like Ajax, whose tragedy (and madness) results from an inability to come to terms with the interior world of 'nature.' Antigone, on the other hand, is in essence *all* interior for Hegel. Her 'pathos' coincides with that more primordial region of the psyche which most of us have repressed. She is the other of culture, its underground woman, so to speak, who is denied only at great cost to the health of communal life. Hence her tragic situation promises to teach us more about ourselves than Creon's situation does, more about the domain of the unconscious, of instinct, of nature, which Hegel sees as the 'presupposition' of all spirit, the originary scene of life which is gradually sublimated and hence lost from view and darkened over in the developmental progression of spirit.[19] Here too, as in the case of madness, it is through acquaintance with what lies on the outside, or the underside, of the everyday, that we are able to learn more fully about the contours of the 'normal.'

ISSUES OF PATRIARCHY. It must be said, however, that what we learn from Antigone is made problematic by Hegel's persistent ten-dency to move beyond the general psychological principles entailed by her immersion in nature, to make claims about gender. In Hegel's reading, it is not accidental that the human law is repre-sented in the tragedy by a man, Creon, but is *essentially* male; and the divine law is not merely coincidentally represented by a woman, Antigone, but is *essentially* female. Thus Hegel associates the opposing principles of human and divine, culture and nature, light and darkness, with essential gender distinctions. As such, we do not remain simply within the concerns of a literary and psycho-logical theory of tragic action per se, but shift to the terrain of so-cial and political commentary on gender. Antigone's 'pathos,' her identification with the "infernal regions of nature," her position of otherness in relation to the privileged laws of culture, take on the weight of the "nature of woman" in contest with the "nature of man" (PR § 166; PS 267ff). While the son eventually passes from the bonds of the family (blood ties, emotion, nature) to the sphere of human law (the universal, rational, political), the daughter is never able to transcend nature (PS 275). Hegel speaks of the "nat-ural antithesis" of man and woman (PS 276), and categorizes "womankind in general" as the "internal enemy" and "everlasting irony" of the state, of culture, of the laws of the political community (PS 288). It is for this reason that Luce Irigaray describes Hegel's conception of the feminine as implying the exclusion of women from genuinely historical action, just as we have seen that madness is conceived by Hegel to be ahistorical. "Women do not take an active part in the development of history," Irigaray writes, for theirs is a purely "underground subsistence, powerless on earth," incapable of "achiev[ing] the enunciatory process of the discourse of History."[20]

This reading of the *Antigone* clearly opens itself to feminist critique. Whether one looks to post-modern feminist theories (such as those of Irigaray, Julia Kristeva, and Hélène Cixous), or to object-relations theories within the feminist psychoanalytic movement (for example, D. W. Winnicott, James Masterson, Nancy Chodorow, Dorothy Dinnerstein), Hegel's Antigone carries with her the burden of a patriarchal reduction of the feminine to the status of other. Irigaray makes this argument particularly forcefully in the chapter of her *Speculum of the Other Woman* on "The Eternal Irony of the Community." She speaks of the *"Hegelian dream"* of Antigone as "the effect of a dialectic produced by the discourse of patriarchy," and contends that this is not simply a neutral description on Hegel's part of Greek patriarchal society as reflected in the Sophoclean tragedy, since "in the work of Sophocles, . . . things are not yet that clear. No decision has yet been made about what has more value."[21] By this reading, then, it is not Sophocles (or at least not clearly so) but Hegel himself who imposes a patriarchal schema upon the *Antigone.*

According to this schema, maturity is viewed as a male prerogative (only the son will truly grow up and emerge into the daylight world of culture), where maturity is defined as independence from the immanence of the female, the body, and nature in general. Woman comes to represent the enticements of nature which are seen as distractions from, or even threats to, the purity and autonomy of spirit, mind, and civilization. The whole series of dualisms Hegel's interpretation of the *Antigone* presents—of woman/ man, earth/spirit, body/mind, lower/upper, feeling/reason, subjectivity/objectivity, darkness/light, and nature/culture—configures woman as the space into which the male projects his own abandoned qualities, his rejected otherness, localizing all that is feared and repressed and in need of transcendence.[22]

To the extent that feminist critique clearly is called for in response to Hegel's account of the *Antigone,* it might seem that it could be extended to a critique of his theory of madness itself, given our claim that Antigone's situation so closely parallels Hegel's description of madness. By this interpretation, Hegel's anatomy of madness would be seen as a patriarchal inscription of derangement as paradigmatically feminine, much as the fifteenth century Inquisitor's manual, the *Malleus Maleficarum* (The Hammer of Witches), strongly associated demonic collusion with "female nature."[23]

While this line of interpretation deserves further exploration, it is not clear how far it would lead, for three reasons. First, Hegel never refers to the withdrawals into nature characteristic of madness as a "retreat to the feminine." Indeed, his account of the various forms of madness is virtually devoid of references to gender, and as already noted, he insists that 'nature' is the presupposition of all spirit.[24] Of course, his emphasis on rationality over feeling, and of spirit over nature, need not be explicitly framed in the vocabulary of gender to be seen as basically recapitulating traditional gender distinctions. But it should be remarked that Hegel's notions of 'Reason' and 'Spirit' tend to dislocate traditional concepts: he emphasizes such characteristics as organicity, mediation, and community, while unmercifully critiquing the "logic of the understanding" with its fixed and rigid categories, as well as of the expression of desire in terms of the domination or mastery of the other. Thus it is not at least obviously the case that Hegel's general metaphysics of spirit and phenomenology of rationality, nor his more specific theory of the 'derangement' of reason, implies an essentially masculine logic. There is no doubt, however, that such a logic is employed in his reading of the *Antigone,* and that Hegel's account of 'nature' as it emerges in his interpretation of Oedipus' daughter is made problematic by this logic.

The second point to be made is that the equation of a withdrawal into nature with the feminine which we see in Hegel's reading of the *Antigone* is not an equation he extends (at least in any explicit way) to his readings of other tragedies. The "collisions" of opposites which animate the tragic stage are collisions of universal human principles, conflicts which underlie the human condition as a whole. Clearly, it is crucial to see just how these collisions are interpreted and given expression by Hegel. Certainly, at least with respect to the *Antigone,* they are expressed in a straightforwardly chauvanistic vocabulary. But it is not clear that this in itself discredits the thematic conceptualization of universal human conflicts which underlies Hegel's account of tragic action.

Third, and perhaps most interesting, the tragic figure Hegel most often compares with Antigone is not a woman, but that paragon of the purportedly "masculine" values of rationality, "wisdom, discretion, temperance, moderation, justice, courage, inflexibility, . . . [and] sobriety" (HP 1: 394)—*Socrates*. Socrates, like Antigone, represents "the tragedy of Greece itself" for Hegel, namely the irreconcilable collision of two opposed formulations of law, the divine and the human, the principle of individual conscience as opposed to the privileged "legalized conscience" of the state (HP 1: 443–47). Just as Antigone is the "everlasting irony" of the state, Socratic irony represents a direct challenge to the status quo.

True, Socrates is not tied to the underworld gods as Antigone is. Indeed he is guilty of creating new gods, 'rational' gods. Nor is he tied to the family, but represents a "disrespect to parents"(HP 1: 445) insofar as he challenges traditional wisdom. As Kierkegaard puts it, Socrates "neutraliz[ed] the validity of family life"; his ironic strategy is to:

> rise above the validity of the substantial life of the state, so [that] the life of the family likewise had no validity for him: the state and family were for him a sum of individuals, and he related himself to the members of the family and state as individuals, every other relationship being to him a matter of indifference.[25]

The fact remains, however, that Socrates shares with Antigone her defining characteristic, the principle of "inward subjectivity" or individual conscience in opposition to the daylight world of accepted, legalized norms. In this, Antigone is no more necessarily 'feminine' than Socrates, nor Socrates any more essentially 'masculine' than Antigone. The condition for their parallel tragic situations is their withdrawal from the outer world of law into an inward world which stands related to the daylight world as other, to be denied, repressed, and hidden from sight. Thus while Hegel's interpretation of the *Antigone* invites, even demands, feminist critique, it seems less obvious that this critique may be extended to the more general principles of his theories of madness and tragic action.

MYTH AND HISTORY. One further point deserves mention before we close our discussion of the theme of withdrawal into nature: the way in which the tragic actor's submersion into nature effects a negation of time and history, reminiscent of a similar negation in madness. We saw that Hegel understands madness as a sort of re-

turn to origins, to that "eternal basic text of *homo natura*" which
lies before historical time. To the extent that tragic action also incorporates the movement of withdrawal into nature, it shares with
madness this opposition to history. Froma Zeitlin argues very persuasively about the detemporalization of tragic action in her essay
"Thebes: Theater of Self and Society in Athenian Drama."[26]
Thebes, the city which all three of the great Greek dramatists
choose as the "tragic terrain" for many of their plays, is a "city of
myth as opposed to a city of history"; "a world that obeys the law of
the Eternal Return in contrast to one where history can unfold"; a
city "closed back upon itself as the circular walls that are the city's
most distinctive architectural feature in space"; a place where
change, development, and transformation are negated by a perpetually regressive turn back to the past.[27] Antigone's very name—literally, "generated in place of another"—may be interpreted as
"antigeneration,"[28] just as Ajax's name is tied to "*aei*," always: Ajax
wishes to be always the same and "must therefore hate time."[29]
And Oedipus is on a quest for origins whose historical location is
hidden by the mystery of his birth; further, his act of incest is "the
quintessential act of return, . . . the paradigmatic act that destroys
time by collapsing the necessary temporal distinctions between
generations."[30]

Just as Hegel sees classical Greek sculpture as the idealized
representation of figures "in which there is nothing temporal and
doomed" (A 2: 720), the ancient tragic poet's affinity for motholog-
ical rather than historical representation serves the purpose of a
negation of time. We may recall here Aristotle's famous contrast
between poetry and history: history merely describes what has oc-
cured, the singular, while poetry is "something more philosophic
and of graver import" because it represents the universal (*Poetics*
1451ᵃ36–1451ᵇ7). For Hegel, the universals which are portrayed in
tragic poetry—the "universal ethical powers" which enter into col-
lison with each other—are always embodied in the pre-historical
'pathos' of individual actors. Thus the gods and furies of Greek
tragedy are only symbolically external, and hence only symbolically 'historical': the gods are universal powers which are personi-
fied as "external to man" but are actually "imminent in him as his
spirit and character" (A 1: 227); "[man encloses] in his heart all the
powers which are dispersed in the circle of the gods; the whole of
Olympus is assembled in his breast." In this vein, Hegel approv-
ingly cites the words of "someone in antiquity": " 'O man, out of
thine own passions thou hast created the gods" (A 1: 236–7).

The tragic universal is thus ultimately the human heart itself, the domain of nature, which is prior to historical time. This is the same universal to which the self withdraws in madness, and while the particular symptoms of madness and tragic action will require different typologies, both madness and tragedy lead us back to the domain of psychic origins, the infernal regions of nature, whose dynamics entail a suspension of ordinary time.

Inversion, Ambiguity, and Guilt

We have already noted a number of similarities between Hegel's portraits of madness and tragic action: their characteristically double centers of reality, their affinities with the unhappy consciousness, their tendencies to withdraw into nature, and their negations of history. In this final section of the chapter, we will look at two remaining points of contact: the way in which the decentered realities of madness and tragedy evoke a world of inversion and double meanings, and how they serve to illuminate Hegel's theory of guilt.

The Inverted World

Both madness and tragic action involve particularly dramatic enactments of a form of experience Hegel sees as a recurring encounter of 'normal' consciousness: the experience of the "inverted world" (*die verkehrte Welt*). In the "Understanding" chapter of the *Phenomenology,* Hegel argues that consciousness is inevitably confronted by the "turning upside down" of the world of common sense, resulting in a convolution and reversal of meanings. The common categories of reality and appearance, inner and outer, essence and accident, things in themselves and things for-consciousness, the world "behind the scenes" and the world open to view, are discovered to be tenuous, to collapse into each other, to "turn round" their meanings (PS 96–98).

There is nothing pathological about this process of inversion and reversal of meanings. Indeed, Hegel says in an 1812 letter to his Dutch friend Peter van Ghert that his own philosophical standpoint, that of absolute idealism or speculative philosophy, must appear "[t]o the uninitiated . . . as *the upside-down world,* contradicting all their accustomed concepts and whatever else appeared valid to them according to so-called sound common sense."[31] More generally, the process of inversion is unavoidable within the very nature of the understanding (*Verstand*), insofar as the common sense perspective that 'the apparent is the real' is unstable, undermined by the repeated exposure of the merely apparent character of what is held to be real.[32]

But while this is a perfectly ordinary, if undoubtedly frustrating and uncanny, experience of consciousness, in madness and tragedy the encounter with inversion and double meanings takes on a much deeper existential significance. While the 'normal' understanding's experience of the inverted world is ultimately a lesson in epistemology—indeed the subtext of the 'inverted world' section of the *Phenomenology* is Hegel's critique of Kant's epistemology—in madness and tragic action the inverted world becomes a *way of being*, and we must move from logic to psychology in order to account for this. Put differently, there is an essentially epistemological or logical resolution of the understanding's dilemma of the inverted world in the *Phenomenology*: reason (*die Vernunft*) comes to see that the 'two worlds' of appearance and reality are in fact a dialectically united harmony. In knowing appearance (*Erscheinung*), we are already knowing the way in which reality shows (*scheint*) itself; there is no "curtain" of appearance intervening between knowing and being.[33] But in madness and tragedy, the decentering of reality we have seen to be essential to them both prevents any such resolution—they resist any logic of reconciliation and are left to *live* the consequences of an inverted, convoluted world.

In madness, the doubling of the center of reality effects a basic inversion of the normal ordering of the world. The mad consciousness "communes merely with its *interior* states," which are regarded as essential reality, while the external, objective world is seen as merely apparent, accidental, and insubstantial, emerging as a mere "shadow cast by the mind's own light." In madness, the logic of dreaming displaces the laws of the understanding and the reality principle, reversing the categories of subjective and objective, apparent and real, darkness and light.

THE LAW OF THE HEART AND TRAGIC INVERSION. A good example of this process of inversion is seen in Hegel's analysis of the 'law of the heart,' which we have mentioned several times in passing in earlier chapters. The law of the heart is a perfectly normal form of consciousness which, however, descends into madness (*Verrücktheit*) when carried to its extreme. The law of the heart is that perspective which views all value as stemming from the individual's own passions, and views the external world as an "alien necessity" to be remade in its own image (PS 221). But this consciousness becomes "entangled" in (*sich verwickeln in,* W 3: 277) the consequences of its actions; in attempting to bring about a reality that would correspond to its own personal, subjective value, and therefore convert the intuition of its heart into a genuinely universal significance, it ironically denies the merely personal character of that value, which was precisely the source of its purity and worth for the heart. Thus the law of the heart's act "has the reverse significance" (*die verkehrte Bedeutung*) of what was intended, and it "reveals itself to be [the] inner perversion [*innere Verkehrung*] of itself, to be a deranged consciousness" (*die Verrücktheit des Bewußtseins*), equally "perverted" (*Verkehrte*) and "perverting" (*Verkehrende*) (PS 225, 226 / W 3: 280, 281).

The inverted world is equally a feature of Hegel's theory of tragic action. The tragic stage depicts a world "rent asunder" (*die zerrissene Welt*) and "shattered" (*zersprungen*) (PS 265, 289 / W 3: 327, 354) into mutually hostile powers: human and divine laws, public and private spheres, culture and nature, light and darkness, consciousness and the unconscious. Central to Hegel's analysis of tragedy is his view that each power, in being put into action, becomes destroyed by its opposite. The significance of the tragic act is to solicit its opposite, revealing an inversion or reversal (*Verkehrung*) of meaning. "[T]hrough the deed a transition of opposites" occurs "in which each proves itself to be the non-reality, rather than the authentication, of itself" (PS 279). This is because each side of the tragic collision is ultimately "linked in [its] essence with its opposite," so that "the fulfilment of the one evokes the other, . . . calls it forth as a violated and now hostile entity demanding revenge" (PS 283). Agamemnon's act calls forth the furies of his slain daughter; Clytaemestra's justice evokes the justice of her son; Orestes' honor is converted into shame by "the Furies arising from his deed" (A 1: 278); Creon and Antigone are equally one-sided and their deeds elict the mutual destruction of each other; and Oedipus' insistence on his own lucidity can only temporarily conceal the power of the unconscious which, when revealed, unhinges him.

The tragic stage is thus explicitly defined as an inverted world: tragic action is "this inversion [*diese Verkehrung*] of the *known* [that is, of the 'pathos' which the tragic actor identifies with] into its opposite, . . . the changing-round [*das Umschlagen*] of the rightness based on character ['pathos'] . . . into the rightness of the very opposite" (PS 447/ W 3: 538). All tragic action is fundamentally ambiguous and double in meaning. What is intended, the expression of the purity of the character's own 'pathos,' inevitably reveals its own one-sidedness and the justice of its opposite. Thus Hyllus explains his mother Deianira's crime to his skeptical father Heracles: "In all that she did wrong she had intended good" (*Women of Trachis* l. 1136). And the chorus of Euripides' *Orestes* expresses its bewilderment at the double meaning of the characters' deeds, and the inverted world they beget: "Just the act, crime unjust. / Right and wrong confounded / in a single act. . . . And what had seemed so right, / as soon as done, became / evil, monstrous, wrong!" (*Orestes* ll. 193, 818). We see here dramatic instances of what we discussed in chapter 6 as the inherent role of the unintentional in action, the way in which action inevitably recoils back upon the subject's intended meaning.

In large measure, there is nothing new about Hegel's portrait of the tragic stage as an 'inverted world.' It is a commonplace of aesthetic theory to emphasize the fundamental role of peripety or reversal in tragedy. What is distinctively Hegelian is the way he works out his theory of equally justified universal 'powers,' embodied in the 'pathos' of individual actors, 'soliciting' or 'evoking' their opposites when put into action. More generally, this theory perhaps goes further than others in not merely emphasizing peripety on the level of character—the fate of individual characters to realize "How strange in their reversals are our lives" (*Hecuba* l. 846)—but in expanding the idea of reversal or inversion to characterize the *world* of tragedy itself. When the chorus in Euripides' *Medea*, for example, calls out desperately, "Flow backward to your sources, sacred rivers, / And let the world's great order be reversed" (ll. 410–11), it is expressing a sense of the world itself being out of joint, inverted, a place of poisonous daemonic madness and fury. It is this larger sense of inversion, above and beyond the reversals of fortune that befall individual characters, which interests Hegel. Finally, it is really not Antigone or Creon or Oedipus as characters that preoccupy Hegel—much less even than they do Aristotle, who emphasizes plot over character—but what their acting out of the collision between cosmic forces tells us about "the broken and confused" world (*die zerrissene verworrene Welt*) (W 13: 234) in which these collisions occur.[34]

THE UNCONSCIOUS. But setting aside questions of Hegel's contribution to an understanding of reversal in tragedy, what is of greatest interest for our purposes is how this portrait of the inverted world of tragic action may be linked in an important way to the inverted world of madness. Essential to Hegel's anatomy of inversion in madness is his psychology of the regressive turn into nature, where the logic of the unconscious supplants and enters into opposition with the logic of rationality. We have already discussed the role of the unconscious with respect to Antigone, and may now add that Hegel proposes as one of the main forms of tragic collision the conflict between consciousness and the unconscious (A 1: 213f; A 4: 1214–16). In this "antithesis of the conscious and the unconscious" (PS 280), the act brings out into consciousness what was hidden in the unconscious, an opposite power "that conceals itself and lies in ambush" (PS 446). This power is really 'nature' itself, the domain of instinct, passion, and unconscious drives, the life of the 'feeling soul' which we have seen to be the primordial center of existence in madness.

Oedipus and Ajax are Hegel's favorite examples of this conflict. Both "stand in the power of the unconscious" (LR 354n), so that an explicit dichotomy arises between intended action—Oedipus killing a "stranger," Ajax slaughtering the "Greek leaders"—and the *real* act that remains unconscious—Oedipus has killed his father, and Ajax has really slaughtered the Greeks' cattle. Reality and appearance are here completely inverted, when consciousness, the world of lucidity and light, is revealed as a mere surface veiling the deeper reality of the unconscious, the world of concealment and darkness. Both Oedipus and Ajax are forced to confront their darker, hidden selves. "This darkness is my world," Oedipus says (*Oedipus the King* l. 1325), and Ajax sings a haunting song to his new homeland, Darkness:

> O
> Darkness that is my light,
> Murk of the underworld, my only brightness,
> Oh, take me to yourself to be your dweller,
> Receive and keep me. (*Ajax* ll. 395–7)

And for both, this new, dark underworld of the unconscious is the homeland of madness:

> Madness has seized our noble Ajax;
> He has come to ignominy in the night.
> . . . Insanity stands here revealed indeed! (*Ajax* ll. 215–16, 355)

> Darkness!
> Horror of darkness enfolding, resistless, unspeakable . . .
> madness and stabbing pain and memory
> of evil deeds I have done! (*Oedipus the King* ll. 1314–17)

Evil and Guilt

Oedipus' linking of the unconscious with madness, and of his madness with the "memory of evil deeds," brings us to the final point of this chapter, an exploration of Hegel's conception of evil and guilt in his accounts of madness and tragic action. Oedipus has undergone a process of discovery analogous in some respects to the course of psychoanalytic therapy, of gradually uncovering relevant unconscious memories.[35] His "memory of evil deeds" occurs when he has finally revealed the true meaning of his act, which lay hidden in the unconscious. This revelation is a "link[ing] together," Hegel says, of "the unconscious and the conscious. . . . The deed is brought out into the light of day as . . . what is one's own." And the recognition of one's ownership of the deed—Oedipus' recollection that this was *his* act—entails his guilt. The actor "cannot deny his guilt":

> Guilt is not an indifferent, ambiguous affair, as if the deed as actually seen in the light of day could, or perhaps could not, be the action of the self, as if . . . there could be . . . something external and accidental that did not belong to it, from which aspect, therefore, the action would be innocent. On the contrary, . . . innocence . . . is merely non-action, like the mere being of a stone. . . . (PS 282–3)

Indeed Oedipus accepts his guilt: after initially blaming the gods, he finally refuses this as an excuse and declares that "to this guilt I bore witness against myself" (*Oedipus the King* l. 1384). And just as Oedipus appropriates the whole weight of his deed, identifying himself with his unconscious, so too does Ajax: while Ajax's conscious intention was not to slaughter the cattle, he refuses the fatalistic option of Teucer, that "this was the gods' contrivance" (*Ajax* l. 1037), and accepts Tecmessa's harsh claim that it is "you yourself and no one else" that is responsible; he stands "naked" in his guilt (*Ajax* ll. 261, 463).

In his *Aesthetics,* Hegel makes a great deal of "our modern"-day "repugnance" to the idea that someone might take responsibility for an act which he or she did not intend due to ignorance of the circumstances, or acting under a delusion or in madness. The Greek tragic hero, however, "is answerable for the entirety of his act with his whole personality." "Nowadays," however, "everyone . . . shuffles guilt off himself so far as possible" (A 1: 188). We must learn "above all [to] reject the false idea that . . . tragic conflicts . . . have anything to do with guilt or innocence," an idea which leads us to see tragic actors as innocent because, after all, they didn't know what they were doing. "No worse insult could be given to such a hero than to say that he had acted innocently. It is the honor of these great characters to be culpable" (A 2: 1214–15).[36]

What then is guilt for Hegel? A little patience is required here, since our initial response will turn out to be misleading, in that it will seem to suggest that Hegel simply incorporates a highly moralistic reading of the Christian notion of original sin. It will turn out, however, that Hegel's position is characteristically idiosyncratic, and that nothing could be farther from the truth than to cast Hegel's interpretation of the guilt of madness and tragic action in a moralistic or orthodoxly Christian light.

We have seen that in his discussion of madness, Hegel characterizes the reversion to the unconscious as a return to the "infernal regions" of nature and a liberation of "the dark, infernal powers of the heart." Now Hegel identifies these "earthly elements" of the unconscious with *"that evil which is always latent in the heart,"* and says that *"the evil genius of man . . . gains the upper hand in insanity"* (PM § 408, emphasis added). It is thus the unconscious—or more generally, *nature*—which is identified with evil for Hegel, and which is the source of guilt. So too, with Oedipus and Ajax it is the domain of nature and the unconscious that harbors their guilt, and with Antigone, whom Hegel calls an example of pure guilt (PS 284), it is her perfect coinciding (as Hegel sees it) with nature, her association with the *Dei inferi* of the underworld, situating her in direct collision with the laws of the upper world, which defines her guilt.

Guilt, then, arises through the reversion and submission to 'nature,' the feeling soul, the domain of instinct and passion and the heart. In his *Encyclopædia* Logic, Hegel directly ties this notion of guilt to "the theological dogma that man's nature is evil, tainted with what is called Original Sin." And he says that he "accepts this dogma," since—to cite again a passage we looked at in chapter 4 in the context of Hegel's reading of the biblical Fall—

> the very notion of spirit is enough to show that man is evil by nature, and it is an error to imagine that he could ever be otherwise. To such extent as man is and acts like a creature of nature, his whole behavior is what it ought not to be. (SL § 24 Z)

Yet all is not what it seems. Appearances to the contrary, Hegel never falls into the stance of contrasting 'nature' and 'spirit'

on moralistic grounds, nor ever suggests that the goal of spiritual
life is to seek to distance oneself as fully as possible from the body,
nor ever claims that the 'good life' is to be found in a denial of the
instincts. In chapter 5 we discussed Hegel's theory of the sublimation of nature and the unconscious, and saw that he is no more a
"slanderer of nature," to use Nietzsche's phrase,[37] than is Nietzsche
himself. The point to be made here is that Hegel avoids all moralistic interpretations of guilt and evil for the unimpeachable reason
that guilt and evil are not essentially moral phenomena for him at
all! They are *ontological* terms. Hegel thus anticipates Heidegger's
idea that human beings "*are* guilty in the very basis of their
Being," so that " 'Being-guilty' cannot be defined by morality, since
morality already presupposes [guilt] for itself."[38]

'Evil,' for Hegel, means finitude, incompletion, and disunity
(see, e.g., SL § 24 Z; HP 3: 5; PS 468–74). This is why nature is
'evil,' because it awaits the "awakening of consciousness," the "education and culture" (*Bildung*) of spirit, to complete it (SL § 24 Z). It
is 'evil' because it is embryonic, a mere beginning, not yet subject
to the historical enactment of "the labor of its own transformation"
(PS 6). And given this understanding of evil, *guilt* for Hegel is an
inescapable ontological feature of human existence, our being
grounded in nature and hence our being eternally subject to incompleteness.

The guilt of tragedy and madness shows this state of dishar-
mony in poignant and extreme ways. But we go seriously wrong
when we morally condemn the tragic hero or the insane. Tragic figures are guilty, but their guilt does not show a lack of moral integrity. They are not 'evil' in the common ethical sense. Hegel explicitly asserts that the depiction of evil in this sense is "inartistic,"
something merely "repugnant" which could never serve as the subject of tragedy (A 1: 222). Rather, the tragic protagonist's guilt exposes the existential fact of a world in which fundamental collisions of value are unavoidable, a world inwardly divided between
culture and nature, consciousness and the unconscious, the 'upper'
and 'lower' aspects of our being.[39]

The insane are guilty too for Hegel, but their guilt is not an
ethical guilt.[40] While Hegel follows Pinel's call for a 'moral treatment' of the insane, he makes it clear that the assumptions of this
treatment are not that the insane are suffering from a moral lapse,
but that we must treat them morally, and presuppose that they are
moral beings (PM § 408 Z). The guilt of madness is, like that of the
tragic protagonist, an extreme expression of the ontology of disunion

which characterizes us all, a particularly dramatic constituting of the double center of reality which is incipient in all human experience. Ours is a broken world, a world where every achievement of harmony is evanescent and subject to collapse into the experience of loss, despair, and alienation.

Ontology and Anguish: The Logic and Horror of Evil

Our consideration of Hegel's view of evil invites a new look at our earlier discussion, in chapter 3, of William Desmond's argument that the Hegelian dialectic finally is unable to account for the existential 'intimacy' of 'otherness': 'otherness' is always 'sublated' or *aufgehoben,* literally 'raised up' into the abstract shapes or figures (*Gestalten*) of consciousness which together form the gallery of logical, rational moments of Hegel's system. We saw how Desmond, like Kierkegaard, believes that such a preoccupation with the logic by which reason perpetually restores its internal unity inevitably leaves out of account the existential anguish of states of being which cannot be reduced to such a logic. The upshot of the debate in chapter 3 was this: while agreeing with Desmond that in Hegel's letters we may find a very different Hegel from the author of the published works—a private Hegel who, when confronted by the pain of dying children or the madness of his sister Christiane, refused to take refuge in the consoling logic of his philosophical works, and admitted that "I do not know what I am to say"—it was suggested that in fact it might be possible to see it as a great *virtue* of Hegel's philosophic system that it did *not* seek to encompass the intimacy of grief within its categories and schematisms, that it *refused* to speak philosophically about a domain of experience which can only be encountered authentically on a purely intimate, personal level.

Our present discussion of Hegel's ontologizing of the 'evil' of madness and tragedy allows us to look at Desmond's critique from another angle. Indeed, one of Desmond's most central interests is to provoke questions about the adequacy of Hegel's dialectic to account for the 'otherness' of evil.[41] Thus we may ask whether, in his reduction of 'evil' to an essentially formal, structural, ontological condition of human being—the fact of human finitude, incompletion, and disunity—Hegel abandons any possibility for understanding a much more existentially profound sense of the evil to which madness and tragedy are condemned. This would be the sort of evil that Euripides' Hecuba cries out against, for example, when she speaks of the "awful dirge," "the fiend, the fury, / singing, wailing in me now, / shrieking madness!" (*Hecuba* ll. 683–86). Hecuba is hardly tormented by the 'wailing' of an ontological structure within her—ontological structures do not wail—but by the horror of a world infected with monstrosity and senseless brutality, by an anguish which is absolutely intimate, "unspeakable, unimaginable" (l. 714), delivering "blow after blow" such that she "cannot cope at all" (ll. 582, 589).

It is this sense of evil that Desmond describes as "a wall" which the "speculative mind seems to run against" and "cannot scale, can never scale." We must not "rest satisfied with a dialectical logic of evil," or else we risk "covering up the recalcitrant reality of evil by dialectical sorcery."[42] Unlike Kierkegaard, Desmond acknowledges a "strongly existential side to Hegel's treatment of evil," namely, his emphasis on the concepts of anguish and suffering, but argues that "over the long run" the existential reality of evil gets sublated into the "logicist" and "world-historical" rhythm of Hegel's dialectic. Evil becomes a "logical necessity, . . . simply an ontological structure inherent in the being of the human self," and as such gets "rational[ly] justif[ied]."[43] By this reading, Hegel is ultimately impatient with the existential; he "does not *dwell with* the inwardness of anguish as an inwardness," but "dialectically displaces" it into the logical and world-historical. Thus Hegel's philosophy is finally silent about "the gratuitousness in evil, . . . a sickening gratuitousness, . . . resist[ing] [any] dialectical *Aufhebung*."[44]

According to this account, the Hegelian dialectic is alternatively silent about the 'idiocy' and monstrousness of evil—"Hegel's system tries to play mum about th[is] idiocy"[45]—or else is inappropriately intrusive, not allowing Hecuba the intimacy of her confrontation with an anguish which is "unspeakable, unimaginable." Paraphrasing Pascal, "[T]he heart has reasons, not of which reason knows nothing, but of which Hegelian reason will want to know everything."[46] True, the private Hegel, the Hegel whose personality emerges through his correspondence, is "the Hegel of existential intimacy," and this private Hegel "exhibits a different wisdom" in which "the idiocy of evil is allowed some place." But for Hegel "the magister of the logical *Begriff*," for Hegel the philosopher, this idiocy is always silenced, either directly (through its absence) or indirectly through its "dialectical encasement."[47]

I think we ought to agree with Desmond that Hegel's system is mum about the 'idiocy' of evil—the deeply intimate experience of being crushed by the monstrous—but to disagree that Hegel "*tries to play* mum." His philosophy is not a 'playing' mum, not a surreptitious attempt to conceal its silence; rather it calls attention to this silence. Hegel knows, with Desmond, that the intimacy of evil is "a wall" that the "speculative mind . . . cannot scale." He knows, with Hecuba, that the 'inwardness' of evil and madness and tragedy are "unspeakable, unimaginable," just as he knows that in his own anguish over his sister's plight he "do[es] not know what [he is] to say." He never promises to comprehend philosophically the element of the immediacy and intimacy of anguish, nor to "rationally justify" it by a "dialectical sorcery," because he knows that this is not philosophically possible, let alone desirable. Hence he insists that in the *art* of the tragedians, evil must *not* be presented as brute anguish or moral horror, which are not appropriate *aesthetic* objects at all (A 1: 222). Similarly, in his ontology of madness he is very clear about his account being a purely formal and structural explanation: his project is never intended to offer a sort of poetics of the grief of madness, nor an existential lyricism of affliction or anguish or evil, but to examine what the human self must be like to be capable of such grief, and to develop an ontology which might account for certain typical patterns of response such as regression, withdrawal, separation from reality, and projection.

"There is no logic of being crushed," Desmond insists,[48] and he is absolutely right about this. This is just what Hegel knows and takes to heart. He does not "want to know everything" about the human heart in his philosophy, he does not wish to speak at all about those most intimate reaches of the heart in which suffering is an irreducibly personal confrontation, much less to "dialectically encase" those reaches. Here he has the sense to remain silent, here he has the wisdom and courage to have nothing philosophically to say.

It should be clear that this wisdom does not contradict Hegel's general theory of language, which (as we saw in chapter 6) is committed to the idea that what cannot be expressed linguistically cannot be true, or that language is 'more honest' than mere intentionality. For in having the wisdom to have nothing *philosophically* to say about the intimacy of suffering, Hegel is by no means left without language. The language he uses, in his letters for example, is not philosophical language but the language of Hecuba—or the closest Hegel can come to it!—a much more personal (but not 'private' and inchoate) language than can be expressed within the constraints of a scientific ontology.

The great value of a philosophy which is *knowingly, consciously* reticent about the intimacy and idiocy of madness—or of existential tragedy and evil—is that it allows for such voices as those of Hecuba, and Christiane, and Hegel's own personal voice in his letters, to be heard on their own terms. There is no pretense of capturing these voices in his 'logic' of madness, and so far from abandoning these voices to silence—an abandonment which is asserted to be the inevitable consequence of any 'medical model' of mental illness by such anti-psychiatric authors as Michel Foucault and Thomas Szasz, an argument we will consider in our concluding chapter—this absence of philosophic pretense frees them to speak. What Hegel's ontologizing of the evil of madness and tragedy achieves is a warning against the dangers of a moralizing discourse which reduces the worlds of insanity and tragedy to the domain of ethical lapse, and hence the world of therapy to the domain of moral correction. This is hardly to diminish or somehow explain away the existential horror of evil or madness, but quite the contrary, to respect it by refusing to comprehend it philosophically.

Darkened Mirrors

For Hegel, every human being must struggle with the anguish of existence, and every pursuit of self-realization must ultimately risk the 'pathway of doubt' and 'way of despair.' While there are many different strategies Hegel sees open to us for meeting this challenge, the prospects of tragedy and madness are constantly real possibilities. This is perhaps why Hegel characterizes what he calls the "absolute position" of spirit as itself intrinsically tragic, and writes of "the tragedy which the Absolute eternally enacts with itself" (NL 108, 104). The tragedy spoken of here is the unavoidable "surrender" of spirit to self-division, and "the Absolute" is explained as the ultimately "doubled-nature" (*gedoppelte Natur*) of spirit, its constant striving for unity, reconciliation, and self-harmonization, and yet its perpetual "self-othering" or "place[ment] outside itself" (*sich gegenüberstellen*) (NL 104–9 / HW 1: 386–91).

While there is something inherently tragic about the Hegelian perspective, we have already rejected the idea that Hegel would see the human condition as inherently insane. Still, given the tragic dimension of existence, consciousness forever will be confronted with the lure of withdrawal from reality into a communing with the more primordial harmony of the feeling soul. In the extreme case, where this withdrawal amounts to a severing of the connections with the outer world, and reality is reduced to a shadow of the mind's own projection, our attempt at healing the wounds of spirit will lead directly to madness. Madness and tragedy are in this way not in fact direct contraries of 'normality' or 'rationality' or 'health,' but rather extreme potentialities of our entirely normal encounter with alienation. They are mirrors—broken, perhaps, and darkened, but mirrors nonetheless—of our normal selves.

CHAPTER EIGHT

Madness and Society:
Coming to Terms with Hegel's Silence

Psychiatry is not a medical, but a moral and political enterprise.

> (Thomas Szasz, *The Myth of Mental Illness*)

This kind of "diagnostician"—whether he be priest or physician—does not find witches or madmen; he creates them.

> (Thomas Szasz, *The Manufacture of Madness*)

Pascal [once said] "Men are so necessarily mad, that not to be mad would amount to another form of madness." . . . We have yet to write the history of that other form of madness, by which men, in an act of sovereign reason, confine their neighbors, and communicate and recognize each other through the merciless language of non-madness. . . .

> (Michel Foucault, *Madness and Civilization*)

The Absent Stage Setting

After having examined a wide range of themes and applications of Hegel's theory of madness, and having gained, it is hoped, an appreciation for its subtlety and scope, the time has come to call attention to a glaring absence in this theory. Given the strongly historical emphasis of Hegel's philosophical temperament, it is remarkable how thoroughly his theory of madness is divorced from considerations of social, political, and historical contexts. Just who *are* the insane? How have they been defined, classified, and understood in different historical periods? Who fills the asylums? What is their class and social status, and how have these populations changed through time? How have different theories of madness and therapeutic practice reflected the cultural and political ideas of their times?

When Hegel considers such universal human phenomena as morality, or law, or religion, or art, or philosophy itself, he never strays far from placing them in a social and historical frame of reference. Indeed, he sees such straying as the sure mark of wandering into a barren formalism, which abstracts away from the inherently developmental, historical character of spirit. Even Hegel's logic, which in one respect is precisely designed to deal "only and solely with . . . thoughts *as thoughts*, in their complete abstraction" (L 34), cannot be appreciated fully apart from its allusions to the historical development of basic categories of thought. We must never forget, Hegel warns, that these categories "serve as *abbreviations*" for a whole "host of particulars of outer existence and actions" (L 34), lest we lose sight of the connection between the form and the content of thought (L 38–39, 43ff). And we must learn to see the "*immanent coming-to-be*" of these categories, as opposed to the typical tendency of the formal logic of the schools—the "dead bones of logic" (L 53)—to fix them as static and stable (L 55).

More to the point, even the most basic ontology of Hegel's *Phenomenology*—his account of such constitutive structures of spirit as consciousness, self-consciousness, reason, desire, and language—is historically oriented, since the basic terms of his ontology are perpetually reconfigured through successive social and historical phases. In his theory of madness, however, the basic ontology is all-encompassing, never opening itself to the historical and social turn that is otherwise so typical of his way of thinking. Thus upon encountering the key idea of his account of madness, that insanity is a necessary stage in the development of spirit, the reader familiar with Hegel's usual inclinations would naturally expect to find an inquiry into the social and historical contexts in which this 'stage' becomes set. But no such inquiry is given; there is no stage-setting, only pure ontology.

In this concluding chapter, we will explore the ways in which Hegel's uncharacteristic silence on social and historical themes leaves his discussion of madness vulnerable to the critiques of the madness-idea by two of the most important twentieth century writers on the history of psychiatry and the concept of mental illness, Michel Foucault and Thomas Szasz. While these two authors are temperamentally, philosophically, and methodologically poles apart, they share a basic perspective of madness as essentially constituted or even invented by historically changing social and political interests. Madness, from this point of view, is not finally a medical phenomenon at all, but a phenomenon of social engineering, manipulation, and coercion, and of the politically motivated labeling of deviant behavior.

It should be stressed that even if Hegel did provide a social-historical framework for his philosophy of madness, this would still not be sufficient to make his position compatible with Foucault or Szasz, for he would never completely reduce madness to a socially constituted phenomenon. Like desire, which Hegel shows to be subject to constant reshaping through different cultural and historical contexts—but which he also insists remains a basic, essential, underlying feature of all self-consciousness, possessing universal components—so too there are certain necessary 'inner determinations' of madness which define its essence, notwithstanding any possible elaborations or shadings of meaning which might reshape these properties as they unfold in social and historical time.

But such an account of the historical and political dimensions of madness would allow for a more complete debate with writers like Foucault and Szasz. The debate is in fact marked by silence on both sides, since for their part, neither Foucault nor Szasz apply their critiques of the medicalization of madness to Hegel. Szasz never speaks of Hegel at all, and while Foucault studied under the great Hegelian scholar Jean Hyppolite, and in post-*Madness and Civilization* works partly defined his own project in terms of detaching himself from certain basic Hegelian tendencies, he never spoke of Hegel's theory of madness. But Szasz's and Foucault's social construction arguments are tailor-made to throw Hegel's pure ontology of madness into question. Hegel's virtual silence on the historical and political themes which are so central to their critiques opens his theory to the suspicion of not being able to account for the socially changing reconfigurations of madness, and the possibly constitutive role of political factors.

After sketching out the basic lines of the Foucaultian and Szaszian critiques, we will turn to offer various hypotheses about Hegel's silence, reexamining some of the main premises of his madness theory and some of the consequences of locating this theory within his anthropology. We will consider the plausibility of rethinking Hegel's discussion so that it is in fact compatible with a view which sees madness as importantly constituted by social and political forces, but will show that even this possible reconciliation would be too tame to meet the commitments of Foucault's and Szasz's radical positions. The conflict between Hegel and social labeling theorists like Foucault and Szasz will come to a head in our examination of their competing interpretations of the role of the body in madness, and in their strong disagreements over the nature of the Pinelian 'moral treatment' of the insane. Finally, we will look at Hegel's thoughts on poverty, criminality, and social marginalization, since these are themes which Foucault and Szasz make central to their histories of mental illness and psychiatry, and which are striking for their absence from Hegel's discussion of madness. It will be argued, however, that many of Hegel's ideas about these themes can be applied to his theory of madness in such a way as to reinforce the prospects for integrating a modest version of the labeling perspective with his own ontology of insanity.

Foucault and Szasz: The Social-Political Invention of Madness

Some Differences and Similarities

Michel Foucault and Thomas Szasz were two of the first, and certainly two of the most persistent and influential twentieth century thinkers seriously to call into question reigning assumptions about the history and nature of psychiatry and the whole concept of mental illness. The debates between the eighteenth- and nineteenth-century somatic and psychic schools and the proponents of Romantic and empirical medicine, as also such twentieth century contests as those between psychoanalysis and behaviorism, for all the weighty issues which have hung in the balance, have all been internecine in nature. All sides of these debates have agreed that madness is a real disease with essential properties, however fervently they have disagreed about what these properties are, and have agreed that psychiatry is the science of treating these diseases. Foucault and Szasz are radical outsiders to these debates, true heretics, challenging the very reality of madness as a disease and the description of psychiatry as the science of treating disease.

It must be said at the outset that these two heretics are very different thinkers in many ways. Szasz's positions are much easier to classify. Indeed, he takes great pride in having his guiding principles appear completely transparent to view, a virtue he finds conspicuously absent amongst the practitioners, past and present, of the "manufacture of madness," whose basic commitments remain covert.[1] Foucault, for his part, seems to have taken equal pride in his elusiveness: he defined himself by an absence of definition—or at least by a constant shifting of and toying with self-descriptions— and by denial of all labels attached to him, whether structuralist, Marxist, Nietzschean, or historian. Szasz is an uncompromising libertarian, while Foucault, who joined the Communist Party only to break with it in 1951 at the age of twenty-five, and who for a time edited the leftist weekly *Libération*, may best be character-ized as anarchistic[2]—if only because the label ironically admits the very precariousness of attaching labels to him.[3]

Stylistically there are great differences as well. Szasz writes with a more informal, narrative, even journalistic tone; he is com-pletely at home in and a master of ordinary language. Foucault, for all his literary elegance, is an experimentalist; his language is a language in search of itself, in battle with common forms and regimes. Temperamentally, while both are iconoclastic, transgres-sive thinkers, Foucault is anti-positivistic, anti-Enlightenment, and anti-humanist; Szasz is positivistic, sympathetic to Enlighten-ment ideals, and thoroughly humanistic. Methodologically, al-though neither may be said to be writing normal histories—both are out to demystify the normal historiographic stories of culture, and to look beneath the historical record to hidden motivations of social discourses—Szasz never develops the highly technical lan-guage and principles of an archaeology or a genealogy; his is a self-stylized 'common sense' debunking of historical myths.

Finally, while Szasz's lifework, his hundreds of articles and score or so of books in addition to his social activism, has been sharply focused on the critique of the institution of psychiatry and the decoding of the history of 'mental illness,'[4] Foucault's interests are much more sweeping. Like Szasz, Foucault was trained in the field of psychology—Szasz studied at the Chicago Institute of Psychoanalysis, where he later became a staff member from 1950–1954; Foucault received his Diplôme de Psycho-Pathologie at the Sorbonne in 1952—and his first published works were on the topic of psychiatry and madness (*Maladie mentale et personalité* in 1954 [revised as *Maladie mentale et psychologie* in 1962], and his doctoral dissertation, *Folie et déraison: histoire de la folie à l'âge classique* in 1961[5]). But he soon turned to a much wider field of in-quiry. His work engages the whole compass of the discursive archives of modernity: he writes an archaeology of knowledge, ra-tionality, and science, a genealogy of power, a history of the social practices of medicine, linguistics, and economics, and of social attitudes on the body, sexuality, confinement, punishment, and domination.

The differences between Szasz and Foucault are many and profound. This no doubt explains why the two, although contemporaries (Szasz was born in 1920, while Foucault, who died in 1984, was born in 1926), and whose first major texts on madness were published at almost the same time (Szasz's *Myth of Mental Illness* in 1960, Foucault's *Folie et déraison* just a year later), never developed a dialogue. They were aware of each other—thus Szasz would occasionally cite a passage from Foucault,[6] and Foucault supported the translation of Szasz's books into French, as well as encouraging various anti-psychiatric movements[7]—but always from a distance, neither offering commentary on the other. Notwithstanding these differences, the two share a number of basic claims in their critiques of the idea of madness. By whatever different routes, different methodologies, differences of nuance and purpose, both arrive at a view of madness as a social construction, and of the medical model of insanity as a moral and political mythology.

The Semantics of Madness

In *The Myth of Mental Illness*, Szasz explains his task as "laying bare the socio-historical and epistemological roots of the modern concept of mental illness." By examining the "economic, moral, political, and social forces [which] helped to mold" the idea of the "so-called mental illnesses," his method will be "an essentially 'destructive' analysis of the concept of mental illness and of psychiatry as a pseudomedical enterprise."[8] For his part, Foucault describes the purpose of *Madness and Civilization* to be an "archaeology of [the] silence" to which the coercive "language of psychiatry" has reduced those it has identified as mad. Leaving aside the important issue of how such an 'archaeology' will differ methodologically from Szasz's work of 'laying bare,' Foucault shares with Szasz a focus on the social, political, economic, and moral forces which they both feel have historically constituted the idea of mental illness.

Foucault traces the "constitution of madness as mental illness"[9] from the founding of the Hôpital Général in 1657 through William Tuke's establishment of a Quaker 'Retreat' for the insane near York in 1792 and Pinel's 'liberation' of the inmates of the dungeons of Bicêtre in 1794, to the 'thaumaturgic' wizard-psychology of Freud. Szasz more briefly covers this same territory, especially in *The Manufacture of Madness,* where his purpose is to uncover common themes in the intersecting histories of witchcraft and madness, the Inquisition and psychiatric practice. But throughout his work, Szasz concentrates on the nineteenth century, and particularly on Jean Charcot (1825–1893), the neurologist, head physician at Salpêtrière, and one of Freud's teachers. Both Foucault and Szasz see the nineteenth century as the decisive period of the medicalization of madness, and notwithstanding differences of emphasis—Foucault, for example, is most interested by the great 'reformers' Tuke and Pinel, Szasz by Charcot—each see a basic continuity from Pinel (1745–1826) to his student Esquirol (1772–1840) to Charcot and Freud in the project of casting madness into a new language of medicine. As Szasz puts it, "Pinel, Esquirol and Charcot . . . were the founders not only of the French school of psychiatry but of all of modern psychiatry as a positivistic-medical discipline."[10]

A basic claim of both Foucault and Szasz is that this work of configuring madness as a medical disorder involved a process of *semantic transformation.* Thus in his *Mental Illness and Psychology,* Foucault identifies the medicalization of madness as the consequence of an "artifice of language,"[11] and in *Madness and Civilization* he speaks of the need to study the ways "in which the exchange between madness and reason modifies its language, and in a radical manner."[12] Szasz often speaks of psychiatry's "playing of language games,"[13] effecting a "semantic transformation"[14] or "semantic and social reclassification"[15] of various forms of human suffering as illness, and of the way in which names create values. As he writes in an entry to the 1974 *Encyclopaedia Britannica Yearbook*:

> All too often, the language in which a personal or social problem is couched subtly but inexorably supplies its solution. Nowhere is this more evident than in the field of so-called mental illness.
> In earlier times, when 'the problem' was witchcraft—that is, when persons who provoked punishment for certain antisocial actions, or who were scapegoated for other reasons, were said to be witches possessed by demons—the solution was exorcism and burning at the stake. Today, when 'the problem' is mental illness—that is, when such persons are said to be psychiatric patients suffering from mental diseases—the solution is to imprison them in buildings called hospitals and torture them in the name

of treatment. . . . I submit that this problem is primarily linguistic, . . . a matter of how words are used to shape popular
opinion and to justify legal action and political policy.[16]

Foucault's and Szasz' shared commitment to viewing categories of mental illness as semantic constructions symptomatic of
moral and political interests situates them both within the general
perspective of *labeling theory*. As Carol Warren puts it in her study
of the role of the courts in the lives of those diagnosed as mentally
ill, "labeling theory points to both the economic and the power dimensions of laws and ideas, and to the socially constructed nature
of deviance labels. . . . At its outer limits, the phenomenon of deviance labeling is a matter of the power to create and sustain the
categories through which the social control of deviance becomes
possible."[17]

Foucault sees the history of psychiatry as a series of systems
of discourse whose linguistic terms, as J. G. Merquior puts it, "in
fact 'invent' their objects so that [human beings] . . . can be better
controlled."[18] And Szasz speaks of the ways in which the "labeling
of individuals displaying or disabled by problems in living as 'mentally ill' has only impeded and retarded the recognition of the essentially moral and political nature" of human suffering and the
tactics employed by psychiatry to manage it.[19] Thus both Foucault
and Szasz seek to apply Nietzsche's dictum about the creative
power of language to their histories of madness: "[T]o realize that
what things *are called*," Nietzsche writes in *The Gay Science*, "is
incomparably more important than what they are; . . . it is enough
to create new names and estimations . . . in order to create in the
long run new 'things.' "[20] This is precisely the argument of Szasz
and Foucault: by medicalizing the vocabulary used to define and
manage madness, the nineteenth century reformers created new
names for behaviors which effectively become new 'things,' mental
illnesses.

The Politics of Semantic Transformation

Foucault and Szasz alternate between moods of cool detach-
ment and pathos in their accounts of the essentially political and
social motivations underlying the semantic transformation of varieties of human misery into categories of mental illness. Both see
the first state-sponsored mass incarceration of the 'mad,' with the
institution of the French Hôpital Général in the mid-seventeenth

century, to have been straightforwardly politically coercive, without any hint of medical rationale: "From the very start, one thing is clear," Foucault writes:

> The Hôpital Général is not a medical establishment. It is rather a sort of semijudicial structure, an administrative entity which, along with the already constituted powers, and outside of the courts, decides, judges, and executes. . . . A quasi-absolute sovereignty, jurisdiction without appeal, a writ of execution against which nothing can prevail—the Hôpital Général is a strange power that the King establishes between the police and the courts, at the limits of the law: a third order of repression.[21]

Szasz writes in precisely the same vein in his *Encyclopaedia Britannica* essay:

> Modern psychiatry began in the seventeenth century with the building of insane asylums in which all sorts of troublesome and unwanted persons were incarcerated. Originally, then, psychiatry was 'institutional'; it was a kind of extralegal penology.[22]

And in a passage from *The Manufacture of Madness* which includes one of the very rare occasions where Szasz quotes Foucault, he speaks of the absence of any medical pretense behind the Hôpital Général: "It was enough to be abandoned, destitute, poor, unwanted by parents or society. . . . Institutional psychiatry came into being, as had the Inquisition earlier, to protect [society] from [the] threat . . . [of] the nonconformist, the objector, in short, all who denied or refused to affirm society's dominant values. . . ." The original asylums thus were basically transparent means of "social control and of the ritualized affirmation of the dominant social ethic."[23]

For Foucault and Szasz, the new language game which transfigured madness into a disease beginning in the late eighteenth century with people like Pinel and Tuke, developing further in the nineteenth century with the whole panoply of somatic and psychic, empirical and Romantic theories of medicine, and perfected by people like Charcot and Freud, was not at all the result of an accumulation of new scientific knowledge—as though there were a truly medical essence of madness awaiting the discoveries of ever more sophisticated scientific theories and technologies. On the contrary, the medicalization of madness was grounded in no discoveries at all; it was an invention, an "artifice of language" designed not to liberate the mad from political coercion and manipulation into social conformity, but to disguise and rationalize it. "In the course of [the asylum's] 300-year history," Szasz writes, "immense and unceasing efforts have been directed at redefining psychiatric confinement as 'hospitalization' and psychiatric control as 'treatment.' " But "this medicalization of human problems" only allows for a more complete method of "persecut[ion]" and "coercive control by means of the police power of the state."[24]

Thus the medicalization of madness, so far from displacing the earlier coercive and disciplinary rationale of incarceration, only displaced the transparency of this rationale by creating a new way of speaking about the mad. The language of medicine must be decoded as only a façade over the old language of coercion. "This is not the least of the paradoxes of Pinel's 'philanthropic' and 'liberating' enterprise," Foucault writes, "this conversion of medicine into justice, of therapeutics into repression. . . . This is the essential point, the doctor's intervention is not made by virtue of a medical skill or power that he possesses in himself and that would be justified by a body of objective knowledge. It is not as a scientist that *homo medicus* has authority in the asylum; . . . if the medical profession is required, it is as a juridical and moral guarantee, not in the name of science."[25] The psychiatrist, for all the trappings of his scientific authority, "functions as an *agent of society*,"[26] Szasz says, empowered to control and engineer the conduct of the poor, the deviant, the discontented and dissenting.

Foucault and Szasz thus set out to uncover what they see as one of the great grotesqueries of history, the apotheosis of the psychiatrist as savior of the sick. In *Madness and Civilization*, Foucault concentrates on Tuke and Pinel, seeking to expose their legends as the great liberators of the insane as shams. Tuke and Pinel emancipated the mad from their physical chains only to bind them the more securely by the chains of "pure morality, of ethical uniformity, . . . all the acknowledged virtues" of the established social order.[27] Foucault sees their 'moral therapies' as operating by the principles of fear, of perpetual judgment, of humiliation and shame.[28]

Szasz does for Charcot what Foucault does for Tuke and Pinel. "There was nothing therapeutic, in the contemporary medical sense of this word," about Charcot's "care" for the patients at the Salpêtrière hospital. His main clinical interest was in fact to classify—"charting . . . human misery and cataloguing it in the language of medicine"—and to manipulate his patients: "Charcot and the other physicians who worked [at Salpêtrière] functioned as rulers vis-à-vis their subjects. Instead of intimacy and trust, their relationship to each other was based on fear, awe, and deception," all the hallmarks of Foucault's image of Tuke and Pinel. The effect of this relationship was "an utterly dehumanized view of the sick person."[29]

Habeas Corpus: You Should Have the Body

Before turning to apply the critiques of Foucault and Szasz to Hegel's theory of madness, the extremest consequence of these critiques should be clearly stated. Some labeling theorists—Thomas Scheff, probably the most influential proponent of labeling theory, is a good example[30]—see their work of exposing the socially constructed nature of such deviance labels as 'insanity' as finally compatible with the medical model of mental illness. That is, they merely seek to call attention to the often neglected, downplayed role of social construction, without denying that there is also an organic or psychopathological basis of mental illness. Alan Horwitz, a sociologist who adopts this more modest labeling view, expresses this idea very clearly:

> I do not contrast a view of mental illness as social deviance with a view of mental illness as a genuine type of illness. . . . [T]he notion of mental illness as a cultural label neither conflicts with nor provides an alternative to the illness concept, but is posed at a different level of analysis. A social control perspective . . . is valuable but does not compete with a psychiatric view of mental illness.[31]

In Szasz and Foucault, there is no such spirit of compromise: Szasz very directly, and Foucault somewhat more obliquely, deny the very existence of 'mental illness' as an ontological entity, and emphasize the radical disanalogy between actual bodily disease and the purely socially constituted 'diseases' of the mind. In effect, they issue a writ of *habeas corpus* to psychiatry, and find that the body—and therefore the illness—is missing.

Thus Szasz claims that "strictly speaking, . . . disease or illness can affect only the body. Hence, there can be no such thing as mental illness. The term 'mental illness' is a metaphor."[32] Similarly, "mental illnesses do not exist," and "indeed they cannot exist, because the mind is not a body part or bodily organ," and there simply is no empirical evidence of any organic, neurological basis of psychiatrically labeled illnesses.[33] Throughout his work he describes 'mental illness' as a myth, a metaphor, a counterfeit, a simulation, and a facsimile.[34]

As for Foucault, while he never makes as clear a statement in *Madness and Civilization* of this extreme view as Szasz does in his works, he consistently denies that successive historical efforts to medicalize madness as illness had any scientific foundation. This is one of the dominant themes of *Madness and Civilization*: from the seventeenth-century Hôpital Général, where no affectation of medical purpose blemished the social and political enterprise of incarceration, to the eighteenth-century Enlightenment, where a new fear arose of mysterious diseases spreading from the asylums into the cities, "a fear formulated in medical terms but animated" instead by a moral "myth," "hallucination" and "fantasy",[35] to the legendary period of Tuke and Pinel at the turn of the eighteenth century, where moral and political coercion masqueraded as medicine, and to Freud and modern psychiatry, where the language of medicine is perfected but the theory and practice of therapy is out and out thaumaturgy—through each new phase of describing and managing the insane, the appeal to scientific, medical language is equally specious.

Moreover, there is direct evidence of the extreme labeling view in Foucault's *Mental Illness and Psychology (Maladie mentale et psychologie)*. This work was a significantly revised version of his first work, *Maladie mentale et personalité* (1954), which he refused to have reprinted in its original form, largely because he came to regard its strongly Marxist interpretation of madness as flawed.[36] Indeed, he later also refused any reprints of the revised work, and unsuccessfully opposed its translation into English,[37] not, however, because of its conclusions about the socially constituted character of mental illness.[38] The revised and retitled work was published in 1962, just after the first publication of *Folie et déraison,* and in fact included a ten page whirlwind tour of the 580 page work. In *Mental Illness and Psychology,* Foucault asks two quintessentially Szaszian questions: "Under what conditions can one speak of illness in the psychological domain?" and "What relations can one define between the facts of mental pathology and those of organic pathology?"[39]

Like Szasz, Foucault's response to these questions is that the analogy between physical and mental pathology is based on a category mistake. The very idea of mental pathology is determined by cultural conditions which lead us to treat certain socially unacceptable behaviors as illnesses. "The analyses of our psychologists and sociologists, which turn the patient into a deviant and which seek the origin of the [clinically] morbid in the [behaviorally] abnormal, are, therefore, above all a projection of cultural themes."[40] In a passage striking for its echoing of Szasz, Foucault describes his "aim . . . [as] show[ing] that mental pathology requires methods of analysis different from those of organic pathology and that it is only by an artifice of language that the same meaning can be attributed to 'illnesses of the body' and 'illnesses of the mind.' "[41] It is absolutely essential that "one must not regard [the phenomena of madness] as ontological forms,"[42] since they are always "historically constituted."[43]

Decoding Hegel's Silence

In seeking now to come to terms with Hegel's silence on the historical and political dimensions of madness, I will not engage in the popular project of adjudicating the accuracy of Foucault's and Szasz's histories of psychiatry and the concept of mental illness. These are extremely controversial histories, with many debunkers and defenders who respectively storm and protect the barricades.[44] But the real issue for Hegel is not whether Foucault and Szasz have all their historical facts straight. The issue is whether the labeling perspective they represent seriously challenges his ontology of madness.

However the history of madness should be written, the sorts of questions Foucault and Szasz raise about the social construction of madness are serious. And even if we were to accept a much milder version of labeling theory which acknowledged an ontological basis of mental pathology while insisting that social, political, and moral factors also play an important role in the construction of our psychiatric theories and practices, Hegel's depiction of madness as a purely ontologically constituted pathology would still raise serious questions about his silence. From the perspective of labeling theory, such a silence about social and political factors only tends to further mystify madness and, indeed, to further silence the voices of the 'insane.' According to the most troubling interpretation, Hegel's own silence might be read as simply reflecting his complicity with the forces of social and political conformity which are so interested in 'correcting,' and therefore silencing, the voices of the poor, the disenfranchised, the disaffected, and the dissenting—in short, just those most vulnerable to being categorized as 'mad.'

It is important to see that the silence we are speaking of here is quite different from the silence we discussed in chapters 3 and 7, where we considered Hegel's philosophical silence about the intimacy of the suffering of the insane. The argument of these previous chapters was that Hegel's reticence about intruding upon the personal inwardness of the grief and sense of being crushed of the insane in fact was a great virtue, and so far from silencing the voices of madness, allowed them to speak by refusing to comprehend them *philosophically*. In fact, it is just this refusal of philosophical comprehension which allowed Hegel himself to speak in a very different way about the madness of his sister in his letters. It would be perfectly possible to agree with this argument and still to agree with Szasz and Foucault that Hegel's quite different silence about the role of social and political forces in defining madness was troubling. For while Hegel may in principle allow the voices of the insane a space of their own, outside the constraints of his philosophical ontology of madness, if he fails to account for the ways in which such persons are subject to social and cultural classification and management, it might seem that the freedom he allows them is a rather small consolation.

To return to Foucault's basic premise, "the language of psychiatry . . . is a monologue of reason *about* madness, [and] has been established only the basis of [the] silence" to which those labeled as mad have been reduced.[45] Hegel, it is true, in a sense also recognizes the 'silence' of the mad, insofar as he sees the language of the insane to be an essentially private (and therefore unintelligible) language to which madness reverts in its regression back to the life of the soul. He has his own method of deciphering that silence, as he develops an ontology of 'the infernal regions' of the unconscious, and a phenomenological psychology of madness as the echo of the universal past of spirit, the primitive origin from which all consciousness arises. But it is just such an ontology and psychology which Foucault and Szasz see as a mystification of madness, by its banishment of any historical, social, and political considerations.

The Context of the "Anthropology" of Madness

THE LIFE OF THE SOUL AS PRE-HISTORY. In order to explain this Hegelian banishment of the historical and cultural dimensions of madness, and to speculate as to how Hegel might respond to the critiques of Foucault and Szasz, we need to review some of the basic premises of his theory of madness, and to further investigate the role of his "Anthropology" in which this theory is placed. The subject of the "Anthropology" is the soul, or "natural mind," mind as purely "immediate or implicit," mind "which is still in the grip of Nature and connected with its corporeity, mind which is not as yet in communion with itself, not yet free" (PM § 387). Madness is a reversion of the mind which has developed into full conscious life back to the life of the soul, fundamentally alienating and disconnecting itself from its concrete reality and all the usual causal connections with it. But as such, the mind withdrawn from its world and reimmersed in its archaic past, communing only with its own interior feeling states and the unconscious play of instincts, has subverted the very conditions for historical, social existence. Madness occurs not in the space of culture, but in a dream-space, "entangled in dreaming away and [only] dimly presaging its individual world" (PM § 405 Z). Indeed, in the 1827 version of Hegel's "Anthropology" lectures, the passages on the feeling soul in which his discussion of madness occurs were titled "The Dreaming Soul."[46]

This view of madness as a reversion to the pre-historical past of spirit partly explains Hegel's dismissal of the tendency of Romantic medicine to historicize madness. There can be no genuine history of the forms of madness, but only an ontology of the human archaic past, the unconscious and instinctive 'infernal regions' of the soul. So too, Hegel would look askance at Foucault's and Szasz's projects of entirely circumscribing madness within the orbit of history. Mental illness is not a symbolic expression of changing social and political constructs, but a sign and symbol of our primitive origins in nature.

Of course, it is just this dehistoricizing, ontologizing tendency which Foucault and Szasz take issue with. Both, for example, are adamant in their skepticism about the Freudian theory of mental illness as a regression to origins. Szasz describes as "quite absurd" the theory of a "human disposition to resume immature or childish patterns of behavior, which Freud called 'regression.' "[47] And Foucault speaks of "the myth . . . of a certain psychological substance (Freud's 'libido,' Janet's 'psychic force')"—and we might well add Hegel's 'feeling soul' to this list—"which is seen as the raw material of evolution and which, progressing in the course of individual and social development, is subject to relapses and can fall back, through illness, to an earlier state." More bluntly, "the pathological structure of the psyche is not a return to origins."[48] We may note that one of Foucault's most persistent reservations about Hegelian epistemology and metaphysics is its absorption in the search for origins, which leads Edward Said to contrast "Foucault's admirably un-nostalgic" temperament with the "metaphysical yearning [for origins] such as one finds in heirs to the Hegelian tradition."[49]

Foucault accurately depicts the Freudian theory as proposing a dynamic of evolutionary and regressive tendencies of the psyche, and this is equally true of Hegel's position. Whether this is a mythologizing of psychological life is precisely the question at issue. Foucault and Szasz tend to adopt an uncompromising stance in describing mental illness as solely constituted by historical forces, and Hegel's silence about the possibility of historical constitution might imply that his own stance is equally uncompromising on the side of ontologizing madness. At the very most, we might see him as allowing a study of the labeling of mental illness only as illuminating changing cultural perspectives on the same basic, universal, ontologically underlying phenomena of madness, that is, as reflecting the purely contingent shifting of social, political, and scientific interpretations of insanity. But this would be a study of social fashions, not of madness itself. As such, labeling theory would be analogous to nosology, which we have seen Hegel to be philosophically impatient with: how to classify symptoms is not the task of a philosophical psychology, but rather how to explain the inner determinations, or ontology, of the soul; similarly, how to account for changing social and political classifications of the insane would miss the true heart of madness.

FROM ANTHROPOLOGY TO PHENOMENOLOGY: FROM ORIGINS TO HISTORY. We will return to this debate shortly, since there may be a stronger sense in which Hegel could allow, and indeed should allow, the labeling theory an entry into his account of madness. But first we should mention a second way—beyond Hegel's description of madness as a return to pre-historical origins—by which to explain his silence on historical and political themes. The basic idea is this, that Hegel's anthropology is a way-station to his phenomenology, a propaedeutic for the real work of his philosophy, and as such defers exploration of the social, political, and historical themes which so interest Foucault and Szasz until 'the real work' is begun.

From this perspective, the real role of the "Anthropology" discussion of madness is not really to illuminate the structures of madness for the sake of explaining madness itself, but to lead to a fuller illumination of the structures and dynamics of the 'normal' or 'developed' mind. This is why Hegel says of the question, "How does the mind come to be insane?"—the question Foucault and Szasz attack, and answer according to their theories of social labeling—that "it is rather the converse of this question that should be asked, namely, How does the soul which is shut up in its inwardness . . . emerge . . . and attain to the . . . truly objective intellectual and rational consciousness?" (§ 408 Z)—a question which points beyond the ontology of madness to the nature of the healthy mind.

Hegel presents a thoroughly developmental theory of the psyche, moving from the most immediate, undeveloped characteristics of the mind through a progressive *Bildung* to ever more mediated, evolved forms. Thus he describes his "Anthropology" as a study of the soul's emergence into consciousness, the path towards "the *awakening of consciousness*" (PM § 387), an inquiry into "the struggle for liberation which the soul has to wage against the immediacy of its . . . content in order to become completely master of itself" (PM § 402 Z). It is this self-mastered self which is the subject of Hegel's phenomenology, and the discussion of madness is meant to explain what it is about this 'normal' self which accounts for its "still [being] susceptible of disease" (§ 408). It is only in this context, where the real object of inquiry is the developed, rational mind, that the first question above, "How does the mind come to be insane?" takes on significance.[50]

Madness is "an *essential* stage" (PM § 408 Z, emphasis added) in the development of spirit precisely because it holds the key to the mystery and riddle of spirit's integration with nature, of mind with body, of consciousness with the unconscious. The whole discussion of madness is placed within this context of explaining the developed, rational mind's vulnerability to illness as a result of retaining its origins in nature:

> It will be sufficiently clear why insanity must be discussed before the healthy, intellectual consciousness, although it has that consciousness for its *presupposition* and is nothing else but the extreme limit of sickness to which the latter can succumb. We [must] discuss insanity already in Anthropology because in this state . . . the natural self . . . gains the mastery over the objective, rational . . . consciousness. . . . (PM § 408 Z)

Our first attempt to explain Hegel's silence about the historical and social dimensions of madness, by appeal to his theory of the pre-historical nature of the soul, is thus only half the answer. The soul is not somehow left behind in the emergence of conscious human spirit, but is retained and integrated within it. It does not have a history or social existence of its own—any more than Hegel views 'Being,' the first category of his logic, as having a determinate existence (*Dasein*) of its own, or *an sich*—but the soul does become implicated in and subject to historical, social existence insofar as it is an integral part of the whole of spirit—just as 'Being' may be analyzed in terms of 'Becoming' insofar as it emerges into determinate existence.

This suggests a new reading of Hegel's silence: he is silent not because he is indifferent to the historical and cultural dimensions of madness, but because in the context in which his discussion of madness occurs—in his "Anthropology," where he has not yet reached the level of development of the mind into consciousness, which is the subject of his phenomenology—there is nothing to be said. It is only when we reach a fundamentally different level of analysis, where we no longer abstract away from the concrete conditions under which the developed consciousness, or 'free mind,' becomes imprisoned in the shapes of madness that such a discourse about history and culture could make sense.

Furthermore, it is hardly the case that Hegel's phenomenology is only interested in historical analysis by way of revealing purely contingent shifts in cultural fashions. There is a very real sense in which the social and political labeling of reality is constitutive, since it is a basic axiom of Hegel's idealism, repeatedly insisted upon, that reality is not ultimately definable separately from cultural projections. This axiom explains Hegel's whole effort of "divest[ing] . . . the objective world that stands opposed to us of its strangeness" (SL § 194 Z), by seeing reality as the "externalization" of mind, of "the object [as the mind's] own production" (PS 492). Reality is not a completely given, unchanging structure, but constantly restructured as it is historically and culturally rethought.

Thus Hegel's system can accommodate a theory of the historical constitution of reality (albeit not an extreme version which disallows any givenness of reality, a crucial qualification we will return to). The question now shifts from why Hegel was silent on this point in his "Anthropology," where, as we have argued, it would be inappropriate, to why he never got around to the task of applying his usual historical and cultural analyses to the concept of madness within his phenomenology, where presumably it would be appropriate.

HEGEL'S ONTOLOGY OF MADNESS AS AN 'ABBREVIATION'? Now in a certain sense, it could be said that Hegel did offer such an analysis. Thus we have seen that madness makes its appearance—sporadically to be sure, but nevertheless at important junctures—throughout his *Phenomenology*, for example in the descriptions of skepticism, the law of the heart, virtue, absolute freedom and terror, and the beautiful soul, as well as indirectly in the far-reaching affinities between madness and the 'unhappy consciousness,' the central shape of spirit in the *Phenomenology*. True, we have rejected the claim of Jean Hyppolite—the person, incidentally, with whom Foucault studied Hegel and whom Foucault often referred to as his greatest influence[51]—that madness is a key underlying theme of the *Phenomenology*. But we have also asserted that, as an exposure of the fate of human consciousness to be continually subject to the experience of infinite pain, the *Phenomenology* helps prepare an understanding of the reversion into madness as one of a number of human strategies for responding to this pain.

But this is not enough. For while such forms of consciousness as the law of the heart and the beautiful soul are crucially implicated in and shaped by historical and cultural contexts, the allusions to their connections with madness are just too few, too general, and too undeveloped. It may be that Hegel elevates the principle of recognition (*Anerkennen*) to a level of paramount importance in his philosophy of self-identity, so that it is only in being recognized by an other that the self's identity is shaped—"self-consciousness exists in and for itself when, and by the fact that, it so exists for another; that is, it exists only in being acknowledged [*es ist nur als ein Anerkanntes*]" (PS 111 / W 3: 145). But this principle never gets applied to the specific issue of how society recognizes, and therefore shapes, the identity of the insane. Thus Hegel's comments on the psychopathological elements of various shapes of consciousness never speak clearly to the question that most concerned Foucault and Szasz: what are the social and political interests involved in constituting certain sorts of behavior as mental illness?

The question is whether and to what extent Hegel's philosophy is compatible in principle with such concerns as these. One way of answering this question would be to say that Hegel might well accept these concerns, but as being essentially empirical matters lying outside the scope of his philosophical 'history' of spirit. There are a number of places in his *Philosophy of Right* where Hegel considers the relation between philosophical analysis and empirical or 'positive' history which are suggestive in this regard. For example, he says that "the historical meaning of coming to be—the historical method of portraying it and making it comprehensible—is at home in a different sphere from the philosophical

survey of the concept of the thing and of a thing's coming to be. . . ."
History has to do with the particular, with purely empirical circumstances, while philosophy is concerned with the interpretation
of meanings, or the 'concept' underlying these events (PR § 3 A).
This entails that:

> If we ask what is or has been the historical origin . . . of any par-
> ticular state, or its rights and institutions, . . . or finally if we ask
> in what light the basis of the state's rights has been conceived
> and consciously established, whether this basis has been sup-
> posed to be positive divine right, or contract, custom, etc. . . .—all
> these questions are no concern of the Idea of the state. We are
> here dealing exclusively with the philosophic science of the state,
> and from that point of view all these things are mere appearance
> and therefore matters for history. . . . The philosophical treatment
> of these topics is concerned only with their inward side, with the
> thought of their concept. (PR § 258 A)

It must be emphasized that such passages need to be read in
conjunction with many others which show Hegel to be far from indifferent to historical content. We have already noted in chapter 2
Hegel's denial of writing an *a priori* style of history, his persistent
critique of purely formalistic philosophies, and his insistence that
genuinely speculative philosophy must begin with the empirical.
Indeed, in the *Philosophy of Right* as in all his other works, he insists that in "philosophical science . . . content is essentially bound
up with form," and that "the philosophical Idea" is precisely "the
known identity of . . . form and content" (PR Preface, 2, 12). In the
same 1805 letter to Heinrich Voss in which Hegel announced his
desire to teach philosophy to speak German, he reflected that "just
as philosophy pushes the sciences [to compensate] for their conceptual deficiency, so they drive philosophy to give up the lack of real-
ization [*Erfühlung*] stemming from its abstraction."[52] These comments are of a piece with what we have seen to be Hegel's search
for a middle path between the overly abstract theories of Romantic
medicine—which is "so much at home" in its abstractions that it
"feels an innate indifference to descend to particulars" (SL § 12)—
and the overly particularistic theories of the empirical school,
which collect a hoard of brute data without ever raising them to
the level of speculative thinking and therefore comprehensibility.

It seems certain that Foucault and Szasz would find Hegel to
have lost his way on this supposedly middle path, to have wan-
dered much too far in the direction of abstract and formalistic
thinking, and to have revealed (perhaps unwittingly) his actual

disdain for historical and social questions in such passages as the one just cited from the *Philosophy of Right* where he says that "all these things are mere appearance and therefore matters [merely] for history," being of "no concern of the Idea." By this view, Hegel's ontology of madness would be exposed as analogous to his logic, which we have seen him to describe as dealing "only and solely with thoughts *as thoughts*, in their complete abstraction," where these thoughts "are nevertheless meant to serve as *abbreviations*" for a whole "host of particulars of outer existence and actions." The problem, to continue this line of critique, is that the abstract presentation of forms of consciousness leaves them as mere abbreviations, forgetting the host of historical specificity in which Foucault and Szasz insist the key to understanding 'madness' must be found—a fatal forgetfulness which renders the 'abbreviations' wholly cryptic, mystifying signs, symbols without substance, cryptographic forms without a key to their translation.

On similar grounds, Marx faulted Hegel's anatomy of alienated labor in the master/slave dialectic for abstracting away from the actual historical and social conditions of labor, thereby mythologizing the concrete processes of alienation.[53] But Marx and Engels nevertheless acknowledged the true "revolutionary kernel" of Hegel's philosophy, and the way in which their own thoughts on alienated labor and class struggle were contained in principle within this kernel.[54]

My own feeling is that Hegel's theory of madness is also open, in principle, to a certain version of the labeling theory which seeks to reveal the contribution of social and political forces in the constitution of madness. This would not discount the sorts of questions Foucault or Szasz might raise about the purely 'abbreviated' character of Hegel's ontologizing of madness—it would not, in short, explain away Hegel's silence about the implication of historical and cultural factors in the construction of insanity. But it would deny that a fundamental ontology is essentially mystifying, and that any such project is antithetical to a more historically and politically oriented theory. The version of labeling theory which is compatible with Hegel's ontology is not, however, that of Foucault or Szasz, for reasons we may now turn to.

Satisfying the Writ of Habeas Corpus: We Have the Body

We have noted that the most extreme consequence of Foucault's and Szasz's positions is the reduction of 'mental illness' to a socially and politically constituted phenomenon, denying any ontological foundation of madness in organic pathology. The fact that Hegel was entirely convinced of the role of somatic factors in madness disallows any possibility of reconciliation with this reductionistic version of labeling theory, and means that if his ontology of madness is to be reconciled at all with an account of the social construction of madness, we must look to a much less radical version of it.

We should recall that Hegel was developing his theory of madness during a time of the growing prestige of empirical and somatic theories of insanity, where the process of medicalizing madness was in full swing. In France, the 1790 edict of the Revolutionary Constituent Assembly prohibiting incarceration by the purely political contrivance of a *lettre de cachet*,[55] and mandating that those imprisoned on grounds of insanity be medically examined and subsequently either released or placed within medical hospitals, opened the way for such reformers as Pinel (1745–1826), director of the asylum at Bicêtre and consulting physician to Napoleon; Michel Thouret (1748–1810), first director of the medical school founded in Year III of the Republic, one of the first members of the Royal Society of Medicine in 1776, and brother of Jacques Thouret, who helped draw up the Constitution and later met his end at the blade of the guillotine; the medical writer Pierre Roussel (1742–1802); Pierre Cabanis (1757–1808), Minister of Education and administrator of the Paris hospitals after the Reign of Terror; Jean-Baptiste Delecloy (1747–1807), a member of the National Convention and author of the plan for reorganizing public assistance and the hospitals; and Antoine François de Fourcroy (1755–1809), a member of the Committee of Public Instruction and the Committee of Public Safety, a chemist who worked with Lavoisier, a professor at the École de Medicine in Paris, and, with Cabanis, the person most responsible for instituting the practice of teaching medicine at the bedside of patients.[56]

Although differing in important ways, these reformers were united in seeing mental illness as a physical disorder, requiring a radical transformation of the whole procedure of diagnosis and treatment. Pinel's *Philosophical Nosography* (*Nosographie philosophique ou la méthode de l'analyse appliquée à la médicine,* 1798) and *Medical and Philosophic Treatise* (*Traité médico-philosophique sur l'aliénation mentale ou la manie,* 1801), along with Cabanis' work on the *Relations Between the Physical and Moral Aspects of Man* (*Rapports du physique et du moral de l'homme,* 1802), recast psychiatry within a new clinical, medical context. In 1791, Guillotin proposed to the National Assembly that medical schools be connected with hospitals, and in the next few years, *Écoles de santé* were established throughout France.[57]

In Germany, similar medical reforms began in the 1790s.[58] At about the same time as Cabanis' and Pinel's work in France, Christian Reil's *Rhapsodies* (*Rhapsodien über die Anwendung der psychischen Curmethode auf Geisteszerrüttungen*) was published (1803), marking the beginning of German medical psychiatry. While Reil was a proponent of the Romantic school of medicine, he was also firmly committed to explaining insanity as a physiological illness. He practiced medicine as an internist, surgeon, and ophthalmologist, made important contributions to the fields of anatomy, pathology, physiology, chemistry, and pharmacology, was Professor of Medicine at Halle and later at the University of Berlin, and founded three journals of physiological medicine.[59]

Interestingly, Reil offered a critique of the complicity of "the priests" with the political powers of the old regime which squares very well with Szasz's and Foucault's labeling theory: "The priestlings in particular used [madness] as their special weapon and mask to trick the rabble and force it into the yoke of their religious despotism."[60] And it was precisely in order to counteract this politico-religious constitution of madness that he developed a plan for sweeping medicalization of the German asylum system on the basis of his physiological theory that all mental disease is the result of an "abnormal vital process in the brain."[61] Indeed, by the time of Hegel's lectures on madness (1816–30), most of the asylums in Germany as well as France were headed by physicians who supported the somatic basis of madness and the close clinical observation and description of medical symptoms.

For Szasz and Foucault, of course, this great momentum towards the medicalization of madness was just a front, like the "mask" Reil refers to as "the special weapon" of "the priestlings." The real motive was to make the socially marginal yet more subject to the dominant cultural and political ethic. By defining the problem in medical terms, society could cloak its project of the social engineering of those who were perceived to threaten the values and stability of the state—the poor and disenfranchised, the dissenters and outsiders of all varieties—under appeal to the authority of medicine and the philanthropic enterprise of 'curing' 'diseases.' And in fact, Foucault and Szasz are able to marshall quite impressive evidence of the essentially moral and social purposes of therapy on the part of the great medical reformers of the early nineteenth century and in the treatment programs of the asylums they helped to institute, some of which we will discuss in the next section when we turn to examine the influence of Pinel on Hegel's therapeutics.

Critics of Foucault and Szasz, and of labeling theory in general, point to the skepticism about organic bases of mental illness as the weakest premise of their arguments. One might agree that much of the supposed evidence for the physical roots of madness supplied by the medical reformers and researchers of the turn of the eighteenth century was speculative and even rather mysterious: Gall's phrenology, Mesmer's magnetic fluid, John Brown's Romantically conceived 'vital energy,' as well as much of the postmortem evidence correlating organic lesions with specific forms of insanity, will hardly satisfy the most stringently construed standards of experimental verifiability. But supporters of the medical model claim that current evidence for the complicity of organic pathology in mental illness is overwhelming.[62]

I do not wish to enter into this stormy debate, not out of timidity about showing my own hand—I am inclined to disagree with Foucault and Szasz and the most reductionistic labeling proponents, and to believe that the evidence for physical complicity in many categories of mental illness is persuasive—but for another (more honorable, I hope!) reason. Even if we accept the medical model, and agree that there are certain underlying ontological characteristics of madness, this would not absolve Hegel for his silence on political and cultural themes, since any version of the medical model which was so extreme as to simply deny any contribution of social and political factors in the construction of madness, would itself conflict with formidable evidence to the contrary.

This evidence is supplied by a wide range of labeling studies including work by sociologists and anthropologists, political scientists and medical historians. The historical studies of Foucault and Szasz, in addition to those of such scholars as Andrew Scull, Richard Hunter and Ida Macalpine, Michael MacDonald, Robert Castel, and Klaus Doerner,[63] together demonstrate how social and political ideology has continually influenced the diagnosis and treatment of mental illness. And the evidence of these historical examinations is augmented by a huge amount of empirical research in the field of the sociology of psychiatry and 'deviance theory' documenting the greatly increased vulnerability to being labeled as mentally ill of such groups as the homeless, the poor, the lower classes, and ethnic minorities.[64]

There is nothing in principle that would prevent Hegel's

theory of madness from being compatible with a modest version of the labeling theory which, unlike Szasz' and Foucault's, acknowledged an ontological basis of mental illness while also recognizing the historical role of social and political factors in the construction of madness labels. This is the view of people like Thomas Scheff, Alan Horwitz, and Carol Warren, each of whom, in different ways and with different emphases, seeks to uncover the interaction between the dynamics of social control and what Warren calls the "existential reality" of madness.[65]

Moreover, this compatibility would square nicely with basic commitments of Hegel's larger philosophical perspective, which sees all human consciousness as a dialectical interplay between inner and outer reality, or social and phenomenological factors: all consciousness is formed by both social reality and underlying ontological reality. Thus, for example, the unhappy consciousness, or despair, which we have seen to share with madness many of its intrinsic phenomenological structures, is not only described as the "center" of all the shapes of spirit, "permeating them all" (PS 456)—and thus as a fundamental form of consciousness possessing certain universal ontological features—but is configured differently according to the different social and cultural circumstances it occurs in. As a constantly recurring form of mental life, despair can only be understood according to an analysis of both its basic ontology and the varying historical contexts which serve to reshape it and give it its cultural specificity. By analogy, Hegel's conception of the basic ontology of madness should also be open to, and would certainly profit from, the augmentation of an account of the ways in which insanity has been historically and socially reconceived and reconfigured.

Therapeutics: Coercion or Liberation?

For someone like Foucault or Szasz who denies any reality to madness above and beyond its social constitution, any form of psychiatric therapy will, *ex hypothesi*, have no medical foundation but be a mask for social control and coercion. If, on the other hand, it is plausible to see Hegel's ontology of madness as compatible with a more modest labeling view, then while he would have to acknowledge the historical evidence of the abuses of therapy for the purposes of social manipulation—as in fact he comes close to doing in his references to Bedlam (PM § 408 Z)—he will still be able to speak of a genuinely medical foundation of the liberatory function of therapy. Still, we must return to look more closely at the principles of Hegel's therapeutics, since they were so influenced by Pinel's 'moral therapy,' a phrase which people like Foucault and Szasz see as oxymoronic, straightforwardly confusing medical cure with moral and social 'correction' or re-education.

Hegel's Pinelian Heritage: 'Moral Therapy' and the Imperative of Labor

The key to understanding Hegel's therapeutics is found in his definition of insanity as an inwardly divided, double-centered personality, where on the one hand the self has sunk back into the archaic life of the soul, but on the other it still retains the trace of its rational consciousness. "The right psychical treatment therefore keeps in view the truth that insanity is not an abstract *loss* of reason (neither in the point of intelligence nor of will and its responsibility), but only derangement, only a contradiction in a still subsisting reason" (PM § 408). The therapist must seek to establish contact with this obscured but still present rational center of the self, drawing the patient out of their fixation on inward feeling states, much as in animal magnetism the magnetizer establishes a 'rapport' with the patient so that the self is "brought back to itself" out of its inward absorption (PN § 373 Z; and see PM § 406 Z). It is precisely because "along with an insanity . . . there also exists a consciousness which . . . is rational," that the "skillful psychiatrist [*Seelenarzt*] is able to develop sufficient power to overcome the particular fixed idea" by means which reinforce and liberate the rational side of the self (PM § 408 Z), "just as in the case of bodily disease the physician bases his treatment on the vitality which as such still contains health" (PM § 408).

The therapy Hegel recommends is therefore a "humane [*menschliche*] treatment, no less benevolent than reasonable," which "presupposes the patient's rationality." Hegel explicitly mentions "the services of Pinel" in this regard, "which deserve the highest acknowledgement" (PM § 408).[66] Pinel's 'moral treatment' is one which makes sparing use of physical remedies. As he says in his *Treatise on Insanity*, "in diseases of the mind . . . it is an art of no little importance to administer medicines properly: but, it is an art of much greater and more difficult acquisition to know when to suspend or altogether to omit them."[67] Pinel stresses "the value of consolatory language, kind treatment, and the revival of extinguished hope."[68] Moral therapy is adamantly opposed to the exercise of cru-

elty, violence, and despotism, which for so long had been the
defining marks of the asylum.[69] Pinel will resort to such physically
coercive measures as "straight waistcoats, superior force, and seclusion for a limited time" only with great reluctance for "the most violent and dangerous maniacs," and then only so long as is necessary
to protect themselves and others from their own violence.[70]

For both Pinel and Hegel, the basic goals of moral therapy—to
reinforce the patient's rationality, their sense of hope, and their
ability to reestablish connections to the outer world—are most effectively realized through the use of labor. We have already noted
Hegel's claim that "by working, [the insane] are forced out of their
diseased subjectivity and impelled towards the real world" (PM §
408 Z). For his part, Pinel placed enormous stock in the "labor
cure," which he put into practice at Bicêtre. "It was pleasing to observe," he says, "the silence and tranquility which prevailed in the
Asylum de Bicêtre, when nearly all the patients were supplied by
the tradesmen of Paris with employments which fixed their attention, and allured them to exertion by the prospect of a trifling
gain."[71] So convinced of the curative powers of labor, Pinel put it
forward as:

> no longer a problem to be solved, but the result of the most con-
> stant and unanimous experience, that in all public asylums as
> well as in prisons and hospitals, the surest, and, perhaps, the
> only method of securing health, good order, and good manners, is
> to carry into decided and habitual execution the natural law of
> bodily labour, so contributive and essential to human happiness.[72]

Indeed, "those whose condition does not place them above the necessity of submission to toil and labour, are almost always cured;
whilst the grandee, who would think himself degraded by any exer-
cises of this description, is generally incurable."[73]

Pinel insists that "the application of moral regimen" is a "department of experimental medicine," completely "independent of
social institutions," grounded in a "pure and enlightened philanthropy."[74] For such labeling theorists as Szasz and Foucault, however, this is a ludicrous claim.

Robert Castel, for example, speaks of moral therapy as "a matter
of deploying strategies for subjugation" and as "represent[ing] the
paradigm of every authoritarian pedagogy." It employs an "ar-
moury of disciplinary techniques" which surreptitiously conflates
the concept of a recovery of reason into the ideal of "subduing the
people (i.e., causing them to internalize the rules that ensure the

reproduction of the bourgeois order)."[75] Klaus Doerner similarly speaks of the "downright draconian rules of morality" implicit in Pinel's moral treatment, which were employed "to teach the values of the bourgeois order, social morality, work, and family."[76]

Foucault is merciless in his attempt to expose the philanthropic and medical pretenses of moral treatment as cloaks over a coercive enterprise of 'educating' the 'insane' into the rules of the social order. "The asylum reduces differences, . . . eliminates irregularities. It denounces everything that opposes the essential virtues of society. . . . The asylum sets itself the task of the homogeneous rule of morality, its rigorous extension to all those who tend to escape from it." The goal of moral treatment is to "guarantee bourgeois morality a universality of fact and permit it to be imposed as a law upon all forms of insanity."[77] Most particularly, the labor cure must be singled out as emblematic of this project of social and moral reeducation: labor "possesses a constraining power superior to all forms of physical coercion" since it is "imposed only as a moral rule; a limitation of liberty, a submission to order, an engagement of responsibility, with the single aim of disalienating the mind lost in the excess of a liberty" which threatens the status quo.[78]

In fact, Pinel does speak quite often about the value of "the strictest discipline and order in every department of [the] management [of] maniacs,"[79] and intersperses his many case studies with remarks about the "happy effects of intimidation, without severity; of oppression, without violence."[80] Foucault's point is precisely that the moral treatment no longer requires overt 'severity' or violence: it perfects the operations of intimidation and oppression by the much more effective means of moral judgment and reeducation, reinforced by the disciplinary practice of forced physical labor.

Against such critiques as these, it seems almost naive to point out that Hegel, in his discussions of moral therapy, never mentions the aim of restoring the patient to the moral status quo, nor the social and political value of labor, but always emphasizes the restoration of individual health. For writers like Foucault, the mere fact that a psychiatric theory or practice does not advertise itself as a means of social coercion is irrelevant: implicit in the rhetoric about a restoration of 'health' or 'rationality' are covert associations with the prevailing values of the social order. And certainly the conservative nature of Hegel's political philosophy, where the values of rationality and even freedom itself are intimately related to the internalization of standardized social norms, might well be taken as giving credence to such an interpretation.

This interpretation deserves serious consideration, and it is not unreasonable to assume that Hegel's strong reliance on Pinelian principles included at least some degree of approval of the purpose of resocialization into the bourgeois order which Foucault and others so persuasively reveal as underlying Pinel's therapeutic project. At the same time, there are two considerations which tend to make any such approval tentative. First, we have shown that in Hegel's theory of madness, the ideal of rationality which it is the goal of the therapist to restore is entirely divorced from moral vocabulary. Or rather, the *apparently* moral vocabulary of 'evil' which Hegel uses to describe the 'dark, infernal powers of the heart' which are 'set free' in insanity, turns out to be a purely ontological vocabulary: this 'evil' is only the immediacy and one-sidedness of nature, the absence of integration of the soul with rational consciousness, the inward 'division' and 'contradiction' between two centers of the self. As Timo Airaksinen says, for Hegel "evil means suffering, not moral condemnation; . . . there remains no trace of treating the insane as wicked, in a moralistic sense of the term."[81] This strongly implies that to restore the rationality of the insane is not fundamentally to restore morality—Hegel may or may not have approved of this as a secondary consequence of therapy, but his very silence on this topic shows that it is not a primary therapeutic goal—but to overcome the mind's imprisonment in fixed ideas. Similarly, moral treatment is not in principle moral education, but treating those who suffer morally, recognizing their personhood.

The second point to be made regards the role of labor in Hegel's phenomenology. Whatever its value for Pinel, for Hegel labor is not predominantly tied to the function of reproducing or reinforcing the social order, but rather to the prospects for liberation and creativity. As Shlomo Avineri puts it, labor for Hegel "represents man's power to create his own world. . . . In labor there always exists an intrinsic moment of liberation."[82] This is not to deny that labor also has the value of social labor, that the product of labor becomes estimated and regulated within a communal order. But first of all, the role of labor is to confirm the creative freedom of the individual, which Hegel regards as "the worthiest and holiest thing in man" (PR § 215 Z). In this sense, the place of labor in the moral treatment of madness need not be seen as simply reconnecting the self to the established order, but equally as reawakening the self's knowledge of its capacity to transform and remake its world—just as we have seen Hegel to insist this is the value of labor for the slave, and for Adam and Eve.

Labor is in essence liberatory, and speaks to the 'struggle for liberation' from 'imprisonment' which Hegel sees as intrinsic to the life of madness. By way of further exploring this liberatory, non-coercive potentiality of the labor cure, we may now turn to a comparison of madness with another sphere of life which Hegel views as fundamentally imprisoning: the life of poverty, of destitution, of social marginalization. What makes this comparison particularly interesting is that it is just such an analysis of the socially marginalized which labeling theorists insist must be central to any account of the institution of psychiatry and the decoding of the meanings of insanity. While we have seen that Hegel fails to meet this requirement in his philosophy of madness, he is very interested in the issue of poverty and destitution in his political philosophy. It is my feeling that his political commentary on social marginalization suggests a way of reconstructing his theory of madness in such a way as to give further credence to our argument that it is in fact compatible with a modest, non-reductionistic version of labeling theory.

The Missing Link: Poverty, Destitution, Social Marginalization

Contemporary proponents of labeling theory all point to the overwhelming correlation between the population of those identified as mentally ill and those who are living on the margins of society: the poor, the destitute, the indigent, the vagrant—precisely those, we may note, who are excluded from the liberatory potential of labor. Hegel's own analysis of poverty and destitution also reveals some important connections with his analysis of madness, although as we have stated, he does not draw out these connections himself. Like madness, poverty is radical alienation. "The poor still have the needs common to civil society, and yet since society has withdrawn from them the natural means of acquisition [of property and personal welfare] . . . their poverty leaves them more or less deprived of all the advantages of society, of the opportunity of acquiring skill or education of any kind, as well as of the administration of justice, the public health services, and often even of the consolations of religion, and so forth" (PR § 241). The acute "distress" of the poor "entail[s] [the] inability to feel and enjoy the broader freedoms . . . of civil society" (PR § 243).

The distress of the poor is not merely lamentable, and is not merely a deprivation of "the advantages of society," but amounts to a deprivation of personhood itself: for the destitute, "self-consciousness no longer has any rights, freedom has no existence" (PR/1819–20, 195).[83] Hegel defines the right to personhood, or "personality itself" (*das Recht der* Persönlichkeit *als* solcher) as an inalienable right to my own body, to "my universal freedom of will," to my conscience ("my ethical life"), and to my status as end-in-itself, or self-possession without being possessed by another (PR §§ 40 A, 66). To be alienated from personhood is to be subjected to a damage which is "infinite" (PR § 77 A). Thus the poor are not simply placed in an unfortunate circumstance by their exclusion from rights and their loss of access to the benefits of civil society; their alienation from personhood amounts to a fundamental injustice. "Poverty immediately takes the form of a wrong [*eines Unrechts*] done to one class by another," and the "question of how poverty is to be abolished is one of the most disturbing problems which agitate modern society" (PR § 244 Z).

The destitute thus share with the insane the alienation of personhood: just as madness forces the self out of "its own free subjectivity" (PM § 408) into to a state of imprisonment in disease, the poor are estranged from the conditions for genuinely free action into a life of desperation. We might even see the destitute as taking on a sort of double personality, analogous to that of the insane. They too retain the marks of humanity, but only in principle, as an abstract potentiality for freedom and rationality—just as the slave is in principle a free self-consciousness, and the mad are in principle rational beings—while at the same time being reduced to a desperate existence which effaces their humanity. Also, as in madness, those whom poverty exiles from civil society have been effectively severed from normal connections with the external world; they too are forced into themselves in their struggle for survival. True, this is not a withdrawal into the archaic life of the unconscious soul—poverty and destitution are not literally madness, but only analogues—and yet even here there may be certain similarities to be explored in what Marx calls the reversion to primitive "animal existence" into which the socially marginal are forced.[84]

Hegel's own account of the exile of the destitute from all the ordinary systems of rights and duties of civil society lends support to a comparison with the severing of connections with normal causal relations in madness. The poor are forced into desperate action, into crime, into a topsy-turvy underworld of deeds which have no place within the rational economy of the state. This is a world of 'evil,' but, as with the insane, it is an evil without meaningful moral connotations; for someone without rights there are no corresponding duties (VR 1: 322), and for someone whose life "falls below a certain subsistence level, . . . there is a consequent loss of the sense of right and wrong," a moral sense which has meaning only within the context of the social order from which such a person has been excluded (PR § 244).

This last point is particularly important, and leads us to the recognition that Hegel straightforwardly proposes a labeling view of the evil of crime which is so much a part of the environment of poverty. The codes of the criminal law actually constitute certain acts as being crimes: 'crime' indeed cannot be understood apart from the cultural and historical conditions which serve as the context for the writing of a criminal law.[85] Thus Hegel writes in his *Philosophy of Right*:

> There is, therefore, no inherent line of distinction between what is and what is not injurious, even where crime is concerned, or between what is and what is not suspicious, or between what is to be forbidden or subjected to supervision and what is to be exempt from prohibition. . . . These details are determined by custom, the spirit of the rest of the constitution, contemporary conditions, the crisis of the hour, and so forth. Here nothing hard and fast can be laid down and no absolute lines can be drawn. (PR § 234 & Z)

More succinctly, "a penal code, then, is primarily the child of its age and the state of civil society at the time" (PR § 218 A). What Hegel states here so matter of factly with respect to crime is just what we have been looking for in vain in his discussion of madness. Moreover, he uses language which is strikingly close to that of Foucault and Szasz in describing what crimes amount to; just after stating that "a criminal code cannot hold good for all time," he suggests that *"crimes are only shows of reality* which may draw on themselves a greater or lesser degree of disavowal" (PR § 218 Z, emphasis added). Crimes are only "shows of reality"—Hegel's term is *Scheinexistenzen*: pseudoexistences, simulations, simulacra—precisely the sort of term Szasz and Foucault use in their descriptions of 'mental illness.'

As for poverty itself, the role of social constitution is paramount. Poverty is brought about—Hegel's most usual words are "produced" and "created"—by the economic and political conditions of society. "The complications of civil society itself produce poverty"

(PR/1817–19, 138), and "the emergence of poverty is in general a consequence of civil society and on the whole arises necessarily out of it" (PR/1819–20, 193). Both in his lectures on *Realphilosophie* at Jena between 1803 and 1806, and later in his lectures at Heidelberg and Berlin on the *Philosophy of Right* (published in 1821), Hegel offers an incisive analysis of modern capitalist-industrial society which, Shlomo Avineri says, "reveals Hegel as one of the earliest radical critics of the modern industrial system," and as offering "one of the most acute insights into the working of modern, industrial society," an analysis "almost identical," he adds, "in its systematic structure with Marx's program forty years later."[86]

In these lectures, Hegel looks carefully at the conditions of factory labor, the emergence of mechanization, and the ever-increasing extension of the division of labor as factors which inherently intensify human alienation. "Factories and manufacturers base their existence on the misery of a class," he writes, and the power of the market economy "condemns a multitude to a raw life and to dullness in labor and poverty, so that others could amass fortunes" (JR 257, 238).[87] In modern economies, inequities of wealth are inevitable due to the very processes of commodity production. "Conditions . . . greatly facilitate the concentration of disproportionate wealth in a few hands," which leads to "a large mass of people fall[ing] below a certain subsistence level," and "the result is the creation of a rabble [*Pöbel*] of paupers" (PR § 244).

Notwithstanding the radical nature of Hegel's critique of capitalist society, his political conservativism prevents him from anticipating Marx's call for a revolutionary transfiguration of society. As Avineri puts it, "It is precisely at the point where Hegel shows how modern society abandons whole masses to poverty and destitution, that the possibility of a radical transformation of society presents itself to Hegel—only to be discarded. . . . At the height of his critical awareness of the horrors of industrial society, Hegel ultimately remains quietistic, searching for a solution that would incorporate this horrifying reality into a system that could integrate and accommodate it."[88] Thus while we have seen Hegel to say that "the important question of how poverty is to be abolished is one of the most disturbing problems which agitate modern society" (PR § 244 Z), finally, he despairs of solving it.[89]

But even if, for the sake of argument, we grant Hegel his conviction that the modern state is the most perfectly rational embodiment of human freedom, so that whatever flaws or 'distressing' consequences it may have must be accommodated rather than seeking to create a fundamentally new form of society—even so, why can't the problem of poverty be solved within the modern state? Here, as with madness, the goal would be a 'labor cure': it is precisely the liberatory power of labor that the socially marginalized are cut off from.

The problem is that poverty is a *necessary* consequence of the modern state. As Allen Wood puts it, "It is the basic principles of civil society itself that stand in the way of the state's attempts to prevent poverty or remedy it."[90] In the first place, due to the pressures for mechanization and intensified division of labor, much labor is alienated labor, socially productive in the creation of wealth but individually deadening (see PR § 243). And second, neither of the two main ways in which society could alleviate poverty are open to it:

> When the masses begin to decline into poverty, (a) the burden of maintaining them at their ordinary standard of living might be directly laid on the wealthier classes, or they might receive the means of livelihood directly from other public sources of wealth. . . . In either case, however, the needy would receive subsistence directly, not by means of their work, and this would violate the principle of civil society and the feeling of individual independence and self-respect in its individual members. (b) As an alternative, they might be given subsistence indirectly through being given work. . . . In this even the volume of production would be increased, but the evil [of poverty] consists precisely in an excess of production . . . [which] is simply intensified [by this proposal]. It hence becomes apparent that despite an excess of wealth civil society is not rich enough, i.e., its own resources are insufficient to check excessive poverty. . . . (PR § 245)

Note that the first alternative, a sort of welfare proposal, is excluded essentially because it does not respond to the real problem, namely, that people must work in order to be fully free. The second alternative, while promising the possibility of labor, is excluded because of the very conditions of commodity production whose health depends upon the pauperization of the masses.

Our inquiries into the possible reconciliation of Hegel's theory of madness with a labeling view may now be brought to a close, with the aid of two basic conclusions drawn from our consideration of Hegel's thoughts on the nature of poverty. The first centers on the labor cure, and suggests that Hegel's divorce of his therapeutics from social and political issues risks highly unexpected consequences; the second proposes a way to integrate the labeling perspective with Hegel's basic ontology of madness.

A Revolutionary Therapeutics?

We have seen that the possibility of a labor cure for poverty is ruled out by Hegel with a tone of regret, given the inability of the modern state to accommodate it. Poverty is a tragic necessity of the capitalist economy, which could not function without the existence of an unemployed and pauperized segment of the population. Given the fact that throughout history the great majority of those diagnosed as mentally ill have been members of the impoverished class, this suggests that Hegel's Pinelian therapeutics, which relies so strongly on the labor cure, could not be successful on a large scale without at the same time endangering capitalist society! For just to the extent that such a therapy succeeded in preparing its subjects for a reintegration into society and the labor force, the already existing pressures on the conditions of production would be exacerbated. Those who were cured would be turned out into a world which could not accept them, so that moral therapy in fact would be creating a whole population of people qualified for the rights and duties of society but excluded from them, a whole population encouraged to labor but unable to do so—a whole population, that is, unwittingly and ironically prepared for profound discontentment with the social order.

This unnerving paradox was already noted by the Revolutionary Constituent Assembly in France in the 1790s, just during the period Pinel was inaugurating his labor cure. Early on, the Assembly's Committee on Begging argued that the state should proclaim a universal and absolute right to work. "Work is the sole aid that the State should employ to assuage indigence," Jean-Baptiste Bô stated before the Convention, "for *man is not precisely poor because he possesses nothing, but because he does not work*. . . . [We must] eradicate, either by property or by industry, even the very notion of misery."[91] Another member of the Committee, Bernard d'Airy, asserted that "every man has a right to his subsistence, by his labour if he is fit, by free assistance if he is unable to work"[92]—precisely the two possibilities we have seen Hegel to declare inconsistent with the basic principles of capitalist society. Very quickly, however, the Assembly realized that such a policy would be dangerous indeed. Hence the Comte Charles Marie Tanneguy Duchâtel remarked many years later (1829), in reflecting back on the perilous course considered by the Assembly, that "the principle of the right to work shakes the foundations of the social order."[93] As Castel argues, "In the final analysis, the right to work might represent the equivalent in the social order of a right to insurrection in the political order: the recognition of a right turns its violation into arbitrary despotism. Popular violence would then be rendered legitimate, since it would do no more than reestablish the right."[94]

Hegel's attachment to moral therapy thus ironically points to a destabilization of the political state he was so enamored of. Moral therapy, understood in the most generous sense as a liberation of the creative personality of the individual, turns out to be a revolutionary therapeutics. What this suggests is not that Hegel's commitment to moral therapy should be rejected—barring, of course, the most cynical acceptance of an alternative therapeutics which consciously would seek to repress individual rights and to maintain a population of socially marginalized people in a state of destitution and often incarceration—but that his commitment to the economic and political regime which characterized the bourgeois Prussian state should be questioned. We would need, that is, to reject Hegel's political conservativism so as to free labor from the conditions of its alienation.

Much the same conclusion is reached by a number of commentators on Hegel's political philosophy who are similarly troubled by the opposition between his acute awareness of the failures of the commodity-producing industrialized economy on the one hand, and, on the other hand, the pessimism and paralysis about any solution to the evils of alienated labor, poverty, and social marginalization to which he is delivered by his attraction to the political state which makes that economy possible. We have already noted Avineri's feeling that "it is precisely at the point where Hegel shows how modern society abandons whole masses to poverty and destitution, that the possibility of a radical transformation of society presents itself to Hegel—only to be discarded." John McCumber goes further, and suggests that Hegel's exposure of the necessary evils of the modern state in fact involves a "covert" but nevertheless "radical and systematic indictment of the state," one which would encourage "the rage of a justified revolution"[95]—exactly the situation the French Constituent Assembly, back in the 1790s, came to fear would ensue if it adopted the Committee on Begging's policy of a universal right to work.

Allen Wood is surely right in saying that McCumber goes too

far: it may be true that "Hegel's theory of poverty in modern civil
society . . . support[s] an indictment against [the capitalist state],
but not one that Hegel was ever inclined to draw up," covertly or
otherwise.[96] Wood himself, however, also questions Hegel's failure
to draw the radical consequences implied by his critique of the
modern state: Hegel's analysis of poverty "leads to the conclusion
that the poor have neither rights nor duties. . . . This suggests
some . . . drastic conclusions. [For Hegel,] it is a fundamental principle of modern ethical life that all individuals are equal persons
with rights. If civil society systematically produces a class whose
existence violates that principle, then that tends to undermine the
rationality of the ethical order as a whole." Thus while "Hegel's reflection on the modern state [is] positive in intent, [it] may also
begin to reveal the limits of its principle."[97]

We have been led to the same irony by exploring the consequences of Hegel's endorsement of a moral therapy for the insane
which stresses the emancipating power of labor. For such a
therapy to be rational, it would have to liberate its patients into a
different sort of society than the one Hegel supports, given his own
analysis of the dependence of that society on alienated labor, social
marginalization, and destitution. If moral therapy is to be truly
moral in the sense that Hegel meant it, namely, treating its patients morally, recognizing their personhood, and seeking to emancipate them from a life of darkness into a life where they might
flourish through the creative potential of labor, then moral therapy
is in principle a revolutionary therapeutics, calling for an evolution
of social and political existence beyond the conditions which stifle
the prospects for equality, freedom, and creativity.

*Extending Hegel's 'Middle Path': Reconciling the Social Constitution
of Madness with Ontology*

The second conclusion to be drawn from our examination of
Hegel's thoughts on poverty and crime—beyond the unexpectedly
radical political consequences of his embracing Pinelian moral
therapy—is the need to augment his ontology of madness with a
social labeling model. Given the close association between the socially marginalized and those diagnosed as mentally ill, and given
the ways in which this marginalized population is produced by economic and political interests and forces, there is without doubt a
crucial role to be played by a labeling perspective in the examination of madness. Just as what is to count as crime, for example, as

a form of social deviance into which the poor are often driven, is simply "determined by custom," and "a penal code . . . is primarily the child of its age and the state of civil society at the time"—so too what is to count as madness, as a form of social deviance into which those who suffer most from the alienating conditions of society are sometimes driven, will shift according to the changes in social and political reality. Without a study of how these shifts occur, no theory of madness can be complete.

What this would entail is that we look closely at the relations between the tendency to label as mad those who deviate from social norms and the structures of Hegel's ontology of madness. Such an accommodation of the labeling view need not call that ontology into question, any more than the ontology of desire or of the unhappy consciousness is made problematic by the recognition that the contexts in which human desire and despair are manifest are historically and socially influenced. We have already cited the sociologist Alan Horwitz's contention that "the notion of mental illness as a cultural label neither conflicts with nor provides an alternative to the illness concept, but is posed at a different level of analysis." Hegel, after all, is primarily offering an ontological theory of madness, aiming at a philosophical understanding of the underlying meanings of disease and its structures—analogous in many ways to Freud's 'metapsychology'—and not an account of the place of madness within society. That is, he develops only one level of the complete analysis.

True, the integration of an examination of the social contexts in which madness labels become employed would make the application of any ontological theory to the task of diagnosis more complex and less certain. But Hegel was already perfectly well aware of the difficulties of such an application; as we saw in chapter 2, he recognizes that the "particular content" of madness is "something infinitely manifold and therefore contingent," which can never be "deduced" by any philosophical ontology, but can only be approximately understood by the current state of clinical and empirical research. Hegel never thought that a speculative philosophy of medicine could determine in advance the laws governing the empirical data of illness, including its etiology and diagnosis. It is this acknowledgment of the contingency and empirical vagaries surrounding the constitution of madness that separated Hegel from such Romantic medical theories as those of John Brown. And it is in the space left open by these contingencies and vagaries that the labeling theory is best suited to operate.

Moreover, the accommodation of the labeling view would make Hegel's theory of madness more in tune with many of his larger philosophic commitments, such as his theory of recognition—that self-identity is crucially shaped by whom and how I am recognized as being, and by whom does the recognizing—and the primary importance he gives to the role of historical and cultural contexts for the specification or making concrete of such universal phenomenological structures of consciousness as reason and desire, and such basic human capacities as moral conscience, artistic creation, and religious sensibility.

As an ontology, Hegel's theory of madness is subtle, intricate, and capable of yielding new perspectives on a long list of themes which are central to his larger philosophic project: the nature of the mind-body relationship and the role of the unconscious, nature, and instinct within the life of spirit; the vicissitudes of desire, intentionality, and language; the place of despair, tragedy, and alienation in the world of human action; the nature of evil and guilt; and the dynamics of labor and historical being. More generally, Hegel's ontology of madness reveals a fascinating interplay between the nature and structures of 'normal' mental life and the mind which has sunk back into disease. Much of this interplay anticipates Freudian insights, and allows for the opening of an important dialogue between Hegel and psychoanalytic theory.

The argument of this last chapter has been that however sophisticated and intriguing Hegel's ontology of madness may be in its own right, we must rectify his silence about historical and cultural dimensions of the madness question by integrating a labeling perspective that seeks to uncover the role of social and political interests in the identification of certain behaviors as mentally ill. This would not be enough for the most radical labeling proponents, like Foucault and Szasz, for whom no compromise with ontology is possible. But for those who acknowledge the likelihood of an essential reality to madness in addition to the reality it has as a socially constituted phenomenon, such an integration of two levels of analysis should be welcome.

More, Hegel's philosophy seems a particularly welcoming home for this integrated approach. For all the innovative and creative power of Hegel's philosophy, it has an equal power in its remarkable spirit of unification and reconciliation. Hegel is tireless in his exposure of one-sidedness and exclusiveness, ingenious in his continual proposals for a unification of apparent opposites, and famous for the myriad of ways he seeks to demonstrate that truth is found only in the whole. We see this in the very position he developed for his theory of madness, a middle way between the polarities of the somatic/psychic and empirical/Romantic medicines of his day, a way of synthesis and reconciliation between positions which were trenchant in the rejection of their opposites. To correct Hegel's silence about the undeniable role of cultural factors in the definition and management of madness would thus not only be compatible with the commitment he makes in his larger philosophy to uncovering the crucial play of historical and social forces in the making concrete of ontological realities, but would reinforce the very spirit of synthesis which is one of the most telling and productive features of his philosophic vision.

Notes

1. Introduction

1. K. H. Scheidler, "Über das Verhältnis der Philosophie überhaupt und der Psychologie insbesondere zur Medicin," *Minerva Medica* 1 (1829): 245–46. Cited in Dietrich von Engelhardt, "Hegel's Philosophical Understanding of Illness," in R. S. Cohen and M. W. Wartofsky, eds., *Hegel and the Sciences* (Dordrecht, Holland: D. Reidel, 1984), 138n.

2. M. J. Petry writes of Boumann (1801–1871):

> His father was ennobled [by Frederick the Great], but Boumann himself relinquished the title, deeming it to be incompatible with the sedentary and retired life of a scholar and man of letters. He . . . studied languages and philosophy at Berlin University. In May 1827 he submitted *'De physiologia Platonis'* for his doctorate, and was backed by Hegel, but the classicists objected so violently that he subsequently decided to withdraw the thesis. He submitted *'Expositio Spinozismi'* in the August of 1827, again backed by Hegel, and despite complaints about the obscurity of the work, was eventually awarded his doctorate in August 1828. . . .
>
> A certain donnish ineptitude evidently prevented him from carving out a career for himself. He worked thoroughly, but slowly, and wrote very little—mainly articles on aesthetics and literature, but including the translation of a life of Marlborough.

Petry, *Hegel's Philosophy of Subjective Spirit*, 3 vols. (Dordrecht, Holland: D. Reidel, 1979), 2: 142.

3. On Boumann's method of compiling these additions, see his Foreword to the third volume (*Philosophie des Geistes*) of the *Encyclopædia*, HW 7: part 2, v–vii.

See also Petry's comments in his Introduction to *Hegel's Philosophy
of Subjective Spirit,* 1: cxi-cxv; and J. N. Findlay's Foreword to *Hegel's
Philosophy of Mind,* tr. W. Wallace (Oxford: Clarendon, 1978), vi.
Finally, see the "Note on the *Zusätze* to Hegel's Lectures" above, pp.
xv-xvii.

4. Von Engelhardt, 138n.

5. See Foucault's *Histoire de la Folie* (Paris: Librairie Plon, 1961) /
Madness and Civilization: A History of Insanity in the Age of Reason, tr. R.
Howard (New York: Random House, 1965); *Maladie Mentale et
Psychologie* (Paris: Presses Universitaires de France, 1962) / *Mental
Illness and Psychology,* tr. Alan Sheridan (Berkeley: University of
California Press, 1987); and *Naissance de la Clinique* (Paris: Presses
Universitaires de France, 1963) / *The Birth of the Clinic,* tr. A. M.
Sheridan Smith (New York: Random House, 1973).

See also Franz Alexander and Sheldon Selesnick, *The History of
Psychiatry* (New York: Harper, 1966); Robert Castel, *L'Ordre psychiatrique*
(Paris: Les Editions de Minuit, 1976) / *The Regulation of Madness,* tr. W. D.
Halls (Berkeley: University of California Press, 1988); Klaus Doerner,
Bürger und Irre (Europäische Verlagsanstalt, 1969) / *Madmen and the
Bourgeoisie,* tr. Joachim Neugroschel and Jean Steinberg (Oxford: Basil
Blackwell, 1981); Richard Hunter and Ida Macalpine, *Three Hundred Years
of Psychiatry, 1535–1860* (New York: Oxford University Press, 1963); Roy
Porter, *Social History of Madness* (New York: Dutton, 1989); George Rosen,
Madness in Society: Chapters in the Historical Sociology of Mental Illness
(Chicago: Chicago University Press, 1968); David Rothman, *The Discovery
of the Asylum: Social Order and Disorder in the New Republic* (Boston:
Little, Brown, 1971); and Andrew Scull, *Museums of Madness* (New York:
St. Martin's, 1979), and Scull, ed., *Madhouses, Mad-Doctors, and Madmen:
The Social History of Psychiatry in the Victorian Era* (Philadelphia:
University of Pennsylvania Press, 1981).

6. The exceptions are as follows. In 1930, Nathan Fialko published
"Hegel's Views on Mental Derangement" in the *Journal of Abnormal and
Social Psychology* 25, no. 2 (1930): 241–67. Fialko very loosely situates
Hegel in the context of eighteenth- and nineteenth-century psychiatry,
and argues (rather overambitiously, no doubt) that his theory of
Verrücktheit "contains . . all the ideas that modern psychiatry has
evolved" (263).

Darrel Christensen published two articles in 1968: "The Theory of
Mental Derangement and the Role and Function of Subjectivity in Hegel,"
The Personalist 49 (1968): 433–53, and "Hegel's Phenomenological
Analysis and Freud's Psychoanalysis," *International Philosophical
Quarterly* 8, no. 3 (1968): 356–78. In the first of his articles, Christensen is
concerned to show how Hegel's discussion of madness helps illuminate his

theory of subjectivity, and to defend Hegel against the common interpretation of his philosophy as downplaying the importance of subjective experience. In his second article, Christensen makes a number of interesting comparisons between Hegel and Freud, centering especially on the concepts of anxiety, the nature of evil, guilt, repression, projection, dream theory, transference, and the typology of mental disease.

Dietrich von Engelhardt (note 1 above) writes about Hegel's general theory of illness, and although he makes only passing remarks about mental illness, he is very helpful in his presentation of Hegel's position between the conflicting schools of medicine of his day.

Timo Airaksinen's 1989 article on "Insanity, Crime and the Structure of Freedom in Hegel" shows the close connections between Hegel's concepts of madness, wickedness, and crime. *Social Theory and Practice* 15 (1989): 155–78.

Finally, Alan M. Olson has included a chapter on Hegel's theory of madness in his very fine study of *Hegel and the Spirit: Philosophy as Pneumatology* (Princeton: Princeton University Press, 1992). He closely links Hegel's *Encyclopædia* discussion of madness with the insanity of Hegel's friend, the poet Friedrich Hölderlin, suggesting that Hegel's discussion is in part "an attempt to come to terms somehow with the fate of the poetic genius sunk into the dark night of his emotions," and that "Hölderlin provides Hegel with the exigent question for a detailed analysis of this topic" (96, 104). Olson situates Hegel's theory of madness within the larger context of his philosophy, and argues that Hegel's "persistent fear of Madness," as represented by his friend Hölderlin and his sister Christiane, also helps explain his "critique of the subjectivist Enlightenment" (12).

I have benefitted greatly from all of these essays, and will discuss them each in the course of this work. The major commentaries on Hegel give at most fleeting mention to the theme of madness.

7. W. T. Stace, *The Philosophy of Hegel* (New York: Dover, 1955), 336.

8. Darrel Christensen prefigures my claim. He writes that "Hegel's theory of mental disease provides a fresh and informative point of access to a number of themes within his philosophy" ("Theory of Mental Derangement," 433).

9. Christensen, "Hegel's Phenomenological Analysis and Freud's Psychoanalysis," 372, 376. Dietrich von Engelhardt makes a similar point when he says that for Hegel, "illnesses show the structure of reality in especially sharp relief, more so than does health" (130).

10. All references to Freud will be to the *Standard Edition of the Complete Psychological Works of Sigmund Freud,* 24 vols., ed. James Strachey (London: Hogarth, 1953ff); henceforth 'SE.' The present citation is from the metapsychological paper "On Narcissism," SE 14: 82.

2. Hegel's Place in Early Nineteenth Century Views of Madness

1. Petry (2: 578, 604, 623–24) and von Engelhardt (123–25, 137) make this point as well, Petry in passing, in some historical notes on the conflict between the 'somatic' and 'psychic' schools, and von Engelhardt more centrally, in his presentation of the conflict between empirical and Romantic medicine, although his focus is not so much on madness as on the general theory of illness. The present discussion is much indebted to both of these writers.

2. Fialko, 246.

3. See Foucault, *Madness and Civilization,* 40ff.

4. Royal Edict of 1656, article XII. Cited in Foucault, *Madness and Civilization,* 40.

5. Pinel, *A Treatise on Insanity,* tr. D. D. Davis (Sheffield: W. Todd, 1806), 4.

6. Cited in Doerner, 201.

7. Cited in Doerner, 142.

8. Cited in Kathleen Jones, *Lunacy, Law, and Conscience 1744–1845* (London: Routledge and Kegan Paul, 1955), 41–42, n 2. See also Ida MacAlpine and Richard Hunter, *George III and the Mad-Business* (London: Allen Lane, 1969).

Willis' manuscripts include a remark by George III which Willis puts down to delirium: "Sir," the King exclaimed, "I will never forgive you whilst I live." British Museum Add. mss. 41692–3; cited in Petry 2: 611. Willis became celebrated throughout Europe for his reputed cure of George III, and he subsequently treated Queen Maria of Portugal as well, although with less success (see Pinel, *Treatise on Insanity,* 55). Willis referred to his method as "moral management" (see Doerner, 74), and indeed Pinel cites him as an influence (Pinel, *Treatise,* 50, 184–5), while also lamenting certain "imperfections" in Willis' practices which are "inconsistent with the principles of a pure and rigid philanthropy" (65–66).

9. Ministère de l'intérieur et des cultes, *Législation sur les aliénés et les enfants assistés* (Paris, 1880), 1: 1. Cited in Castel, 1.

10. This phrase is taken from Jules-Philippe Falret's 1864 description of "the asylum that is suitably organized," *Des maladies mentales et des asiles d'aliénés* (Paris: Baillière, 1864), 685. Cited in Castel, 102.

11. Foucault, *Madness and Civilization,* 270 (my emphasis).

12. Doerner, 198–202, 252.

13. See Doerner, 49–50, 196.

14. Doerner, 234ff. Hegel, incidentally, corresponded with of many of these men.

15. See Doerner, 227–34.

16. "Ideen und Erfahrungen über den thierischen Magnetismus," and "Weitere Betrachtungen über den thierischen Magnetismus, und die Mittel ihn näher zu erforschen," in *Jahrbücher der Medicin als Wissenschaft,* ed. A. F. Marcus and F. W. J. Schelling (Tübingen, 1807), 2: 3–46, 158–90.

17. See Hegel's correspondence to his sister, *Hegel: The Letters,* tr. Clark Butler and Christiane Seiler (Bloomington: Indiana University Press, 1984), 406–22 (letters beginning April 9, 1814). See also Petry, 2: 561–63.

18. Doerner, 241.

19. See Werner Liebbrand, *Die spekulative Medizin der Romantik* (Hamburg: Claassen Verlag, 1956), 271–89; and Von Engelhardt, 127. See also pp. 29, 155, 191 below.

   For example, see Heinroth's *Lehrbuch der Störungen des Seelenlebens vom rationalen Standpunkt aus entworfen* (1818), and J. M. Leupoldt's *Allgemeinen Geschichte der Heilkunde* (1825).

20. See Von Engelhardt, 129; Doerner, 238–39; and Liebbrand, 282, 300ff.

21. Cited in Doerner, 202.

22. C. W. Hufeland, *System der practischen Heilkunde,* 2 vols. (Frankfurt, Leipzig, Jena: F. Frommann, 1800–05), 1: viii; A. F. Hecker, *Kunst, die Krankheiten der Menschen zu heilen* (Erfurt: Henning, 1804), v–vi; Candidus, "Nicht Anklage, sondern Klage," *Journal der practischen Heilkunde* 33 (1816): 110–16; and P. C. Hartmann, *Theorie der Krankheit* (Vienna: Gerold, 1823), 60. All citations are taken from von Engelhardt, 124–25.

23. Thomas Sydenham, *Works,* 2 vols., tr. R. G. Latham (London: Sydenham Society, 1848), 1: 13, 20; 2: 83–84. Cited in Esther Fischer-Homberger, "Eighteenth–Century Nosology and its Survivors," *Medical History* 14, no. 4 (1970): 397–98.

24. Locke, *De arte medica* (1669), Public Record Office, London 30/24/472. Cited in David E. Wolfe, "Sydenham and Locke on the Limits of Anatomy," *Bulletin of the History of Medicin* 35 (1961): 209. And see Kenneth Dewhurst, *John Locke, Physician and Philosopher: A Medical Biography with an Edition of the Medical Notes in His Journals* (London: Wellcome Historical Medical Library, 1963).

25. See Petry, 2: 604–5.

26. See Doerner, 154–55; and Liebbrand, 149ff, 167ff.

27. Castel, 91.

28. Doerner, 155.

29. Bayle, *Recherches sur les maladies mentales* (Paris, 1822), cited in Doerner, 156.

30. For example, Friedrich Bird and Wilhelm Richartz at Siegburg, Karl von Flemming at Sachsenberg, Karl Roller at Illenau, Baden, E. A. Zeller at Winnenthal, Württemberg, and Friedrich Nasse at Bonn. Zeller also edited the school's main periodical, *Zeitschrift für psychische Aerzte.* See Doerner, 257–58; and Petry, 2: 578.

31. Ideler, *Grundriss der Seelenheilkunde,* 2 vols. (Berlin: Enslin, 1835–38); cited in Doerner, 253.

32. Heinroth, *Lehrbuch der Störungen des Seelenlebens,* 2 vols. (Leipzig, 1818), 1: 179. Cited in Petry, 2: 579.

33. Cited in Liebbrand, 300.

34. Doerner, 212–13.

35. Harper, *Observations on Insanity* (London, 1790), 10. Cited in Petry, 2: 578–79.

36. For more on Hegel's critique of rational and empirical psychology, see Willem DeVries, *Hegel's Theory of Mental Activity: An Introduction to Theoretical Spirit* (Ithaca: Cornell University Press, 1988), 18–24.

37. See, for example, Paul Redding, "Absorbed in the Spectacle of the World: Hegel's Criticism of Romantic Historiography," *Clio* 16 (1987): 297–315; and Robert Solomon, *In the Spirit of Hegel: A Study of G. W. F. Hegel's Phenomenology of Spirit* (Oxford: Oxford University Press, 1983), 49–51, 96–97, 506–10.

38. Hegel, *Maximen des Journals der deutschen Literature,* in *Sämtliche Werke (Jubiläumsausgabe),* 4th ed., ed. H. Glockner (Stuttgard-Bad Cannstatt, 1965), 1: 545.

39. For more general discussions of Hegel's critique of 'formalism,' see Joseph Flay, *Hegel's Quest for Certainty* (Albany: State University of New York Press, 1984), 155–56; F. V. Freier, "Kritik der Hegelschen Formalismusthese," *Kantstudien* 83, no. 3 (1992): 304–23; Quentin Lauer, *A Reading of Hegel's Phenomenology of Spirit* (New York: Fordham University Press, 1976), 290–93; and Sally Sedgwick, "On the Relation of Pure Reason to Content: A Reply to Hegel's Criticism of Formalism in Kant's Ethics," *Philosophy and Phenomenological Research* 49 (1988): 59–80.

40. Freud, *Introductory Lectures on Psycho-Analysis*, SE 16: 260.

41. Cited without reference in George Brett, *A History of Psychology* (London: Allen & Unwin, 1921), 3: 93.

42. *Letters*, 565 (letter of April 11, 1824).

43. Petry, 2: 624.

44. Pinel, 2–3, 134.

45. For more on Hegel's typology of madness, see Darrel Christensen, "Hegel's Phenomenological Analysis," and Alan Olson, *Hegel and the Spirit*, 98–100.

46. Kant, *Anthropologie in pragmatischer Hinsicht* (1798), in *Werke*, 6 vols., ed. Wilhelm Weischedel (Frankfurt am Main: Wissenschaftliche Buchgesellschaft Darmstadt, 1960–64), 6: 395–690. Cited in Doerner, 185–86.

47. Adolf Meyer, "A Few Trends in Modern Psychiatry," *The Psychological Bulletin* 1 (1904): 217–40. Cited in Fialko, 255.

48. Von Engelhardt, 124, 125.

49. Thomas Bole, "John Brown, Hegel, and Speculative Concepts in Medicine," *Texas Reports on Biology and Medicine* 32, no. 1 (1974): 292.

50. Bole, 289–92.

51. Crawford Elder gives an interesting account of the Hegelian solution to the mind–body problem, although he concentrates on the *Logic*, in his *Appropriating Hegel* (Aberdeen University Press, 1980). See also Elder, "Hegel's Teleology and the Relation between Mind and Brain," *Southern Journal of Philosophy* 17 (1979): 27–45; Errol Harris, "Hegel's Theory of Feeling," in Warren E. Steinkraus, ed., *New Studies in Hegel's Philosophy* (New York: Holt, Rinehart and Winston, 1971): 77–78, 81; John McCumber, "A Mind-Body Problem in Hegel's *Phenomenology of Spirit*," *International Studies in Philosophy* 12 (1980): 41–52; Stefano Poggi, "Mind and Brain in Medical Thought During the Romantic Period," *History and Philosophy of the Life Sciences* 10 (1988): 41–53; and Michael Wolff, *Das Körper-Seele Problem* (Frankfurt am Main: Klostermann, 1992).

52. Cited in Petry, 2: 580.

53. Pinel, *Philosophie de l'homme aliené;* cited in Fialko, 245.

54. Pinel, *Treatise on Insanity*, 5.

55. Murray Greene gives a very helpful account of Hegel's theory of the soul in his *Hegel on the Soul: A Speculative Anthropology* (The Hague:

Martinus Nijhoff, 1972). See also Errol Harris, "Hegel's Theory of Feeling."

56. Freud, *The Interpretation of Dreams*, SE 5: 613, 620; and *Introductory Lectures*, SE 16: 368.

57. Freud, *Introductory Lectures*, SE 16: 368, 359.

58. Darrel Christensen argues that Hegel's notion of the "soul" is in many respects analogous to Freud's concept of "libido": "the two concepts contain . . . the notion of a center and core of the mind's life which determines or becomes attached to definite feeling content." "Hegel's Phenomenological Analysis," 361–62.

59. Freud, *Introductory Lectures*, SE 15: 88.

60. Foucault, *Madness and Civilization*, 94, 103–4.

61. Cited in Foucault, *Madness and Civilization*, 103.

62. Kant, *Gesammelte Schriften*, 23 vols., Preussische Akademie der Wissenschaften edition (Berlin: Georg Reimer, 1902–55), 2: 265. Kant published the *Versuch über die Krankheiten des Kopfes* in the *Königsberger Zeitung* in 1764.

63. "Das zweite Gesicht," *Archiv für den thierischen Magnetismus* (Leipzig and Halle, 1817–24), 6: 93–94.

64. As, for example, in the writings of Heinrich Damerov, Ludwig Friedländer, Johann Heinroth, Karl Richard Hoffmann, Friedrich Jahn, J. M. Leupoldt, Lorenz Oken, Christian Reil, Karl Wilhelm Stark, and R. W. Volz.

65. *Rapport des commissaires chargés par le Roi de l'examen du magnétisme animal* (Paris, 1784). Cited in Petry, 2: 505; and see Doerner, 110. See also *Rapport des commissaires de la Société Royale de Médecine, nommés par le Roi pour faire l'examen du magnétisme animal* (Paris, 1784).

For attacks on the Franklin and Royal Society of Medicine reports, see Jean-Baptiste Bonnefoy, *Analyse raisonnée des rapports des commissaires chargés par le Roi de l'examen du magnétisme animal* (Lyons: Prault, 1784), and J.-M.-A. Servan, *Doutes d'un provincial proposés à MM. les médecins commissaires chargés par le Roi de l'examen du magnétisme animal* (Lyons: Prault, 1784). These reports are summarized and discussed in Alexandre Bertrand, *Du magnétisme animal en France, . . . avec le texte des divers rapports faits en 1784 par les commissaires de l'Academie des sciences, de la Faculté et de la Société royale de médecine . . .* (Paris: J. B. Baillière, 1826); A. Binet and C. Féré, *Animal Magnetism* (London: D. Appleton, 1888); Robert Darnton, *Mesmerism and the End of the Enlightenment in France* (New York: Schocken Books, 1970); and

Frank Podmore, *From Mesmerism to Christian Science* (New York: University Books, 1963).

66. "Mesmerismus oder System der Wechselwirkungen," and "Erläuterungen zum Mesmerismus" (Berlin: Rikolais, 1814, 1815); "Report of the Experiments on Animal Magnetism made by a Committee of the Medical Section of the French Royal Academy of Sciences" (Paris, 1831). Cited in Petry, 2: 505.

67. Doerner, 110.

68. Doerner, 110.

69. Hegel discusses water divining in his *Encyclopædia*, PM § 406 and PN § 371. For Hegel's correspondence with Schelling and others on this topic, see Petry 2: 517–19.

70. See Doerner, 197; and Karl Jaspers, *Schelling: Grösse und Verhängnis* (Munich: Piper, 1955), 16.

71. Puységur, *Du magnetisme animal, considéré dans ses rapports avec diverses branches de la physique générale* (Paris: Desenne 1807), 8. See also Puységur's *Mémoires pour servir à l'histoire et à l'établissement du magnétisme animal* (Bayonne: [n. p.], 1784). Puységur's dates are 1751–1825.

72. *Letters,* 590 (letter of October 15, 1810).

73. Freud, "Review of August Forel's Hypnotism," SE 1: 97.

74. See Ernest Jones, *The Life and Work of Sigmund Freud,* 3 vols. (New York: Basic Books, 1953), 1: 207–220. See also Freud, "Report on my Studies in Paris and Berlin," SE 1: 5–15; "Preface to the Translation of Bernheim's Suggestion," SE 1: 75–85; "Review of August Forel's Hypnotism," SE 1: 91–102; "Hypnotism," SE 1: 103–14; and "A Case of Successful Treatment by Hypnotism," SE 1: 117–28.

75. Freud, "Preface to the Translation of Bernheim's Suggestion," SE 1: 75.

76. This 'hence' needs some thinking through. Hegel believes he can account for the bizarre phenomena of the magnetic state on the level of theory, since his analysis of the abeyance of the conditions pertaining to normal perceptual life entailed by the reversion to the domain of the unconscious allows us to conceive of alternative states of perception (perhaps on the model of 'dream–work'). But Hegel never claimed to possess an explanation of these magnetic phenomena on the level of physiology—that is, an account of the actual sensory processes by which one could see without light or perceive smells or tastes experienced by the magnetizer. He was convinced that these phenomena actually occurred, but left it to empirical research eventually to discover the physical mechanisms which underlay them. His claim that only speculative philosophy could explain the magnetic state is thus a claim for a theoretical explanation only.

3. Madness as the Decentering of Reason

1. Darrel Christensen also makes this connection when he speaks of how "Hegel's theory of mental disease [is] a useful, and, for the most part, neglected point of access to his phenomenological method." "Hegel's Phenomenological Analysis and Freud's Psychoanalysis," 356–7.

2. *Intelligenzblatt der Jenaischen Allgemeinen Litteraturzeitung,* October 28, 1807. Cited in Walter Kaufmann, ed. and tr., *Hegel: Texts and Commentary* (Garden City, New York: Doubleday, 1965), 4. See also Hegel, W 3: 593.

3. *Intelligenzblatt,* cited in Petry, 3: 361.

4. Quentin Lauer gives a very helpful discussion of Hegel's use of phenomenology in "Phenomenology: Hegel and Husserl," in Frederick Weiss, ed., *Beyond Epistemology: New Studies in the Philosophy of Hegel* (The Hague: Nijhoff, 1975): 174–96. For other comparisons with Husserl, see J. N. Mohanty, *The Possibility of Transcendental Philosophy* (*Phaenomenologica,* vol. 98) (Dordrecht: Martinus Nijhoff, 1985); and Robert R. Williams, *Recognition: Fichte and Hegel on the Other* (Albany: State University of New York Press, 1992), 6–10, 96–103, 285–301.

5. *Intelligenzblatt,* cited in Kaufmann, *Texts and Commentary,* 4–5. See Hegel, W 3: 593.

6. Darrel Christensen, in his article on "Hegel's Phenomenological Analysis and Freud's Psychoanalysis," gives a nice summary of Hegel's typology and its similarities to Freud's three–fold distinction between hysteria, obsessional neurosis, and "mental conflict" (*Konfliktbildung*—i.e., schizophrenia or psychosis). See 373–76.

7. Freud, *The Interpretation of Dreams,* SE 5: 612, 620.

8. The status of language in madness will be discussed in chapters 5 and 6.

9. Jean Hyppolite, "Hegel's Phenomenology and Psychoanalysis," tr. Albert Richer, in Steinkraus, *New Studies,* 70. For an interesting commentary on Hyppolite's article, see Alphonse De Waelhens, "Réflexions sur une problématique Husserlienne de l'inconscient, Husserl et Hegel," in *Edmund Husserl 1859–1959* (*Phaenomenologica* 4), La Haye: Martinus Nijhoff, 1959: 221–37. De Waelhens compares Hegel's notion of an unconscious (very much following Hyppolite's grounding of the unconscious in the 'natural consciousness') with Husserlian phenomenology and psychoanalytic theory.

10. See, e.g., *Introductory Lectures,* SE 15: 88.

11. Recall Foucault's discussion mentioned in chapter 2 of how com-

monly authors of this period saw madness as "the night of the mind," where the self is "confiscated" by the world of dreams. *Madness and Civilization,* 93–104.

12. See Petry, 2: 503.

13. Christensen, "Hegel's Phenomenological Analysis and Freud's Psychoanalysis," 372.

14. Hyppolite, "Hegel's Phenomenology and Psychoanalysis," 59, 60.

15. The unhappy consciousness is the "grief and longing [which] . . . permeates [all the shapes of consciousness], and is the center and common birth–pang" of all mind (PS 456–57).

Jean Wahl, in his *Le malheur de la conscience dans la philosophie de Hegel* (Paris: Presses Universitaires de France, 1951), first published in 1911, was the first of many to argue for the centrality of the unhappy consciousness in Hegel's philosophy. Hyppolite also claims that the "unhappy consciousness is the fundamental theme of the *Phenomenology*." *Genesis and Structure of Hegel's Phenomenology of Spirit,* tr. Samuel Cherniak and John Heckman (Evanston: Northwestern University Press, 1974), 190.

16. Jean Hyppolite uses this same image of self–escape in describing the despairing self as engaged in a "continuous escape from oneself" (*Genesis,* 203). Hyppolite's whole discussion of the unhappy consciousness is well worth reading (190–215). For other important commentaries, see Eugen Fink, *Hegel* (Frankfurt–am–Main: Vittorio Klostermann, 1977), 179–201; Flay, 101–11; Findlay, *Hegel: A Re-examination* (London: George Allen & Unwin, 1958), 100–103; Murray Greene, "Hegel's 'Unhappy Consciousness' and Nietzsche's 'Slave Morality,' " in Darrel Christensen, ed., *Hegel and the Philosophy of Religion* (The Hague: Martinus Nijhoff, 1970): 125–41; Alexandre Kojève, *Introduction to the Reading of Hegel,* tr. James Nichols (Ithaca: Cornell University Press, 1980), 55ff; Lauer, *A Reading,* 117–24; Philippe Muller, "Connaissance concrète de l'homme chez Hegel," *Studia philosophica* 30–31 (1970–1971): 207–24; Stanley Rosen, *Hegel: An Introduction to the Science of Wisdom* (New Haven: Yale University Press, 1974), 151–82; Solomon, *In the Spirit,* 465–70; Jon Steward, "Die Rolle des unglücklichen Bewusstseins in Hegels *Phänomenologie des Geistes,*" *Deutsche Zeitschrift für Philosophie* 39, no. 1 (1991): 12–21; Charles Taylor, *Hegel* (Cambridge: Cambridge University Press, 1977), 57–59, 159–61, 206–8, 497–8; and Donald Phillip Verene, *Hegel's Recollection: A Study of Images in the Phenomenology of Spirit* (Albany: State University of New York Press, 1985), 70–79.

17. Sartre, *Being and Nothingness,* tr. Hazel Barnes (New York: Washington Square Press, 1973), 707.

18. Hyppolite, *Genesis,* 189.

19. Kojève, 55.

20. Rosen, 151–52.

21. See also Alan Olson: "one is not *at home* in one's madness; indeed, it is precisely *not–being–at–home* that makes the condition of madness the deformed, visible sign that something is wrong." Olson, *Hegel and the Spirit,* 102.

22. Freud, *Introductory Lectures,* SE 16: 457.

23. Freud, *Introductory Lectures,* SE 16: 358.

24. Hyppolite, "Hegel's Phenomenology and Psychoanalysis," 64, 66.

25. See pp. 85, 124.

26. Hyppolite, *Genesis,* 181.

27. Flay, 99.

28. Rosen, 167: "Stoicism, then, is the first effort of the slave to transform himself into a master, but by *dreaming,*" insofar as it is the position of "thought separated from life."

29. For commentaries on Hegel's view of stoicism, see Findlay, 98–99; Hyppolite, *Genesis,* 179–84; Kojève, 53–54; Rosen, 154–55, 164–72; Solomon, 457–61; and Taylor, *Hegel,* 157–59.

30. Kojève, 54.

31. Hegel in fact associates skepticism with ancient comedy, which seeks to show the vanity of all value outside itself. See Hyppolite's discussion of skepticism on this point (*Genesis,* 184–89); also William Desmond, *Beyond Hegel and Dialectic: Speculation, Cult, and Comedy* (Albany: State University of New York Press, 1992), 279–81.

32. For commentaries on Hegel's view of skepticism, see Findlay, 99–100; Michael N. Forster, *Hegel and Scepticism* (Cambridge, MA: Harvard University Press, 1989); Hyppolite, *Genesis,* 184–89; Kojève, 54–55; Rosen, 164–72, 178–79; Heinz Röttges, *Dialektik und Skeptizismus* (Frankfurt: Athenaum, 1987); Solomon 461–65; and Robert Williams, "Hegel and Skepticism," *Owl of Minerva* 24, no. 1 (1992): 71–82.

33. Rosen, 152.

34. Kierkegaard, *Concluding Unscientific Postscript,* tr. David Swenson and Walter Lowrie (Princeton: Princeton University Press, 1968), 100, 375–6.

35. Foucault, *Madness and Civilization,* ix.

36. Aristotle, *Physics* 220a27.

37. William Desmond, *Beyond Hegel and Dialectic*, 11.

38. Robert Williams, *Recognition: Fichte and Hegel on the Other* (Albany: State University of New York Press, 1992), 142, 150.

39. Williams, 155.

40. Desmond, 113–14.

41. Desmond, 114. We will return to this idea in chapter 4, in the context of Wilfried Ver Eecke's critique of Hegel's purported indifference to what Ver Eecke calls "failed" forms of consciousness. See p. 85 below.

42. Desmond, 218.

43. Desmond, 232.

44. See, for example, Hegel's 1812 letter to his friend Friedrich Niethammer (who in 1808 had appointed Hegel to the rectorship of a gymnasium in Nuremberg), speaking of the death of his daughter shortly after her birth. Hegel speaks of his "double" suffering, from the pain of the loss, and the pain of his wife's suffering. See also Hegel's 1831 letter, just weeks before his death, to his friend Heinrich Beer, who had just lost a son. Hegel describes his own "incalculable pain" on learning of "the crushing blow of misfortune" his friend has suffered; he "lament[s] with [Beer] such an irreparable loss"; and offers to "hold your hand in the depth of a pain borne of friendship." *Letters*, 270–72.

45. Desmond, 237.

46. Foucault, *Madness and Civilization*, x–xi.

47. Hegel, *Letters*, 414.

48. See Olson, *Hegel and the Spirit*, 100.

49. *Letters*, 407–8, letter of April 9, 1814.

50. See Karl Rosenkranz, *G. W. F. Hegels Leben* (Berlin: Duncker und Humblot Verlag, 1844; reprint, Darmstadt: Wissenschaftliche Buchgesellschaft, 1977).

51. Kierkegaard, *Postscript*, 109.

52. See Martin Brecht, "Hölderlin und das Tübinger Stift 1788–1793," *Hölderlin-Jahrbuch* 18 (1973–74): 20–48; Wilhelm Michel, *Das Leben Freidrich Hölderlins* (Frankfurt am Main: Insel Verlag, 1967); Rosenkranz, *Hegels Leben*; and Emil Staiger, *Der Geist der Liebe und das Schicksal: Schelling, Hegel und Hölderlin* (Frauenfeld: Huber, 1935).

For studies of the intellectual and philosophic connections between Hölderlin and Hegel, see Ernst Cassirer, "Hölderlin und der Deutsche Idealismus," in *Idee und Gestalt* (Darmstadt: Wissenschaftliche

Buchgesellschaft, 1971): 113–56; Wilhelm Dilthey, "Friedrich Hölderlin," in *Das Erlebnis und die Dichtung,* 14th ed. (Göttingen: Vandenhoeck und Ruprecht, 1965): 242–317; Klaus Düsing, *Das Problem der Subjektivität in Hegel's Logik* (Bonn: Bouvier, 1976); Dieter Henrich, "Hegel und Hölderlin," in *Hegel im Kontext* (Frankfurt: Suhrkamp, 1971): 9–40; and Otto Pöggeler, "Hegel's Jugendschriften und die Idee einer Phänomenologie des Geistes" (Habilitation, Heidelberg, 1966).

53. See Adolf Beck, ed., *Hölderlins Diotima, Susette Gontard* (Frankfurt: Insel Verlag, 1980).

54. For descriptions of Hölderlin's life in the *Turm,* see *Hölderlin: Sämtliche Werke,* 7 vols., ed. Friedrich Beissner and Adolf Beck (Stuttgart: Kohlhammer, Cotta, 1943ff) (the *Grosse Stuttgarter Hölderlin-Ausgabe*), vol. 7.

55. Wilhelm Lange, *Hölderlin: Eine Pathographie* (Stuttgart: Enke, 1909). See also Helm Stierlin, "Lyrical Creativity and Schizophrenic Psychosis as Reflected in Friedrich Hölderlin's Fate," in Emery E. George, ed., *Friedrich Hölderlin, An Early Modern* (Ann Arbor: The University of Michigan Press, 1972): 192–215; Rudolf Treichler, "Die seelische Erkrankung Friedrich Hölderlins in ihren Beziehungen zu seinem dichterischen Schaffen," *Zeitschrift für die gesamte Neurologie und Psychiatrie* 155 (1936): 40–144; and Stephan Wackwitz, *Friedrich Hölderlin* (Stuttgart: J. B. Metzlersche Verlagsbuchhandlung, 1985), 43–46. Exceptions are very few. Pierre Bertaux's biography of Hölderlin follows the anti–psychiatric perspective of people like R. D. Laing, David Cooper, and Thomas Szasz, and argues that Hölderlin's purported schizophrenia was only a "mask" and "metaphor" for a way of living he chose in resistance to the bourgeois order: *Friedrich Hölderlin* (Frankfurt am Main: Suhrkamp, 1978). Alan Olson speculatively suggests that Hölderlin may have suffered from Alzheimer's disease (Olson, 86).

56. See Olson, 84; and Johannes Hoffmeister, ed., *Briefe von und an Hegel,* 4 vols. (Hamburg: Felix Meiner, 1952–81), 1: letters 38, 97.

57. Hölderlin, *Sämtliche Werke,* 7 vols., ed. Friedrich Beissner and Adolf Beck (Stuttgart: Kohlhammer, Cotta, 1943ff), 4: 129. The translation is by Stierlin (212). The original reads:

> Und wagtest dich ins Heiligtum des Abgrunds,
> Wo duldend vor dem Tage sich das Herz
> Der Erde birgt und ihre Schmerzen dir
> Die dunkle Mutter sagt, o du der Nacht
> Des Aethers Sohn! ich folgte dir hinunter.

58. Christoph Jamme, "Hegel and Hölderlin," tr. Richard Findler and Clark Butler, *Clio* 15 (1986): 375.

59. Olson, 85.

60. Olson, 104, 96.

61. Olson, 100.

62. Olson, 89.

63. Olson, 12, 104–5.

64. Olson, 12.

65. Kant, *Critique of Pure Reason,* tr. Norman Kemp Smith (London: Macmillan, 1973), B xxx.

66. See note 44 above to *Letters,* 270–72.

67. For a fuller treatment of Hegel's idealism as animated by the theme of the quest for unity in the midst of discord, see Daniel Berthold-Bond, *Hegel's Grand Synthesis: A Study of Being, Thought, and History* (Albany: State University of New York Press, 1989).

68. Robert Pippin, *Hegel's Idealism: The Satisfactions of Self-Consciousness* (Cambridge: Cambridge University Press, 1989). See especially 8, 35, 93, 98, 99, 131, 149, 157, 186, 187, 229, 230, and 252 for Pippin's claim that Hegel's idealism involves the rejection of realism. Kenneth Westphal offers an important criticism of Pippin's claim in "Hegel, Idealism, and Robert Pippin," *International Philosophical Quarterly* 33, no. 3 (1993): 263–72, while in the same issue of IPQ Pippin responds, reasserting the merits of his "anti-realist" Hegel (285-95). Both articles were originally presented at a symposium at the Central Division Meeting of the American Philosophical Association in Chicago, April 1992.

69. Kenneth Westphal, *Hegel's Epistemological Realism* (Dordrecht, Holland: Kluwer, 1989). See my review of this book in *The Review of Metaphysics* 45, no. 1 (1991): 157–8.

70. In *Hegel's Grand Synthesis,* 57–63.

71. See also Kojève, 150–58. Kojève claims that "Hegelian absolute idealism has nothing to do with what is ordinarily called 'idealism.' And if terms are used in their usual senses, it must be said that Hegel's system is 'realist'" (150). I discuss this claim of Kojève's in *Hegel's Grand Synthesis,* 61–63.

72. Albert Camus, "An Absurd Reasoning," in *The Myth of Sisyphus and Other Essays,* tr. Justin O'Brien (New York: Random House, 1955), 5, 21.

73. Georg Lukács, *The Young Hegel: Studies in the Relations between Dialectics and Economics,* tr. Rodney Livingstone (Cambridge, MA: MIT Press, 1975), 477.

74. Kojève, 51, 53.

4. Madness and the Second Face of Desire

1. See especially Donald Phillip Verene's book, *Hegel's Recollection.* See also Daniel Berthold-Bond, *Hegel's Grand Synthesis,* 109–12, 135–44.

2. Rosen, 139.

3. Kierkegaard, *The Sickness Unto Death,* tr. Walter Lowrie (Princeton: Princeton University Press, 1974), 158.

4. For the relation between consciousness and self-consciousness, see *Hegel's Grand Synthesis,* 57–58, 61–63, 134.

There are many fine discussions of the role of desire in the transition from consciousness to self-consciousness, and I have relied on all of the following: Judith Butler, *Subjects of Desire: Hegelian Reflections in Twentieth-Century France* (New York: Columbia University Press, 1987), 24–35; Joseph Flay, 80, 170, 228; Hans-Georg Gadamer, *Hegel's Dialectic: Five Hermeneutical Studies,* tr. P. Christopher Smith (New Haven: Yale University Press, 1976), 54ff; Martin Heidegger, *Hegel's Phenomenology of Spirit,* tr. Parvis Emad and Kenneth Maly (Indianapolis: Indiana University Press, 1980), 131–36; Jean Hyppolite, *Genesis and Structure,* 143ff; Pierre-Jean Labarrière, *Structures et mouvement dialectique dans la Phénoménologie de l'esprit de Hegel* (Paris: Aubier-Montaigne, 1968), 76–80; Quentin Lauer, *A Reading,* 90–97; and Herbert Marcuse, *Reason and Revolution: Hegel and the Rise of Social Theory* (Boston: Beacon, 1969), 112–13.

5. Jacques Lacan, *Écrits: A Selection,* tr. Alan Sheridan (New York: Norton, 1977), 307.

6. Lacan, *Écrits,* 301, 302.

7. Judith Butler presents a very thoughtful reading of Lacan's critique of Hegel in *Subjects of Desire,* 186–204.

8. Freud, "On Narcissism: An Introduction," SE 14: 100 (emphasis added).

9. Freud, "On Narcissism," SE 14: 75.

10. Freud, "Instincts and Their Vicissitudes," SE 14: 136.

11. Parmenides, "The Way of Truth," in Kathleen Freeman, ed., *Ancilla to the Pre-Socratic Philosophers* (Cambridge, MA: Harvard University Press, 1957), 43–44.

12. Hyppolite also makes this point: "the end point of desire is . . . the unity of the I with itself." *Genesis,* 160.

13. Butler, 25, 34. See also Flay, 81: "Desire is always interest in some-

thing other than itself"; and Hyppolite, *Genesis,* 158: "The movement of self-consciousness, without which it would not exist, requires otherness."

14. See Rosen, 30: "We become alienated from ourselves or regard our true self as contained in the object outside us, which we desire to assimilate. Desire is thus fundamentally desire for myself . . . from which I have become detached"; Lauer, *A Reading,* 94: "appetition [desire] is a mode of consciousness which does in fact aim at the assimilation and, thus, the gradual negation of its object"; and Kojève, 37–38: "Now what is Desire . . . but the desire to *transform* the contemplated thing by an action, to overcome it in its being that is unrelated to mine and independent of me, to *negate* it in its independence, and to assimilate it to myself, to make it *mine,* to absorb it in and by my I?"

15. Kojève, 40.

16. Freud, "On Narcissism," SE 14: 100. We may note that Freud describes the original state of inwardness as one in which there is a primitive identification of the external as "the bad" (*das Schlechte*): "What is bad, what is alien to the ego and what is external are, to begin with, identical." *Negation,* SE 19: 237. Jean Hyppolite develops a highly provocative interpretation of this idea in his contribution to one of Jacques Lacan's seminars on Freud: "A Spoken Commentary on Freud's *Verneinung,*" in Jacques-Alain Miller, ed., *The Seminar of Jacques Lacan, Book I: Freud's Papers on Technique 1953–1954,* tr. John Forrester (New York: Norton, 1988): 289–97. The paper was originally published as "Commentaire parlée sur la *Verneinung* de Freud," *La Psychanalyse* 1 (1956): 29–40, and reprinted as an Appendix to Lacan's *Écrits.*

17. This is seen most clearly in traumatic neurosis and obsessional neurosis. See *Beyond the Pleasure Principle,* SE 18: 12–17, 29–30.

18. For example, in many children's games and in all dreams. Again, see *Beyond the Pleasure Principle,* SE 18: 7–11, 17, 26–27, 29–30.

19. Freud, *Beyond the Pleasure Principle,* SE 18: 62, 38.

20. Freud, *Introductory Lectures,* SE 15: 88.

21. Butler, 37. For the association of destruction with consuming and assimilating, see also Kojève, 37–38; and Howard Kainz, *Hegel's Phenomenology, Part I* (University, Alabama: University of Alabama Press, 1976), 120.

Hyppolite compares Freud's notion of 'negation' to the Hegelian master/slave dialectic by way of making a distinction between negation and destruction: in the master/slave dialectic, "the issue becomes that of substituting genuine negativity for that destructive appetite which takes hold of desire" in the life and death struggle. Hence for Hegel (and Hyppolite argues this holds for Freud as well), it is crucial not to reduce all negation to destruction: "to deny is more than to wish to destroy." Hyppolite, "Commentary on Freud's *Verneinung,*" 292–3.

22. See Eugen Fink's discussion of asceticism, *Hegel,* 199.

23. Judith Butler, in her excellent discussion of Jean Hyppolite's reading of Hegel, suggests that "Hyppolite has engaged Freud's vision . . . that all desire is in some sense inspired by a fundamental striving toward death." I follow her in believing that Hegel's position is more optimistic: "death is not an absolute negation [for Hegel], but a determinate one which establishes the boundaries of a new beginning" (91).

For some interesting comments on the role of desire in Hegel and Freud, see Wilfried Ver Eecke, "Negation and Desire in Freud and Hegel," *Owl of Minerva* 15 (1983): 11–22.

24. Martin Luther, "Lectures on Romans," in *The Library of Christian Classics,* tr. and ed. by Wilhelm Pauck (Philadelphia: Westminster, 1961), 15: 42, 240, 331.

25. See Deleuze's *Anti-Oedipus: Capitalism and Schizophrenia,* tr. Robert Hurley, Mark Seem, and Helen R. Lane (New York: Viking Press, 1977), and *Nietzsche and Philosophy,* tr. Hugh Tomlinson (New York: Columbia University Press, 1983).

26. Wilfried Ver Eecke, *Saying "No": Its Meaning in Child Development, Linguistics, and Hegel* (Pittsburgh: Duquesne University Press, 1984), 159.

27. See, for example, Kojève, 145, 148, 259 (n41); Lukács, 462, 519; Solomon, 638–39; Merold Westphal, *History and Truth in Hegel's Phenomenology* (Atlantic Highlands, New Jersey: Humanities, 1979), 221–23. And see Heinrich Heine, *Werke,* ed. Ernst Elster (Leipzig: Bibliographisches Institut, 1922), 4: 148–49:

> *Ich habe hinter dem Maëstro* [Hegel] *gestanden, als er sie* [die Musik des Atheismus] *komponierte, freilich in sehr undeutlichen und verschnörkelten zeichen, damit nicht jeder sie entziffre—ich sah manchmal, wie er sich ängstlich umschaute, aus Furcht, man verstände ihn.*

> (I stood behind the maestro as he composed [the music of atheism], though in very obscure and ornate signs so that not everyone could decipher them—I sometimes saw him anxiously looking over his shoulder, in fear that he had been understood.)

28. W. H. Werkmeister, "Hegel's Phenomenology of Mind as a Development of Kant's Basic Ontology," in Christensen, *Hegel and the Philosophy of Religion,* 102. See also Stephen Crites, *In the Twilight of Christendom: Hegel vs. Kierkegaard on Faith and History* (Chambersburg,

Pennsylvania: American Academy of Religion, 1972), 41; Quentin Lauer, *Essays in Hegelian Dialectic* (New York: Fordham University Press, 1977), 12; and J. Hutchison Sterling, *The Secret of Hegel* (New York: Putnam's, 1898), xxii.

29. All further quotations from Hegel regarding the Fall in this chapter will be from this passage from the *Zusatz* to § 24 of the *Encyclopædia*.

30. Karl Löwith, "History and Christianity," in Robert W. Bretall and Charles W. Kegley, eds., *Reinhold Niebuhr: His Religious, Social, and Political Thought* (New York: MacMillan, 1961): 283.

31. Reinhold Niebuhr, *The Nature and Destiny of Man: A Christian Interpretation* (New York: Scribner's, 1941, 1943), 2: 288 (and see Chapter X, passim). Niebuhr also expresses this view in his *Faith and History: A Comparison of Christian and Modern Views of History* (New York: Scribner's, 1949).

32. Herbert Marcuse discusses the absence of history in 'nature' in *Hegel's Ontology and the Theory of Historicity,* tr. Seyla Benhabib (Cambridge, MA: MIT Press, 1987), 254.

33. For Hegel's critique of Rousseau's notion of the 'state of nature,' see PR § 194. Shlomo Avineri comments perceptively on this critique in *Hegel's Theory of the Modern State* (Cambridge: Cambridge University Press, 1972), 145.

34. Foucault, *Madness and Civilization,* 266.

5. Madness and the Unconscious

1. Freud, *An Autobiographical Study,* SE 20: 31.

2. Nietzsche, *Beyond Good and Evil,* in Walter Kaufmann, ed., *The Basic Writings of Nietzsche* (New York: Random House, 1968), Preface, § 2.

3. Clark Butler, in his edition of Hegel's *Letters,* 407.

4. Errol Harris, "Hegel's Theory of Feeling," 88. See also p. 83: "the great contribution of [Hegel's] theory of feeling, in a measure anticipating Freud," is "the recognition by Hegel of a subconscious psychic life." See also Alan Olson: "By locating the possibility of madness in the . . . 'featureless abyss' of the 'feeling soul,' Hegel anticipated by a hundred years Freud's and Jung's theories of the unconscious" (95).

5. DeVries, 73, 74.

6. Freud, *New Introductory Lectures,* SE 22: 70.

7. Freud, *New Introductory Lectures,* SE 22: 70.

8. Darrel Christensen believes that there is nothing in Hegel resembling Freud's concept of repression ("Hegel's Phenomenological Analysis and Freud's Psychoanalysis," 369, 378). I am not convinced of this, however. I would certainly agree that Hegel does not elaborate an account of the mechanisms by which, as Freud says, "repression proceeds from the ego," so that the ego excludes (rejects, censors) instinctual impulses which are "unwelcome" to consciousness (*Inhibitions, Symptoms, and Anxiety,* SE 20: 91). On the other hand, Hegel's account of madness as the flight of consciousness from painful encounters anticipates Freud's most basic definition of repression: "repression," he says, "is fundamentally an attempt at flight" (*Inhibitions, Symptoms, and Anxiety,* SE 20: 153).

Two other key elements of Freud's idea of repression are also found in Hegel: first, repression operates by way of forcing instincts back along the "path of regression" to archaic psychic formations of the unconscious (e.g. *Interpretation of Dreams,* SE 5: 548); and second, when "the repressed instinctual impulse becomes isolated" or "fixed" in the unconscious, it henceforth "goes its own way," uninfluenced by the parameters of the reality principle (*The Question of Lay Analysis,* SE 20: 203). Hegel's emphasis on regression, on the imprisonment and fixation of the soul in primitive unconscious feeling-states, and on the corresponding separation from reality, all suggests at least a general compatibility of his theory with Freud's idea of repression.

Jean Hyppolite's discussion of Freudian 'negation' as an *Aufhebung* of repression in his "Commentary on Freud's *Verneinung*" also seems to support the idea of a close connection between Hegel and Freud on the nature of repression (see 291).

9. As mentioned in a previous note, Christensen suggests that Hegel's notion of "soul" is actually quite close to Freud's "libido": "the two concepts both contain . . . the notion of a center and core of the mind's life which determines or becomes attached to definite feeling content. . . . Freud's account of the *attachment* of libido to an erogenous zone may be seen to be roughly parallel to Hegel's soul as an abstract identity determining a content for itself at the level of feeling." "Hegel's Phenomenological Analysis and Freud's Psychoanalysis," 361–2.

A Lacanian interpretation of the connections between Hegel and Freud on the centrality of desire may be found in Wilfried Ver Eecke, *Saying "No": Its Meaning in Child Development, Linguistics, and Hegel* (Pittsburgh: Duquesne University Press, 1984).

10. For Hegel's theory of the *List der Vernunft,* see L 746; RH 44; PS 33; and SL § 209.

11. The theme of guilt will occupy us in chapter 7, and intentionality will be the major issue of chapter 6. Hegel's most important discussions of guilt are in the sections of the *Phenomenology* on "The Ethical World;

Human and Divine Law: Man and Woman," and "Ethical Action; Human and Divine Knowledge; Guilt and Destiny" (PS 267–289), and in his *Aesthetics,* A 1: 187–88, 213–14, and 2: 1214–16.

For an interesting comparison of Hegel's theory of guilt with that of Freud, see Christensen's "Hegel's Phenomenological Analysis and Freud's Psychoanalysis," 356–78.

For general passages on the role of the unconscious in intentionality, see PS 220f, 249; and RH 26–36.

12. Nietzsche, *Beyond Good and Evil,* §§ 23, 230.

13. Freud, *The Ego and the Id,* SE 19: 19.

14. Freud, *Civilization and its Discontents,* SE 18: 613.

15. Nietzsche, *The Gay Science,* tr. Walter Kaufmann (New York: Random House, 1974), § 354.

16. Nietzsche, *Daybreak,* tr. R. J. Hollingdale (Cambridge: Cambridge University Press, 1982), § 119.

17. Nietzsche, *Gay Science,* § 179.

18. This citation is taken from Karl Jaspers' *Nietzsche: An Introduction to the Understanding of His Philosophical Activity,* tr. C. F. Wallraff and F. J. Schmitz (Chicago: Henry Regnery, 1965), 115. The translators omit all of Jaspers' references, and in the original German text (*Nietzsche: Einführung in das Verständnis seines Philosophierens,* Berlin: Walter de Gruyter Verlag, 1936), Jaspers refers to the early edition of the collected works prepared by Nietzsche's sister Elisabeth (the so-called *Kleinoktavausgabe,* 16 vols., ed. Elisabeth Förster-Nietzsche, et al., Leipzig: Kröner Verlag, 1899–1912), which I have been unable to locate. Since Jaspers nowhere specifies which of Nietzsche's works correspond to the different volumes of the collected works, I will refer the reader to pages in Jasper's text, and, for those more fortunate in their search for Elisabeth's *Kleinoktavausgabe,* to volume and page numbers of that edition. The present citation is from *Kleinoktavausgabe,* 15: 47.

19. See, e.g., *Beyond Good and Evil,* § 354: "Whatever becomes conscious becomes by the same token shallow, thin, relatively stupid, general, sign, herd signal, . . . falsification, reduction to superficialities. . . . Ultimately, the growth of consciousness becomes a danger; and anyone who lives among the most conscious Europeans even knows that it is a disease." Compare *Beyond Good and Evil,* § 357: "what we call consciousness constitutes only one state of our spiritual and psychic world (perhaps a pathological state). . . ."

20. See my article on "Freud's Critique of Philosophy," *Metaphilosophy* 20 (1989): 274–94.

21. Freud, *Interpretation of Dreams*, SE 4: 54–5. Freud's bibliography lists Spitta's text as *Die Schlaf– und Traumzustände der menschlichen Seele*, first published in Tübingen in 1878.

22. Freud, *Introductory Lectures*, SE 16: 359.

23. Freud, *Introductory Lectures*, SE 16: 368.

24. Freud, "The Unconscious," SE 14: 161–215.

25. Freud, "The Unconscious," SE 14: 186–87.

26. DeVries, 76.

27. Freud, "The Unconscious," SE 14: 186.

28. "The Unconscious," SE 14: 186, 187.

29. See Chapter Seven, pp. 155–56, 162–64.

30. Freud gives a full description of the differences between the primary and secondary processes as early as 1900 in his *Interpretation of Dreams*, SE 5: 588–609.

31. See *Introductory Lectures*, SE 16: 382ff; *The Ego and the Id*, SE 19: 49; and *Inhibitions, Symptoms and Anxiety*, SE 20: 99–100.

32. Nietzsche also often presents a basic duality of instinct, described variously as the will to power and its repression, the will to health and the will to nothingness, affirmation and denial, growth and decadence, the will to life and the "will to death" (*Gay Science*, § 344). We will see, however, that Nietzsche develops his view in a significantly different way from Hegel and Freud.

33. Freud, *Civilization and its Discontents*, SE 18: 117ff.

34. See Hegel, PS 51; and Freud, *Inhibitions, Symptoms and Anxiety*, SE 20, passim. Christensen argues that Hegel's view of anxiety is very similar to Freud's notion of "free-floating anxiety," which sees anxiety as more basic than its attachment to any particular object of fear. "Hegel's Phenomenological Analysis," 364–65.

35. Freud, *Civilization and its Discontents*, SE 18: 76.

36. Freud, *Civilization and its Discontents*, SE 18: 83.

37. Freud, *Beyond the Pleasure Principle*, SE 18: 12ff, 38.

38. I believe that Nathan Fialko is getting at the same point when he writes that "the very fact of the existence of insanity [is] a great problem for Hegel," since the rational, developed consciousness is meant to be entirely "free and . . . not subject to disease." That is, the line of demarcation is too strictly drawn to account for the motivation of the developed con-

sciousness to give up its rationality and sink back into madness. "Hegel's Views on Mental Derangement," 259–60.

39. Freud, *Introductory Lectures,* SE 16: 358.

40. Jaspers, *Nietzsche,* 112; *Kleinoktavausgabe* 5: 159.

41. Nietzsche, *The Will to Power,* tr. Walter Kaufmann and R. J. Hollingdale (New York: Random House, 1967), § 812.

42. Nietzsche, *The Will to Power,* § 47.

43. One complicating factor is that when Nietzsche refers to his own illness he is sometimes speaking of purely physical pains. I have been careful to select passages where he has mental or spiritual factors in mind.

44. Nietzsche, *Gay Science,* § 382.

45. See *Gay Science,* § 382; *Will to Power,* § 1013; *Human, All Too Human,* tr. Marion Faber (London: University of Nebraska Press, 1984), Preface § 4; and *The Genealogy of Morals,* in *The Basic Writings of Nietzsche,* ed. Walter Kaufmann (New York: Random House, 1968), Part II, § 24.

46. Nietzsche, *Gay Science,* § 382.

47. Jaspers, *Nietzsche,* 112; *Kleinoktavausgabe* 1: 193. Note the similarity between Nietzsche's view and those of modern writers like Thomas Szasz, Thomas Scheff, R. D. Laing, and Michel Foucault, who substitute a 'labeling theory' of mental illness for the 'medical model': 'mental illness' is not a medical condition but a socially constructed label for deviance from accepted norms. The labeling view will be discussed in detail in chapter 8.

48. Nietzsche, *Gay Science,* § 382.

49. Nietzsche, *Gay Science,* § 120.

50. Nietzsche, *Human, All Too Human,* Preface, § 4.

51. Nietzsche, *Gay Science,* Preface, § 4.

52. See, for example, *Gay Science,* Preface, §§ 2–3; and *Ecce Homo,* in *The Basic Writings,* Part I, § 2.

53. Nietzsche, *Gay Science,* Preface, § 2.

54. Freud in fact compares metaphysical systems to paranoia: "the delusions of paranoics have an . . . internal kinship to the systems of our philosophers" ("Preface to Reik's *Ritual: Psycho-Analytic Studies,*" SE 17: 261). Both the philosopher and the paranoid schizophrenic share "the belief that the real events in the world take the course which our thinking seeks to impose on them" (*New Introductory Lectures,* SE 22: 165-6).

Compare Nietzsche's description of philosophy as the "tyrannical drive" to "create the world in its own image" (*Beyond Good and Evil*, § 9).

Two general studies comparing the thought of Freud and Nietzsche are about to be published by the State University of New York Press: *Nietzsche's Presence in Freud's Life and Thought: On the Origins of a Psychology of Dynamic Unconscious Mental Functioning,* by Ronald Lehrer (December 1994), and *Nietzsche and Psychoanalysis,* by Daniel Chapelle (July 1994). See also Robert Herrera, "Freud on Nietzsche—A Fantastic Commentary?" *Philosophy Today* (1985): 339–44.

55. Freud, *The Psychopathology of Everyday Life,* SE 6: 259.

56. For a fuller discussion of Hegel's revaluation of truth, see *Hegel's Grand Synthesis,* chapter 2: "Hegel's Theory of Truth," 9–36.

57. For example, *Introductory Lectures,* SE 16: 389.

58. Nietzsche, *Daybreak,* § 312.

59. Nietzsche, *Daybreak,* § 119.

60. Nietzsche, *Twilight of the Idols,* in *The Portable Nietzsche,* ed. Walter Kaufmann (New York: Viking Press, 1984), 486.

61. Nietzsche, *The Birth of Tragedy,* in *Basic Writings,* § 5; see also *Gay Science,* § 107.

62. Nietzsche, *Will to Power,* § 852.

63. Nietzsche, *Birth of Tragedy,* § 7.

64. Nietzsche, *Birth of Tragedy,* § 1.

65. Nietzsche, *Birth of Tragedy,* § 14.

66. See *Birth of Tragedy,* §§ 10-15.

67. See Nietzsche, *Human, All Too Human,* § 13: "Dreams take us back again to distant conditions of human culture and put a means at our disposal for understanding them better." See also *Daybreak,* § 312: "in the fantasizing of dreams and insanity, a man rediscovers his own and mankind's prehistory." Freud speaks of the archaic phylogenetic heritage of the unconscious on many occasions. See, e.g., *Civilization and its Discontents,* SE 18: 13–14; *Ego and the Id,* SE 19: 36–38, 48–49, 55; *Future of an Illusion,* SE 19: 17; *Interpretation of Dreams,* SE 18: 548–49 (where Freud refers to his debt to Nietzsche); and *Introductory Lectures,* SE 15: 179–81, 199, 210–11, 213, 226. Finally, see Robert Herrera's "Freud on Nietzsche," 341.

68. See Hyppolite's analysis of the position of the consciousness which "withdraws to itself and rejects all communication," initiating a "total breakdown of relationship," as the epitome of the death instinct ("Hegel's Phenomenology and Psychoanalysis," 70).

69. Nietzsche, *Gay Science,* § 294.

70. Nietzsche, *Genealogy,* Part I, § 6.

71. Nietzsche, *Beyond Good and Evil,* § 36.

72. Freud, *Civilization and its Discontents,* SE 18: 86, 111, 143–44.

73. Christensen shows how Hegel's key concept of the *Aufhebung* "is compatible with the notion of an unconscious conceived in something like the Freudian way." "Theory of Mental Derangement," 434ff.

74. John Dewey, "Art as Experience," in A. Hofstadter and R. Kuhns, eds., *Philosophies of Art and Beauty* (Chicago: University of Chicago Press, 1976), 604–606.

75. Dewey, 614.

76. Freud, *Leonardo Da Vinci,* SE 11: 136.

77. Ricoeur, *Freud and Philosophy: An Essay on Interpretation,* tr. Denis Savage (New Haven: Yale University Press, 1970), 332.

78. Freud, *Leonardo,* SE 11: 80.

79. Ricoeur, 333.

80. Freud, *Leonardo,* SE 11: 118.

For other discussions by Freud of art and sublimation, see his "Creative Writers and Daydreaming," SE 9: 143–53; "Delusions and Dreams in Jensen's *Gradiva,*" SE 9: 7–95; "Formulations on the The Two Principles of Mental Functioning," SE 12: 224; and "The Moses of Michelangelo," SE 13: 211–36.

See also Jean Hyppolite's "Commentary on Freud's *Verneinung,*" where he speaks of the relation between the affective and intellectual in Freud's account of repression and sublimation (291–3).

81. For discussions of the concept of sublimation in Nietzsche, see Jaspers, *Nietzsche,* 137; Walter Kaufmann, *Nietzsche: Philosopher, Psychologist, Antichrist,* 4th ed. (Princeton: Princeton University Press, 1974), 211–56; and George Morgan, *What Nietzsche Means* (New York: Harper & Row, 1965), 98ff, 128ff, 180–81, 185, 209–10.

82. Nietzsche, *Beyond Good and Evil,* § 188.

83. Nietzsche, *Beyond Good and Evil,* § 225.

84. Nietzsche, *Will to Power,* §§ 382–84.

85. Nietzsche, *Beyond Good and Evil,* §§ 26, 289.

86. Nietzsche, *Beyond Good and Evil,* § 284.

87. Nietzsche, *Ecce Homo,* Part I, § 8.

88. Freud, *Future of an Illusion*, 9.

89. Freud, *Introductory Lectures*, SE 15: 23.

90. This quote appears in an otherwise splendid book by William Chase Greene, *Moira: Fate, Good, and Evil in Greek Thought* (New York: Harper & Row, 1963), 96.

91. Freud, *Introductory Lectures*, SE 15: 216; *Interpretation of Dreams*, SE 5: 561.

92. Nietzsche, *Ecce Homo*, Part I, §§ 1–3.

93. Nietzsche, *Will to Power*, § 811.

94. Nietzsche, *Twilight of the Idols*, 518.

95. Friedrich Grimmlinger, "Zum Begriff des absoluten Wissens in Hegels *Phänomenologie*," in Hans-Dieter Klein und Erhard Oeser, eds., *Geschichte und System: Festschrift für Erich Heintel zum 60. Geburtstag* (München: R. Oldenbourg Verlag, 1972), 291–92.

96. Christensen makes a similar point when he argues that "the unconscious is the subjective ground of the integrity which is potential for the individual," and that Hegel already anticipates Freud's view of the unconscious having "a continuing function in even the normal and mature consciousness." "Theory of Mental Derangement," 444, 440.

See also Yvon Gauthier, "Langage et psychanalyse," *Dialogue* 7 (1969): 633–38. Gauthier shows how the Lacanian thesis that "the unconscious is structured like a language" involves psychoanalysis in a significant dialogue with Hegel. And see Wilfried Ver Eecke, *Saying "No,"* and Alphonse De Waelhens, "Réflexions," 233–36.

97. Fialko, 263.

6. Madness, Action, and Intentionality

1. Nietzsche, *Beyond Good and Evil*, § 32.

2. Murray Greene makes this point as well: "Hegel here [in the "Anthropology" section of the *Encyclopædia*] deals with a realm of the psyche that later came to be explored by depth psychology." "Hegel's Conception of Psychology," in Cohen and Wartofsky, *Hegel and the Sciences*, 173.

3. Christensen, "Theory of Mental Derangement," 440.

4. I will be using the term 'psychology' quite loosely in this chapter, departing from Hegel's technical use of the word. In the "Philosophy of Mind" volume of his *Encyclopædia*, psychology is the last of three sciences

of 'subjective mind,' after anthropology and phenomenology. Psychology here is the study of such mental faculties as intuition, imagination, and memory, and more generally of theoretical and practical reason. Psychology is distinguished from anthropology, which studies 'the soul,' or our pre-conscious immersion in nature (the 'life of feeling'), and from phenomenology, which studies the life of 'consciousness as such,' mind which has emerged from nature and which now stands in opposition to nature. I am using 'psychology' to refer very broadly to the study of the underlying *motives* for action, whether they are conscious or unconscious.

For more on the relation between Hegel's anthropology, phenomenology, and psychology, see Alan Olson, 94–5.

5. *Interpretation of Dreams,* SE 5: 613 (emphasis added).

6. The idea of circularity is of great importance in Hegel's philosophy as a whole. See Tom Rockmore's *Hegel's Circular Epistemology* (Bloomington: Indiana University Press, 1986). See also *Hegel's Grand Synthesis,* 106–12.

7. We will be discussing Hegel's theory of guilt in the next chapter, but should at least note by way of anticipation that guilt, for Hegel, is primarily an *ontological* concept and only secondarily a moral concept. In a word, Hegel sees guilt as the inevitably recurring discord between our being-for-self and our being-for-others, between consciousness and what is experienced as 'other,' between inner reality and outer reality, and between intentionality and "the way of the world" *(der Weltlauf).*

8. Nietzsche, *Beyond Good and Evil,* § 19.

9. For a few of the many discussions of Hegel's critique of Kant's moral theory, see: Karl Ameriks, "The Hegelian Critique of Kantian Morality," in Bernard den Ouden and Marcia Moen, eds., *New Essays on Kant* (New York: Lang, 1987): 179–212; Moltke Gramm, "Moral and Literary Ideals in Hegel's Critique of 'The Moral World-View,'" *Clio* 7, no. 3 (1978): 375–402; David Hoy, "Hegel's Critique of Kantian Morality," *History of Philosophy Quarterly* 6 (1989): 207–32; Jean-François Kervegan, "Le problème de la fondation de l'éthique: Kant, Hegel," *Revue de Métaphysique et de Morale* 95 (1990): 33–55; T. O'Hagan, "On Hegel's Critique of Kant's Moral and Political Philosophy," in Stephen Priest, ed., *Hegel's Critique of Kant* (Oxford: Oxford University Press, 1987): 135–59; Sally Sedgwick, "Hegel's Critique of the Subjective Idealism of Kant's Ethics," *Journal of the History of Philosophy* 26 (1988): 89–105; Paul Stern, "On the Relation Between Autonomy and Ethical Community: Hegel's Critique of Kantian Morality," *Praxis International* 9, no. 3 (1989): 234–48; and Allen W. Wood, "The Emptiness of the Moral Will," *Monist* 72 (1989): 454–83.

10. As Hegel says in his *Philosophy of Right,* "etymologically, *Absicht* [intention] implies abstraction" away from the objective, external side of

action. Hence "the endeavor to justify an action by the intention behind it involves the isolation [or abstraction] of [just] one . . . of [the] aspects" of the whole action (PR § 119).

11. The connection between desire and otherness is put succinctly by Joseph Flay, who remarks that "desire is always interest in something other than itself." *Hegel's Quest for Certainty,* 81.

12. Daisetz T. Suzuki, *Zen and Japanese Culture* (Princeton: Princeton University Press, 1970), 155–6.

13. It is this view which leads Joseph Flay to describe Hegel's theory as ascribing an inherently *historical* character to language: "[language is for Hegel] a historical phenomenon: the unity of the world through language, language as the *Dasein des Geistes.* . . . Through language the individual objectifies himself within . . . culture by the use of language forms which are institutionally public in that culture. . . . Language is the medium which . . . forms concrete links between individuals as they talk and think their way through their tasks." *Hegel's Quest,* 187. Flay sees Hegel as developing "a completely new theory of language as essentially performative in *all* of its modes" (186).

14. Heidegger, *Hegel's Phenomenology of Spirit,* 64.

15. Moritz Schlick, "The Foundation of Knowledge," tr. David Rynin, in A. J. Ayer, ed., *Logical Positivism* (New York: MacMillan, 1959): 226. Schlick, of course, sees this perpetual vanishing of the immediate sensation as precisely its claim to epistemological value: "here everything depends on the characteristic of *immediacy* which is peculiar to observation statements [i.e., statements about sense data], to which they owe . . . their value of absolute validity" (226).

16. Taylor, "The Opening Arguments of the Phenomenology," in Alasdair MacIntyre, ed., *Hegel: A Collection of Critical Essays* (Notre Dame: University of Notre Dame Press, 1972): 165.
    Jean Hyppolite claims that "one of the profound defects in Hegel's thought is revealed perhaps in his philosophy of language," due precisely to the "ineffability" of the purely specific or particular: Hegel "may indeed lead us to a *universal subject* but . . . tends to eliminate *specific existents*" (*Genesis,* 86n). My own feeling is that Hegel's philosophy of language was no more meant to 'eliminate' specific existents than, for example, was Plato's argument for the forms, or was Wittgenstein's argument against private language. His point is to show how the particular must be conceptualized in a different manner than as a brute, immediate, 'given' reality.

17. For other discussions of the "Sense Certainty" chapter, see *Hegel's Grand Synthesis,* 33, 34, 52, 53, 173 (n 83); Heribert Boeder, "Das natürliche Bewußtsein," *Hegel–Studien* 12 (1977): 157–78; Martin De Nys, " 'Sense Certainty' and Universality: Hegel's Entrance into the Phenome-

nology," *International Philosophical Quarterly* 18 (1978): 445–65; Fink, *Hegel,* 57ff; Flay, 29–50; Heidegger, *Hegel's Phenomenology of Spirit,* 45–66; Johannes Heinrichs, *Die Logik der Phänomenologie des Geister* (Bonn: Bouvier Verlag Herbert Grundmann, 1974), 116–22; Hyppolite, *Genesis,* 80–99; Kainz, 61–64; Matthias Kettner, *Hegels "Sinnliche Gewissheit": Diskursanalytischer Kommentar* (Main: Campus, 1990); Lauer, *A Reading,* 3ff; Labarrière, 73–76; Lukács, 596–97; Judith Shklar, *Freedom and Independence: A Study of the Political Ideas of Hegel's Phenomenology of Mind* (Cambridge: Cambridge University Press, 1976), 14–26; Verene, *Hegel's Recollection,* 27–38; Reiner Wiehl, "Über den Sinn der sinnlichen Gewissheit in Hegels *Phänomenologie des Geistes," Hegel-Studien* 3 (1966): 103–34; and W. Wieland, "Hegels Dialektik der sinnlichen Gewissheit," in Dietrich Gerhardt, et al., eds., *Orbis Scriptus: Dmitrij Tschizewskij zum 70. Geburtstag* (München: Wilhelm Fink Verlag, 1966): 933–41.

18. Butler, 198.

19. Sartre, 372, 373.

20. Sartre, 372 / *L'être et le néant,* 422.

21. Sartre, 373 / *L'être et le néant,* 423.

22. Sartre, 374 / *L'être et le néant,* 423.

23. Sartre, 364–412 / *L'être et le néant,* 413–63, passim.

24. Wittgenstein, *Philosophical Investigations,* tr. G. E. M. Anscombe (New York: MacMillan, 1962), 18n.

25. Taylor, "Opening Arguments," 153, 156. The purpose of Taylor's essay is to show that Hegel employs a method of "transcendental argument"—where we "start from some putatively undeniable facet of our experience in order to conclude that this experience must have certain features or be of a certain type" (151)—and he brings in Wittgenstein to indicate a parallel strategy in the *Investigations.*
     See also Caroline Dudeck, "Hegel on Private Experience," *Philosophy Research Archives* 3 (1977): 102–12; David Lamb, "Hegel and Wittgenstein on Language and Sense-Certainty," *Clio* 7 (1978): 285–301, and *Language and Perception in Hegel and Wittgenstein* (New York: St. Martin's Press, 1979); and Solomon, 333–34. For reservations about Taylor's and Lamb's Wittgensteinian readings of Hegel (although not focused on the question of private language), see Robert Pippin's *Hegel's Idealism,* 278 n5, 285–6 n13.
     Stanley Rosen notes a further connection of Hegel with Wittgenstein's arguments against private language, namely Hegel's rejection of intellectual intuition (which is "related or similar to the later Wittgenstein's rejection of private language"). He writes that "in order to be tested by the universal or public criteria of reason, an intuition must be externalized in discourse" (273–74).

Finally, Stanley Cavell's *Must We Mean What We Say?* (New York: Scribner, 1969) addresses many of the same questions that Hegel and Wittgenstein are concerned with.

26. Wittgenstein, *Philosophical Investigations*, § 261.

27. It is interesting to note that Sartre speaks of the "sacred" aspect of language, reminiscent of Hegel's view of the "divine" nature of language, which for Sartre is its ability to "reveal to me the freedom (the transcendence) of the one who listens to me in silence" (374).

28. See also SL § 20; PS 308f, 395; and PM § 396 Z.

29. See Jere Paul Surber's discussion in "Hegel's Speculative Sentence," *Hegel-Studien* 10 (1975): 212–30; also Dietrich Gutterer, "Der Spekulative Satz," *Kodikas / Code* 1 (1979): 235–47.

30. *Letters*, 107.

31. For discussions of Hegel's philosophy of language, see Theodor Bodammer, *Hegel's Deutung der Sprache* (Hamburg: F. Meiner, 1969); Daniel Cook, *Language in the Philosophy of Hegel* (New York: Mouton, 1973); Jacques Derrida, "The Pit and the Pyramid: Introduction to Hegel's Semiology," in his *Margins of Philosophy*, tr. Alan Bass (Brighton: Harvester Press, 1982): 69–108; Gadamer, *Hegel's Dialectic*, 91–96; Heidegger, *Hegel's Phenomenology of Spirit*, 63–66; John McCumber, *Poetic Interaction: Language, Freedom, Reason* (Chicago: University of Chicago Press, 1989); and Richard Winfield, "Logic, Language, and the Autonomy of Reason," *Idealistic Studies* 17 (1987): 109–21.

32. Sartre, *Being and Nothingness*, 554–55.

33. Nietzsche, *Beyond Good and Evil*, § 23.

34. Freud, *An Autobiographical Study*, SE 20: 31.

35. For an excellent discussion of the relation between nature and spirit, see William DeVries, *Hegel's Theory of Mental Activity*, chapter 3.

36. Foucault, *Madness and Civilization*, 100.

37. Freud, *The Claims of Psycho-analysis to Scientific Interest*, SE 13: 176–77.

38. See, for example, *Interpretation of Dreams*, SE 4: 122–3, 305–8, and SE 5: 640–43.

39. See *The Psychopathology of Everyday Life*, SE 6: 257ff; and *New Introductory Lectures on Psycho-analysis*, SE 22: 165ff.

40. See, for example, PM § 402 Z: "the opposition between itself and that which is *for* it [the world], remains still shut up within it."

7. Madness and Tragedy

1. All citations from Greek tragedies are from *The Complete Greek Tragedies*, 4 vols., ed. David Greene and Richmond Lattimore (Chicago: University of Chicago Press, 1959–60). The translators are as follows:

AESCHYLUS:
Agamemnon, Libation Bearers, and *Eumenides*, tr. Richmond Lattimore.

SOPHOCLES:
Antigone, tr. Elizabeth Wyckoff; *Ajax*, tr. John Moore, Jr.; *Oedipus the King*, tr. David Greene; and *Women of Trachis*, tr. Michael Jameson.

EURIPIDES:
Bacchae, Hecuba, and *Orestes*, tr. William Arrowsmith; *Trojan Women*, tr. Richmond Lattimore

2. Bennett Simon, *Mind and Madness in Ancient Greece: The Classical Roots of Modern Psychiatry* (Ithaca: Cornell University Press, 1978), 101.

3. Paul Ricoeur, *History and Truth*, tr. Charles Kelbley (Evanston: Northwestern University Press, 1965), 293.

4. See, for example, Freud's distaste for the moralistic attitude of clinical psychiatry towards neurotics:

> Psychiatry insists that those who suffer from these symptoms are 'degenerates'. This gives small satisfaction; in fact it is a judgment of value—a condemnation instead of an explanation. (*Introductory Lectures*, SE 15: 260)

And for Hegel, see below, pp. 170–71, and chapter 8, p. 205.

5. A 1: 240ff, 2: 229ff, 4: 238ff; PS 267–89, 443ff; NL 104–5, 108; PR §§ 118A, 140A, 163A, 166A, 218A; PH 237ff; LR 330ff; and HP 1: 426ff.

6. For discussions of Hegel's distinction between ancient and modern tragedy, see A. C. Bradley's now classic essay, "Hegel's Theory of Tragedy," in his *Oxford Lectures on Poetry* (London: Macmillan, 1950): 69–95; Stephen Bungay, *Beauty and Truth: A Study of Hegel's Aesthetics* (Oxford: Oxford University Press, 1987), 166–78; and Walter Kaufmann, "Hegel's Ideas about Tragedy," in Steinkraus, *New Studies*, 201–20.

7. The German *Pathos* means 'passionate commitment,' or as Hegel says, "the power of the emotional life." It must not be confused with the English meaning of the word as 'pitifulness.' For this reason I will leave 'pathos' in quotes.

8. These lines are virtually identical to the words of Dionysus to Pentheus in Euripides' *Bacchae*: "You do not know/ what you do. You do not know who you are" (l. 506).

9. It should be noted that while Hegel sees despair as the "center" and "birthpang" of all the shapes of spirit, within the chronological account of his *Phenomenology,* he locates the unhappy consciousness within the Christian era (see PS 454ff).

10. See A 2: 1215, 1228. For discussions of Hegel's reservations about Euripides, see Bungay, 172–73; and Stephen Houlgate, *Hegel, Nietzsche and the Criticism of Metaphysics* (Cambridge: Cambridge University Press, 1986), 199.

11. This citation comes from the *"Kunstreligion"* section of the *Phenomenology,* where Hegel is referring to the general principle of all of the arts of ancient Greece—sculpture, the religious cults and festivals, and epic and comic literature as well as tragedy.

12. Hegel refers to *Antigone* l. 451: "that Justice who lives with *the gods below* [did not] / mark out such laws to hold among mankind" (emphasis added).

13. Marcuse, *Hegel's Ontology,* 302.

14. Marcuse, *Hegel's Ontology,* 302.

15. Marcuse, *Hegel's Ontology,* 303.

16. William Arrowsmith, "A Greek Theater of Ideas," *Arion* 2 (1963): 50.

17. Michael Davis, "Politics and Madness," in *Greek Tragedy and Political Theory,* ed. J. Peter Euben (Berkeley: University of California Press, 1986): 142–61. The following remarks on the *Ajax,* and particularly the idea that the sane Ajax lacks an 'inside,' are indebted to this essay.

18. Stephen Bungay, for example, challenges Hegel's view that "Creon is not a tyrant, but also an ethical power," which Hegel sees as necessary for having the status of tragic figure. Bungay cannot agree with Hegel that Creon is as much in the right as Antigone, and hence has difficulty seeing Creon's situation as fully tragic. *Beauty and Truth,* 166–69. See also, e.g., A. J. A. Waldock, *Sophocles the Dramatist* (Cambridge: Cambridge University Press, 1966), 30–31: Creon does *not* represent the "justified power" of the state, he is simply a tyrant, and simply "morally wrong."

On the other hand, Hegel is equally opposed to commentators like H. D. F. Kitto who read the play as "primarily the tragedy of Creon." *Greek Tragedy: A Literary Study* (Garden City, New York: Doubleday, 1954), 132.

19. Thus Hegel could not be further from someone like Kitto who says that Antigone's situation is "terrible," to be sure, and her part in the tragedy is "impressive and affecting enough," but who insists that Creon's role "has the wider range and is the more elaborate" and "significant" (Kitto, 130, 131). See also Walter Kaufmann's critique of Kitto's "unfair" treatment of Hegel's interpretation of the *Antigone* in "Hegel's Ideas about Tragedy," 202.

20. Luce Irigaray, *The Speculum of the Other Woman*, tr. Gillian C. Gill (Ithaca: Cornell University Press, 1985), 224, 225. See also Allen Wood's brief but lucid discussion of how Hegel's differentiation of gender roles effectively excludes women from participation in the "actualization of personhood" within civil society: *Hegel's Ethical Thought* (Cambridge: Cambridge University Press, 1993), 244–46. For more general discussions of feminist concerns surrounding Hegel's reading of the *Antigone*, see Martin Donougho, "The Woman in White: On the Reception of Hegel's *Antigone*," *Owl of Minerva* 21 (1989): 65–89; Patricia Jagentowicz Mills, "Hegel's *Antigone*," *Owl of Minerva* 17 (1986): 131–52; Raymond Piertercil, "Antigone and Hegel," *International Philosophical Quarterly* 18 (1978): 289–310; Stuart Swindle, "Why Feminists Should Take the *Phenomenology of Spirit* Seriously," *Owl of Minerva* 24, no. 1 (1992): 41–54, and Heidi Ravven's "Response" to Swindle in the same issue (63–68); and Cynthia Willett, "Hegel, Antigone, and the Possibility of Ecstatic Dialogue," *Philosophy and Literature* 14, no. 2 (1990): 268–83.

21. Irigaray, 217.

22. For a few of the many discussions of the idea of 'rationality' as the transcendence of the feminine, see Mary Field Belenky, Blythe Clinchy, Nancy Goldberger, and Jill Tarule, *Women's Ways of Knowing* (New York: Basic Books, 1986); Jane Flax, *Thinking Fragments: Psychoanalysis, Feminism, and Postmodernism in the Contemporary West* (Berkeley: University of California Press, 1990); Susan Griffin, *Woman and Nature: The Roaring Inside Her* (New York: Harper & Row, 1978); Alison Jagger and Susan Bordo, *Gender / Body / Knowledge: Feminist Reconstructions of Being and Knowing* (New Brunswick, NJ: Rutgers University Press, 1991); Genevieve Lloyd, *The Man of Reason: "Male" and "Female" in Western Philosophy* (Minneapolis: University of Minnesota Press, 1984); and Sherry Ortner and Harriet Whitehead, eds., *Sexual Meanings: The Cultural Construction of Gender and Sexuality* (New York: Cambridge University Press, 1981).

Gila Hayim argues that Hegel's account of desire and labor does not give enough recognition to certain basic differences between the nature of desire and the conditions surrounding labor for men and women, and hence that he does not consider the possibility of different "cognitions of estrangement." "Hegel's Critical Theory and Feminist Concerns," *Philosophy and Social Criticism* 16, no. 1 (1990): 1–21.

Julia Kristeva criticizes what she sees as Hegel's rationalistic, logo-centric interpretation of desire, which fails to account for its essentially embodied and gendered character, so that the masculine (rationalistic) appropriation of desire will always be privileged over the feminine. See *Revolution in Poetic Language,* tr. Margaret Walker (New York: Columbia University Press, 1984).

Jacques Lacan's remarks on the subjection of women to a phallocentric system of meaning, the "Law of the Father" or the patriarchal "Symbolic Order," are also pertinent here. See, e.g. *Feminine Sexuality: Jacques Lacan and the École Freudienne,* ed. Juliet Mitchell and Jacqueline Rose, tr. Jacqueline Rose (New York: Norton, 1985), 109.

23. Thomas Szasz quotes several appropriate passages from the *Malleus*: "[It is women who are] chiefly addicted to Evil Superstitions"; "All witchcraft comes from carnal lust, which is in women insatiable"; "Blessed be the Highest who has so far preserved the male sex from so great a crime." Szasz, *The Manufacture of Madness: A Comparative Study of the Inquisition and the Mental Health Movement* (New York: Harper & Row, 1970), 8.

The *Malleus Maleficarum* was published in 1486, implementing a Papal bull of 1484.

24. On nature as the presupposition of spirit, see Herbert Marcuse, *Hegel's Ontology,* 312–14.

25. Kierkegaard, *The Concept of Irony, With Constant Reference to Socrates,* tr. Lee Capel (Bloomington: Indiana University Press, 1965), 212, 210.

26. Froma I. Zeitlin, "Thebes: Theater of Self and Society in Athenian Drama," in Euben, 101–41.

27. Zeitlin, 126–28.

28. Zeitlin, 126, citing Seth Bernadete, "A Reading of Sophocles' *Antigone: I,*" *Interpretation* 4 (1975), 156.

29. Zeitlin, 154–55.

30. Zeitlin, 128.

31. *Letters,* 591 (letter of December 18, 1812), emphasis added.

32. For commentaries on Hegel's discussion of the "inverted world" in the "Understanding" section of the *Phenomenology,* see W. H. Bossart, "Hegel on the Inverted World," *Philosophical Forum* 1 (1982): 326–41; Joseph Flay, "Hegel's 'Inverted World'," *Review of Metaphysics* (1970): 662–78; Gadamer, Chapter Two, "Hegel's 'Inverted World'"; Leon Goldstein, "Force and the Inverted World in Dialectical Retrospection," *International Studies in Philosophy* 20 (1988): 13–28; Murray Greene,

"Hegel's Notion of Inversion," *International Journal of the Philosophy of Religion* 1 (1970): 161–75; Lauer, *A Reading*, 84–87; Rosen, 140–50; Solomon, 376–85; Verene, *Hegel's Recollection*, 39–58; and Robert Zimmerman, "Hegel's 'Inverted World' Revisited," *Philosophical Forum* 1 (1982): 342–70.

33. See also the "Appearance" chapter of the *Encyclopædia* Logic (§§ 131ff): "The essence must appear or shine forth. . . . Essence accordingly is not something beyond or behind appearance" (§ 131); "The appearance shows nothing that is not in the essence, and in the essence there is nothing but what is manifested" (§ 139).

34. Walter Kaufmann makes this point as well: "[Antigone's] character is not at issue any more than Creon's; their positions are." "Hegel's Ideas about Tragedy," 202.

35. Freud himself draws this analogy in his *Introductory Lectures,* SE 16: 330.

36. For further discussions by Hegel of the theme of tragic guilt and innocence, see HP 1: 445–46 (Socrates' tragic situation is that it is his very "innocence which is guilty"), and SC 233 (the "most exalted form of guilt" is "the guilt of innocence").

37. Nietzsche, *Gay Science,* § 294.

38. Heidegger, *Being and Time,* 332.

39. Walter Kaufmann believes that the "*mot juste*" for Hegel's conception of the tragic hero is not tragic *guilt* but tragic *responsibility*, since "'guilt' is not the right word where guilt feelings are not appropriate; and we do not really admire those who harbor such feelings in a situation in which they are not to be blamed" ("Hegel's Ideas about Tragedy," 210–11). I think this view misses Hegel's ontologizing of the concept of guilt, a move which is meant to remove the moralistic talk of 'blame.'

40. Timo Airaksinen makes this same point. He argues that "insanity and evil are, at least structurally, one and the same thing, . . . two mutually convergent phenomena," but that "no moralistic overtones apply [here]" (160–62).

41. See especially chapter 4 of *Beyond Hegel and Dialectic,* "Dialectic and Evil: On the Idiocy of the Monstrous," 189–250.

42. Desmond, 189–90.

43. Desmond, 203–4.

44. Desmond, 207, 212.

45. Desmond, 238.

46. Desmond, 230. The famous line from Pascal's *Pensées* is, "Le coeur a ses raisons que la raison ne connaît point" (The heart has its reasons of which reason knows nothing). *Pensées,* ed. Robert Barrault (Paris: Librairie Larousse, 1965), 141 (Brunschvicg numbering, # 277).

47. Desmond, 237.

48. Desmond, 232.

8. Madness and Society: Coming to Terms with Hegel's Silence

1. The phrase, "manufacture of madness," serves as the title of Szasz's 1970 book comparing the "myth" of mental illness with the superstition of witchcraft and the institution of psychiatry with the Inquisition. *The Manufacture of Madness: A Comparative Study of the Inquisition and the Mental Health Movement* (New York: Harper and Row, 1970).

2. Foucault has often been described as an anarchist, both in terms of his politics as well as his epistemology and archaeological and genealogical methods. See discussions by Michael Walzer ("The Politics of Michel Foucault"), Richard Rorty ("Foucault and Epistemology"), and Ian Hacking ("The Archaeology of Foucault") in David Couzens Hoy, ed., *Foucault: A Critical Reader* (Oxford: Basil Blackwell, 1986); also J. G. Merquior, *Foucault* (Berkeley and Los Angeles: University of California Press, 1985), 154–56. Some of Jürgen Habermas' comments in his *Lectures on the Discourse of Modernity* (Cambridge, MA: Harvard University Press, 1985), delivered at the Collège de France in 1983, are also appropriate, although Habermas does not explicitly refer to Foucault as an anarchist. Hayden White's *Tropics of Discourse* (Baltimore: The Johns Hopkins Press, 1990) similarly captures one sense of Foucault's anarchism without using this label: "Foucault celebrates the spirit of creative *dis*ordering, *de*structuration, *un*naming. His whole effort as a historian can be characterized as a sustained promotion of the '*dis*remembrance of things past'" (233).

Several authors see Foucault's reputed anarchism as implying an essentially nihilistic standpoint. Merquior, for example, speaks of Foucault being "the founding father of our *Kathedernihilismus*" (160), and Walzer regards Foucault's attempt to radically question all the forms of modern society as inherently fatalistic and nihilistic: "Either there will be nothing left at all, nothing visibly human; or new codes and disciplines will be produced, and Foucault gives us no reason to expect that these will be any better than the ones we now live with. Nor, for that matter, does he give us any way of knowing what 'better' might mean" (61). Finally, see also Sylvie Le Bon, who says that for Foucault, history is reduced to "*le moment du chaos, celui où, par une mutation obscure, le non-savoir explose en savoir et le savoir s'abîme en non-savoir. De toute manière, elle est liquidée comme telle, car rien jamais ne devient."* "Un positiviste désespéré: Michel Foucault," *Les Temps Modernes* 248 (1967): 1319.

My own use of the term 'anarchist' does not in any way imply a view of Foucault as a nihilist, whether of an 'armchair' *(Katheder)* variety or otherwise.

3. While I am (somewhat hesitantly, always recalling the ironical sense alluded to) using this term largely by way of characterizing Foucault's intellectual temperament, the political shadings of his 'anarchism' may be seen in his 1971 television debate in Amsterdam with Noam Chomsky, where he asserted that the purpose of revolutionary practice is simply constantly to resist power, not to bring about some ideal of justice: "It seems to me that the idea of justice in itself is an idea which in effect has been invented and put to work in different types of societies as an instrument of that power; . . . one can't, however regrettable it may be, put these notions forward to justify a fight which should . . . overthrow the very fundaments of our society." "Human Nature: Justice versus Power,'' in Fons Elders, ed., *Reflexive Water: The Basic Concerns of Mankind* (London: Souvenir Press, 1974), 187.

4. Szasz has also written on issues of sexuality (e.g., sexual preference, sex education), censorship, civil liberties and the ACLU, alcohol and drug addiction, and a variety of topics of biomedical ethics (e.g., birth control, the right to die). But the vast majority of his essays, articles, lectures, and books are on the topic of psychiatry and mental illness.

5. In its original edition, *Folie et déraison* was 580 pages long. *Madness and Civilization* (299 pages) is a translation of an abridged edition Foucault published in 1964, with the addition of some passages from the original, most importantly the chapter on "Passion and Delirium." See the Vintage Books edition, tr. Richard Howard (New York, 1965), publisher's note, iv.

6. For example, twice in *The Manufacture of Madness,* 13, 42.

7. See Didier Eribon, *Michel Foucault,* tr. Betsy Wing (Cambridge, MA: Harvard University Press, 1991), 126; and Robert Castel, "Les Aventures de la pratique," *Le Débat* (1986): 47.

8. Szasz, *The Myth of Mental Illness: Foundations of a Theory of Personal Conduct,* revised edition (New York: Harper & Row, 1974), xiv, 9.

9. Foucault, *Madness and Civilization,* x.

10. Szasz, *Manufacture of Madness,* 71.

11. Foucault, *Mental Illness and Psychology,* 10.

12. Foucault, *Madness and Civilization,* xii.

13. Szasz, *Myth of Mental Illness,* 8.

14. Szasz, *Myth of Mental Illness,* x.

15. Szasz, *Myth of Mental Illness,* 25.

16. Szasz, "Medicine and Madness," *The Encyclopaedia Britannica Yearbook* (1974): 454–55. Reprinted in *The Therapeutic State: Psychiatry in the Mirror of Current Events* (Buffalo, NY: Prometheus Books, 1984), 16. On the idea of names creating values, see also *The Myth of Mental Illness,* 38.
Andrew Scull also comments on the semantics of madness:

> The Victorian age saw the transformation of the madhouse into the asylum into the mental hospital; of the mad-doctor into the alienist into the psychiatrist; and of the madman (and mad-woman) into the mental patient. And while it would be a grave error to confuse semantics with reality, it equally will not do to treat these verbal changes as no more than a succession of euphemisms masking a fundamentally static reality. As with all mythical representations, the progressive images that this succession of terms is designed to conjure up bear a significant, albeit distorted, relationship to the social order they purport to describe.

Andrew Scull, "The Social History of Psychiatry in the Victorian Era," in Scull, ed., *Madhouses, Mad-Doctors, and Madmen* (Philadelphia: University of Pennsylvania Press, 1981): 6.

17. Carol Warren, *The Court of Last Resort: Mental Illness and the Law* (Chicago: University of Chicago Press, 1982), 2–3. Warren includes discussions of some of the theoretical and experimental underpinnings of labeling theory (44–68), especially the work of Thomas Scheff (*Being Mentally Ill: A Sociological Theory,* 2nd edition, New York: Aldine, 1984) and such now-classic studies as the Temerlin and Rosenhan experiments: Maurice Temerlin, "Suggestion Effects in Psychiatric Diagnoses," *Journal of Nervous and Mental Diseases* 147 (1968): 349–58; and David Rosenhan, "On Being Sane in Insane Places," *Science* 179 (1973): 250–8.

18. Merquior, 146.

19. Szasz, *Myth of Mental Illness,* 25.

20. Nietzsche, *The Gay Science,* § 58.

21. Foucault, *Madness and Civilization,* 40.

22. Szasz, "Medicine and Madness," in *The Therapeutic State,* 17.

23. Szasz, *Manufacture of Madness,* 13–15.

24. Szasz, "Medicine and Madness," in *The Therapeutic State,* 17.

25. Foucault, *Madness and Civilization*, 266, 270.

26. Szasz, *Myth of Mental Illness*, 61.

27. Foucault, *Madness and Civilization*, 257.

28. Foucault, *Madness and Civilization*, chapter 9, "The Birth of the Asylum," passim.

29. Szasz, *Myth of Mental Illness*, 17–24.

30. Scheff describes his position as being that "most chronic mental illness is at least in part a social role" (14), or that "labeling and the processes of social interaction play a crucial role" in the constitution of mental illness (143–4). He points out that "[t]his is not to claim, of course, that some symptoms of mental illness are not caused by disease. . [Mental illness] may have its origins in complex combinations of two or more of these sources: organic causes, environmental stress, psychological causes, or volition" (189). For Scheff's critique of Szasz, see 49ff.

31. Alan Horwitz, *The Social Control of Mental Illness* (New York: Academic Press, 1982), 6–7.

32. Szasz, *Myth of Mental Illness*, ix.

33. Szasz, "Mental Illness: A Myth?" in *The ABC of Psychology*, ed. Leonard Kristal (London: Michael Joseph, 1981): 150–55.

34. For a few good examples, see *Myth of Mental Illness*, 5, 10, 34, 43.

35. Foucault, *Madness and Civilization*, 202–5.

36. See Hubert Dreyfus' forward to *Mental Illness and Psychology*, vii–xl.

37. See Eribon, 70.

38. The reasons are complex, but basically, the revised edition remained a theoretical mishmash (a "mongrel," as Eribon puts it [Eribon, 70]), overlaying a history of forms of experience on top of what Herbert Dryfus calls "an unstable combination of Heideggerian existential anthropology and Marxist social history" (Foreword to *Mental Illness and Psychology*, viii).

39. Foucault, *Mental Illness and Psychology*, 1.

40. Foucault, *Mental Illness and Psychology*, 63.

41. Foucault, *Mental Illness and Psychology*, 10.

42. Foucault, *Mental Illness and Psychology*, 84.

43. Foucault, *Mental Illness and Psychology*, 64–75.

44. For discussions of the lines of division between the labeling and medical models, see Walter Gove, "Societal Reaction as an Explanation of Mental Illness: An Evaluation," *American Sociological Review* 35 (1970): 873–84, and *The Labelling of Deviance: Evaluating a Perspective* (New York: Wiley, 1975); and Thomas Scheff, "The Labelling Theory of Mental Illness," *American Sociological Review* 39 (1974): 444–52.

45. Foucault, *Madness and Civilization*, x–xi.

46. See Petry, 2: 215n.

47. Szasz, *Myth of Mental Illness*, 163.

48. Foucault, *Mental Illness and Psychology*, 24, 26.

49. Edward Said, "Foucault and the Imagination of Power," in Hoy, ed., *Foucault: A Critical Reader*, 149.

50. Alan Olson emphasizes this point as well. Olson, 88.

51. Hyppolite was a major influence in Foucault's intellectual life. In his first lecture at the Collège de France in 1970 (*L'ordre du discours*), Foucault speaks of Hyppolite's work as having "traversed and formulated the most fundamental problems of our age. . . . It is because I have borrowed both the meaning and the possibility of what I am doing from him; . . . [and] because I would like to dedicate my work to him, that I end this presentation of my projected work by invoking the name of Jean Hyppolite." Translated as "The Discourse on Language" by Rupert Swyer, and included in an Appendix to *The Archaeology of Knowledge*, tr. A. M. Sheridan Smith (New York: Pantheon Books, 1972).

We may also cite the inscription of a copy of his *Discipline and Punish* Foucault sent to Hyppolite's widow in 1975: "For Madame Hyppolite, in memory of the man to whom I owe everything." Cited in Eribon, 18.

52. *Letters*, 106 (letter of March 1805).

53. For example, *Economic and Philosophical Manuscripts*, in Rodney Livingstone and Gregor Benton, tr. and ed., *Karl Marx: Early Writings* (New York: Random House, 1975), 383–400.

54. See, for example, Friedrich Engels, *Ludwig Feuerbach and the Outcome of Classical German Philosophy*, ed. C. P. Dutt (New York: International Publishers, 1978), 10–13.

55. The *lettre de cachet*, under the law of the French *ancien régime*, was a letter bearing the official seal of the king authorizing imprisonment (or sometimes exile) without trial.

56. See Castel, 60–69; and Doerner, 119–27. Various biographical details were found in J. Balteau, M. Barroux, and M. Prevost, eds.,

Dictionnaire de biographie française (Paris: Librairie Letouzey et Ané, 1933–89), and François Furet and Mona Ozouf, eds., *Dictionnaire critique de la révolution française* (Paris: Flammarion, 1988).

57. Doerner, 122.

58. See Doerner, 207–26.

59. Doerner, 198. Reil's journals were the *Archiv für Physiologie,* the *Magazin für die psychische Heilkunde,* and the *Beyträge zur Beförderung einer Kurmethode auf psyschischem Wege* (Doerner, 198, 327 n110).

60. Reil, *Über die Erkenntnis und Kur der Fieber,* 4: 43. Cited in Doerner, 203.

61. Reil, *Fieber,* 4: 45. Cited in Doerner, 199.

62. For example, see David Ausebel, "Personality Disorder *is* Disease," *American Psychologist* 16 (1961): 69–74; Robert Spitzer, "More on Pseudoscience in Science and the Case for Psychiatric Diagnosis," *Archives of General Psychiatry* 33 (1976): 459–70; and John Wing, *Reasoning about Madness* (London: Oxford University Press, 1978).

For general critiques of the labeling theory, see Walter Gove's works, already cited ("Societal Reaction as an Explanation of Mental Illness: An Evaluation," and *The Labelling of Deviance: Evaluating a Perspective*); Jack Gibbs, "Issues in Defining Deviant Behavior," in Robert Scott and Jack Douglas, eds., *Theoretical Perspectives on Deviance* (New York: Basic Books, 1972): 39–68; and Nanette Davis, "Labeling Theory in Deviance Research: A Critique and Reconsideration," *Sociological Quarterly* 13 (1972): 447–74.

63. Castel's *The Regulation of Madness* and Doerner's *Madmen and the Bourgeoisie* we have already mentioned (see especially chapter 2). Andrew Scull has published a great deal on the social history of madness, four of his most important works being *Museums of Madness* (London: Heinemann, 1978), "From Madness to Mental Illness: Medical Men as Moral Entrepreneurs," *European Journal of Sociology* 16 (1975): 219–61, "Madness and Segregative Control: The Rise of the Insane Asylum," *Social Problems* 24 (1977): 337–51, and (as editor and contributor of three articles) *Madhouses, Mad-Doctors, and Madmen: The Social History of Psychiatry in the Victorian Era* (Philadelphia: University of Pennsylvania Press, 1981). Richard Hunter and Ida Macalpine wrote the massive (over eleven hundred pages) *Three Hundred Years of Psychiatry, 1535–1860* (New York: Oxford University Press, 1963). Michael MacDonald's *Mystical Bedlam: Madness, Anxiety, and Healing in Seventeenth-Century England* (Cambridge: Cambridge University Press, 1981) is a detailed study of the seventeenth-century "astrological physician" Richard Napier and the social and cultural factors of early modern England which helped to shape his conception of madness.

64. In addition to the works of Thomas Scheff and Carol Warren already mentioned, some of the most representative labeling studies are: Norman Brill and Hugh Stornow, "Social Class and Psychiatric Treatment," *Archives of General Psychiatry* 3 (1960): 340–44; Phyllis Chesler, *Women and Madness* (New York: Avon, 1972); Peter Conrad and Joseph Schneider, *Deviance and Medicalization: From Badness to Sickness* (St. Louis: Mosby, 1980); Bruce Ennis, *Prisoners of Psychiatry* (New York: Harcourt, Brace & World, 1972); Bernard Gallagher, *The Sociology of Mental Illness* (Englewood Cliffs, NJ: Prentice-Hall, 1980); Erving Goffman, *Asylums* (Garden City, NJ: Doubleday, 1961); James R. Greenley, "Alternative Views of the Psychiatrist's Role," *Social Problems* 20 (1972): 15–26; Gerald Grob, *The State and the Mentally Ill* (Chapel Hill: University of North Carolina Press, 1966), and "Rediscovering Asylums: The Unhistorical History of the Mental Hospital," *Hastings Center Report* 7 (1977): 33–41; J. L. Hardisty, "Mental Illness: A Legal Fiction," *Washington Law Review* 48, no. 4 (1973): 735–62; August Hollingshead and Fredrick Redlich, *Social Class and Mental Illness: A Community Study* (New York: Wiley, 1958); and H. R. Lamb, Alvin P. Sorkin, and Jack Zusman, "Legislating Social Control of the Mentally Ill in California," *American Journal of Psychiatry* 138 (1979): 201–7.

See also Ronald Leifer, *In the Name of Mental Health: The Social Functions of Psychiatry* (New York: Science House, 1969); Alexander Leighton, "Cultural Relativity and the Identification of Psychiatric Disorders," in W. Caudill and T.-Y. Lin, eds., *Mental Health Research in Asia and the Pacific* (Honolulu: East-West Center Press, 1969): 448–62; Jane Mercer, *Labeling the Mentally Retarded: Clinical and Social System Perspectives on Mental Retardation* (Berkeley: University of California Press, 1973); Jane Murphy, "Psychiatric Labeling in Cross-Cultural Perspectives," *Science* 191 (1976): 1019–28; D. L. Rosenhan, "On Being Sane in Insane Places," *Science* 179 (1973): 250–58; Theodore Sarbin, "The Scientific Status of the Mental Illness Metaphor," in S. C. Plog and R. B. Edgerton, eds., *Changing Perspectives in Mental Illness* (New York: Holt, 1969); John Schwab and Mary Schwab, *Sociocultural Roots of Mental Illness: An Epidemiologic Survey* (New York: Plenum, 1978); Edwin Schur, *Labeling Deviant Behavior: Its Sociological Implications* (New York: Harper & Row, 1971); Steven P. Segal, Jim Baumohl, and Elsie Johnson, "Falling Through the Cracks: Mental Disorder and Social Margin in Young Vagrant Population," *Social Problems* 24 (1977): 387–400; and Nancy Waxler, "Culture and Mental Illness: A Social Labeling Perspective," *Journal of Nervous and Mental Disease* 159 (1974): 379–95.

For general discussions of labeling theory, see, in addition to Scheff's *Being Mentally Ill* and "The Labelling Theory of Mental Illness" (already cited), Edwin Schur, *Interpreting Deviance: A Sociological Introduction* (New York: Harper & Row, 1979); and George Bridges, "Deviance Theories," in Edgar Borgatta and Marie Borgatta, eds., *The Encyclopedia of Sociology* (New York: MacMillan, 1992): 476–87.

65. Warren, 6.

66. Pinel stresses the importance of the rationality of his patients throughout his *Treatise on Insanity* (e.g. 103, 135, 150, 156). See also Samuel Tuke, who in his own psychiatric practice insisted upon "treating the patient as much in the manner of a rational being as the state of his mind will possibly allow" (cited by Andrew Scull, "Moral Treatment Reconsidered: Some Sociological Comments on an Episode in the History of British Psychiatry," in Scull, ed., *Madhouses, Mad-Doctors, and Madmen,* 110). Bob Fine points out that this assumption was equally present in the early nineteenth-century prison reformers: "The prisoner was to be treated as a person, *who possessed a reason in common with all other persons,* in contrast to animals and objects. However hardened the prisoner was, beneath the surface of his or her criminality an irreducible reason still remained." "Objectification and the Contradictions of Bourgeois Power," *Economy and Society* 6, no. 4 (1977): 429.

67. Pinel, *Treatise,* 10. Compare Hegel: "The curative method . . . is partly physical and partly psychological. In some cases the former alone is sufficient; but in most cases it is necessary to supplement this by psychological treatment which, in its turn, can sometimes effect a cure by itself. . . . But the most effective treatment is always psychological" (PM § 408 Z).

68. Pinel, *Treatise,* 100.

69. Pinel, *Treatise,* 4, 89–90.

70. Pinel, *Treatise,* 68, 92.

71. Pinel, *Treatise,* 193–4.

72. Pinel, *Treatise,* 216.

73. Pinel, *Treatise,* 195.

74. Pinel, *Treatise,* 5, 107, 229.

75. Castel, 121. Castel further elaborates his argument in "Le traitement moral, thérapeutique mentale et contrôle social au XIXè siècle," *Topique,* no. 2 (1970).

76. Doerner, 134.

77. Foucault, *Madness and Civilization,* 258–59.

78. Foucault, *Madness and Civilization,* 247–48. See also Castel, *The Regulation of Madness,* 211: the value of labor in moral treatment is precisely its effectiveness in "the learning of order, regularity, and discipline."

79. Pinel, *Treatise,* 205.

80. Pinel, *Treatise,* 63.

81. Airaksinen, 162.

82. Avineri, 89, 144.

83. Translations of passages from PR/1819–20, as also from PR/1817–19 (the *Philosophy of Right* lectures of 1819–20 and 1817–19 respectively) are from Allen Wood, *Hegel's Ethical Thought,* chapter 14.

This idea recapitulates Thomas Hobbes' famous claim that prior to society, "nothing can be Unjust; the notions of Right and Wrong, Justice and Injustice have there no place. Where there is no common Power, there is no Law: where no Law, no Injustice, . . . [for these] are Qualities that relate to men in Society, not in Solitude." Hobbes, *Leviathan, or The Matter, Forme, and Power of a Common-Wealth Ecclesiasticall and Civill,* ed. C. B. MacPherson (New York: Viking Penguin, 1985), 188.

While Hegel never refers to Hobbes in his *Philosophy of Right,* in his lectures on the *History of Philosophy* he speaks of Hobbes' *Leviathan* and *De cive* as "contain[ing] sounder reflections on the nature of society and government than many now in circulation" (HP 3: 316). Hegel's discussion of Hobbes in these lectures is unusual for its relatively positive nature, departing from his more predictable polemical attitude towards British empiricist philosophy (Locke's school "calls itself Philosophy, although the object of Philosophy is not to be met with here"; Hume's philosophy "has been given a more important place in history than it deserves from its intrinsic nature"; and in general, the period of British empiricism is a period of "the decadence of thought" [*das Verkommen des Denkens*]: HP 3: 295, 369, 361 / W 3: 267).

84. See, for example, Marx, *Manuscripts,* in *Early Writings,* 327–29.

85. See also Airaksinen, 169: "If there is no state, no crimes or even wicked acts can be defined."

86. Avineri, 93–94.

87. Translations of JR passages (the *Jenaer Realphilosophie* lectures of 1805–1806) are from Shlomo Avinieri, *Hegel's Theory of the Modern State,* chapter 5.

88. Avineri, 98–99.

89. On this striking disparity between Hegel's radical critique of modern society and his conservative commitment to retaining an allegiance to it, see also Klaus Hartmann, "Towards a New Systematic Reading of Hegel's *Philosophy of Right,*" in Z. A. Pelczynski, ed., *The State and Civil Society: Studies in Hegel's Political Philosophy* (Cambridge: Cambridge University Press, 1984): 114–36; John McCumber, "Contradiction and Resolution in the State: Hegel's Covert View," *Clio* 15 (1986): 379–90; and Allen Wood, *Hegel's Ethical Thought,* 247–55.

90. Wood, *Hegel's Ethical Thought,* 249.

91. Jean-Baptiste Bô, *Rapport et projet de décret sur l'extinction de la mendicité, présenté à la Convention au nom du Comité de secours publics*; cited in Castel, 107.

92. Bernard d'Airy, *Rapport et projet sur l'organisation générale des secours publics, présenté à l'Assemblée nationale le 12 juin 1792*; cited in Castel, 107.

93. Comte Charles Marie Tanneguy Duchâtel, *De la charité dans ses rapports avec l'état moral et le bien-être des classes inférieures de la société* (Paris, 1829); cited in Castel, 108.

94. Castel, 108.

95. McCumber, 382.

96. Wood, *Hegel's Ethical Thought*, 250.

97. Wood, *Hegel's Ethical Thought*, 255.

Bibliography

Hegel

Hegel, Georg Wilhelm Freidrich, *Aesthetics: Lectures on Fine Art,* 2 vols., tr. T. M. Knox, Oxford: Clarendon Press, 1975.

———, *Briefe von und an Hegel,* 4 vols., ed. Johannes Hoffmeister, Hamburg: Felix Meiner, 1952–81.

———, *The Difference Between Fichte's and Schelling's System of Philosophy,* tr. H. S. Harris and Walter Cerf, Albany: State University of New York Press, 1977.

———, *Early Theological Writings,* ed. T. M. Knox, Philadelphia: University of Pennsylvania Press, 1977.

———, *The Encyclopædia Logic* (Part I of the *Encyclopædia*), tr. T. F. Geraets, W. A. Suchting, and H. S. Harris, Indianapolis: Hackett, 1991.

———, *Enzyklopädie der philosophischen Wissenschaften im Grundrisse,* ed. Friedhelm Nicolin und Otto Pöggeler, Hamburg: Felix Meiner Verlag, 1959.

———, *Essay on Natural Law,* tr. T. M. Knox, Philadelphia: University of Pennsylvania Press, 1975.

———, *Faith and Knowledge,* tr. Walter Cerf and H. S. Harris, Albany: State University of New York Press, 1977.

———, *Hegel: The Letters,* tr. Clark Butler and Christiane Seiler, Bloomington: Indiana University Press, 1984.

———, *Hegel's Logic* (Part I of the *Encyclopædia*), tr. William Wallace, Oxford: Clarendon Press, 1975.

———, *Hegel's Philosophy of Mind* (Part III of the *Encyclopædia*), tr. William Wallace, with translations of the *Zusätze* by A. V. Miller, Oxford: Clarendon Press, 1978.

264   *Bibliography*

——, *Hegel's Philosophy of Nature* (Part II of the *Encyclopædia*), tr. A. V. Miller, Oxford: Clarendon Press, 1970.

——, *Hegel's Philosophy of Nature* (Part II of the *Encyclopædia*), 3 vols., tr. M. J. Petry, London: Allen & Unwin, 1970.

——, *Hegel's Philosophy of Right*, tr. T. M. Knox, London: Oxford University Press, 1976.

——, *Hegel's Philosophy of Subjective Spirit* (Part III of the *Encyclopædia*), 3 vols., tr. M. J. Petry, Dordrecht, Holland: D. Reidel, 1979.

——, "Hegels Selbstanzeige," *Intelligenzblatt der Jenaer Allgemeinen Literatur-Zeitung*, 28 Oktober, 1807. Announcement of publication of *Die Phänomenologie des Geistes*.

——, *Hegel's Werke*, 18 vols., ed. P. Marheineke, J. Schulze, E. Gans, L. Henning, H. Hotho, K. Michelet, F. Förster, Berlin: Duncker und Humblot, 1832–45.

——, *Jenaer Realphilosophie (1805–1806)*, ed. J. Hoffmeister, Hamburg: Felix Meiner Verlag, 1969. (Previously titled *Jenenser Realphilosophie II: Die Vorlesungen von 1805–1806.*)

——, *Lectures on the History of Philosophy*, 3 vols., tr. E. S. Haldane and F. H. Simson, New York: Humanities Press, 1974.

——, *Lectures on the Philosophy of History*, tr. J. Sibree, New York: Willey Book Co., 1900.

——, *Lectures on the Philosophy of Religion*, 3 vols., tr. E. B. Speirs and J. B. Sanderson, London: Kegan Paul, Trench, Trübner, 1895.

——, *Phenomenology of Spirit*, tr. A. V. Miller, Oxford: Oxford University Press, 1979.

——, *Philosophie des Rechts: Die Mitschriften Wannenmann (Heidelberg 1817–1818) und Homeyer (Berlin 1818–1819)*, ed. Karl-Heinz Ilting, Stuttgart: Klett-Cotta Verlag, 1983.

——, *Philosophie des Rechts: Die Vorlesung von 1819/1820*, ed. Dieter Henrich, Frankfurt: Suhrkamp Verlag, 1983.

——, *The Philosophy of Fine Art*, 4 vols., tr. F. P. B. Osmaston, London: G. Bell and Sons, 1920.

——, *Reason in History* (the Introduction to the *Philosophy of History*), tr. Robert S. Hartman, Indianapolis: Bobbs-Merrill, 1953.

——, *Sämtliche Werke, Jubiläumsausgabe*, 26 vols., ed. H. Glockner, Stuttgart: Frommann Verlag, 1965–68.

——, *The Science of Logic*, tr. A. V. Miller, New York: Humanities Press, 1969.

———, *Vorlesungen über Rechtsphilosophie*, 6 vols., ed. Karl-Heinz Ilting, Stuttgart: Frommann Verlag, 1974.

———, *Werke*, 20 vols., ed. Eva Moldenhauer and Karl Markus Michel, Frankfurt am Main: Suhrkamp Verlag, 1970–79 (Theorie Werkausgabe).

Works on Hegel

Adorno, Theodor, "Aspekte," in *Drei Studien zu Hegel*, Frankfurt-am-Main: Suhrkamp, 1963: 11–65.

Airaksinen, Timo, "Insanity, Crime and the Structure of Freedom in Hegel," *Social Theory and Practice* 15 (1989): 155–78.

Ameriks, Karl, "The Hegelian Critique of Kantian Morality," in Bernard den Ouden and Marcia Moen, eds., *New Essays on Kant*, New York: Lang, 1987: 179–212.

Avineri, Shlomo, *Hegel's Theory of the Modern State*, Cambridge: Cambridge University Press, 1972.

Beierwalter, Werner, "Differenz, Negation, Identität: Die reflexive Bewegung der Hegelschen Dialektik," *Philosophische Abhandlungen* 49 (1980): 241–68.

Berthold-Bond, Daniel, "The Decentering of Reason: Hegel's Theory of Madness," *International Studies in Philosophy* 25, no. 1 (1993): 9–25.

———, "Freud's Critique of Philosophy," *Metaphilosophy* 20, nos. 3 & 4, 20th Anniversary Issue (1989): 274–94.

———, "Hegel on Madness and Tragedy," *History of Philosophy Quarterly* 11, no. 1 (1994): 71–99.

———, "Hegel, Nietzsche and Freud on Madness and the Unconscious," *The Journal of Speculative Philosophy* 5, no. 3 (1991): 193–213.

———, "Hegel's Eschatological Vision (Does History Have a Future?)": *History and Theory* 27, no. 1 (1988): 14–29.

———, *Hegel's Grand Synthesis: A Study of Being, Thought, and History*, Albany: State University of New York Press, 1989.

———, "Intentionality and Madness in Hegel's Psychology of Action," *International Philosophical Quarterly* 32, no. 4 (1992): 427–41.

———, Review of Kenneth Westphal's *Hegel's Epistemological Realism*, in *Review of Metaphysics* 45, no. 1 (1991): 157–8.

———, "The Two Faces of Desire: Evolution and Nostalgia in Hegel's Phenomenology of Desire," *Clio* 19, no. 4 (1990): 367–88.

Bodammer, Theodor, *Hegels Deutung der Sprache,* Hamburg: F. Meiner, 1969.

Boeder, Heribert, "Das natürliche Bewußtsein," *Hegel-Studien* 12 (1977): 157–78.

Bole, Thomas, "John Brown, Hegel, and the Speculative Concepts in Medicine," *Texas Reports on Biology and Medicine* 32, no. 1 (1974): 287–97.

Bonsiepen, Wolfgang von, "Dialektik und Negativität in der *Phänomenologie des Geistes*," *Hegel-Jahrbuch* (1974–5): 263–7.

Bossart, W. H., "Hegel on the Inverted World," *Philosophical Forum* 1 (1982): 326–41.

Bradley, A. C., "Hegel's Theory of Tragedy," in his *Oxford Lectures on Poetry,* London: Macmillan, 1926, 69–95.

Bungay, Stephen, *Beauty and Truth: A Study of Hegel's Aesthetics,* Oxford: Oxford University Press, 1987.

Butler, Judith, *Subjects of Desire: Hegelian Reflections in Twentieth-Century France,* New York: Columbia University Press, 1987.

Cassirer, Ernst, "Hölderlin und der deutsche Idealismus," in *Idee und Gestalt,* Darmstadt: Wissenschaftliche Buchgesellschaft, 1971: 113–56.

Christensen, Darrel E., "Hegel's Phenomenological Analysis and Freud's Psychoanalysis," *International Philosophical Quarterly* 8, no. 3 (1968): 356–78.

⸻, ed., *Hegel and the Philosophy of Religion,* The Hague: Martinus Nijhoff, 1970.

⸻, "The Theory of Mental Derangement and the Role and Function of Subjectivity in Hegel," *The Personalist* 49 (1968): 433–53.

Cohen, R. S., and M. W. Wartofsky, eds., *Hegel and the Sciences,* Dordrecht, Holland: D. Reidel, 1984.

Cook, Daniel, *Language in the Philosophy of Hegel,* New York: Mouton, 1973.

Crites, Stephen, *In the Twilight of Christendom: Hegel vs. Kierkegaard on Faith and History,* Chambersburg, PA: American Academy of Religion, 1972.

De Nys, Martin, " 'Sense Certainty' and Universality: Hegel's Entrance into the Phenomenology," *International Philosophical Quarterly* 18 (1978): 445–65.

Derrida, Jacques, *Margins of Philosophy,* tr. Alan Bass, Brighton: Harvester Press, 1982.

———, "Speech and Writing According to Hegel," tr. Alphonso Lingis, *Man and World* 11 (1978): 107–30.

Desmond, William, *Beyond Hegel and Dialectic: Speculation, Cult, and Comedy,* Albany: State University of New York Press, 1992.

DeVries, Willem, *Hegel's Theory of Mental Activity: An Introduction to Theoretical Spirit,* Ithaca: Cornell University Press, 1988.

Donougho, Martin, "The Woman in White: On the Reception of Hegel's *Antigone,*" *Owl of Minerva* 21 (1989): 65–89.

Dudeck, Caroline, "Hegel on Private Experience," *Philosophy Research Archives* 3 (1977): 102–12.

Düsing, Klaus, *Das Problem der Subjektivität in Hegel's Logik,* Bonn: Bouvier, 1976.

Elder, Crawford, *Appropriating Hegel,* Aberdeen University Press, 1980.

———, "Hegel's Teleology and the Relation between Mind and Brain," *Southern Journal of Philosophy* 17 (1979): 27–45.

Engelhardt, Dietrich von, "Hegel's Philosophical Understanding of Illness," in R. S. Cohen and M. W. Wartofsky, eds., *Hegel and the Sciences,* Dordrecht, Holland: D. Reidel, 1984: 41–54.

Fialko, Nathan, "Hegel's Views on Mental Derangement," *Journal of Abnormal and Social Psychology* 25, no. 2 (1930): 241–67.

Fink, Eugen, *Hegel,* Frankfurt-am-Main: Vittorio Klostermann, 1977.

Flay, Joseph, "Hegel's 'Inverted World'," *Review of Metaphysics* (1970): 662–78.

———, *Hegel's Quest for Certainty,* Albany: State University of New York Press, 1984.

Forster, Michael N., *Hegel and Scepticism,* Cambridge, MA: Harvard University Press, 1989.

Freier, F. V., "Kritik der Hegelschen Formalismusthese," *Kantstudien* 83, no. 3 (1992): 304–23.

Gadamer, Hans-Georg, *Hegel's Dialectic: Five Hermeneutical Studies,* tr. P. Christopher Smith, New Haven: Yale University Press, 1976.

Goldstein, Leon, "Force and the Inverted World in Dialectical Retrospection," *International Studies in Philosophy* 20 (1988): 13–28.

Gram, Moltke, "Moral and Literary Ideals in Hegel's Critique of 'The Moral World-View,'" *Clio* 7, no. 3 (1978): 375–402.

Greene, Murray, *Hegel on the Soul: A Speculative Anthropology,* The Hague: Martinus Nijhoff, 1972.

———, "Hegel's Conception of Psychology," in R. S. Cohen and M. W. Wartofsky, eds., *Hegel and the Sciences,* Dordrecht, Holland: D. Reidel, 1984: 161–91.

———, "Hegel's Notion of Inversion," *International Journal of the Philosophy of Religion* 1 (1970): 161–75.

———, "Hegel's 'Unhappy Consciousness' and Nietzsche's 'Slave Morality,'" in Darrel Christensen, ed., *Hegel and the Philosophy of Religion,* The Hague: Martinus Nijhoff, 1970: 125–41.

Griesheim, K. G. J. von, *Philosophie des Geistes, vorgelesen von Professor Hegel, Sommer 1825,* Staatsbibliothek Preussischer Kulturbesitz, Handschriftenabteilung, Archivstrasse 12–14, 1 Berlin 33.

Grimmlinger, Friedrich, "Zum Begriff des absoluten Wissens in Hegels Phänomenologie," in Hans-Dieter Klein and Erhard Oeser, eds., *Geschichte und System: Festschrift für Erich Heintel zum 60. Geburtstag,* München: R. Oldenbourg Verlag, 1972.

Gutterer, Dietrich, "Der Spekulative Satz," *Kodikas/Code* 1 (1979): 235–47.

Harris, Errol E., "Hegel's Theory of Feeling," in Warren E. Steinkraus, ed., *New Studies in Hegel's Philosophy,* New York: Holt, Rinehart, Winston, 1971: 71–91.

Hartmann, Klaus, "Towards a New Systematic Reading of Hegel's *Philosophy of Right,*" in Z. A. Pelczynski, ed., *The State and Civil Society: Studies in Hegel's Political Philosophy,* Cambridge: Cambridge University Press, 1984: 114–36.

Harvey, Irene, "The Linguistic Basis of Truth for Hegel," *Man and World* 15 (1982): 285–97.

Heidegger, Martin, *Hegel's Phenomenology of Spirit,* tr. Parvis Emad and Kenneth Maly, Indianapolis: Indiana University Press, 1980.

———, *Hegel's Concept of Experience,* tr. Kenley Royce Dove, New York: Harper & Row, 1970.

Heinrichs, Johannes, *Die Logik der Phänomenologie des Geistes,* Bonn: Bouvier Verlag Herbert Grundmann, 1974.

Henrich, Dieter, "Formen der Negation in Hegels Logik," in R.-P. Horstmann, ed., *Seminar: Dialektik in der Philosophie Hegels,* Frankfurt am Main: Philosophische Abhandlungen, 1978: 241–68.

———, "Hegel und Hölderlin," in *Hegel im Kontext,* Frankfurt: Suhrkamp, 1971: 9–40.

Hotho, Heinrich, *Philosophie des Geistes, nach dem Vortrage des herrn Professor Hegel, im Sommer 1822,* Staatsbibliothek Preussischer Kulturbesitz, Handschriftenabteilung, Archivstrasse 12–14, 1 Berlin 33.

Houlgate, Stephen, *Hegel, Nietzsche and the Criticism of Metaphysics,* Cambridge: Cambridge University Press, 1986.

Hoy, David, "Hegel's Critique of Kantian Morality," *History of Philosophy Quarterly* 6 (1989): 207–32.

Hyppolite, Jean, *Genesis and Structure of Hegel's Phenomenology of Spirit,* tr. Samuel Cherniak and John Heckman, Evanston: Northwestern University Press, 1974.

———, "Hegel's Phenomenology and Psychoanalysis," tr. Albert Richer, in Warren E. Steinkraus, ed., *New Studies in Hegel's Philosophy,* New York: Holt, Rinehart, Winston, 1971: 57–70.

Jamme, Christoph, "Hegel and Hölderlin," tr. Richard Findler and Clark Butler, *Clio* 15 (1986): 359–77.

Kainz, Howard, *Hegel's Phenomenology, Part I,* University, AL: University of Alabama Press, 1976.

Kaufmann, Walter, ed. and tr., *Hegel: A Reinterpretation,* Notre Dame: University of Notre Dame Press, 1965.

———, *Hegel: Texts and Commentary,* Garden City, NY: Doubleday, 1965.

———, "Hegel's Ideas about Tragedy," in Warren E. Steinkraus, ed., *New Studies in Hegel's Philosophy,* New York: Holt, Rinehart, Winston, 1971: 201–20.

Kehler, H. von, *Philosophie des Geistes nach Hegel, Sommer 1825,* Universitätsbibliothek, Goethealle 6, 69 Jena.

Kervegan, Jean-François, "Le problème de la fondation de l'éthique: Kant, Hegel," *Revue de Métaphysique et de Morale* 95 (1990): 33–55.

Kettner, Matthias, *Hegels "Sinnliche Gewissheit": Diskursanalytischer Kommentar,* Main: Campus, 1990.

Kojève, Alexandre, *Introduction to the Reading of Hegel,* tr. James Nichols, ed. Allan Bloom, Ithaca: Cornell University Press, 1980.

Labarrière, Pierre-Jean, *Structures et mouvement dialectique dans la Phénoménologie de l'esprit de Hegel,* Paris: Aubier-Montaigne, 1968.

Lamb, David, "Hegel and Wittgenstein on Language and Sense-Certainty," *Clio* 7 (1978): 285–301.

——, *Language and Perception in Hegel and Wittgenstein,* New York: St. Martin's Press, 1979.

Lauer, Quentin, *Essays in Hegelian Dialectic,* New York: Fordham University Press, 1977.

——, "Phenomenology: Hegel and Husserl," in Frederick Weiss, ed., *Beyond Epistemology: New Studies in the Philosophy of Hegel,* The Hague: Nijhoff, 1975: 174–96.

——, *A Reading of Hegel's Phenomenology of Spirit,* New York: Fordham University Press, 1976.

Leary, David E., "German Idealism and the Development of Psychology in the Nineteenth Century," *Journal of the History of Philosophy* 18 (1980): 299–317.

Lukács, Georg, *The Young Hegel: Studies in the Relations Between Dialectics and Economics,* tr. Rodney Livingstone, Cambridge, MA: MIT, 1975.

MacIntyre, Alasdair, ed., *Hegel: A Collection of Critical Essays,* Notre Dame: University of Notre Dame Press, 1972.

Marcuse, Herbert, *Hegel's Ontology and the Theory of Historicity,* tr. Seyla Benhabib, Cambridge, MA: MIT Press, 1987.

——, *Reason and Revolution: Hegel and the Rise of Social Theory,* Boston: Beacon, 1969.

McCumber, John, "Contradiction and Resolution in the State: Hegel's Covert View," *Clio* 15 (1986): 379–90.

——, "A Mind–Body Problem in Hegel's *Phenomenology of Spirit,*" *International Studies in Philosophy* 12 (1980): 41–52.

McTaggart, J. E., "Hegel's Theory of Punishment," *International Journal of Ethics* 6 (1896), reprinted in Gertrude Ezorsky, ed., *Philosophical Perspectives on Punishment,* Albany: State University of New York Press, 1972.

Michalewski, Czeslaw, "La négativité de l'action," *Les Etudes Philosophiques* (1978): 291–5.

Mills, Patricia Jagentowicz, "Hegel's *Antigone,*" *Owl of Minerva* 17 (1986): 131–52.

Mohanty, J. N., *The Possibility of Transcendental Philosophy* (*Phaenomenologica,* vol. 98), Dordrecht: Martinus Nijhoff, 1985.

Muller, Philippe, "Connaissance concrète de l'homme chez Hegel," *Studia Philosophica,* nos. 30–31 (1970–71): 207–24.

Nicholson, Peter, "Hegel on Crime," *History of Political Theory* 3 (1982): 103–21.

O'Hagan, T., "On Hegel's Critique of Kant's Moral and Political Philosophy," in Stephen Priest, ed., *Hegel's Critique of Kant,* Oxford: Oxford University Press, 1987: 135–59.

Olson, Alan, *Hegel and the Spirit,* Princeton: Princeton University Press, 1992.

Pelczynski, A., ed., *The State and Civil Society: Studies in Hegel's Political Philosophy,* Cambridge: Cambridge University Press, 1984.

Piertercil, Raymond, "Antigone and Hegel," *International Philosophical Quarterly* 18 (1978): 289–310.

Pippin, Robert B., *Hegel's Idealism: The Satisfactions of Self-Consciousness,* Cambridge: Cambridge University Press, 1989.

———, "Hegel's Original Insight," *International Philosophical Quarterly* 33, no. 3 (1993): 285–95.

Pöggeler, Otto, "Hegel's Jugendschriften und die Idee einer Phänomenologie des Geistes," Habilitation, Heidelberg, 1966.

Ravven, Heidi, "A Response to Stuart Swindle's 'Why Feminists Should Take the *Phenomenology of Spirit* Seriously'," *Owl of Minerva* 24, no. 1 (1992): 63–68.

Rockmore, Tom, *Hegel's Circular Epistemology,* Bloomington: Indiana University Press, 1986.

Rosen, Stanley, *Hegel: An Introduction to the Science of Wisdom,* New Haven: Yale University Press, 1974.

Rosenkranz, Karl, *G. W. F. Hegels Leben,* Berlin: Duncker und Humblot Verlag, 1844; reprint, Darmstadt: Wissenschaftliche Buchgesellschaft, 1977.

Röttges, Heinz, *Dialektik und Skeptizismus,* Frankfurt: Athenaum, 1987.

Sedgwick, Sally, "Hegel's Critique of the Subjective Idealism of Kant's Ethics," *Journal of the History of Philosophy* 26 (1988): 89–105.

———, "On the Relation of Pure Reason to Content: A Reply to Hegel's Critique of Formalism in Kant's Ethics," *Philosophy and Phenomenological Research* 49 (1988): 59–80.

———, "Pippin on Hegel's Critique of Kant," *International Philosophical Quarterly* 33, no. 3 (1993): 273–83.

Shklar, Judith, *Freedom and Independence: A Study of the Political Ideas of Hegel's Phenomenology of Mind,* Cambridge: Cambridge University Press, 1976.

Solomon, Robert, *In the Spirit of Hegel,* Oxford: Oxford University Press, 1985.

Stace, W. T., *The Philosophy of Hegel,* New York: Dover, 1955.

Staiger, Emil, *Der Geist der Liebe und das Schicksal: Schelling, Hegel und Hölderlin,* Frauenfeld: Huber, 1935.

Steinkraus, Warren E., ed., *New Studies in Hegel's Philosophy,* New York: Holt, Rinehart, Winston, 1971.

Sterling, J. Hutchison, *The Secret of Hegel,* New York: Putnam's, 1898.

Stern, Paul, "On the Relation Between Autonomy and Ethical Community: Hegel's Critique of Kantian Morality," *Praxis International* 9, no. 3 (1989): 234–48.

Steward, Jon, "Die Rolle des unglücklichen Bewusstseins in Hegels *Phänomenologie des Geistes,*" *Deutsche Zeitschrift für Philosophie* 39, no. 1 (1991): 12–21.

Surber, Jere Paul, "Hegel's Speculative Sentence," *Hegel-Studien* 10 (1975): 212–30.

Swindle, Stuart, "Why Feminists Should Take the *Phenomenology of Spirit* Seriously," *Owl of Minerva* 24, no. 1 (1992): 41–54.

Taylor, Charles, *Hegel,* Cambridge: Cambridge University Press, 1977.

————, "The Opening Arguments of Hegel's Phenomenology," in Alasdair MacIntyre, ed., *Hegel: A Collection of Critical Essays,* Notre Dame: University of Notre Dame Press, 1972: 151–87.

Ver Eecke, Wilfried, "Negation and Desire in Freud and Hegel," *Owl of Minerva* 15 (1983): 11–22.

————, *Saying "No": Its Meaning in Child Development, Psychoanalysis, Linguistics, and Hegel,* Pittsburgh: Duquesne University Press, 1984.

Verene, Donald Phillip, *Hegel's Recollection: A Study of Images in the Phenomenology of Spirit,* Albany: State University of New York Press, 1985.

De Waelhens, Alphonse, "Réflexions sur une problématique Husserlienne de l'inconscient, Husserl et Hegel," in *Edmund Husserl 1859–1959 (Phaenomenologica* 4), La Haye: Martinus Nijhoff, 1959: 221–37.

Wahl, Jean, *Le malheur de la conscience dans la philosophie de Hegel,* Paris: Presses Universitaires de France, 1951.

Webb, Thomas, "Scepticism and Hegelian Science," *Dialogue* 16 (1977): 139–62.

Weiss, Frederick, ed., *Beyond Epistemology: New Studies in the Philosophy of Hegel*, The Hague: Nijhoff, 1975.

Werkmeister, W. H., "Hegel's Phenomenology of Mind as a Development of Kant's Basic Ontology," in Darrel Christensen, ed., *Hegel and the Philosophy of Religion*, The Hague: Martinus Nijhoff, 1970: 93–107.

Westphal, Kenneth, *Hegel's Epistemological Realism*, Dordrecht, Holland: Kluwer, 1989.

———, "Hegel, Idealism, and Robert Pippin," *International Philosophical Quarterly* 33, no. 3 (1993): 263–72.

Westphal, Merold, *History and Truth in Hegel's Phenomenology*, Atlantic Highlands, NJ: Humanities, 1979.

Wiehl, Reiner, "Über den Sinn der sinnlichen Gewissheit in Hegels *Phänomenologie des Geistes*," *Hegel-Studien* 3 (1966): 103–34.

Wieland, W., "Hegels Dialektik der sinnlichen Gewissheit," in Dietrich Gerhardt et al., eds., *Orbis Scriptus: Dmitrij Tschizewskij zum 70. Geburtstag*, München: Wilhelm Fink Verlag, 1966: 933–41.

Willett, Cynthia, "Hegel, Antigone, and the Possibility of Ecstatic Dialogue," *Philosophy and Literature* 14, no. 2 (1990): 268–83.

Williams, Robert, "Hegel and Skepticism," *Owl of Minerva* 24, no. 1 (1992): 71–82.

———, *Recognition: Fichte and Hegel on the Other*, Albany: State University of New York Press, 1992.

Wood, Allen W., "The Emptiness of the Moral Will," *Monist* 72 (1989): 454–83.

———, *Hegel's Ethical Thought*, Cambridge: Cambridge University Press, 1993.

Zimmerman, Robert, "Hegel's 'Inverted World' Revisited," *Philosophical Forum* 1 (1982): 342–70.

Other Works

d'Airy, Bernard, *Rapport et projet sur l'organisation générale des secours publics, présenté à l'Assemblée nationale le 12 juin 1792*, Paris: L'Imprimerie nationale, [1793?].

Alexander, Franz, and Sheldon Selesnick, *The History of Psychiatry*, New York: Harper, 1966.

Arac, Jonathan, ed., *After Foucault: Humanistic Knowledge, Postmodern Challenges*, New Brunswick, NJ: Rutgers University Press, 1988.

Arrowsmith, William, "A Greek Theater of Ideas," *Arion* 2 (1963): 32–56.

Ausebel, David, "Personality Disorder *is* Disease," *American Psychologist* 16 (1961): 69–74.

Balteau, J., M. Barroux, and M. Prevost, eds., *Dictionnaire de biographie française*, Paris: Librairie Letouzey et Ané, 1933–89.

Bayle, Antoine Laurent Jessé, *Recherches sur les maladies mentales*, Paris: [n. p.], 1822.

Beck, Adolf, ed., *Hölderlins Diotima, Susette Gontard*, Frankfurt: Insel Verlag, 1980.

Belenky, Mary Field, and Blythe Clinchy, Nancy Goldberger, Jill Tarule, eds., *Women's Ways of Knowing*, New York: Basic Books, 1986.

Bernadete, Seth, "A Reading of Sophocles' *Antigone: I,*" *Interpretation* 4 (1975): 148–96.

Bertaux, Pierre, *Friedrich Hölderlin*, Frankfurt am Main: Suhrkamp, 1978.

Bertrand, Alexandre Jacques Francois, *Du magnétisme animal en France,* ... *avec le texte des divers rapports faits en 1784 par les commissaires de l'Academie des sciences, de la Faculté et de la Société royale de médecine* ... , Paris: J. B. Baillière, 1826.

Binet, A., and C. Féré, *Animal Magnetism*, London: D. Appleton, 1888.

Bô, Jean-Baptiste, *Rapport et projet de décret sur l'extinction de la mendicité, présenté à la Convention au nom du Comité de secours publics*, Paris: L'Imprimerie nationale, [1793?].

Bonnefoy, Jean-Baptiste, *Analyse raisonnée des rapports des commissaires chargés par le Roi de l'examen du magnétisme animal*, Lyons: Prault, 1784.

Brecht, Martin, "Hölderlin und das Tübinger Stift 1788–1793," *Hölderlin-Jahrbuch* 18 (1973–74): 20–48.

Brett, George, *A History of Psychology*, London: Allen & Unwin, 1921.

Bridges, George, "Deviance Theories," in Edgar Borgatta and Marie Borgatta, eds., *The Encyclopedia of Sociology*, New York: MacMillan, 1992: 476–87.

Brill, Norman, and Hugh Stornow, "Social Class and Psychiatric Treatment," *Archives of General Psychiatry* 3 (1960): 340–44.

Camus, Albert, "An Absurd Reasoning," in *The Myth of Sisyphus and Other Essays*, tr. Justin O'Brien, New York: Random House, 1955.

Candidus (pseudonym), "Nicht Anklage, sondern Klage," *Journal der practischen Heilkunde* 33 (1816): 110–16.

Castel, Robert, *L'Ordre psychiatrique*, Paris: Les Éditions de Minuit, 1976. / *The Regulation of Madness: The Origins of Incarceration in France*, tr. W. D. Halls, Berkeley: University of California Press, 1988.

——, "Les Aventures de la pratique," *Le Débat* (1986).

——, "Le traitement moral, thérapeutique mentale et contrôle social au XIXè siècle," *Topique*, no. 2 (1970).

Cavell, Stanley, *Must We Mean What We Say?* New York: Scribner, 1969.

Chapelle, Daniel, *Nietzsche and Psychoanalysis*, Albany: State University of New York Press, 1994.

Chesler, Phyllis, *Women and Madness*, New York: Avon, 1972.

Conrad, Peter, and Joseph Schneider, *Deviance and Medicalization: From Badness to Sickness*, St. Louis: Mosby Press, 1980.

Cooper, David, *Psychiatry and Anti-Psychiatry*, London: Tavistock, 1967.

Darnton, Robert, *Mesmerism and the End of the Enlightenment in France*, New York: Schocken Books, 1970.

Davis, Michael, "Politics and Madness," in J. Peter Euben, ed., *Greek Tragedy and Political Theory*, Berkeley: University of California Press, 1986: 142–61.

Davis, Nanette, "Labeling Theory in Deviance Research: A Critique and Reconsideration," *Sociological Quarterly* 13 (1972): 447–74.

Deleuze, Gilles, *Anti-Oedipus: Capitalism and Schizophrenia*, tr. Robert Hurley, Mark Seem, and Helen R. Lane, New York: Viking Press, 1977.

——, *Nietzsche and Philosophy*, tr. Hugh Tomlinson, New York: Columbia University Press, 1983.

——, *Un nouvel archiviste*, Paris: Fata Morgana, 1972.

Dewey, John, *Art as Experience*, in A. Hofstadter and R. Kuhns, eds., *Philosophies of Art and Beauty*, Chicago: University of Chicago Press, 1976.

Dewhurst, Kenneth, *John Locke, Physician and Philosopher: A Medical Biography with an Edition of the Medical Notes in His Journals*, London: Wellcome Historical Medical Library, 1963.

Dilthey, Wilhelm, "Friedrich Hölderlin," in *Das Erlebnis und die Dichtung,* 14th ed., Göttingen: Vandenhoeck und Ruprecht, 1965: 242–317.

Doerner, Klaus, *Bürger und Irre,* Europäische Verlagsanstalt, 1969. / *Madmen and the Bourgeoisie: A Social History of Insanity and Psychiatry,* tr. Joachim Neugroschel and Jean Steinberg, Oxford: Basil Blackwell, 1981.

Dreyfus, Hubert L., and Paul Rabinow, *Michel Foucault: Beyond Structuralism and Hermeneutics,* with an Afterword by Michel Foucault, Chicago: University of Chicago Press, 1982.

Duchâtel, Comte Charles Marie Tanneguy, *De la charité dans ses rapports avec l'état moral et le bien-être des classes inférieures de la société,* Paris: A. Mesnier, 1829.

Engels, Friedrich, *Ludwig Feuerbach and the Outcome of Classical German Philosophy,* ed. C. P. Dutt, New York: International Publishers, 1978.

Ennis, Bruce, *Prisoners of Psychiatry,* New York: Harcourt, Brace & World, 1972.

Eribon, Didier, *Michel Foucault,* tr. Betsy Wing, Cambridge, MA: Harvard University Press, 1991.

Euben, Peter, ed., *Greek Tragedy and Political Theory,* Berkeley: University of California Press, 1986.

Ezorsky, Gertrude, ed., *Philosophical Perspectives on Punishment,* Albany: State University of New York Press, 1972.

Falret, Jules-Philippe, *Des maladies mentales et des asilees d'aliénés,* Paris: Baillière, 1864.

Fine, Bob, "Objectification and the Contradictions of Bourgeois Power," *Economy and Society* 6, no. 4 (1977): 408–35.

Fischer-Homberger, Esther, "Eighteenth-Century Nosology and its Survivors," *Medical History* 14, no. 4 (1970): 397–98.

Flax, Jane, *Thinking Fragments: Psychoanalysis, Feminism, and Postmodernism in the Contemporary West,* Berkeley: University of California Press, 1990.

Foucault, Michel, *L'Archéologie du Savoir,* Paris: Éditions Gallimard, 1969. / *The Archaeology of Knowledge,* tr. A. M. Sheridan Smith, New York: Pantheon Books, 1972.

————, *Folie et déraison: histoire de la folie à l'âge classique,* Paris: Librairie Plon, 1961. / *Madness and Civilization: A History of*

Insanity in the Age of Reason, tr. Richard Howard, New York: Random House, 1965.

———, "Human Nature: Justice versus Power," transcript of televised debate with Noam Chomsky (Amsterdam, 1971), in Fons Elders, ed., *Reflexive Water: The Basic Concerns of Mankind*, London: Souvenir Press, 1974.

———, *Maladie Mentale et Psychologie*, Paris: Presses Universitaires de France, 1962. / *Mental Illness and Psychology*, tr. Alan Sheridan, Berkeley: University of California Press, 1987.

———, *Naissance de la Clinique: une archéologie du regard médical*, Paris: Presses Universitaires de France, 1963. / *The Birth of the Clinic: An Archaeology of Medical Perception*, tr. A. M. Sheridan Smith, New York: Random House, 1973.

———, *L'ordre du discours*, Paris: Gallimard, 1971. / *The Discourse on Language*, tr. Rupert Swyer, in the Appendix to A. M. Sheridan Smith's translation of *The Archaeology of Knowledge*.

———, *Surveiller et punir: naissance de la prison*, Paris: Gallimard, 1975. / *Discipline and Punish: the Birth of the Prison*, tr. Alan Sheridan, New York: Pantheon, 1977.

Franklin, Benjamin, et al., *Rapport des commissaires chargés par le Roi de l'examen du magnétisme animal*, Paris: L'Imprimerie royale, 1784.

Freeman, Kathleen, ed., *Ancilla to the Pre-Socratic Philosophers*, Cambridge, MA: Harvard University Press, 1957.

French Royal Society of Medicine, *Rapport des commissaires de la Société Royale de Médecine, nommés par le Roi pour faire l'examen du magnétisme animal*, Paris: L'Imprimerie royale, 1784.

Freud, Sigmund, *Standard Edition of the Complete Psychological Works of Sigmund Freud*, 24 vols., ed. James Strachey, London: Hogarth, 1953ff.

———, *An Autobiographical Study*, in the *Standard Edition*, vol. 20: 7–74.

———, *Beyond the Pleasure Principle*, in the *Standard Edition*, vol. 18: 7–64.

———, *A Case of Successful Treatment by Hypnotism*, in the *Standard Edition*, vol. 1: 117–28.

———, *Civilization and its Discontents*, in the *Standard Edition*, vol. 21: 64–145.

———, *Creative Writers and Daydreaming*, in the *Standard Edition*, vol. 9: 143–53.

————, *Delusions and Dreams in Jensen's* Gradiva, in the *Standard Edition*, vol. 9: 7–95.

————, *The Ego and the Id*, in the *Standard Edition*, vol. 19: 12–66.

————, *Formulations on the The Two Principles of Mental Functioning*, in the *Standard Edition*, vol. 12: 218–26.

————, *The Future of an Illusion*, in the *Standard Edition*, vol. 21: 5–56.

————, *Hypnosis*, in the *Standard Edition*, vol. 1: 105–14.

————, *Inhibitions, Symptoms and Anxiety*, in the *Standard Edition*, vol. 20: 87–174.

————, *Instincts and Their Vicissitudes*, in the *Standard Edition*, vol. 14: 117–40

————, *The Interpretation of Dreams*, in the *Standard Edition*, vols. 4, 5: xxiii–xxxii, 1–621.

————, *Introductory Lectures on Psycho-analysis*, in the *Standard Edition*, vols. 15, 16: 9–463.

————, *Leonardo Da Vinci and a Memory of his Childhood*, in the *Standard Edition*, vol. 11: 63–137.

————, *The Moses of Michelangelo*, in the *Standard Edition*, vol. 13: 211–36.

————, *On Narcissism*, in the *Standard Edition*, vol. 14: 73–102.

————, *Negation*, in the *Standard Edition*, vol. 19: 235–39.

————, *New Introductory Lectures on Psycho-analysis*, in the *Standard Edition*, vol. 22: 5–182.

————, "Preface to Reik's *Ritual: Psycho-Analytic Studies*," in the *Standard Edition*, vol. 17: 259–63.

————, "Preface to the Translation of Bernheim's *Suggestion*," in the *Standard Edition*, vol. 1: 75–85.

————, *On Psycho-analysis*, in the *Standard Edition*, vol. 12: 207–11.

————, *The Psychopathology of Everyday Life*, in the *Standard Edition*, vol. 6: 1–279.

————, *The Question of Lay Analysis*, in the *Standard Edition*, vol. 20: 183–258.

————, *Report on my Studies in Paris and Berlin*, in the *Standard Edition*, vol. 1: 5–15.

————, "Review of August Forel's *Hypnotism*," in the *Standard Edition*, vol. 1: 91–102.

————, *The Unconscious,* in the *Standard Edition,* vol. 14: 166–215.

Furet, François, and Mona Ozonf, *Dictionnaire critique de la révolution française,* Paris: Flammarion, 1988.

Gall, Franz Joseph, *Sur les fonctions du cerveau et sur celles de chacune de ses parties,* 6 vols., Paris: Schoell, 1809.

Gallagher, Bernhard, *The Sociology of Mental Illness,* Englewood Cliffs, NJ: Prentice-Hall, 1980.

Gauthier, Yvon, "Langage et psychanalyse," *Dialogue* 7 (1969): 633–38.

Gibbs, Jack, "Issues in Defining Deviant Behavior," in Robert Scott and Jack Douglas, eds., *Theoretical Perspectives on Deviance,* New York: Basic Books, 1972: 39–68.

Goffman, Erving, *Asylums,* Garden City, NJ: Doubleday, 1961.

Gove, Walter, "Labelling and Mental Illness: A Critique," in Walter Gove, ed., *The Labelling of Deviance: Evaluating a Perspective,* New York: Wiley, 1975: 35–81.

————, "Societal Reaction as an Explanation of Mental Illness: An Evaluation," *American Sociological Review* 35 (1970): 873–84.

Greene, William Chase, *Moira: Fate, Good, and Evil in Greek Thought,* New York: Harper & Row, 1963.

Greenley, "Alternative Views of the Psychiatrist's Role," *Social Problems* 20 (1972): 15–26.

Grene, David, and Richmond Lattimore, eds., *The Complete Greek Tragedies,* 4 vols., Chicago: Chicago University Press, 1959–60.

Griffin, Susan, *Woman and Nature: The Roaring Inside Her,* New York: Harper & Row, 1978.

Grob, Gerald, "Rediscovering Asylums: The Unhistorical History of the Mental Hospital," *Hastings Center Report* 7 (1977): 33–41.

————, *The State and the Mentally Ill,* Chapel Hill, NC: University of North Carolina Press, 1966.

Habermas, Jürgen, *Lectures on the Discourse of Modernity,* Cambridge, MA: Harvard University Press, 1985.

Hacking, Ian, "The Archaeology of Foucault," in David Couzens Hoy, ed., *Foucault: A Critical Reader,* Oxford: Basil Blackwell, 1986: 27–40.

Hampton, Jean, "The Moral Education Theory of Punishment," *Philosophy and Public Affairs* 13 (1984): 208–38.

Hardisty, J. L., "Mental Illness: A Legal Fiction," *Washington Law Review* 48, no. 4 (1973): 735–62.

Harper, Andrew, *Observations on Insanity*, London: [n. p.], 1790.

Hartmann, P. C., *Theorie der Krankheit*, Vienna: Gerold, 1823.

Hayim, Gila, "Hegel's Critical Theory and Feminist Concerns," *Philosophy and Social Criticism* 16, no. 1 (1990): 1–21.

Hecker, A. F., *Kunst, die Krankheiten der Menschen zu Heilen*, Erfurt: Henning, 1804.

Heidegger, Martin, *Being and Time*, tr. John Macquarrie and Edward Robinson, New York: Harper & Row, 1962.

Heine, Heinrich, *Sämtliche Werke*, 7 vols., ed. Ernst Elster, Leipzig: Bibliographisches Institut, 1922.

Heinroth, Johann Christian, *Lehrbuch der Störungen des Seelenlebens vom rationalen Standpunkt aus entworfen*, 2 vols., Leipzig, 1823–24. / *Textbook of Disturbances of Mental Life*, 2 vols., Ann Arbor, MI: Books on Demand, 1975.

Herrera, Robert, "Freud on Nietzsche—A Fantastic Commentary?" *Philosophy Today* (1985): 339–44.

Historische Commission bei der Königl. Akademie der Wissenschaften, *Allgemeine Deutsche Biographie*, 56 vols., Leipzig: Duncker und Humblot, 1875–1912.

Hobbes, Thomas, *Leviathan, or The Matter, Forme, and Power of a Common-Wealth Ecclesiasticall and Civill*, ed. C. B. MacPherson, New York: Viking Penguin, 1985.

Hölderlin, Friedrich, *Sämtliche Werke*, 7 vols., ed. Friedrich Beissner and Adolf Beck, Stuttgart: Kohlhammer, Cotta, 1943ff (the *Grosse Stuttgarter Hölderlin-Ausgabe*).

Hollingshead, August, and Fredrick Redlich, *Social Class and Mental Illness: A Community Study*, New York: Wiley, 1958.

Horwitz, Allan V., *The Social Control of Mental Illness*, New York: Harcourt Brace Jovanovich, 1982.

Hoy, David Couzens, ed., *Foucault: A Critical Reader*, Oxford: Basil Blackwell, 1986.

Hufeland, Christoph Wilhelm, *System der practischen Heilkunde*, 2 vols., Frankfurt, Leipzig, and Jena: F. Frommann, 1800–05.

———, et al., "Mesmerismus oder System der Wechselwirkungen," and "Erläuterungen zum Mesmerismus," Commission reports to the Prussian Government, Berlin: Rikolais, 1814, 1815.

Hume, David, *An Enquiry Concerning Human Understanding*, Indianapolis: Hackett, 1977.

Hunter, Richard, and Ida Macalpine, *Three Hundred Years of Psychiatry, 1535–1860*, New York: Oxford University Press, 1963.

———, *George III and the Mad-Business*, London: Allen Lane, 1969.

Hyppolite, Jean, *Figures de la pensée philosophique*, 2 vols., Paris: Presses Universitaires de France, 1971.

———, "A Spoken Commentary on Freud's *Verneinung*," in Jacques-Alain Miller, ed., *The Seminar of Jacques Lacan, Book I: Freud's Papers on Technique 1953–1954*, tr. John Forrester, New York: Norton, 1988: 289–97.

Ideler, Karl, *Grundriss der Seelenheilkunde*, 2 vols., Berlin: Enslin, 1835–38.

Irigaray, Luce, *The Speculum of the Other Woman*, tr. Gillian C. Gill, Ithaca: Cornell University Press, 1985.

Jacobi, Maximilian, *Beobachtungen über die Pathologie und Therapie der mit Irresein verbundenen Krankheiten*, Elberfeld: Schoeniänsche Buchhandlung, 1830.

Jagger, Alison, and Susan Bordo, eds., *Gender / Body / Knowledge: Feminist Reconstructions of Being and Knowing*, New Brunswick, NJ: Rutgers University Press, 1991.

Jaspers, Karl, *Schelling: Grösse und Verhängnis*, Munich: Piper, 1955.

———, *Nietzsche: Einführung in das Verständnis seines Philosophierens*, Berlin: Walter de Gruyter Verlag, 1936. / *Nietzsche: An Introduction to the Understanding of His Philosophical Activity*, tr. C. F. Wallraff and F. J. Schmitz, Chicago: Henry Regnery, 1965.

Jones, Ernest, *The Life and Work of Sigmund Freud*, 3 vols., New York: Basic Books, 1953.

Jones, Kathleen, *Lunacy, Law, and Conscience 1744–1845*, London: Routledge and Kegan Paul, 1955.

Kant, Immanuel, *Anthropologie in pragmatischer Hinsicht*, 1798, in *Werke* 6: 395–690.

———, *Critique of Pure Reason*, tr. Norman Kemp Smith, London: Macmillan, 1973.

———, *Gesammelte Schriften*, 23 vols., ed. by the Preussische Akademie der Wissenschaften, Berlin: Georg Reimer, 1902–55.

———, *Versuch über die Krankheiten des Kopfes*, 1764, in *Werke* 1: 885–902.

———, *Werke*, 6 vols., ed. Wilhelm Weischedel, Frankfurt am Main: Wissenschaftliche Buchgesellschaft Darmstadt, 1960–64.

Kaufmann, Walter, *Nietzsche: Philosopher, Psychologist, Antichrist*, 4th ed., Princeton: Princeton University Press, 1974.

Kierkegaard, Søren, *The Concept of Irony, with Constant Reference to Socrates*, tr. Lee Capel, Bloomington: Indiana University Press, 1965.

———, *The Concluding Unscientific Postscript*, tr. David Swenson and Walter Lowrie, Princeton: Princeton University Press, 1968.

———, *The Sickness Unto Death*, tr. Walter Lowrie, Princeton: Princeton University Press, 1974.

Kieser, Dietrich, "Das zweite Gesicht," *Archiv für den thierischen Magnetismus* 6 (1817–24).

Kitto, H. D. F., *Greek Tragedy: A Literary Study*, Garden City, NY: Doubleday, 1954.

Kristeva, Julia, *Revolution in Poetic Language*, tr. Margaret Walker, New York: Columbia Univesity Press, 1984.

Lacan, Jacques, *Écrits*, Paris: Éditions du Seuil, 1966. / *Écrits: A Selection*, tr. Alan Sheridan, New York: Norton, 1977.

———, *Feminine Sexuality: Jacques Lacan and the École Freudienne*, ed. Juliet Mitchell and Jacqueline Rose, tr. Jacqueline Rose, New York: Norton, 1985.

Laing, R. D., *The Divided Self: An Existential Study of Sanity and Madness*, Baltimore: Penguin, 1973.

———, *The Politics of Experience*, New York: Ballantine Books, 1972.

Lamb, H. R., Alvin P. Sorkin, and Jack Zusman, "Legislating Social Control of the Mentally Ill in California," *American Journal of Psychiatry* 138 (1981): 334–39.

Lange, Wilhelm, *Hölderlin: Eine Pathographie*, Stuttgart: Enke, 1909.

Le Bon, Sylvie, "Un positiviste désespéré: Michel Foucault," *Les Temps Modernes* 248 (1967): 1299–1319.

Lehrer, Ronald, *Nietzsche's Presence in Freud's Life and Thought: On the Origins of a Psychology of Dynamic Unconscious Mental Functioning*, Albany: State University of New York Press, 1994.

Leifer, Ronald, *In the Name of Mental Health: The Social Functions of Psychiatry*, New York: Science House, 1969.

Leighton, Alexander, "Cultural Relativity and the Identification of Psychiatric Disorders," in W. Caudill and T.-Y. Lin, eds., *Mental Health Research in Asia and the Pacific,* Honolulu: East–West Center Press, 1969: 448–62.

Leupoldt, J. M., *Allgemeinen Geschichte der Heilkunde,* Erlangen: Palm und Enke, 1825.

Liebbrand, Werner, *Die spekulative Medizin der Romantik,* Hamburg: Claassen Verlag, 1959.

Lloyd, Genevieve, *The Man of Reason: "Male" and "Female" in Western Philosophy,* Minneapolis: University of Minnesota Press, 1984.

Locke, John, *De arte medica,* 1669, Public Record Office, London 30/24/472.

Logan, Marie–Rose, "The Renaissance: Foucault's Lost Chance?" in Jonathan Arac, ed., *After Foucault: Humanistic Knowledge, Postmodern Challenges,* New Brunswick, NJ: Rutgers University Press, 1988: 97–109.

Löwith, Karl, "History and Christianity," in Robert Bretall and Charles Kegley, eds., *Reinhold Niebuhr: His Religious, Social, and Political Thought,* New York: Macmillan, 1961: 281–90.

Luther, Martin, "Lectures on Romans," in Wilhelm Pauck, tr. and ed., *The Library of Christian Classics,* Philadelphia: Westminster, 1961, vol. 15.

MacDonald, Michael, *Mystical Bedlam: Madness, Anxiety, and Healing in Seventeenth-Century England,* Cambridge: Cambridge University Press, 1981.

Marx, Karl, *The Economic and Philosophical Manuscripts,* in Rodney Livingstone and Gregor Benton, tr. and ed., *Karl Marx: Early Writings,* New York: Random House, 1975.

McCumber, John, *Poetic Interaction: Language, Freedom, Reason,* Chicago: University of Chicago Press, 1989.

Mercer, Jane, *Labeling the Mentally Retarded: Clinical and Social System Perspectives on Mental Retardation,* Berkeley: University of California Press, 1973.

Merquior, J. G., *Foucault,* Berkeley and Los Angeles: University of California Press, 1985.

Meyer, Adolf, "A Few Trends in Modern Psychiatry," *The Psychological Bulletin* 1 (1904): 217–40.

Michel, Wilhelm, *Das Leben Friedrich Hölderlins,* Frankfurt am Main: Insel Verlag, 1967.

Midelfort, H. C. Erik, "Madness and Civilization in Early Modern Europe: A Reappraisal of Michel Foucault," in Barbara C. Malament, ed., *After the Reformation: Essays in Honor of J. H. Hexter,* Philadelphia: University of Pennsylvania Press, 1980: 247–65.

Montaigne, Michel de, *Complete Works,* tr. Donald M. Frame, Stanford: Stanford University Press, 1957.

Morgan, George, *What Nietzsche Means,* New York: Harper & Row, 1965.

Murphy, Jane, "Psychiatric Labeling in Cross–Cultural Perspectives," *Science* 191 (1976): 1019–28.

Niebuhr, Reinhold, *Faith and History: A Comparison of Christian and Modern Views of History,* New York: Scribner's, 1949.

———, *The Nature and Destiny of Man: A Christian Interpretation,* 2 vols., New York: Scribner's, 1941, 1943.

Nietzsche, Friedrich, *Beyond Good and Evil,* in Walter Kaufmann, ed., *The Basic Writings of Nietzsche,* New York: Random House, 1968.

———, *The Birth of Tragedy,* in *Basic Writings.*

———, *Daybreak,* tr. R. J. Hollingdale, Cambridge: Cambridge University Press, 1982.

———, *Ecce Homo,* in *Basic Writings.*

———, *The Gay Science,* tr. Walter Kaufmann, New York: Random House, 1974.

———, *The Genealogy of Morals,* in *Basic Writings.*

———, *Human, All Too Human,* tr. Marion Faber, London: University of Nebraska Press, 1984.

———, *Kleinoktavausgabe,* 16 vols., ed. Elisabeth Förster–Nietzsche, et al., Leipzig: Kröner Verlag, 1899–1912.

———, *Sämtliche Werke,* 15 vols., ed. Giorgio Colli and Mazzino Montinari, Berlin: Walter de Gruyter, 1967–77.

———, *Twilight of the Idols,* in Walter Kaufmann, ed., *The Portable Nietzsche,* New York: Viking, 1984.

———, *The Will to Power,* tr. Walter Kaufmann and R. J. Hollingdale, New York: Random House, 1967.

Ortner, Sherry, and Harriet Whitehead, eds., *Sexual Meanings: The*

Cultural Construction of Gender and Sexuality, New York: Cambridge University Press, 1981.

Parmenides, "The Way to Truth," in Kathleen Freeman, ed., *Ancilla to the Pre-Socratic Philosophers,* Cambridge, MA: Harvard University Press, 1957.

Pascal, Blaise, *Pensées,* ed. Robert Barrault, Paris: Librairie Larousse, 1965.

Peacock, Ronald, *Hölderlin,* London: Methuen & Co., 1938.

Pinel, Phillipe, *Traité médico-philosophique sur l'aliénation mentale,* 2nd edition (1809), Salem, NH: Ayer, 1976. / *A Treatise on Insanity,* tr. D. D. Davis, Sheffield: W. Todd, 1806.

————, *La nosographie philosophique: Ou, la méthode de l'analyse appliquée à la médicine,* 6th ed., Paris: Brosson, 1818.

Podmore, Frank, *From Mesmerism to Christian Science,* New York: University Books, 1963.

Poggi, Stefano, "Mind and Brain in Medical Thought During the Romantic Period," *History and Philosophy of the Life Sciences* 10 (1988): 41–53.

Porter, Roy, *Social History of Madness,* New York: Dutton, 1989.

Puységur, Armand M. Jacques, marquis de Chastenet, *Du magnetisme animal, considéré dans ses rapports avec diverses branches de la physique générale,* Paris: Desenne, 1807.

————, *Mémoires pour servir à l'histoire et à l'établissement du magnétisme animal,* Bayonne: [n. p.], 1784.

Reil, Christian, *Rhapsodien über die Anwendung der psychischen Kurmethode auf Geisteszerrüttungen,* Halle: Curt, 1803.

————, *Über die Erkenntnis und Kur der Fieber,* 5 vols., Wien: Ghelenschen Schriften, 1800–1802.

Redding, Paul, "Absorbed in the Spectacle of the World: Hegel's Criticism of Romantic Historiography," *Clio* 16 (1987): 297–315.

Ricoeur, Paul, *Freud and Philosohy: An Essay on Interpretation,* tr. Denis Savage, New Haven: Yale University Press, 1970.

————, *History and Truth,* tr. Charles Kelbley, Evanston: Northwestern University Press, 1965.

Rorty, Richard, "Foucault and Epistemology," in David Couzens Hoy, ed., *Foucault: A Critical Reader,* Oxford: Basil Blackwell, 1986: 41–50.

Rosen, George, *Madness in Society: Chapters in the Historical Sociology of Mental Illness,* Chicago: Chicago University Press, 1968.

Rosenhan, David L., "On Being Sane in Insane Places," *Science* 179 (1973): 250–58.

Rothman, David, *The Discovery of the Asylum: Social Order and Disorder in the New Republic,* Boston: Little Brown, 1971.

Said, Edward W., "Foucault and the Imagination of Power," in David Couzens Hoy, ed., *Foucault: A Critical Reader,* Oxford: Basil Blackwell, 1986: 149–56.

Sarbin, Theodore, "The Scientific Status of the Mental Illness Metaphor," in S. C. Plog and R. B. Edgerton, eds., *Changing Perspectives in Mental Illness,* New York: Holt, 1969: 9–31.

Sartre, Jean-Paul, *L'être et le néant,* Paris: Éditions Gallimard, 1943. / *Being and Nothingness,* tr. Hazel Barnes, New York: Washington Square Press, 1973.

Scheff, Thomas, *Being Mentally Ill: A Sociological Theory,* Chicago: Aldine, 1966.

———, *Labelling Madness,* Englewood Cliffs, NJ: Prentice-Hall, 1975.

———, "The Labelling Theory of Mental Illness," *American Sociological Review* 39 (1974): 444–52.

Scheidler, K. H., "Über das Verhältnis der Philosophie überhaupt und der Psychologie insbesondere zur Medicin," *Minerva Medica* 1 (1829): 211–48.

Schelling, Karl, "Ideen und Erfahrungen über den thierischen Magnetismus," *Jahrbücher der Medicin als Wissenschaft* 2 (1807): 3–46.

———, "Weitere Betrachtungen über den thierischen Magnetismus, und die Mittel ihn näher zu erforschen," *Jahrbücher der Medicin als Wissenschaft* 2 (1807): 158–90.

Schlick, Moritz, "The Foundation of Knowledge," tr. David Rynin, in A. J. Ayer, ed., *Logical Positivism,* New York: MacMillan, 1959: 209–27.

Schopenhauer, Arthur, *The World as Will and Representation,* 2 vols., tr. E. F. J. Payne, New York: Dover Publications, 1966.

Schur, Edwin, *Interpreting Deviance: A Sociological Introduction,* New York: Harper & Row, 1979.

———, *Labeling Deviant Behavior: Its Sociological Implications,* New York: Harper & Row, 1971.

Schwab, John J., and Mary E. Schwab, *Sociocultural Roots of Mental Illness: An Epidemiologic Survey,* New York: Plenum, 1978.

Scull, Andrew, "From Madness to Mental Illness: Medical Men as Moral Entrepreneurs," *European Journal of Sociology* 16 (1975): 219–61.

———, ed., *Madhouses, Mad-Doctors, and Madmen: The Social History of Psychiatry in the Victorian Era,* Philadelphia: University of Pensylvania Press, 1981.

———, "Madness and Segregative Control: The Rise of the Insane Asylum," *Social Problems* 24 (1977): 337–51.

———, *Museums of Madness: The Social Organization of Insanity in Nineteenth–Century England,* New York: St. Martin's Press, 1979.

Segal, Steven P., Jim Baumohl, and Elsie Johnson, "Falling Through the Cracks: Mental Disorder and Social Margin in Young Vagrant Population," *Social Problems* 24 (1977): 387–400.

Servan, J.-M.-A., *Doutes d'un provincial proposés à MM. les médecins commissaires chargés par le Roi de l'examen du magnétisme animal,* Lyons: Prault, 1784.

Shakespeare, William, *The Complete Works,* 3rd edition, ed. David Bevington, Glenview, IL: Scott, Foresman & Co., 1980.

Simon, Bennett, *Mind and Madness in Ancient Greece: The Classical Roots of Modern Psychiatry,* Ithaca: Cornell University Press, 1980.

Spitzer, Robert, "More on Pseudoscience in Science and the Case for Psychiatric Diagnosis," *Archives of General Psychiatry* 33 (1976): 459–70.

Stierlin, Helm, "Lyrical Creativity and Schizophrenic Psychosis as Reflected in Friedrich Hölderlin's Fate," in Emery E. George, ed., *Friedrich Hölderlin, An Early Modern,* Ann Arbor: The University of Michigan Press, 1972: 192–215.

Suzuki, Daisetz T., *Zen and Japanese Culture,* Princeton: Princeton University Press, 1970.

Sydenham, Thomas, *Works,* 2 vols., tr. R. G. Latham, London: Sydenham Society, 1848.

Szasz, Thomas, *Ideology and Insanity: Essays on the Psychiatric Dehumanization of Man,* Garden City, NJ: Doubleday, 1970.

———, *Law, Liberty, and Psychiatry: An Inquiry into the Social Uses of Mental Health Practices,* New York: Macmillan, 1963.

———, *The Manufacture of Madness: A Comparative Study of the Inquisition and the Mental Health Movement,* New York: Harper & Row, 1970.

———, "Mental Illness: A Myth?" in Leonard Kristal, ed., *The ABC of Psychology,* London: Michael Joseph, 1981: 150–55

————, *The Myth of Mental Illness: Foundations of a Theory of Personal Conduct,* revised edition, New York: Harper & Row, 1974.

————, *Psychiatric Justice,* New York: Macmillan, 1965.

————, *The Therapeutic State: Psychiatry in the Mirror of Current Events,* Buffalo, NY: Prometheus Books, 1984.

Temerlin, Maurice K., "Suggestion Effects in Psychiatric Diagnoses," *Journal of Nervous and Mental Diseases* 147 (1968): 349–58.

Treichler, Rudolf, "Die seelische Erkrankung Friedrich Hölderlins in ihren Beziehungen zu seinem dichterischen Schaffen," *Zeitschrift für die gesamte Neurologie und Psychiatrie* 155 (1936): 40–144.

Tuke, Samuel, *Description of the Retreat,* York, England: Alexander, 1813.

Wackwitz, Stephan, *Friedrich Hölderlin,* Stuttgart: J. B. Metzlersche Verlagsbuchhandlung, 1985.

Waldock, A. J. A., *Sophocles the Dramatist,* Cambridge: Cambridge University Press, 1966.

Walzer, Michael, "The Politics of Michel Foucault," in David Couzens Hoy, ed., *Foucault: A Critical Reader,* Oxford: Basil Blackwell, 1986: 51–68.

Warren, Carol A. B., with contributions by Stephen J. Morse and Jack Zusman, *The Court of Last Resort: Mental Illness and the Law,* Chicago: University of Chicago Press, 1982.

Waxler, Nancy, "Culture and Mental Illness: A Social Labeling Perspective," *Journal of Nervous and Mental Disease* 159 (1974): 379–95.

White, Hayden, *Tropics of Discourse,* Baltimore: The Johns Hopkins Press, 1990.

Winfield, Richard, "Logic, Language, and the Autonomy of Reason," *Idealistic Studies* 17 (1987): 109–21.

Wing, John, *Reasoning about Madness,* London: Oxford University Press, 1978.

Wittgenstein, Ludwig, *Philosophical Investigations,* tr. G. E. M. Anscombe, New York: MacMillan, 1962.

Wolfe, David E., "Sydenham and Locke on the Limits of Anatomy," *Bulletin of the History of Medicin* 35 (1961): 193–220.

Wolff, Michael, *Das Körper-Seele-Problem,* Frankfurt am Main: Klostermann, 1992.

Zeitlin, Froma, "Thebes: Theater of Self and Society in Athenian Drama," in J. Peter Euben, ed., *Greek Tragedy and Political Theory,* Berkeley: University of California Press, 1986: 101–41.

Author Index

Subject Index

Home, at-homeness, and homelessness,
18, 43, 48, 52, 64, 66, 71, 75, 139, 196,
228 n21
Homeopathy, 16
Honest consciousness, 125
Human and divine laws (see also
Antigone), 80–81, 137, 151, 158, 159,
162, 166, 327 n11
Hyllus, 167
Hypnotism, 32, 34

'I', the (see also *the ego*), 26, 43, 65, 76,
109, 131, 232 n12, 233 n14
'I am I' (see also *narcissism*), 43, 46, 52,
56, 75–86, 102, 103, 125, 126, 128,
131
Iago, 149
Idealism, 6, 39, 54, 64–70, 164, 194, 231
n67, 231 n68, 231 n71
and madness (two idealisms), 6, 39,
64–70
Illness (see *disease*)
Illusion, 26, 64, 111, 113
Immediate, immediacy, 19, 20, 43, 67,
69, 86, 88–89, 101, 129, 132, 138, 174,
191, 193, 205, 244 n15
Inchoate, the, the inarticulate, the ineffable, 78, 129, 130, 132, 174, 244 n16
Inhibition (see also *repression*), 111, 133
Innocence (see also *evil; guilt*), 86–91,
93, 123, 169–70
Inquisition, 183, 185, 252 n1
Insanity (see *madness*)
Instincts, drives (see also *the archaic;
death instinct; feeling; nature; the
soul; the unconscious*), 3, 5, 26, 29, 31,
38, 42, 44, 54, 69, 71, 75, 77, 80, 82,
84, 95, 98, 100–3, 106–11, 114–16,
119, 121, 127, 136–38, 148, 149,
154–56, 158, 159, 168, 170, 191, 215,
236 n8, 238 n32
'dark infernal powers', 29, 98, 115,
153–64, 170, 190, 191, 205
'earthly elements' of the soul, 26, 42,
44, 82, 98, 154, 170
Intentionality (see also *meaning*), 5, 6,
78, 97, 115, 119–42, 146, 174, 215,
236 n11, 243 n7, 243 n10
and desire, 78, 115

and language, 120
and the unintentional, 119–42, 149,
167
Intuition, 158, 166, 243 n4
intellectual intuition, 246 n27
Inversion, 3, 124, 125, 127, 132, 144,
146, 164–76
inverted world, 144, 164–68, 250 n32
Irony, 55, 162, 166, 213

Jocasta, 150

King Lear (Shakespeare; see also *Lear*),
143

Labeling theory of mental illness (see
also *madness: socially and politically
constructed*), 7, 179–80, 184, 187–90,
192–94, 197, 199–201, 203, 206, 208,
210–11, 213–15, 239 n47, 254 n17,
255 n30, 256 n44, 257 n62, 258 n64
Labor, work (see also *alienation: alienated labor; madness: therapy: moral
treatment*), 5, 68–69, 83–88, 92–93,
125, 137, 140, 155–56, 171, 197,
202–6, 211–13, 215, 249 n22
division of labor, 209, 210
factory labor, 209
labor cure (see also *madness: therapy:
moral treatment*), 68, 92–93, 140,
202–6, 210–11
as liberation, 92, 140–41, 205, 206,
209, 213
right to work, 211–13
Language (see also *madness: semantics
of; private language; the speculative
proposition*), 5, 6, 29, 42–45, 52,
63–64, 98–100, 109, 112, 120, 124,
128–34, 138–39, 174, 180, 183–86,
189, 202, 215, 226 n8, 242 n96, 244
n13, 244 n16, 246 n27, 246 n31
divine nature of, 132, 246 n27
ordinary language, 181
Law of the heart, 4, 80, 125–26, 138,
145, 165–67, 195
Lear (see also *King Lear*), 150, 156, 157
Lettre de cachet, 198, 256 n55
Libation Bearers (Aeschylus), 152

Made in the USA
Middletown, DE
09 January 2019